THE HISTORY OF FORGETTING

THE HAYMARKET SERIES

Editors: Mike Davis and Michael Sprinker

The Haymarket Series offers original studies in politics, history and culture, with a focus on North America. Representing views across the American left on a wide range of subjects, the series will be of interest to socialists both in the USA and throughout the world. A century after the first May Day, the American left remains in the shadow of those martyrs whom the Haymarket Series honors and commemorates. These studies testify to the living legacy of political activism and commitment for which they gave their lives.

Forthcoming titles

THE INVENTION OF THE WHITE RACE, VOLUME 2: The Origin of Racial Oppression in Anglo-America *by Theodore Allen*

MIAMI *by John Beverley and David Houston*

NOTES FROM UNDERGROUND: The Politics of Zine Culture *by Stephen Duncombe*

THE WAY THE WIND BLEW: A History of the Weather Underground *by Ron Jacobs*

RACE AND POLITICS IN THE UNITED STATES: New Challenges and Responses for Black Activism *edited by James Jennings*

THE PUBLIC BROADCASTING SERVICE *by James Ledbetter*

MESSING WITH THE MACHINE: Modernism, Postmodernism and African-American Fiction *by Wahneema Lubiano*

MASS TRANSIT *by Eric Mann*

WEEKEND IN SILVERLAKE *by Kevin McMahon*

RED DIRT: Growing Up Okie *by Roxanne Dunbar Ortiz*

DECADE OF DESIRE: American Culture and Literature in the Twenties *by Chip Rhodes*

DANCING ON THE BRINK: The San Francisco Bay Area at the End of the Twentieth Century *by Richard Walker*

THE WAR ON THE URBAN POOR: A Manmade Endless Disaster *by Deborah Wallace and Rodrick Wallace*

THE HISTORY OF FORGETTING

Los Angeles and the Erasure of Memory

◆

NORMAN M. KLEIN

VERSO

London · New York

First published by Verso 1997
Reprinted 1998
© Norman M. Klein 1997
All rights reserved

The right of Norman M. Klein to be identified as the author of
this work has been asserted by him in accordance with the
Copyright, Designs and Patents Act 1988

Verso
UK: 6 Meard Street, London W1V 3HR
USA: 180 Varick Street, New York NY 10014-4606

Verso is the imprint of New Left Books

ISBN 1-85984-820-6
ISBN 1-85984-175-9 (pbk)

British Library Cataloguing in Publication Data
A catalogue record for this book is available from the British Library

Library of Congress Cataloging-in-Publication Data
A catalog record for this book is available from the Library of Congress

Typeset in Monotype Bembo by Lucy Morton, London SE12
Printed and bound in Great Britain by Biddles Ltd,
Guildford and King's Lynn

CONTENTS

INTRODUCTION

HISTORIES OF FORGETTING

Just west of downtown Los Angeles, over fifty thousand housing units were torn down in the period 1933 to 1980, leaving an empty zone as noticeable as a meteor's impact. Only some of the lots have since been filled. Many look the same as the day the buildings went down, twenty or thirty years ago. High-rises stand directly beside barren hills, near weedy patches of old foundations. Along Sunset Boulevard, the stone staircases of former Victorian houses now lead to nothing at all.

Virtually no ethnic community downtown was allowed to keep its original location: Chinatown, the Mexican Sonora, Little Italy. In 1930, 20,000 people resided in the four blocks around Olvera Street. Now only a few hundred live there. The overall population downtown is lower than it was in 1890, unless the homeless are included. New plans for revitalization have failed to revive much. Business streets immediately west of Olvera Street remain as dead as a violated graveyard – a warning that downtown will be forgettable even while it continues to be built.[1]

And yet the clues are still there. Two tunnels exit from downtown, but there is no hill above them, as if a large bird has flown away with it. Numerous lots west along Sunset Boulevard have steps on to what clearly used to be a house. Creaky Victorian cottages are stranded along streets just south of Sunset, cut short by a roaring freeway.

Most of this book centers on neighborhoods just west of downtown, on interviews with residents from 1979 to 1994. This is their imaginary map of community life under fire, while the world around them is being systematically erased.

The need to chronicle their responses is very pressing in Los Angeles, particularly since the impact of Mike Davis's *City of Quartz* has staked new ground in the history of how communities are destroyed by failed policies.

But their responses are very changeable, similar to memoirs after a political shock: new information drops in, old details disappear. And to add even more complication, in city hall, the myths that propel urban planners to demolish neighborhoods can be utterly phantasmagorical. And finally, there is the inattention from the public at large. Every morning for over thirty years, over 200,000 cars passed the bulldozing of these neighborhoods. Despite a few organizations that tried to rally support against these urban plans, there is virtually no record of complaint on a mass level. Most Angelinos I interview, even those who live immediately in the areas affected, have barely a dim memory that these neighborhoods stood at all. The overall effect resembles what psychologists call "distraction," where one false memory allows another memory to be removed in plain view, without complaint – forgotten.

PHANTOM LIMBS[2]

In 1974, when I first moved to the neighborhoods west of downtown Los Angeles, I was soured by the omens I sensed there. One vacant store had been a kosher butcher shop in the fifties, now with a rusted sign, but very similar to the dismal store my father had run in Brooklyn for thirty years. In an utter reversal of Proust sipping tea, I remembered the smell of raw meat in the sawdust on the floors, the armies of cockroaches under the display cases, the look of chicken guts stuck to the sides of garbage pails out back.

I learned that across the street from my apartment, on Glendale Boulevard, Tom Mix used to ride a horse to work from his ranch in Mixville (now a Hughes market shopping center). But no recognition could be found anywhere that the entire film industry had once been centered there (1912–20). It was clear that the city of Los Angeles would never announce formally that the movie business had started in what was now, forgettably, a "Mexican" neighborhood. At first, the sheer neglect left me dreary, reminding me of family repression during my own childhood. It took at least a year for me to realize how much vitality existed west of downtown.

In 1979, I bought what had formerly been a gang house in Angelino Heights, with no plumbing that worked, leaking drains flooding the basement, dank old carpets everywhere, graffiti carved into some of the wood trim, and practically no working electricity. It took twelve years to restore. During that time, I gradually made peace with the absurdity of my Brooklyn memories, and discovered I had a lifelong fascination with high urban decay, and with the gradual uncovering of urban ruins. By 1986, I was running a series of lectures about the level of public neglect and bad faith in Los Angeles, entitled "Beneath the Myths." I started taking students on what I called "anti-tours." I would stop at locations where no buildings existed any longer, tell them what had been there once: a movie studio, a whorehouse, whatever. We would get out, look around, and agree that it was gone all right. I showed them as many interiors as I could find, but only if they were inhabited; no museum artifacts allowed.

Clearly, those anti-tours and lectures were the origins of this book. I was learning about contractors, ordinances, old and new tenants, shifting demographics – the chain of production that generates the image of a city street. At the same time, while researching on animation for ten years, I noticed that the drawings and pencil tests made before a cartoon was finished often betrayed more about the real intentions than what finally showed on the movie screen, even though the earlier versions usually were just thrown in the trash. "As film, pencil tests can look very unsteady and not always flattering, though I find them exciting and vulnerable to watch. They are a record of how a scene is built, virtually from the first line."[3] The sheer numbers of erased versions, and the many animation crafts people I interviewed utterly changed my understanding of what takes place when mass culture is produced: that a pecking order had to be studied – who came first, who finished up, who controlled the budget. The same clearly was true of Los Angeles' history: the final version was the whitewash, or the conciliation, the ad that went public.

I realized how utterly inefficient this chain of production was, no matter how much greed and corporate ideology lay behind it. Throwing out mistakes, or even successes (but from the "wrong" people) was another source of erasure. Also, the sheer ineptitude very often generated worse problems. The direction of a "rumor made solid" resembled a labyrinth of missteps more than a demonic process, even when the results were demonic indeed.

In the minds of consumers, the source of these erasures resembled what psychologists call an *imago*, an idealized face left over from childhood

– a photograph, the color of mother's dress on the day she took ill (the photological trace). For example, we see in our mind's eye the war in Vietnam primarily as two photographs: a general shooting a man in the head; a naked girl running toward the camera after being napalmed.

These imagos are preserved inside a mental cameo frame (itself a fiction: who knows what is inside?). If we concentrate, the imago seems to be waiting for us intact: a photo, a document, a table of statistics, an interview. It remains where we put it, but the details around it get lost, as if they were haunted, somewhat contaminated, but empty. Imagos are the sculpture that stands in the foreground next to negative space. Imagos are the false light that defines chiaroscuro. They are the rumor that seems haunted with memory, so satisfying that it keeps us from looking beyond it. The imago contains, as Kristeva describes so vividly, "once upon blotted-out time," when "forgotten time crops up suddenly and condenses into a flash of lightning."[4] However, when the flash is over, much of what remains as urban history is picturesque,[5] in itself a form of erasure.

Therefore, very soon into this project I realized that imagos – or phantom limbs, or whatever one called them – are extremely deceptive. They make poor evidence, even when one finds the "imago" photo or video, as I will show when I try to follow the perverse journey that the George Holliday video of the Rodney King beating has taken. The shock value obscures entire stages in the political history of collective memory. And the traces from one reception to the next are too faint in themselves to build much of a case. The mystery therefore is not how to find clues to an "abject" crime. It is about perception itself – as a political context. Why do people fail to see "the obvious?" Why is imaginary identification so difficult for things so clearly in one's best interest? Like Poe's famous "purloined letter," the clues sit openly on the mantelpiece, but are utterly unfindable.[6] Something in the obviousness of them makes them instantly forgettable.

In the chapters to follow in this book, the "phantom limb" is often an empty lot where a building once stood, perhaps on Sunset Boulevard.[7] Scraps of lathe and façade mix in piles with broken brick. The foundation is momentarily a ruin, like a photo of someone's toothless mouth held wide open. The grading left by the bulldozers form ridges along the dust. It seems that if you could simply rest your ear close enough to the point where the blades have sheared away the joists, there might be the faint echo of a scream, or a couple talking at breakfast. Your imagination tries to see those people, based on the evidence, but doesn't find enough at first. A car passes. Someone watches through the windshield for an instant, as if they knew who used to live here. But no conversation is supposed to take place. The cars graze at the light, and disappear.

POPULAR MEMORY IN FLASHBACK: DOWNTOWN BEFORE IT WAS ERASED

To locate what these empty lots had been, I asked dozens of old-timers to describe the downtown Los Angeles of their youth. Gradually, as my research expanded, an utterly different popular memory emerged, mostly from the twenties into the fifties. As of 1930, downtown – seen from the western edge – was a buzz cut of wood-frame gingerbread houses near ten-storey office buildings on a very steep terrain that sloped directly into the western neighborhoods: easy to walk to, take a trolley into, in the midst of gridlocked traffic.

It had an arc without a skyline, like a miniature landlocked San Francisco. At the western promontory was Bunker Hill, "the brow" of the city so-called, where many of the wealthiest had lived, above the desert haze, in what had been Olympian grandeur until the noise and density took over. As one old man told me in the 1970s: "We always dressed to go downtown. My parents were Serbian farmers. I think they thought it was Vienna." Not quite. This was by no means a very beautiful downtown. Many complained that it seemed dusty and ill-conceived. The housing stock made a curious cityscape, where one block might resemble Chicago, with stone-façade mansions, hotels, close to wooden rooming houses; and another a twenties farm-town securities district.

But in its jaggedness, streets angled by hills, as well as in the tumble of different classes and races, it was the equal certainly of downtowns in many "middle-sized" cities of the time. It bore the traces of quick money, buildings stranded by tourism and rapid turnover. It did look ramshackle on many streets, because houses not part of new boosterism were often neglected entirely, like the card parlors in the Italian district north of Sunset; the darker corners along Main, the liquor stores just off Second Street; a few major hotels not far from sleazebags where prostitutes serviced sailors, just around the corner from major investment houses.

Into the forties, visitors often described the effect as quaint more than raw, like a coat made of twill – too stiff, too hick to fit quite right, but sturdy and appointed with humility. The parks were badly planned, partly because farmland was close by anyway. Even as late as the forties, downtown was still described as the capital of a farming city. It was famous for its lack of skyscrapers, and of cultural monuments "for a city of its size," like large museums or grand opera houses. The suburbs were mostly rustic bedroom communities with just a strip of shops. Some of these suburbs were very wealthy, like San Marino or Bel Air; but most were simply midwest colonies carved out of former orange groves.

Signs of decentralization were unmistakable by the late twenties, but again, not as I had imagined. Some major shopping had already relocated about two miles west of downtown, on Wilshire primarily, to allow for cars and easy parking. Nonetheless, in most of the literature, film and history as late as 1960, downtown still had a much stronger profile than the myths of rapid suburbanization suggest. Crime films shot on location during the fifties show crooks filing past busy pharmacies filled with downtown residents, and hotels with random foot traffic late at night, past antique entryways for elegant office buildings. Most of the fanciest stores were still downtown until about 1950; also the best doctors, or so many residents assumed. Certainly the major law firms were there, and twelve of the major first-run movie theaters. Downtown was busy enough to stay open day and night; not quite like Manhattan, but certainly enough to keep some streets dressy and full in the evening. I would estimate that a steady flow of over 200,000 people used these services continuously, simply because it was accessible to a dozen neighborhoods just west of it. I say "west" because the eastern section (past the river) had been isolated essentially in the twenties, as too Mexican.

This policy of shutting out downtown to non-whites is an important theme in Part I of this book. From 1930 onward, gradually and then rapidly, urban plans strangled the access from westerly directions in particular, taking out key walking streets. The irony of course is that, finally, all this planning shut off street life itself; it pruned out more than just the non-white. But who among the elite could imagine 200,000 people forgetting to show up? It seemed impossible to foresee that all this density could ever go away, no matter how radical the surgery.

WRITING AND STRUCTURING ERASURE

In the early eighties, as I began writing about these contrasts, I noticed that my scholarship began to resemble fiction. There seemed no strictly empirical form of history that did justice to the fictional side of booster-ism, to stories about urban myths that are built. Fiction became "history's handmaid," like novels of the 1830s,[8] Balzac's and Scott's in particular, where chapters of historical narration would be inserted whole. Also, in histories by Carlyle, Guizot Michelet or Macauley, the ear of the novelist was unmistakable.[9] While sorting out this project, I often wondered if the rash of novels by historians in the 1990s represented a return to that crossed identity, to make the scholar both reader and character within the same text.

Also, I found that the structure of chapters often required inserts of fiction, to document the chain of popular memory. To keep each layer properly and honestly in place, I decided to use my evidence at an earlier state of production, before it is synthesized into a single chronicle,[10] fictional or scholarly. In many ways, the materials I have assembled look like research gathered by a novelist before the novel is written, before the writer turns the contradictions into a character-driven story. Like blending notes with a diary, I plan to leave the chronicle often, to break off into essays on the social history of media, and of Los Angeles. That way I can I describe the rumors and hearsay more as I received them, in the literary spirit in which they were delivered, as fictions. At the same time, I can take my leave of the fictive regularly, and write as an urban mass-culture historian.

Obviously, this enters the divide of postmodern writing. And that generally requires a full medley of critical citations. However, what inter-ests me most about postmodern debates is their permissions for new writing – new literary experiments possible as a result of decades of ground-breaking work. There are clear signs that both critical theory and cultural studies have generated what amounts to a new category of litera-ture (as yet unnamed). What names there are sound a bit early in the cycle right now, clearly not what this "genre"(?) might be called ten years from now:[11] docu-novels, "mockumentaries," false autobiographies, public autobiography; "faction;" phonebooks or chat lines as variations of per-sonal essay; public autobiography; "witnessing" as Dick Hebdige describes his new work of the nineties (the structure of his books, along with his advice, were an influence on this project); historiographic metafiction.[12]

I would rather not add more labels. Instead, I'll stick to the term "history." That is problematical and fictive enough already.[13] More specifically, I am interested in the history of mass culture as an alternate form of literature, how popular memory makes for a very uneasy form of research. In this book, my primary sources are urban planning reports, local interviews, the detritus of neighborhood conversations, urban legends, movie locations, and so on. Primary or otherwise, sources of this type, even when they look more empirical inside scholarly articles, are unstable and fundamentally fictional. Therefore, to be honest, the text I produce must be partly autobiographical. What else can a history of collective memory be but a rigorous diary about unreliable documents?

The documents are a mix of history, fiction and urban anthropology: more a form of historicized ethnography, always cooked, certainly never raw.[14] Like the ethnographer, the historian of urban mass culture is the outsider who takes a reflexive journey into the vagaries of diary, of the destabilized text. The people who are interviewed sense the researcher studying from outside. They change their memory to be helpful, like an uncertainty principle, which becomes doubly uncertain once the historian writes their story down. The page in print becomes a contagion of fictions, a form of literature.[15]

This trope that compares memory to contagion resembles a diasporic journey, where the "past" is "reinscribed and relocated."[16] It can be identified as the axis between colonization and decolonization.[17] Or the tension between objectivity and objectification.[18] Most of all, the structure of chapters resembles the dialogues within a city street, continuously in a state of interference and restatement. They cannot be recorded as a fixed object, only as traffic through intersections, invaded by noises, interrupted by other conversations.[19] These are studies on how memory is "contaminated" by imagery.

Critics as sources: In a project of this sort, little is accomplished by simply itemizing talmudically the dozens of authors and art makers whose work fits into the broad category of "forgetting." The writers who have been the most valuable to me while working on this project were Virginia Woolf,[20] Foucault, Barthes, Baudelaire and Benjamin,[21] more a cosmology than a bibliography.

Perhaps no historian of mass culture has detailed the trope of memory/ contamination more thoroughly than Foucault, even down to his continual use of phrases that suggest binaries erasing each other, a "perpetual state of decomposition and recomposition." One false memory "is present, while the other has ceased, perhaps a long time ago," inside the web of "impressions, reminiscence, imagination, memory – all that involuntary background which is, as it were, the mechanics of the image in time."[22] That sense of binaries breaking down is crucial to this project.

Another source for me has been a colleague, Sande Cohen, anti-historiographer and Nietzschean anarchist, in statements like the following: "I am involved in the production of anti-production, to prove there is nothing there to be lost." What is received has already dissolved, or never was, except as text. The fiction of memory is incontrovertible and unprovable.

Also, after over twenty years teaching in art schools, I have begun to see historical writing, at least about mass culture, as an installation piece harking back to synthetic Cubism. By installation I mean history as decomposition, about the anxiety of representation, about excisions. Evidence is a remnant left over by chance. Very often, historical documents survive because they were not important enough to destroy at the time. They are what was not consumed by the rhythm of events. To follow this analogy, the historian's writing should include an open-ended diagram of what information cannot be found: the document that was tossed away; the cracks in the sidewalk where the roots of trees, now gone, lifted the street. For example, when I research mainstream cinema, I look for ruptures more than coherence. I don't mind if the scenes fail to match, or the effects are uneven; and not because that is a Brechtian device, but because I like to sense the scars, perhaps where a cut was made — objects removed during the chain of production, at different stages of participation. The final version for me is only the survivor. It is the last step in a coping mechanism.

USING PRIMARY SOURCES ABOUT POPULAR MEMORY

In the first section, I employ the term *social imaginary*,[23] but not in the Lacanian, or in the post-Hegelian sense, which seemed too elusive for research on urban planning or neighborhood politics in Los Angeles. Instead, I preferred a version of social imaginary specifically about the built environment, particularly sites that were destroyed or severely altered: office towers where houses once stood; abandoned tunnels like the famous Belmont entrance to the vanished twenties subway in Los Angeles;[24] consumer simulations of neighborhoods, like Citywalk, near the Universal Tours. Documents sorted out by this model make the fictions of erasure easier to describe.

That is not to say that a social imaginary uncovers the "true" collective memory, as if it were a Dead Sea Scroll. There is no empirical way to beam up the "actual" picture in one person's mind, much less in a group; it is a disappearing phosphene.[25] So what does a construct about popular memory accomplish? It maps erasures mostly, what in memory is lost when language intervenes – the sensation left by the unfindable. Castoriadis calls that place "the night of the world, the power of drawing images out of this night or of letting them slip away."[26] It is always fundamentally visual, and yet not visual at all, a "specular" site that escapes any category, and can be found only by the trail it leaves, by its evacuation.

The social imaginary, therefore, is a built environment that also contains an evacuation. It is charming, because in part it erases. That missing part induces suspense. In lectures to students I always summarize the social imaginary in a phrase: "A collective memory of an event or place that never occurred, but is built anyway." Then, to warm up discussion, I give examples that are as tangible as the built environment, often not simply from Los Angeles. After all, L.A. is merely one paradigm for crises in mass culture throughout the world. The example that seems to spark the most focused response is the vampire.

Vampires are a *Victorian* social imaginary (*c.* 1840–1900). That is, in British novels and plays, vampire stories come out of a Victorian memory of a medieval folklore that never existed. Many of the details in the vampire's dress, manner and power belong more to Victorian superstitions than Hungarian ones. When I guess which superstition that might be, I compare Dracula rising from the undead to Victorian male phobias about sexual performance. For Stoker at least, Dracula was very likely the incarnation of syphilis. In the Murnau film *Nosferatu*, he is the plague of cholera stalking victims in their sleep. Dracula's powers, to gain sperm *after* sex, probably refer more obviously to myths about sperm and scarcity – what one historian has called "the spermatic economy."[27] But I have no space here to examine what went through the fevered brain of Stoker, or Sheridan Le Fanu, or their readers. Suffice it to say that Eastern Europeans certainly had next to nothing to do with the fiction itself. And yet, each year, thousands of tourists visit a castle in Romania that happens to bear the name Dracula – a title that Bram Stoker essentially pulled out of a reference book at the British Museum, perhaps because the syllables had marquee value. Popular memory has reinscribed the name with a historical space it never inhabited, not unlike the myths surrounding the potboiler novel *Ramona* that brought millions to Southern California after 1885, looking for a fictional mestiza, Ramona herself, and the imaginary mission where she lived.

From *Ramona*, I shift toward examples much closer to myths about cities like Los Angeles: policies toward slums often operate as a social imaginary. Consider who writes these policies. Often, they are responding to fears of upscale professionals afraid to enter a seemingly dangerous street. The professional middle class generally avoids slums like the plague, or escapes from them to greener suburbs, or mystifies them in crime films. Slums are a vital part of noir imagination, but rarely visited. Even their popular history – how they declined – tends to be very apocryphal, littered with half-baked theories that say more about white male panic, or fears of the Great Depression, than life in neighborhoods. Generally in films, and often in public documents, the "causes" of urban decay that are presented will amount to little more than rumor. And yet, freeways based on many of these rumors have been built, as I will show.

Nearly all forms of urban planning involve a social imaginary, and certainly those I describe in Part I. That point can be extended infinitely, it seems, to include nostalgia in architecture, whether the buildings are homages in the sixteenth century to classical Rome, or citywalks in the 1990s – homages to imaginary L.A. neighborhoods. Nostalgia convinces the viewer *because* the actual events of the past have been forgotten. In fact, the past is not the issue at all; it serves merely as a "rosy" container for the anxieties of the present. Political ideology uses nostalgia in much the same way as architecture, ironically enough. It builds the unremembered. For example, trickle-down theories in conservative Republican politics are built on paramnesiac fantasies about fifties economics. These imply that business during the fifties boom was utterly unregulated (though taxes were in fact higher, and business was very much on a tight leash, pressured by much larger unions, asked to pay for vast government programs, from freeways to hospitals to public housing). However, since 1982 myths about an age when government was "off our backs" have been written into tax laws, shifting hundreds of billions of dollars from public infrastructure to corporate investment portfolios.

Social imaginaries can be extremely cruel. And it is very pleasant to attack them. But that will easily miss the mark. It is important to see social imaginaries as very practical as well. Venomous or not, they are clinical tools. Academic and medical disciplines will build social imaginaries that doctors and scientists use in surgery, in space programs. Any scientific map of the unseen that leads to treatment can be called a social imaginary: Freud's imagined maps of the unconscious; maps of the atom; maps of the birth of the universe; maps for the faithful. However, if a prayer humanizes the believer, is salvation imaginary? All cosmologies, teleologies, cargo cults, probably all forms of history and anthropology, require belief in an event or holy place that never existed in any provable way. And, finally, the future is a clinical map (a topology) that we visit in advance, hypothetically.

All forms of the "future," when they are built, whether it is the Starship Enterprise or the acid rain on a cyberpunk movie set, fit as social imaginaries, what I call the future-perfect. They deliver a shared memory of an event that has never occurred – yet. Game theory, when the army uses it to game-plan for maneuvers in the Middle East or at NATO, is a social imaginary (clinical if they actually take it to war). The military claims that game theory is very clinical. What if occasionally they are right? Never underestimate the horse-and-plow uses of the map, no matter how perverse its signage or epistemology.

There is a proverb in my family which I repeat continuously to my son, while we commute from one L.A. tourist trap to another: the best way to lie is with the truth. To prove my point, I show him photos of the muddy Main Street that Disney knew as a child, and compare that to the nostalgic Main Street that was approved by Walt for Disneyland. My son stares at me intolerantly, and says: "Dad, all the kids know this already. They just don't care as much as you do." I try to remember this mild humiliation whenever I play with material involving mass culture. The social imaginary has just enough "truth" to make the false worth savoring, or else no one cares. The audience already senses, very consciously, that it is false, but buys it anyway, simply as the thrill of sharing in the magic trick. The gag can be blatantly awkward (big lies in shopping malls), and succeed brilliantly, simply because its map "feels" useful. It is useful precisely *because* it is defiantly false. The hyper-real edge announces how false; it is fashioned out of a sensation of difference, of a *lost* memory. The object can be touched, but it stands in for what is off the map. Simulation is not a copy, but a blur between memory and signifier.

To describe that sensation, I prefer the metaphor of a *scar*. The hand touches the welt of an old scar on the side of the face. The mass feels unnatural. It bears the memory of surgical violence – a physical piece of evidence, but evacuated of meaning. To repeat a popular example in Los Angeles,[28] the abandoned tunnel off Glendale Boulevard, where a subway spur used to run from downtown, is a scar. As a historian, I was taught to invent a clean, linear story to explain how this tunnel was abandoned: the greed, the racism. But there are tours of the tunnel, and a mythology

12

around it, though very few people are quite certain how it was used. This uncertainty allows the historian to find a narrative hook, like the opening page of a novel. It is a specular (visual) site that escapes its own origins, and can be found only by the trail (the sensation) it leaves, by its evacuation.

I return to the theme of this introduction: as historical text, the social imaginary presents a literary problem as well. The scholar cannot write down precisely what a group remembers – the mental picture they share: the face of God, the look of the future. If individuals are asked directly, their testimony involves an act of forgetting as much as remembering. But in this case, social imaginary is not a tool, only a document. The principle *literary* tool for the historian has to be considerably more precise: to re-evoke an historical event in the context of these fleeting memoirs – what one philosopher called "the hearing of deaf actions, the seeing of the blind."[29] The term I use for this tool is distraction, amended from theories on how the individual forgets, then applied as a literary technique, to how a collective forgets.

SIMULTANEOUS DISTRACTION: THE INDIVIDUAL

Research on "forgetting" is mostly a subfield within cognitive psychology – the study of how memory "decays." However, many of these same issues resonate in art and literary theory as well, about modernity, simultaneity. Effaced memory has been an appropriately postmodern subject. It brings to mind contemporary debates in cultural studies, ethnohistory, anthropology, and urban history – and seems to make reasonably charming video games. At the very least, it is a literary conceit perversely suitable for a study on street memory in Los Angeles.

The core issue – for theories on how the individual forgets – once again is *distraction*: the quiet instant when one imago covers over another. Philosophically, if not experientially, this sensation can be summed up by two paradoxes, which I underline because they reappear often over the past 2,500 years in the West: first, *In order to remember, something must be forgotten*; second, *The place where memories are stored has no boundaries*. In other words, forgetting is a twin; its tandem effect is best called "*simultaneous*" *distraction*, the instant when one memory defoliates another. This fuzzy double – one devouring the other – presumably inhibits learning. Models of how "distraction" looks have rediscovered this paradox consistently, even when they seem to look so different on first viewing. In the end, with grave reluctance, the passages that point out how binaries erase each other are cautionary, in the form of a warning, often not much more than a paragraph long, saved for somewhere near the end of a lengthy analysis.

BRIEF INTERRUPTION

This subject utterly absorbs me, but the details over centuries do not take us directly into Parts I and II. Also, to split hairs surgically, to point out how distraction is not quite what Webster's dictionary says it is – about confusion merging into entertainment – would take a lengthy review. The only solution for this introduction is a kind of hypertext (click to page 301). For the reader who is also interested in memory theory – tropes (clinical maps) about how the individual forgets – I have included an Appendix, entitled "Where is Forgetting Located?" Read it now or later, whenever it suits you. In it, I review how the "rhetoric of memory" has operated as a social imaginary, at least in the West, in systems of mnemonics, in theories of the unconscious, in cultural theory. I have centered the debate on this principle of simultaneous distraction; philosophers, clinicians and critics have observed the same binary paradox for millennia – how remembering scars. When one recalls a memory, one is also simultaneously forgetting to some degree, or effacing another memory, or simply watching the clarity decay. But to stay on track – how the collective forgets – let me merely summarize what is in the Appendix.

THE LOCATION OF FORGETTING[30]

Even the topologies and tropes used to describe the "place" where memory is stored in the brain imply erasure. Over the centuries, this "place" has been imagined as a waxen tablet, an electrical trace, a cluster sparking on a network, a library made of eroding fabric, a mental theater with painted doors. In practically every version, the site is "built" from a highly malleable substance, or moves along a very slippery trail. Memories tend to efface easily, or lose track.

Most of all, they distract: if one memory happens to resemble another, one of these will be inhibited; in other words, distorted or simply "misplaced." When a memory is recalled like a car part from storage, there is no scientific certainty as to how it is put back, probably not as it was. Certainly the packing is disturbed. Therefore short-term memory means just that. Over 70 per cent decays within the hour generally. Long-term memory – events and ideas – vanish even more elaborately, inside yet another practical but imaginary construct, the unconscious, where forgetting and dream theory apparently meet, as parallel systems of displacement and condensation, or as language evaporating as it speaks.

These tropes make for marvelous fictions (even literally in the Surrealist sense of "the marvelous"). They conjure up images of leaky batteries misfiring, organic radio towers sending up bent signals. And among these fictions, displacement is the most ironic, most sardonic of them all, a system of flaking and growing, dead cells and new cells surfacing at the same metabolic instant.

According to the ancients and many of the moderns, the only hope for retaining short-term memory in particular (numbers, names, dates, nonsense syllables) – to protect against distraction – is through mnemonic systems, where cues like place, sound, or contiguity are assembled mentally in order to bring the picture back ("Where did I park that car again?"). But even here, memory is a distracted imaginary, essentially a filing system where information disappears or reforms itself whenever you touch it. Episodic and semantic memory are even less stable. They mutate simply as a result of what is present around them, like plants of different species making friends when you're not looking.

Test: can you remember the five examples of short-term memory in parenthesis above? If for some perverse reason you can, how long before it will disappear, unless you package it in some way? Like this test, most work on memory theory in the West is fundamentally empiricist, primarily linked to salvaging memory. That has been the pattern since the Romans essentially. Save as much as possible. Keep the mental bookkeeping accurate. Civilization seemed to depend on immense recall. However, that attitude represents only a small portion of the literature on "forgetting." In our century most of all, for reasons all too brutally obvious, at least as many writers have taken an anti-empirical position, that mnemonics was futile, even dangerous. The short story by Borges, "Funes the Memorious," may be the classic position: a man afflicted by complete recall, who eventually is driven mad by his gift.[31] In place of obsessive retention, Borges advises selective forgetting; and that essential argument has re-emerged in contemporary theory.[32] Barthes summarized the argument best with a quote from Kafka: "We photograph things in order to drive them out of our minds."[33]

What Barthes is warning us is that the Borgesian/Kafkaesque strand of criticism, above all, is a form of literature. "Selective forgetting" is a *literary* method more than a scholarly one. It is "distractive" history, where "presence and absence"[34] infect each other inside the same object – like a Joseph Cornell installation or a Jan Svankmejer film.

In terms of this book, selective forgetting is a literary tool for describing a social imaginary: how fictions are built into facts, while in turn erasing facts into fictions. I call this *literary* device "distraction," to remind myself that no matter how fancy my urban research, this is merely a story about how one person decides to forget – voluntarily or involuntarily.[35]

When this technique – distraction – dominates a "story" utterly, when the contradictory impact of a social imaginary is the sole object, the "factive" result is what I call a docufable, for lack of a better term (it seemed the most innocent label that I could find, but there is not much music to it). A docufable is generally short, often ethnographic, a passage no longer than 5,000 words surely. I'll provide a few examples of docufable in Part III, but will use distractive techniques throughout, to a greater or lesser degree, depending on the subject.

DOCUFABLE

To narrow further: Docufable is a brief essay in a fictive voice that captures, through distraction, the instant when a memory is being erased. Visually, I'd compare it to special effects, a morphing program in slo-mo, when the simulation is naked, when the tiger obviously is three frames away from turning human. Or a documentary on a historical subject that ignores the historical photographs, and instead simply uses digital simulations that morph into photos, because the film is about an imaginary about to be built (for example, a casino, a theme mall, a movie set, a new expressway, plastic surgery on a body).

The term is merely another literary conceit that sharpens some of the issues for me. The word itself sounds passive, like a soft landing after a steep fall. I remember hearing someone's dying message on an answering machine – before he took his life. It sounded stricken, but amazingly polite. So, too, my mother said goodbye to me on the phone right before she died. The theater of possibilities disappear. A frenzy and shadow take over. The tone of voice is distracted, as in many of the interviews for this book. The speaker is reminded of a personal shock, a grave loss from war or immigration; and speaks gently, as if trying not to move a bandage. The writer takes this information, adds social context and theory; but what results will read more like a novel about collective paramnesia than empirical history.

I will provide examples in Part III; however, the technique of simultaneous distraction reappears throughout, so the reader is officially "put on alert." The writing style has to be more changeable than is usual in scholarship; it shifts to match the tone of the evidence. As Huck Finn said of Mark Twain: "There was things which he stretched, but mainly he told the truth."[36]

OUTLINE

In the chapters that follow (Part I), I will examine the map of what is left out in downtown Los Angeles, how urban myths (social imaginaries) have been used as public policy. In the second part, I present a docu-novel (or novella) based on Vietnamese immigrants who live in areas affected by these policies. In the third part, I present docufables from other residents in these communities, particularly about how their memories are affected by public traumas: drive-by shootings, racist neglect, policies toward immigrants, the Uprising of 1992, and so on. And in the final parts, I examine how literature and now media use techniques of the "unreliable narrator," and how the corporate uses of "unreliable" memory are transforming the cultures in Los Angeles.

IDENTITY / COMMUNITY

I should add a paragraph on my own "unreliability," my tendencies. Much of this book is about the uneven decay of Anglo identity in Los Angeles, how the instability of white hegemonic culture leads to bizarre over-reactions in urban planning, in policing, and how these are mystified in mass culture. However, I do not want to exoticize the pain that this violent uncertainty causes. I would rather honor the nobility I see in those who are left to deal with what remains afterward. Admittedly, I am sentimental about the virtues of community cohesion, particularly in poor neighborhoods. I admire whatever survives in the face of utter neglect.

That includes even a blunt, empty city lot. As I write this, however, I notice what a weepy side of my nature this suggests. If I painted myself as a parody, I probably would be staring at a construction site in a Caspar David Friedrich painting.

My garage office even suggests the fetishes of a Romanticist, despite my obsession with ruthless compression in writing and research. I store everything that looks like a pile of dirt left on the side of a hole. On one shelf, I keep a piece of the Berlin Wall next to a fossil of a Pleistocene bug, and beside that a pint whiskey bottle that was buried by a doctor during Prohibition, to keep his neighbors from knowing how much he drank. Next to that I have an eroded coke bottle dropped seventy years ago into Echo Park Lake, by a teenage girl forced to spoon with her oafish boyfriend, while wishing she could toss him into the lake instead. They don't make much of a community, nor an identity – more like a collection of string; but they are satisfactorily in a state of absence. They remind me that most crimes are nearly not committed, and that only a fraction of crimes are ever discovered, or even considered worth remembering.

NOTES

1. Beyond the secondary sources on downtown's removal since the thirties – e.g. Mike Davis, *City of Quartz* (London and New York: Verso, 1990); Klein and Schiesl, eds, *Twentieth Century Los Angeles* – infinitely more is available through primary sources in various collections, from articles to pamphlets to ephemera: Los Angeles Regional History Collection at USC, Special Collections at UCLA, various archival sources under Los Angeles history at the central branch of the Los Angeles Public Library, the morgues for the *Los Angeles Times*, the *Los Angeles Herald*, the *Los Angeles Examiner*, and through the key photo collections in each of these sources, as well as the William Reagh collection. The most extensive bibliography for the earlier twentieth century is *Los Angeles and Its Environs in the Twentieth Century: A Bibliography of a Metropolis*, edited by Doyce Nunis (Los Angeles: The Ward Ritchie Press, 1973).

2. "Phantom limb" is another term that clarifies the issues for me. While it fits into this section of the text, it is also utterly phallocentric, but that can be useful, a reminder that much of this study is about men in power. From boosterism to noir, the sources are filled with phrases that sound priapic, comically omnipotent, and frequently destructive, simple as that. So the reader is invited to let all the double entendres "fly." For example, why did "phantom limb," a term commonly used in "polite" society during the period I discuss, not suggest the hidden penis? In the Victorian era, close to where I begin my diegesis, limb was considered a more polite word than leg. Roaches did not have cocks. Pianos had "limbs."

3. Norman M. Klein, *Seven Minutes: The Life and Death of the American Animated*

Cartoon (London:Verso, 1993), p. 95. Samples of some of these are among the illustrations.

4. Julia Kristeva, *Powers of Horror: An Essay on Abjection*, trans. L. Roudiez (New York: Columbia University Press, 1982), p. 8.

5. Picturesque: a term associated with Ruskin, and with nineteenth-century aesthetics, about the sublime within the *pictural* representation of landscape. I also see it as the distractive qualities of tourism – the imago that the tourist brings to a real space, or that a real space brings to an imago (simulations of the picturesque in urban planning).

6. The incriminating letter was stuffed behind visiting cards on a mantelpiece. It is so soiled, as to be "hyper-obtrusive," yet invisible even "in full view," easy to steal or replace. Poe's purloined letter is identified as an evacuated presence, in discussions of this story by Lacan and Derrida. Its presence is distracted by the speech of the narrator, standing in for the observer. See: John Muller and William Richardson, eds. *The Purloined Poe: Lacan, Derrida and Psychoanalytic Reading* (Baltimore: Johns Hopkins University Press, 1988). Also: Stuart Schneiderman, "Fictions," in the anthology edited by Ellie Ragland-Sullivan and Mark Bracher, *Lacan and the Subject of Language* (London: Routledge, 1991).

7. Field work about urban erasure – the "empty" vessel in the built environment. – is essential for the subfield Industrial Archaeology: see the journal *IA* and the writings of Patrick Malone, Robert Vogel, Robert Gordon, Lawrence Gross, Sandra Norman, Mathew Roth. Also, *The Urban Text*, edited by Mario Gandelsmas (Chicago: Chicago Institute for Architecture, 1991), on "real and unreal grids" (pp. 39–42), the "ghost" of the Chicago River (51–9); and writings of Grady Clay.

8. David Lowenthal, *The Past is a Foreign Country* (Cambridge: Cambridge University Press, 1985), p. 225. Fiction as "history's handmaid" is Lowenthal's phrase, but is very much in the spirit of Scott's project as novelist in the 1820s, and Balzac's for that matter, though in a different sense clearly. Lowenthal argues that the late Renaissance marks the point of divergence between history and fiction, on behalf of "accuracy" (p. 225). With that as the theme, memory is presented as a construct that is antithetical to history. Memory is too debased by its own political concerns to locate – except by distraction – the past that is a foreign country (see also footnote 29). By contrast, I simply narrow to areas of mass culture where "historical documents" stand in for the trail left by an absence; the record that is always, in itself, an act of erasure – not quite what Lowenthal means. Nor what Raphael Samuel discusses so well: power grids that build (objectify) historical memory, and the marketing of urban heritage, in *Theatres of Memory*, Volume I (London: Verso, 1994).

9. For a brief discussion of nineteenth-century historians who owed a great deal to the novel, see Linda Hutcheon, *A Poetics of Postmodernism: History, Theory and Fiction* (London: Routledge, 1988), pp. 105–7. One of the classic examples is Thomas Carlyle's *The French Revolution* as a source for Dickens' *A Tale of Two Cities*, referring to the criticism of Barbara Foley (*Telling the Truth* [Ithaca: Cornell University Press., 1986]). Of course, Carlyle's source was the notes left him by John Stuart Mill, which were in turn deeply limited by the censorship of British journalism. So indeed, there seems no point within that process where the fictionalizing of a historical event did not interfere.

10. By "chronicle," I am suggesting aspects of the debate on narrativity associated with Hayden White and others; for example, in White's *The Content of the Form: Narrative Discourse and Historical Representation* (Baltimore: Johns Hopkins University Press, 1987). I suppose a more appropriate term might be *recit*, as in White's chapter on

Foucault (p. 125), but I decided that the fuss I might make by laboring over epistemology could confuse the reader. I am trying, with as much modesty as possible, to identify a form of literature that is not simply "hybridized," or "de-narrated," and certainly not deconstructed – not a blend of others, but a structure in itself, a structure that is evolving, in a way similar to what generated the novel in the 1820s. By structure, I mean *how to generate alternatives within the text itself, within the style itself.* So instead of writing a paragraph about the differences between chronicle, annals and history, I simply took the term that returned the problem to historical writing at a point in transition, like the 1820s (as in Stendhal's use of the term "chronicle," or ironic references in historical novels back to Froissart's chronicles). I refer to the 1820s merely as an instructive parallel, one instance when writers were acutely aware of how the new fashion for the historical novel was "historicizing" memory.

11. On faction, etc.: I suppose the term that wins will be the one that makes the most singular impact on the racks of a new section in the bookstore. The trick, of course, lies in identifying the solidity of the imaginary somewhere in the word itself.

12. Historiographic metafiction is a term in Linda Hutcheon's *A Poetics of Postmodernism* (pp. 108–23): the fictionalizing of famous people in historical novels, where the status of the "facts" are presented ironically in the narrative.

13. Historians John Demos (*The Unredeemed Captive*), and Simon Schama (*Landscape Memory, Dead Certainties*) have both written historical fiction, and have drawn some criticism for and against, much as Natalie Davis did in the sixties with her documentary novel (*The Return of Martin Guerre*), and the work of Robert Darnton and Jonathan Spence. One critic observed: "Of course Daniel Defoe had been blending fact and fiction long before Oliver Stone or before Schama set pen to paper" (David Samuels, "The Call of Stories," *Lingua Franca*, May 1995, p. 39). That makes sense: that historian/fictioneers are retrieving an old practice, the moment for readers in 1719 when Crusoe's diary refers back to the shipwreck of Henry Selkirk only ten years earlier. That becomes a moment (among many) when the novel as literary form begins, as a hybrid of documentation and invention. And scholarship may be at such a point again, like the epistolary novel of 1720, or a post-historicist novel of the 1990s.

14. A useful summary of "postmodern" ethnography is to be found in Susan Hegeman, "History, Ethnography and Myth: Some Notes on the 'Indian-Centered' Narrative," Part II, *Social Text*, No. 23, Fall/Winter 1989, pp. 154–8. Many of the sources are taken from the anthology *Writing Culture: The Poetics and Politics of Ethnography*, edited by James Clifford and George Marcus (Berkeley: University of California Press, 1986). The essays there by Marcus, Fischer, Rabinow and, of course, Clifford are very suggestive. Michael Fischer offers a precise summary: "The ethnic, the ethnographer, and the cross-cultural scholar in general often begin with a personal empathetic 'dual tracking,' seeking in the other clarification for processes in the self" (p. 199). Another useful summary is Johannes Fabian, "Ethnographic Objectivity Revisited: From Rigor to Vigor, in *Rethinking Objectivity*, edited by Allan Megill (Durham: Duke University Press, 1994).

15. As general sources, to clarify what I had already been discovering – beyond the wealth of anthropological field studies on tall tales and oral memory – I found the anthology *Anthropology and Autobiography* (edited by Judith Okely and Helen Calloway [London: Routledge, 1992]) useful, particularly the essay by Kirsten Hastrup, "Writing Ethnography: The State of the Art." See also, James Fentress and Chris Wickham, eds, *Social Memory* (Oxford: Blackwell, 1992). The anthology edited by Clifford and Marcus,

Writing Culture, has become a classic resource, as has Clifford's *The Predicament of Culture* (Harvard: Harvard University Press, 1988). Finally, I found Richard Bauman's *Story, Performance, and Event: Contextual Studies of Oral Narrative* (Cambridge: Cambridge University Press, 1986) filled with valuable reminders.

16. As used by Homi Bhaba in his review of sources: "Postcolonial Authority and Postmodern Guilt," in Lawrence Grossberg, Cary Nelson, Paula Treichler, eds, *Cultural Studies* (London: Routledge, 1992), pp. 56–68, particularly p. 63ff.

17. Ruth Frankenberg and Lata Mani, "Crosscurrents, Crosstalk: Race: 'Postcoloniality' and the Politics of Location," *Cultural Studies*, May 1993, p. 301: "the postcolonial axis of memory – of the memories and legacies of colonization/decolonization…"

18. See feminist critiques of "objectivity in the research sciences." Jill McCalla Vickers: "Objectifying [women's] pains in words which hide the identity of their oppression" (from "Memories of an Ontological Exile," quoted in Angela R. Miles and Geraldine Finn, eds, *Feminism in Canada: From Pressure to Politics* (Montreal: Black Rose Books, 1982), p. 40). Also, Mary E. Hawksworth, "From Objectivity to Objectification," in Allan Megill, ed., *Rethinking Objectivity* (Durham: Duke University Press, 1994), p. 156.

19. Clearly, I am interpellating here from Bakhtin's theories of the dialogical. It is also important, within this category, to include Certeau's work on the street, the many variations of Benjamin on *flâneur*, interpellated from Baudelaire's essays and diaries: the scholar as empathic tourist, observing the simultaneities of urban street life. And Simmel's essays on "adventure," and on the street.

20. From Woolf's 1931 novel *The Waves* (Bernard speaking):

> Is it Paris, is it London where we sit or some southern city of pink-washed houses lying under cypresses, under high mountains, where eagles soar? I do not at this moment feel certain.
>
> I begin now to forget; I begin to doubt the fixity of tables, the reality of here and now, to tap my knuckles smartly upon the edges of apparently solid objects and say, "Are you hard?" I have seen so many different things, have made so many different sentences. I have lost in the process of eating and drinking and rubbing my eyes along surfaces that thin, hard shell which cases the soul, which, in youth, shuts one in, – hence the fierceness, the tap, tap, tap of the remorseless beaks of the young.

(New York: Harcourt Brace, 1959 paperback edition, p. 288, within ten pages of the end)

21. A Walter Benjamin quote that seemed appropriate. In his essay "The Image of Proust" (in *Illuminations*, trans. Harry Zohn [New York: Schocken Books, 1969] p. 202), Benjamin describes memory and writing as an unraveling process, the "Penelope syndrome":

> The day unravels what the night has woven. When we awake each morning, we hold in our hands, usually weakly and loosely, but a few fringes of the tapestry of lived life, as loomed before us by forgetting… Our purposive remembering each day unravels the ornaments of forgetting.

22. Michel Foucault, *The Order of Things* (New York: Random House, 1971; orig. 1966), p. 69.

23. References to *social* imaginary appeared in French criticism during the seventies, as an amalgam of Lacan's theory of the Imaginary Order and Althusser on ideology. They are central to critiques by the philosopher psychiatrist Cornelius Castoriadis.

Hegel may well be the "originating" source in this chain of theory, as when Castoriadis calls the *imaginary* "the night of the world, the power of drawing images out of this night or of letting them slip away," and then quotes directly from Hegel on the "night" of the self, "the empty nothingness which contains everything in its simplicity: a wealth of representations, images, infinite in number, none of which emerges precisely in his mind, or which are not always present"(p. 263). The imaginary is resemblance in reverse, like anti-matter or anti-memory: "the capacity to see in a thing what it is not, to see it other than it is," because "reality is that in which the do-able and the undo-able reside"(ibid., p. 263).

Another application of social imaginary has been applied from Foucault's theories on popular memory. Stephen Heath, in the conclusion to his book *Questions of Cinema* ([Bloomington: Indiana University Press, 1981], pp. 236–8), describes Foucault's interview on popular memory in *Cahiers du Cinema* in 1970, and its influence on debates in French film theory about the role of memory in cinema, and its role in what was identified as the "Cinema and History fetish". Other writers he cites are Pascal Bonitzer, J. Jourdheuil, Jacques Rancière.

In an interview with Foucault entitled "Film and Popular Memory," in the collection *Foucault Live (Interviews 1966–84)*, edited by S. Lottringer, trans. J. Johnston (New York: Semiotexte, 1989), Foucault describes what sounds to me like a variant of "distraction:" that in the nineteenth century, historical memory was "obstructed" successfully by popular literature (pp. 91–9); and now is obstructed even more effectively through television and cinema. However (in response to a question about Ophuls' *The Sorrow and the Pity*): "it's vital to have possession of this memory, to control it, to administer it, tell it what it must contain" (p. 93). Since 1968, however, the efforts to stifle popular memory have increased considerably, until at last "popular struggles have become for our society, not part of the actual, but part of the possible" (p. 102).

24. See: Alexander Cockburn, "On the Rim of the Pacific Century," in David Reid, ed., *Sex, Death and God in L.A.* (Berkeley: University of California Press, 1994), pp. 16–18.

25. A term used occasionally by Bergson: phosphene is merely the after-image left by bright light, seeing with one's eyes closed, when a deformed specular shock changes colors, then vanishes. See also the Appendix, "Where is Forgetting Located?"

26. Castoriadis, *The Imaginary Institution of Society*, p. 263.

27. Norman M. Klein, "Unearthing the Vampire," *Sulfur*, no. 5. The superstition I refer to is what the American historian Barker-Benfield calls the "spermatic economy," the myth that blood and sperm are produced in the body by the same organs. Therefore excessive sexual ejaculation causes anemia. The vampire's victim is anemic, caught in the sin of excess. The vampire gains blood during the sexual act, defying the laws of mortal sexuality.

28. Not only does Mike Davis mention this tunnel in *City of Quartz*, along with a photo of it looking nasty – graffitied, overgrown, isolated behind a chain link fence – he also uses it often in tours for students interested in research on Los Angeles (also scholars: see note 24). But even more curious to me, the tunnel is undoubtedly the one site that young people whom I interview have seen or visited personally, as the icon of lost downtown. They agree that it looks more cyberpunk than any of the other "lost" sites, like a burial chamber for a lost thought.

29. Martin Farquar Tupper (1810–1915), a rather unremarkable philosopher to us today, a moralist who wrote in blank verse.

30. Again, for more detail on this argument, read the Appendix, "Where is Forgetting Located?"

31. Jorge Luís Borges, *Labyrinths: Selected Stories and Other Writings*, trans. D. Yates and J. Irby (New York: New Directions, 1962). Also, in the same volume, *Tlon, Uqbar, Orbis Tertius*, where the following appears: "All things tend to become effaced and lose their details when they are forgotten," as quoted in David Lowenthal's *The Past is a Foreign Country*. Lowenthal provides a breadth of sources on the role of memory in historical narrative. He narrows to the issue of forgetting specifically on pp. 204–6, by citing *Funes the Memorious*, and writing: "Memories must continually be discarded and conflated; only forgetting enables us to classify and bring chaos into order." My point of view is a bit different: that chaos is a protection against the ideological dishonesty of order; and that chaos is in itself a structural, narrative form in many of the arts, for example in animation (see Klein, *Seven Minutes*).

32. Beside the hundreds of fine-arts installation pieces about memory, starting with Joseph Cornell's work in the forties, this paradoxical erasure of memory is a recurring theme in photo criticism, beginning with Susan Sontag's on photography consuming memory (*On Photography* [New York: Farrar, Strauss & Giroux, 1977]) and recently in the work of William J. Mitchell on digitalized photography consuming meaning: *The Reconfigured Eye* (Cambridge, Mass.: MIT Press, 1992) – which gives the background to how photography has become "natural and normal to us," and "played a crucial role in the creation of collective memory and formation of belief" (p. 59), a thorough and influential source. See also the essays of Lev Manovitch, and certainly the theory of Bourdieu; also the writings of Jonathan Crary (*Techniques of the Observer: On Vision and Modernity in the Nineteenth Century* [Cambridge, Mass.: MIT Press, 1992]); and the section on photography and public memory, in David Chaney, *Fictions of Collective Life*, (London: Routledge, 1993), p. 86ff.

33. Roland Barthes, *Camera Lucida: Reflections of Photography*, trans. R. Howard (New York: Hill & Wang, 1981), p. 53. Barthes is quoting from the diaries of Janouch, which were reassembled years after the fact, somewhat loosely based on memories of what Kafka said – snatches of aphorism, like photographs.

34. I borrow that contrast from Christian Metz, *The Imaginary Signifier: Psychoanalysis and the Cinema*, trans. Britton, Williams, Brewster and Guzzetti (Bloomington: Indiana University Press, 1982), p. 44.

35. Voluntary and involuntary memory, as in Proust's distinctions; a pun referring back to the vast debate on memory during the Symbolist era, mentioned in the Appendix.

36. The opening page of *Huckleberry Finn*.

From *Rob Wagner's California Almanack* (1924)

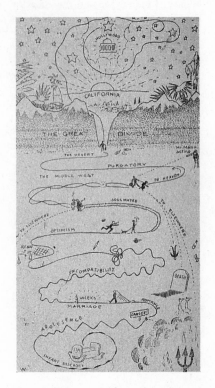

From *Rob Wagner's California Almanack* (1922)

PART I

BUILDING THE SOCIAL
IMAGINARY: 1885–1997

CHAPTER ONE

BOOSTER MYTHS,
URBAN ERASURE

Los Angeles is a city that was imagined long before it was built. It was imagined to avoid city-wide bankruptcy in the 1890s, and has stayed on a knife edge ever since, camouflaged by promotional rhetoric. In 1899, the secretary of the Los Angeles Chamber of Commerce wrote:

> The prosperity of Los Angeles is founded on the immutable forces of nature, combined with the inevitable needs of mankind; and it will remain, as the sea and the clouds and the mountains remain, and will increase as the nation and the race increases.[1]

This is classic boosterist language, like a cross between the Apostles and a salesman's handbook, as if a deal had been cut with God about how to promote real estate. Like many adventurous businessmen of the day, these market managers claimed to be possessed by the evangelical spirit. But they were selling something even grander than leather-tooled editions of the Good Book. They were selling the City on the Hill as prime real estate, in its entirety, including the hill itself, which was located near the new train station immediately downtown, near full city lots for sale, along newly paved streets, with a view of good farmland for sale in the valleys surrounding. It was the new Jerusalem, first come, first served, at the semi-arid, most westerly – and newly civilized – corner of the great frontier. However inflated the language, the strategy was simple enough. Through a consortium of local businessmen and large railroad interests, a small city would be merchandised into a metropolis. A financial disaster would be turned around.

In 1888, following the collapse of a feverish real estate boom, L.A. was losing about a thousand people a month, from a high of about 65,000. By 1890, the population had fallen by a third.[2] Land values had declined by over $14 million (in current dollars, that would be more like $14 billion!). And yet something substantial remained. There were still about 50,000 people left in the city. In only five years, the population had multiplied by 400 per cent. Unfortunately, the business infrastructure had not changed enough to provide jobs for that many people. The economy of L.A. was too primitive for a city of fifty thousand.

In a race against time, the new chamber of commerce turned toward the only industry that promised immediate returns – tourism mixed with real-estate speculation. Other doors were tried in the 1890s: attempts to invite industry into L.A., or to enlarge the citrus market (there was major advertising for both after 1897). But even as late as 1900, tourism still accounted for over a quarter of all business revenues – more than all manufacturing combined, and second only to agriculture.

To keep tourism healthy, as the foundation for economic growth, leading businessmen in Los Angeles personally financed a war chest for large promotional campaigns that went nationwide (a much grander version of what the old Board of Trade had done for L.A.). Exhibitions about exotic and fertile Los Angeles were featured in Chicago, in Iowa, at state fairs and world fairs. Hundreds of brochures reached millions of people,[3] attracting the desired Protestant newcomers from small towns in the midwest, and also attracting movie producers with capital from "back East," and cheap labor from all corners of America. The brochures promised a sunny, "green-acre" city free of urban stress and class warfare – in short, a farm town without unions, and without dark industrial tenements to interfere in the conduct of business.

To maintain the imaginary as the real and make it pay off, some problems were acceptable risks, others were demonized. Business miscues were acceptable. From Venice in 1905 to Mount Olympus in the sixties, there is a long history of failed real-estate projects going gray in the rain like the bones of mammoths. These were understood by civic leaders as the Darwinism of free enterprise. The less fit lose their mortgage. Los Angeles always has a great tolerance for the mess left by speculators. The hype of tourist advertising also brought the hucksters so much associated with the hard edge of Los Angeles: store-front dreamers, white-collar swindlers, and gambling rings. But these sins were also forgiven as a rule, not legislated away. They were essentially bad eggs (white, but a little too hard-boiled), not serious enough to turn off investors.

What presented a far greater risk, it was felt, was the location of slums, where the less white and less middle class lived. Some of these slums emerged out of boosterism itself, as necessary for growth. Agribusiness, oil and the trolley industry campaigned by flyer to bring in Mexicans, Japanese, landless farm workers from the midwest – the cheap labor required to assemble this leviathan. Slums represented the highest negatives for well-heeled tourists who came to stay, and had to be zoned out of sight in some way. But they never disappeared entirely, not when so much activity was bursting at once. As a result, the grand booster campaign built two social imaginaries, not only the Protestant Jerusalem, but also the sinful tourist Babylon. The way these two contraries merged and distracted, from 1890 to the present, may be the easiest way to understand how downtown was erased in plain view.

By 1900, boosterism in Los Angeles had developed virtually into a public-service corporation, centered around three industries: tourism, real estate, and transportation. As those industries changed, the promotional rhetoric shifted considerably. The shifts were most evident during the late 1930s and the Second World War, when much of the background to the freeway city (or industri-opolis) was set up; that is, the planning that altered downtown – from a rural to an industrial imaginary. I will present these as promotional "myths" that were designed by chambers of commerce, city planning, the motor club, and so on; then discussed as self-evident in city council meetings, usually with gusto and active contradiction – half fact, half cloaking device, a collective imaginary shared by those who ran policy. Finally, each myth becomes dated when it no longer fits the market. Then it mutates erratically into other schemes: the myth of the climate (1880s to 1930s); the myth of a freeway metropolis (1936–49); the myths of downtown renewal (1936–49); the myth of the pacific Byzantium (1980s, with the impact of massive immigration, and the internationalization of urban and suburban space).

And then there is *anti*-tourism, the collective "myths" of sleazy Los Angeles created by crime writers, screenwriters, filmmakers, mostly in reaction to the city that these consumerist policies deliver. First I consider the noir impulse (1930–90): apocalyptic myths emerging out of the underside of tourism and consumerism, including the extraordinary importance of the film *Blade Runner* as a collective imaginary, even for architects.

Then I look at noir after 1992: the crime capital of America, though statistically Los Angeles is barely among the twenty most dangerous cities in the country. Then I enter the local myths in and around downtown, particularly after 1980: the fictions being built under the shocks of urban erasure, massive immigration, the Uprising of 1992, the new, panicked media coverage of Los Angeles.

It is noteworthy that research on boosterism plays havoc with the chronology of *post*modernism. L.A. appears more "postmodern" in 1900 than in 1920; that is, "post" before modernism arrives, decades before heavy manufacturing – a peculiar twist to Los Angeles studies.[4]

"Post" as in mass advertising, and a service economy, with exports and tourism integrated through promotion. As of 1900, the elite in L.A. depend on advertising as firmly as Rockefeller depended on railroad cars to freight and burn oil. Even manufacturing was subsumed beneath the ad campaign, in their eyes. Bankers from "back east" had to be promoted to come here, the same as tourists. In 1897, free passage was tendered to industrialists, if they were ready to invest.[5] At the same time, in one more schizoid twist, these same investors could not fail to notice how anti-industrial boosterism tried to sound, promising that L.A. would never turn into another Chicago – no smokestacks, no skyscrapers, no pandering to big rail interests. Climate came first, the "smokeless city."

By the twenties, that ambivalence toward heavy industry had all but disappeared. "Smokeless city" was part of a campaign to sell water power, electric power and big oil, as crucial to booster campaigns as sunshine and citrus.[6] If this equality between machines and the climate sounds schizoid in yet another way, that is because the boosters always changed their pitch when new businesses required different tourists, in this case oil workers. Selling the imaginary was L.A.'s Weberian modernity, the totalizing device that explains how space has been built and perceived.

Therefore boosterism was rarely stable, though on the outside it promised to be. The ads looked deceptively harmonious, the tours as white as kid gloves. Indeed, publicly, the elite could agree on basic principles, to fight unions for example. But in private sessions, there could be grave acrimony and extreme panic. Once dollar investments or city ordinances were at stake, the infighting grew fierce.[7]

Even in boom times, when there seemed enough to go around, behind closed doors investors might go into a feeding frenzy, a free-for-all. For example, every ten years the infrastructure would seem to have become obsolete: roads, water, electric. Businesses would go to war to maximize these improvements profitably, to get breaks at City Hall, to control zoning, city bonds, local ordinances. At the same time, politicians negotiated for pet schemes. Wealthy districts, yet another system of rival power blocs, fought each other over where to put which new road. The result was anything but monolithic: policies were stricken by massive duplication, made worse by contradictory, panicked reversals, and odd "myths."

MYTH OF THE CLIMATE: WHOLESOME HEDONISM (1880s TO 1930s)

Lucky Baldwin was one of many entrepreneurs who arrived in L.A. during the boom of the 1880s. He came with a considerable fortune to invest, bought the land that later became the townships of Baldwin Hills and Santa Anita, juggled bank investments with horse breeding, lived with an opulent disregard for Victorian conventions, and got himself into various financial and moral scrapes (he was shot by a young woman who claimed he forced his attentions on her, was married four times, preferred much younger wives). Often, he stretched his real-estate investments to the edge of bankruptcy, but he died a very wealthy man in 1909. His biographer, a specialist in books about gilded-age plutocrats, wrote:

> In real-estate promotion, Lucky Baldwin unquestionably was ahead of his time; and equally without question he knew his stuff. In reply to one prospect who protested that $200 an acre for some unimproved ground was too much, he answered indignantly: "Hell! We're giving away the land. We're selling the climate."[8]

Sales pitches about "the climate" repeat more often than any other in early brochures about Los Angeles. The boosterism continues in articles into the forties and fifties, and is well remembered in novels, films, critical essays into the present. As Aldous Huxley writes in 1939, the sunshine in Los Angeles worked on tourists like a spotlight, "as though on purpose to show the new arrival all the sights."[9]

The fantasy seems as light as the air itself, deceptively innocent. It is hardly a secret that the climate in Southern California is very moderate, a liberation from winter coats. Of course, the campaign far exceeded that patent observation. First, brochures from the 1890s repeated the claims made famous in travel books on Southern California written during the 1870s and 1880s, particularly by an Eastern journalist named Charles

Nordhoff.[10] To Nordhoff, Los Angeles was a Protestant Eldorado in old Mexico, a magical lotus-land of sleepy adobes and Mediterranean, semi-arid grandeur, but a potential mother lode for someone with Yankee ingenuity.

Then, the brochures promised health miracles. By removing oppressive humidity of all types (particularly industrial humidity), the air could cure tuberculosis, rheumatism, asthma, sleeplessness, even impotence. Indeed, the climate did clear the lungs for many (including Harry Chandler, who slept in an orange grove, and was cured). For a time, L.A. was called "the city for those with one lung." In the winters, as many as 20,000 tubercular and rheumatic patients would take the air, or the hot springs in the Los Angeles area, often within a mile of downtown itself.[11] Health foods and sanatoriums were already a major industry.

Late-Victorians were obsessed about fresh air. What passed through an open window had to be invigorating, but not "emasculating." It had to be fresh enough to keep men "vim and fit." In the very popular medical handbook *The Physical Life of Woman*, the well-known Boston physician George Napheys advised that married couples should not sleep together without an open window, and even then, at least "twenty cubic feet of fresh air a minute are required for every healthy adult."[12] The air space had to be larger than 2,400 square feet, to replace old air once an hour. "Rebreathed air," Dr Napheys warned, "is poisonous."

With such hazards facing even the moral couple at rest, consider how fresh the air had to be if one showed the slightest tendency toward illness, or degeneracy? Late-Victorians suffered from lung diseases much more often than we do. Dry air was considered one of the only cures. With Americans feeling invaded rather suddenly by urban expansion after 1870, by poor sanitation growing worse in expanding cities, by thickening traffic jams fetid with horse-driven carriages, by a plague of syphilis that seemed untreatable, medical texts of the day often described the body as a frail temple threatened by tormenting vapors. Germ theory was understood awkwardly, or not at all. To many, the air itself was a holistic science (like theories about body fluids in the seventeenth century, and medical cures by bleeding, practiced as late as the Civil War).

No wonder, then, that doctors' offices in Los Angeles often were built with porches on all sides, to ventilate the air for patients. What is more, it was air that made the soil curative as well. The air in Los Angeles was not only fresh, it was fragrant, very intense with the smells of what grew here. New arrivals to Los Angeles often mentioned the overpowering aroma of orchards, and of vineyards – that the air smelled like wine. The rustic alternative to city life was not vague at all; it was very sensual, much the way suntans were often described as exotic journeys into the world of brown-skinned races, free from the restraints of Protestant sexual codes. And yet, in the case of L.A., the sensuality was improved by moral order. Not only was L.A. the faraway land of Ramona, of misogynous romance, of missions and ranchos, of banditos like Vasquez; it was also wholesome farm country – and Protestant. One could enjoy the exotic freedom from civilization, and still remain civil and productive, while the desert air sanitized the body.

The promotion of L.A.'s climate had much to camouflage. Certain problems with climate were endemic to Los Angeles in the 1890s and, in fact, well-known to many travelers. Brochures as late as 1910 claimed that crops in Southern California could grow practically without water; and so, apparently, could towns. But the trench irrigation system (called zanja) barely provided enough for a population of 33,000, much less 60,000 at the height of the boom. (Campaigns for improved water from the Los Angeles River were highest on the list of public works by 1900, and remained so for a generation.)

As of 1890, though, the water supply was filthy; it brought on spells of typhoid during the summer, or "fever season." During the rainy season, there were floods. The Los Angeles River would swell into the lowlands, and run directly down Alameda Street, where the trains from Kansas City turned *en route* to the main depot. In winter, many houses in the downtown flatlands would fill up with as much as 2 feet of water.[13] Then, during the dry season, water was desperately scarce, of course, despite reservoirs and pumps for some of the nearby hills.

Perhaps it was best for tourists to look up at the sky, and not down at the hazardous water systems. Despite the new aqueduct in 1913, the city continued to struggle for water. And despite the new sewers, in place by the twenties, there were still floods and mud slides.[14] In the early decades of boosterism, the future had to be promised in imaginary statistics – how large the city was bound to be five years later, how much larger its total assets, to keep the in-migration going.

By 1913, though, much of what had been promised was finally in place: a larger job market, particularly in agriculture, but also in light industry and oil, and finally in the film business. Shipping grew tremendously after the dredging of San Pedro Harbor (reopened in 1913) and, soon after, with the opening of the Panama Canal. Even the search to find more kilowatts to generate this expansion was solved through water power by 1917. The promise of a greenbelt city seemed to survive as well. From 1912 until the mid fifties, Los Angeles was the richest farm county in the nation.

This is all standard information, of course. By the twenties, Los Angeles had become an economic giant, in shipping, petroleum, agriculture and cinema. By the mid forties, it had become an industrial giant, particularly in aeronautics. By the eighties, it had become the banking center of the Pacific world, or, as one frequently quoted article in *The Atlantic Monthly* explained, "The Eastern capital of the Pacific."[15]

Today, the lotus land for Caucasians has become "the new Ellis Island" for the largest influx of non-white immigration in the world, far exceeding the numbers arriving in New York. Many of the old boosterist images become running jokes in conversation, about the toxins of the week, or plans to convert the cement banks of the trickling L.A. River into a freeway alternate. Certainly, the air is no longer alluring, not since the shocks of wartime pollution brought the problem to public attention in 1943.[16] News on the climate looks ominous, with public warnings about earthquakes, the greenhouse effect, inversion layers, and offshore oil spills. But the selling of climate initiated the fantasy of Los Angeles, and continued to dominate promotion into the twenties.

In 1921, to expand summer tourism, the All-Year-Round Club was established as a private company, through the leadership of the *Los Angeles Times*. With county bonds, as well as private donations, it raised a $1 million budget for the first three years, and became the dominant promotional machine for the rest of the decade.[17] During one four-month period, it published more than 90 million separate advertisements, 55 million in local newspapers and 35 million in national magazines.[18] With slogans like "sleep under a blanket every night all summer in Southern California," the promotion worked so well that by 1928 the number of tourists in summer equaled those visiting in the winter, and kept growing until, by the forties, it exceeded it. "But," wrote Carey McWilliams (1943), "like most campaigns of the sort, the All-Year Club has been *too* successful."

> Its seductive advertisements were partly responsible for the great influx of impoverished Okies and Arkies in the thirties. Since 1929 its advertisements carry the caption "Warning! Come to California for a glorious vacation. Advise anyone not to come seeking employment."[19]

During the Depression, the marketing of the climate seemed to back-fire. Promotion about weather was cut back, particularly during the war years, when rationing made tourism impractical anyway, even unpatriotic. Also, the sunshine, lotus-land image was hardly appropriate for selling the new industrial Los Angeles so evident during the Second World War. When the Chamber of Commerce was interviewed by *Life Magazine* in 1943, a shift was apparent. In the modified puff piece based heavily on the interview, the reporter clearly was taking a slant very much in line with the new aggressive strategy of business leaders in Los Angeles. The subheading, provided by editors in New York, read: "The city that started with nothing but sunshine now expects to become the biggest in the world."[20] There was blight evident downtown, a large Mexican presence throughout the city,[21] and many new factories; together, these added a new dimension to the selling of Los Angeles – a city of airplanes, shipping, oil and steel. Through the guidance of the interviews by the Chamber of Commerce, the article is peppered with references to L.A. aggressively promoting heavy industry, particularly Douglas Aircraft, to make the city "the aviation capital of the world." The president of Lockheed was quoted as saying: "In any logical scheme the aviation industry should be back in the manufacturing center of the country and not out in a beautiful resort like this." The city had outgrown its farm-town image.

It also began to outgrow its trolleys, radiating out in lineal fashion from downtown. Public transportation in Los Angeles has been held hostage to real-estate promotion virtually from the beginning. A vast inter-urban and streetcar system was built from the 1880s on, and it was promoted as the largest and most efficient in the world, approximately 1,200 miles of track altogether. However, the leaven that kept the system growing was not public need but land speculation. Most of the profits for Henry Huntington's Pacific Electric empire came from real estate, not the fare box. And Huntington was not the only player. Land syndicates would invest in new streetcar franchises, buy up real estate near the proposed stations, then, after completion of the line, sell off quickly for considerable profit.

The premier builder of streetcars, General Moses Sherman, often formed a land syndicate with realtor/contractor Hobart J. Whitley and *L.A. Times* publisher, Harry Chandler. For example, an inter-urban line to Hollywood (pop. 500) opened in 1903, with considerable fanfare. Up to that time, it was known mostly for cattle ranching, pea farming, lemon groves and tourism (a few inns and the Stritchley Ostrich Farm). Now, however, it was in the path of development.[22] That year, Sunset Boulevard was opened west, past the Edendale area (Echo Park); Sunset was the first predecessor of freeway boulevard attached to downtown, and a signal of what was about to begin. Hollywood was formally incorporated as a city. At the Hollywood Hotel, the only location in the area that cabbies at the Alexandria downtown seemed to know, three real-estate agents established residence, waiting for a land rush into the Ocean View Tract, at the western end of town, north of Hollywood Boulevard between LaBrea and Cahuenga.

A brass band played for the first riders, at the downtown station at Hill and Fourth. Lemonade was dispensed. Then, along the way, riders were invited to meet local celebrities. At Cahuenga Boulevard, they visited the home of French painter Paul de Longpre, who specialized in Impressionist landscapes mixed with the sunshine of Los Angeles; visitors could also study his collection of rare hanging rugs. At the Outpost, the oldest building in Hollywood, General Otis, co-founder of the *Times*, originator of the Chamber of Commerce, leader of the anti-union movement, gave a lecture on the future of the area. Meanwhile, getting down to business, at the Ocean View Tract itself, "promoters piled bricks and lumber on alternative lots, which they marked *SOLD*."[23] Mounds of earth were added strategically, as if houses were about to blossom like sunflowers.

The showpiece of the streetcar system was the Balloon Route, so-called because it made a balloon-shaped circuit from downtown to the beach towns, then back again. In the teens, when the streetcar network reached its maximum efficiency, Balloon Route brochures were quite fancy, with three-color photo-lithos under vellum paper, the sunshine of a watercolor for free. They were pitched at the Sunday workman and his family, riding in imperial splendor to the ocean, where inexpensive property was listed for sale (land along the beach was cheaper than downtown, at that time). Venice was described as "the Coney Island of the West." Redondo Beach was "the happy medium for the masses and attractions." Huntington Beach was "the rendez-vous for the little families."[24]

By the twenties, however, the use of streetcars for weekend leisure diminished. With the quick speculative fortunes already made, the lines at their maximum, both the Pacific Electric (Red Cars) and the Los Angeles Railway (yellow Cars) began to show losses. They asked the city to buy them out, or to allow a penny fare hike, and fund improvements through city bonds.[25] As a privately held trust, the transit system had lost its promotional usefulness, even for its owners. Now it needed public revenues to stay efficient. The city's answer was to back off but keep promising. As a result, little more than commission reports on mass transit were funded for the next fifty years.

The history of how these streetcars were finally destroyed has been rehashed constantly, even in film parodies like *Who Framed Roger Rabbit*.[26] In brief, the trolley system was eclipsed by the automobile. From the twenties on, routes endangered by auto traffic were allowed to go fallow. Attempts to expand the system, add subways, push for elevated lines were blocked, stalled, or deemed too costly – and not in the spirit of the sunshine expansion of Los Angeles.[27] Much of the crisis also involved the three lanes that a trolley line needs on busy streets, so riders could mount the platform without getting swiped by a car. Rivalries between residential and commercial real estate produced a standstill, particularly when plans involved years of noisy construction to widen a key street, like Wilshire Boulevard, or drilling a subway. The result was a steady erasure of the routes, particularly during the Second World War, despite massive decentralization of a growing population into new areas.

In the sixties, finally, the truncated remains of the system were torn up – and with it went much of downtown. The interest groups who lobbied to destroy it after World War II included the auto and industries, railroads, urban planning commissions, suburban chambers of commerce, and, quite frankly, the majority of the voters in Los Angeles, whom it was believed would never support a city bond that helped the traction companies. There is also evidence that streetcars were linked in the public mind to corrupt, grasping railroads, the octopi from San Francisco or back East.[28] During the first decade of the twentieth century, when L.A. leaders were fighting San Francisco railway empires, the Southern Pacific pressured to haul freight along streetcar routes. Streetcar companies were accused of milking city money to get land at brokers' rates. Help the traction companies? The resentment ran very deep, as part of daily conversation. Consider this anecdote: in 1906, oil patriarch Edward Doheny appeared in court to fight a $15 speeding ticket given to his chauffeur. This was the sixth ticket issued to a Doheny driver, and each time the millionaire Doheny, with a touch of the "shanty" Irish, would refuse to pay without first complaining to the judge. "Street car companies are constant violators of the speed laws," Doheny told Judge Austin. "Why don't you arrest them and haul them into these courts?" Judge Austin agreed: "That is ground well taken, Mr Doheny. I suggest that you have warrants issued in a few cases and cause arrests yourself." "I'll do that, your honor," Doheny replied, and paid the fine.[29]

Streetcars were run by the rich, above the law. Even plutocrats who were above the law felt so. Vestiges of this progressivist resentment remained. Even in the thirties, after the streetcars became hostage to bank loans, and hardly a threat to the great leviathan of Los Angeles, headlines still suggested that the traction plutocrats deserved their comeuppance.

The car, on the other hand, was the great liberator, for cruising in the open air, at 40 miles an hour, along wider roads. The car became heir to the sunshine strategy, and the Balloon Route took on a grimmer aspect. Key streets were expanded as parkways: Olympic Boulevard, then by the thirties Wilshire Boulevard, after a decade of resistance by homeowners against commercial investors – the signal victory of the car over residential real estate, the spidery extension of downtown to the zone around the Bullocks Wilshire department store, and then the emergence of rival commercial zones along the Miracle Mile farther west.[30] At the same time, the image of the trolleys continued to sink. By the late thirties, as noted often in virtually every newspaper, the streetcars, without unguarded rights of way, ran much more slowly than before. They were described increasingly as symbols of urban blight, too primitive for the new image of Los Angeles.

What indeed this new image looked like becomes the next focus in this chapter. The next stage of the sunshine strategy, beginning with the late thirties, centered around the automobile, but also involved fantasies about the causes of urban blight, about the end of rustic innocence, about how to replace it with suburban innocence; and finally with no innocence at all. It is a Balloon Route of another sort, from downtown west, and back downtown again, over a period of fifty years.

THE MYTH OF A FREEWAY METROPOLIS:
THE IMPACT OF DECENTRALIZATION (1936–49)

In 1937, just as the Depression seemed to be worsening again, plans for building the first freeways were released to the public. Schemes about what were called "elevated and crossingless motorways" had been in the news before, as early as 1906,[31] seriously in the mid twenties, and occasionally afterward. But now the campaign began in earnest, after a new traffic survey, followed by long articles in the *Times*, brochures from the

Auto Club, meetings of think-tanks and speeches in the City Council. The first freeway, the Arroyo Secco, was funded as part of an elaborate scenario for a new city, even including photo-sketches of an orderly city-scape that bore no resemblance to what actually stood at the time. Then, during the war years, the rest of the Babylonian fantasy was laid out on paper, and the expenses calculated.

Ed Ainsworth,[32] writing for the *Times* in 1937, stated the problem very succinctly: Los Angeles was "ideally situated … for this first great experiment in loosening the strangling noose of traffic." The plan would rehabilitate business, and become "a national model upon which to mold the city of the years to come," clearly a city dedicated to auto-mobility.[33] Roads left over from "the dim days of the pedestrian, the horseman and the horsedrawn vehicle" would be modernized.

It took longer to cross ten blocks downtown by car (14 minutes) than by horse and buggy fifty years earlier. The traffic problem caused quite a furor, so awesome that it became a metaphor for a much deeper anxiety about the future of Los Angeles. The city seemed to be spiralling backwards.

Planning documents from the war years repeat very much the same message – an utter contradiction of the sunshine image of the city. Neighborhoods cannot "just grow, like topsy." Business and housing standards were being damaged by natural forces. In fact, Nature's bounty added stress. Stores and filling stations came too close to residential housing. Office buildings went up where they were not needed. Vacancy rates increased – as did crime. The natural, or unplanned, city was beginning to look more like Chicago than a rustic arcadia.

Like nature gone awry, the language describing these slums used bizarre medical metaphors: Los Angeles was afflicted by urban diseases, like a herd of livestock attacked by mosquitoes or an orchard threatened by the Japanese beetle. Planner Mel Scott writes (1942, in a report widely circulated throughout the forties, then expanded into a book in 1949): circulation is "afflicted by traffic fever," with "sick boulevards," and "high-speed arteries … ruined by straggling roadside businesses."[34] Even more unfortunately, Los Angeles was "blighted," as shown on a map where 20 square miles of urban blight were darkened, like an x-ray of spots on the lung. Actually, blight is more a botanical than a mammalian disease – spots on leaves. In planning jargon, blight was defined as the first step toward slum, or terminal decay.

Despite the rude oversimplifications, many of these models were designed to address the problems of poorer, struggling neighborhoods;

and deeply influenced plans for public housing in the forties. But consider what the model suggests: buildings are the host victims, and therefore alive; poor residents are only *part* of the corpus, seemingly further down the chain. The unique dynamics of specific working-class communities were often ignored, primarily because the brooding problem was, first of all, the body of the city (tax base), and second, the blood system (roads).

Social planning for communities (except to plan leisure for families) was subsumed far below these, often described as part of the tissue that was diseased. To paraphrase the old Dadaist joke, L.A. needed an operation:

> In our dreams the Los Angeles metropolitan community of the future has safe, well-planned streets on which traffic flows smoothly, through convenient, self-contained neighborhoods, numerous regional parks, connected by beautiful parkways, miles of publicly-owned beaches, and prosperous industries... Enchanted by this vision, we sometimes forget that if it is to become more than just a vision, we actually must replace much of the community that exists today. We must create many things still in the imagination. Block after block of buildings must be cleared to make way for freeways. Outworn, dilapidated neighborhoods must be razed, hundreds of new dwellings constructed. Disfiguring roadside stands and signs must come down, so that motorists may enjoy the beauty of the countryside and drive undisturbed by the commercial activities at the side of the road...[35]

To promote this dream, planning campaigns took on the spirit of wartime propaganda, particularly aerial bombings: "Outworn, dilapidated buildings must be razed." Urban decay was compared to cities after blitzkrieg: "Blight had gotten in its deadly work on sections of London long before the blitz came." Finally, and even more tellingly, urban decay suggested the coming of another depression, which many felt was still just around the corner, forestalled only by the wartime prosperity:

> Our cities have decayed so badly that many of them are bankrupt or soon may be. This process is terribly wasteful. It destroys property values. It breeds slums.[36]

In wording reminiscent of recruitment ads, public vigilance was demanded. "Planning, like democracy, needs more than experts." It needs support on the home front, because "cities have stopped growing during the war."

A widely distributed article from *The Architectural Forum* asks: "How can we fix decay?" And answers: "The way a dentist does – by cleaning out the infected area and guarding it against further trouble."[37] What a telling metaphor: poorer neighborhoods as tooth decay. Communities were not described as a delicate balance of institutions, damaged by high un-employment, declining commercial streets, growing absentee landlordism, or the loss of political, religious, and cultural centers of power. Instead, communities were massive urban cavities to scoop out, in order to restore a healthy tax base to the city, and end the looming threat of a new depression after the war. Real-estate prices were indeed slipping in the old metropolitan centers. In 1938, a prestigious committee of ten agents for downtown office buildings complained to county supervisors that vacancy rates were alarmingly high, that businesses were leaving for the suburbs.[38] The downtown area in Los Angeles had clearly suffered a considerable loss of trade since the late twenties, losing out to the Miracle Mile along Wilshire, to chain stores, to neighborhood movies, and to suburban shopping areas, where there were no parking problems.[39]

The image that came with rapid decentralization played havoc with myths about the rustic city. Farm city became casual consumer city, in the *Time* magazine description of 1941 midwestern housewives dressed in pajamas while "shopping in one of the decentralized business centers."[40] Out in the suburbs (often identified as areas west of La Brea), parking restrictions were unnecessary, traffic jams unknown – utterly the reverse of downtown. And yet, since the teens, population growth had been slowing in the already dense downtown area. The downtown share of city-wide shopping had dropped by as much as 50 per cent from 1929 to 1935.[41] However, the decline was not seen as irretrievable. The stores downtown were still mobbed at Christmas season. Major streets down-town were packed with traffic every rush hour – too much traffic.

The war had sped up decentralization. Over fourteen million people were expected to have changed localities by the end of the war. Also, eleven million more had gone into the military. As another planning specialist, Catherine Bauer, explained (1943 – also a very influential article among planners in L.A.; phrases were plagiarized for the Statement of the Greater Los Angeles Citizens Committee, a promotional, planning organization):

All in all, one-quarter to one-sixth of our population are in a state of flux, physically and psychologically. If you ask them where they expect to be five years from now, they shrug their shoulders. When the soldiers stream down the gang-planks to meet their wives and fiancees, the central question for some twenty to thirty million people will be: "Where do we go from here?"[42]

Then Bauer explained how this "state of flux" was "changing cities." "Five or six million people have moved from open country to metropolitan districts since 1940," much faster than earlier. The number of farmers had declined, meaning that "urbanization is still roughly equivalent to economic progress." But what sort of urbanization? While the industrial labor force kept growing, it was not necessarily moving into the old metropolitan centers:

> During the war, twenty billion dollars of streamlined modern war plants have been built, almost doubling the value of industrial plants in the country... Where are they? Not in old city centers nor yet in isolated small towns, but for the most part on the outskirts of metropolitan areas.[43]

Wartime industrialization and decentralization were crippling cities. The concern for these two problems transformed the image of Los Angeles very markedly, with the period after 1936 as the dividing line. From the 1890s on, the number who came from farm areas continued to decline in L.A., until by the forties they became almost insignificant.[44] Then, with the Depression, rural tourists, who had been rich and desirable in the 1890s, when farm prices had zoomed, now became associated with the dispossessed that Steinbeck would describe in *Grapes of Wrath*. From 1936 on, police at the state borders sent back thousands who came to L.A. from the Dust Bowl in particular, the beginning of a rude shift in image and policy, as declining services failed to keep up with the continual in-migration from other parts of America. This policy, called the "bum blockade,"[45] was undertaken with active support from the L.A. Chamber of Commerce. In 1936, for example, the Chamber was invited to send a speaker to the small town of Blythe, about three miles from the state line, where eight LAPD officers were stationed at every highway entrance to the state. After the visitor's lecture, the Chamber at Blythe agreed to send a letter supporting the border checks to L.A. police chief Davis.[46]

Clearly, the L.A. farm-city image had begun to backfire, and became a problem. Promotional imagery, for a time, was tilted away from descriptions of L.A. as a sunshine cornucopia toward L.A. as a home for those with industrial skills. Migration from the Dust Bowl was discouraged, even though that area of the country had once been considered crucial for tourism. Competition to attract government defense money was fierce during the war. L.A. became the center for military industries serving the Pacific, and many of these remained afterward, as part of the huge postwar defense industry here.

By the late thirties, and increasingly in the forties, the promotional image of the city was very much divided. There were two opposites that needed to be blended somehow: first, the sunshine city (1885–1929); second, the Depression, wartime, industrial city (1929–45). Somehow, these two economic strategies would have to be organized into a bivalve organism that was easy to advertise – a new urban model for planning and investment. Stated another way: how were profits made through decentralization going to coordinate with profits needed to save downtown? Suburban real estate was a plum, no doubt, or would be after the war. But most of the investment capital, and investment leaders, were still centered in downtown, along with the financial life blood of the city itself.

Catherine Bauer offered the following solution:

> It's too late, if indeed it ever was possible, to think of "saving" the old city centers in their congested nineteenth century form. A regional organism is striving for birth, with centers and sub-centers and open areas permanently differentiated for varied functions, much more complex and refined than the amoeba-like nineteenth century city and hence requiring more discipline and conscious purpose.[47]

What these biological similes amount to is a plan for orbit cities, to be designed from scratch or enlarged around the knots where freeways would meet. The freeways would radiate from downtown, liberating the center from traffic congestion, while allowing for experiments in ideal city life without the baggage left over from old neighborhoods, with their shabby houses and what Bauer called "the dreary inefficiency of present cities," meaning the roads, the blight and the irrational architecture.[48] In terms of this essay, one image – decentralized suburbs – would be made to coexist with another: a revived downtown center. (The term Bauer used, by the way, was "decentrist."[49])

For lack of a better term, I have decided to call this social imaginary an "Industri-opolis", essentially an *industrial* blueprint laid over a rapidly decentralizing city, like blending the City Efficient or Corbusier's Radiant City with a sunny fantasy of the suburbs. In early L.A. planning (1908 on), downtown was still envisioned as rustic enough to absorb more industry. Industrial districts could be integrated with the landscaped inner city. The focus was still sunshine tourism, to camouflage factories beneath the picturesque, to please the eye of the tourist. Broad "Parisian" boulevards were to be added, along with agricultural parks, for "pleasure drives," by coach more than automobile, and radiating out of downtown along wide, luxuriant streets. Much of this "city beautiful" model survived into the twenties, and the hopes for "garden cities" around downtown.[50]

The hatred of skyscrapers was profound. They caused slums. As one downtown realtor declared in 1910, skyscrapers were "damp dark dreary, dismal, drafty defiles of dim depths with denizens dying of dread disease."[51] Another developer added: "The vital thing in Los Angeles is sunshine and [not tall buildings]. Physicians [should] advise their patients to take the sunny side of the street because of the important difference in temperature between light and shadow."[52]

Slowly the debate shifted. The industrial became more fundamental to the booster message, particularly after 1923. At city planning, directed very forcefully by C. Gordon Whitnall, schemes to industrialize roads were drawn. L.A. would be linked "scientifically" by widened parkways, later called highways, a grandiose transformation to be funded by gas taxes, based on a survey completed and ready to go in 1934 – and very much like the final plan years later. The federal pressure to think industrially was fierce as well. The Bureau of Public Roads was determined to finance a national interstate highway system.[53] By 1937–38, the classic modernist adjective appears, to "rebuild [cities] along *functional* lines."[54] In L.A., "functional" also suited the new reform Mayor Fletcher Bowron, a "clean sweep" of downtown. Functional was honest, disinfecting.

During the war years, I detect a shift, unmistakably: the promise of highways cleansing cities took on the urgency of new defense plants in a war. Not much remained of the sunshine image of downtown anyway. With soldiers away, residential real estate was considered a losing proposition. Councilmen were warned by city planners that shopping and services would keep decentralizing – as indeed city managers were warned throughout the country.[55] Therefore "a gradual change in the character of downtown Los Angeles was inevitable."[56] Better to make downtown "the home of big executive centers of business."

On the surface, this suggested great optimism, but only on the surface. Like the war itself, the slums downtown reminded developers anxiously of the Great Depression, and of wartime shortages and rationing – a world on the edge. Housing shortages were severe. Poverty seemed to be bursting at the seams. Whites were frightened by the rapidly growing black population, 84 per cent larger by 1945 – 60,000 more blacks, with only 3,000 "new units for [Negro] occupancy."[57] Powerful interests pushed for isolating low-income housing in areas like Watts. Others held their breath as whites left much too quickly when many blacks bought into West Adams after 1940. Less than two miles south of downtown, West Adams had been the premier neighborhood in the twenties.

Most of all, the Mexican presence was worrisome, more than ten times what it had been in 1910. From Boyle Heights all the way across northern and western downtown, Mexicans seemed to cast a racially dark shadow across the future of the entire region. Ironically enough, many of these so-called "pachuco" districts were very mixed as a rule, not even pre-dominantly Mexican, but the malaise had become unshakable.

Nor did the end of the war quieten this foreboding all that much. Many downtown leaders remained convinced that the boom had merely been a fluke. The sudden growth of heavy industry might never repeat. Public-works programs would be needed to handle unemployment and housing shortages. By the early fifties the "Eisenhower era" confidence in business finally overcame the morbidity left by the Depression. But even then, there remained in the politics here as elsewhere a brooding anguish. Like the early Nixon campaigns for the Congress and the Senate, it was filled with hysteria about all forms of mass treachery.

Tear down or else: L.A. was by no means alone in this anxiety to rebuild massively. Hundreds of other cities had similar plans; what architect Richard Neutra called "Design for Survival."[58] However, the total commit-ment in Los Angeles was rather unique: "the L.A. penchant for large-scale planning."[59] In 1941, an imaginary – to-scale – Bunker Hill was put on display, at a public exhibition sponsored by the Regional Planning Commission. It promised a geometric wave of entirely new buildings, replacing virtually everything standing downtown. *Time* magazine called it a "Lewis Mumford dreamworld," and added: "If the city planners could burn Los Angeles down they would rebuild it differently."[60] Planning reports described blight as more virulent here than elsewhere (it certainly was not, of course). Neutra asked: "Was this metropolis a paradise, or did there exist here a type of blight which fitted none of the classical descriptions?"[61]

The first projects opened by 1940: Union Station; Arroyo Secco Freeway. But most of the finite details were hatched after 1940, during the Second World War: where to build freeways, what to tear down. The emphasis was on how to strengthen downtown by reducing traffic congestion.[62] These documents do not presume a dying downtown. That is what threw me at first. Beneath all the jargon about suburbs, there remained an unshakable belief in centripetal urbanism. Suburbs tend to strengthen downtown – eventually. Even during the fifties, downtown is treated more as injured than dying. Weed out the bad buildings; put freeways in place to get the traffic flowing. Not much beyond freeways seemed imminent anyway. Who expected these tall buildings in less than thirty years? Even the futuristic models of L.A. that were printed in newspapers looked unborn: blank models, faceless wooden blocks without windows or color – and too extreme to believe entirely. The general public apparently regarded them mostly as intangible. And indeed, for another fifteen years, very little *actually* was built. Many people I have interviewed told me that it seemed nothing ever would be done on Bunker Hill.

Nor had the appeal of downtown disappeared.[63] The population downtown grew between 1939 and 1948, increasing the occupancy rate. The stores showed record profits, up 126 per cent between 1939 and 1948.[64] Broadway and Spring were still lively into the fifties, home to first-run movie theaters, the major department stores, the large legal firms, the corporate headquarters. If you lived in Altadena, ten miles north, your doctor might still be downtown. Throughout the fifties, residents dressed a bit fancier to go "downtown." And, visually speaking, the streets were no more worn than downtowns throughout America.

L.A. actually had outperformed most downtowns after 1930 – higher population growth, less deterioration. Every urban center had been languishing unimproved for twenty years, due to the Depression, the war, and the postwar recession.[65] Midtown Manhattan also looked grievously stricken. I remember that well enough from my childhood. Even gentrifying areas in Chicago during the late sixties felt as slummy to me as much of inner-city Los Angeles. In seventies New Town Chicago, I would see nervous "urban pioneers" mowing new lawns, while only across the street drug addicts waved hello, and at the corner, weary alcoholics emerged from packaged liquor stores, and shoved brown bags under their overcoats when they passed the fancy remodeled Treasure Island supermarket.

We should not imagine throngs of hostile suburbanites running policy in 1950 Los Angeles. That is our reality today perhaps, but not as clearly back then. Downtowns were still seen as the heart that would eventually give life. That is partly why Robert Moses in New York felt comfortable ramming the Bronx Expressway through solid neighborhoods.[66] Urban neighborhoods could survive. They were near all those people downtown. Of course, after a while, there were not enough of these people left in L.A. The hemorrhaging went too far.

But even as late as 1956 writer Gavin Lambert describes a labyrinth of people downtown:

> The noisy populous down-town section with its mixture of Americans and Mexicans, Negroes and Orientals, its glass and concrete new structures jostling fragile wooden slums, its heavy police force and ugly untidy look of sudden industrial growth, is a little like Casablanca. The older parts are exotic but tired, collapsing under the sleek thrust of commerce. There is a modest little Japanese quarter with movie houses, gift shops, *sukiyaki* signs, a steam bath and massage parlour and the Bank of Tokyo; a Chinatown pretty and synthetic as a planner's lifesize model; a Mexican quarter with bullfighters' capes and scented candles always on display. There are oil derricks and power plants massed like geometrical forests, and a thin bitter smog hangs in the air on a windless day.[67]

The absolute vanishing point for downtown came during the mid sixties, or so the documents seem to indicate – much later than I had thought before beginning research and interviewing. By 1968, it was noted, two-thirds of the metropolitan center was devoted to the automobile (garages, roads, filling stations, and so on),[68] an anecdote that spoke directly to the problem: a full-scale depopulation and business exodus, far beyond what the forties "industrial" planners had imagined. L.A. was indeed the city of the future fifteen years too late. To reverse this trend, in the mid sixties, a "growth coalition," in connection with the Community Re-development Agency, created a massive financial district downtown. It was definitely concentrated almost exclusively on the presence of banking and international capital, which made the gap between street and high-rise even vaster – a Wall Street effect.

At the same time, the Growth Coalition/CRA also made awkward stabs at bringing residents back, to reverse the general distrust of down-town as a neighborhood, but with extremely limited results. In fact, the housing that remains may be all that the very narrow infrastructure down-town can bear (limited electric capacity; aging gas and water pipes; limited police and fire protection), at least without getting in the way of high-rise banks, hotels, and insurance companies. The services for a substantial increase in permanent residents downtown certainly would have cost the taxpayers more than the city leaders felt was feasible. And there was clearly no land rush of home buyers heading back to the old center city anyway (not until the late eighties, but cut short by the recession of 1991). For the most part, except for sponsorship of a few condominium garrisons away from the financial district, housing in the downtown area has been systematically ignored, or simply knocked down.

The industri-opolis was re-imagined, based now on the assumption that the general downtown area was unlivable in and crime-ridden – beyond hope – even though many of the neighborhoods nearby were quite stable until the sixties, and still represented a core market of approximately two hundred thousand people. These people would be shut out. A barricaded look developed in the *new* Central City, like a white settlement among the aborigines. For that, I suppose the term "heteropolis" might be more suitable, a suburban nodal "sprawl" that claims to have no center, and no organizing principle except its internationalist collage. In a heteropolis, even the downtown is suburbanized, isolated from the street, less accessible – more like Davis's carceral city.

What consistently amazes me is how anyone in authority remains convinced that this look should be a magnet for tourists. And even if it caught on, tourism would not even pay the postage for a billion-dollar investment like this. First of all, tourists do not spend as consistently as residents. And finally, middle-class residents do not enjoy living inside a concrete canyon designed mostly for foreign bankers and conventioneers. Most of all, the problem is unmistakable at night. Nothing feels eerier than "after hours" at a Wall Street/tourist downtown. The skyline is dead silent. Practically every living soul who has a choice seems to have gone somewhere else.

A busy downtown street has to be dressed at least three times a day: the breakfast rush; lunch through rush hour; nightlife after 8 o'clock. It changes its appearance every five hours, or it is not paying the rent. The only customers who can guarantee that much turnover have to live within two miles. Tourists are only the profit above the line. They come once a day, if at all. So, too, the workers in the tall office towers: they spend their big money elsewhere, and leave in a hurry at 5. A skyline with millions of bulbs glowing along the roof lines does not make a downtown – only a nice effect from miles away.

Despite a campaign planned in the late eighties to encourage museums and ethnic plazas in the northern end of downtown (again tourism, not neighborhoods), the great concrete stockades still dominate, and may never be humanized. Cement pedways resemble a modernist version of the castle town, not unlike sketches of imaginary cities by the Italian Futurist Saint-Elia in 1913 – purely a coincidence, but a revealing one.[69]

The industrial freeway city (industri-opolis) was built upon a profound anxiety about guarding against crime – crime being a code word very often for non-white slums too close by. Much of that anxiety centered, at first, around fears about Mexican neighborhoods close in, then later about African Americans. Soon it became an architectural necessity. Cars moved along guarded freeways. Civic buildings needed security against too many winding alleys or hidden public places. The so-called "International School" found its widely accepted mission after World War II, particularly after 1960, during moments of high urban decay, when cities seemed to need a quarantine. Crime-proof plazas became rather popular, probably not always for the reasons architects envisioned. These plazas removed street-level shopping, made the path up steps very visible, into heavily lit, flat areas, and made unplanned congregations of people far less likely (as we know from the complaints by critic Jane Jacobs and others during the fifties).

By the mid seventies, after the first decade of the Growth Coalition, this passion for safety became essential to the way downtown was promoted (on television, in posters). From a safe height, one saw the glass curtain maze, an overhead helicopter shot of a vertical Oz that was virtually unpopulated at night. From the helicopter, the chalk-white hives of condominiums resembled feudal walls for the great freeway cloverleaf, which became a sculptural medallion in the middle of downtown.

The shocks of the Watts Rebellion (1965) only aggravated the demand for more greater security, as if preparing for a siege, which I suppose finally arrived in 1992.[70] As Davis explains in his chapter on "Fortress L.A.,"[71] the rich districts were walled off very clearly against the poor. This was particularly true of areas west of downtown. During the eighties, with considerable investments left unprotected in real estate between Hancock Park and Fairfax, a wall of safety emerged along the Wilshire Corridor. Continuing into the nineties, plans for a "West Bank" beyond the Harbor Freeway will eventually extend this clear barrier between north and south all the way to downtown. The boundary is supposed to follow the arc of the Metro Rail, from the Wilshire Corridor up Vermont, with a lifeline extended south down Figueroa, past the expanded Convention Center, into South Park, and ultimately, if plans continue, toward the University of Southern California. Again, the shocks of 1992 have stalled that for now.

But the crucial turning was in the late sixties: the industri-opolis seemed at its point of highest efficiency, or at least the freeways were. L.A. was praised worldwide as a city that functioned extremely well. In possibly the most famous homage to industri-opolis, art historian Reyner Banham described the freeway system as a unique ecology. He compared it to a man-made climate, superior to nature, an "autopia."[72] He also meant that playfully: autopia, like the ride in Disneyland.

By contrast, Banham added a tiny "note on downtown, because that is all downtown Los Angeles deserves."[73] He saw no viable architecture there. A few office towers added near the Civic Center only revealed how hopeless the situation had become. Old pedestrian sites like Pershing Square and the pueblo area were corroded, proof that the residents of L.A. no longer cared about downtown at all. Downtown was "a badly planned and badly run suburban shopping center for those who cannot afford cars to get to the 'real' suburbs." In the first illustration of the book, to show how badly planned the old downtown was, Banham included a photo of Echo Park Avenue, near the neon parking display of the Pioneer Market. The nest of store signs looked discombobulated, beyond hope. Even today, that part of Sunset Boulevard is, indeed, quite a jumble. However, the neighborhood around it is one of the most stable in the city, and rather unique in its mixture of classes and ethnicities. In Banham's eyes, except for an overhead photo of the freeway cloverleaf, downtown did not qualify as a modernist architectural superspace, much less an autopia.

As of the early seventies, the industri-opolis presumably had achieved its goal, to fashion L.A. into a national model[74] for the modernist city: efficient, sensually liberating, strangely free of an urban center, like a cognate of abstraction in art, a Rothko painting where the center floats in an existential absence. But it had fundamentally failed in the effect it had on visitors. The French critic Roland Barthes compared downtown Los Angeles to Tokyo: two urban giants evacuated at their center, as a strange liberation from classical codes of urban experience.[75] But, in fact, downtown was not a blank cipher at all, far from it. It was more the scene of the crime, a crisis to ignore, the un-touristed non-image. One might say it was the tree that was designed to fall without anyone watching in the forest. It was a blank because the hotels had turned into flop houses, and they had been removed from the promotion of the city altogether, except in fantasy, as part of a nether world that one found in L.A. literature and film; and also in urban planning documents, as the downtown of no hope, a precursor of the "blade runner" city. It became the polyglot nightmare in people's imagination, as famous in its way as the Sunkist orange.

THE MYTHS OF DOWNTOWN RENEWAL (1936–49)

First Myth: Bunker Hill and Forties Noir –
"Old Town, Lost Town, Shabby Town, Crook Town."

These words, frequently quoted in descriptions of downtown L.A., come from Raymond Chandler's novel *The High Window* (1942).[76] It lays out a romance of urban blight that matches very closely what urban planners during the Second World War saw as beyond redemption. The passage describes the Bunker Hill area downtown:

> Once, very long ago, it was the choice residential district of the city, and there are still standing a few of the jigsaw Gothic mansions... They are all rooming houses now... The wide sweeping staircases are dark with time and with cheap varnish laid on over generations of dirt.[77]

Chandler's version of Bunker Hill is peopled with the hopeless and the criminal: "Landladies bicker with shifty tenants." Old men wearing cracked shoes have "faces like lost battles." It is an old neighborhood, with evil lurking beneath the quaintness, "little candy stores where you can buy even nastier things than their candy." At "ratty hotels ... nobody signs the register except people named Smith and Jones ... The night clerk is half watchdog and half pander..." "Out of the apartment houses come women who should be young but have faces like stale beer." Among the derelict types are "men with pulled-down hats and quick eyes; ... fly cops with granite faces; ... cokies and coke peddlars; people who look like nothing in particular and know it."

Chandler's description of the Florence Apartments, at the northern end of Bunker Hill, is suitably gothic: "dark brick in front, three stories, the lower windows at sidewalk level and masked by rusted screens and dingy net curtains." At the entrance door, only "enough of the names" could be read. Out toward the alley, instead of sunshine fantasy, there were "four tall battered garbage pails in a line, with a dance of flies in the sunlit air above them."

Chandler had lived in Bunker Hill himself, for a short time in 1913, before his career as an oil executive had transformed his finances – also before he was fired (in 1933). Afterward, he plunged into a new career writing detective fiction, living in cheaper districts west of the old metropolitan center, and also in Pacific Palisades.[78] After 1946, with income from screenwriting, and a growing disenchantment with Los Angeles – in his words, "that old whore"[79] – he moved to La Jolla. It is unlikely that Chandler had any direct connection with Bunker Hill after 1913, or even with downtown very much, but only with its reputation.

Bunker Hill had become the emblem of urban blight in Los Angeles, the primary target for redevelopment downtown from the late twenties on. A steep hill, rising from Fourth Street to Temple, from Hill Street west, past Figueroa, it represented 200 acres of impasse.[80] The hill stifled traffic. It offered little opportunity for commercial development, though it had supported a number of elegant hotels for decades. It seemed suitable only for residential housing, despite the Bradbury Mansion, the Melrose Mansion, the Armour House (also called the Castle).[81] By the late twenties, that housing also looked rundown. Its median year of construction was 1895.[82] Some 98 per cent of the homes had been built before 1920. Bunker Hill was the oldest cityscape in Los Angeles, with more showboat Victorians than anywhere else in Southern California, but virtually all of them were being converted into rooming houses.

After 1910, the social elite who had dominated the hill and downtown life started to move away, mostly to the new Adams district near USC. And Mexican immigrants began to take their place. As early as 1912,[83] the first proposals to remove it were made, but were easily resisted by the wealthy residents there. In 1915, rather than add a third tunnel under the hill, City Council offered to make two giant cuts at First and Second Streets, at a cost of $5 million, to prevent what was perceived as the isolation of new housing west of downtown. Again, organized protests by residents, including downtown businessmen, stopped the bond issue. A tunnel at Second Street was started instead, and finished in 1924 – the last formal improvement of Bunker Hill.

In 1928, in the spirit of quick fixes during the oil boom, a man named C.C. Bigelow offered to wash down the entire hill with the same hydraulic equipment used in mining, at a cost of $50 million. The city council took him seriously, and hired a consulting engineer, William H. Babcock to check out the plan. Finally, in 1931, after an elaborate survey, Babcock suggested removing only the crown of the hill, at a cost of $24 million. Then no more cuts would be needed. The plan was to keep most of the residents out of the crown, and make it an "acropolis," a term that reappears often in the thirties,[84] meaning "a citadel of local government:" courthouses, museums, and so on.

But residents living on the hill, particularly the few remaining wealthy families, fought and killed the bond issue in committee. Bigelow announced that "the human equation must be overcome." In 1938, the City Council said: "We'll let the natural force of economics do the job."[85] Depression prices would make the hill cheap enough to remove eventually. It already had been designated a fire hazard since the teens. Strict fire codes allowed very little new housing until the twenties, when a few Mission Revival stucco buildings were permitted.

After 1930, nothing new was built up there. Between 1930 and 1940, the population on the hill increased by 19 per cent to a density above 63 per acre, rivaling eastern cities.[86] As of 1940, over 75 per cent of the residents had less than eight years of schooling. Most were immigrants, predominantly from Mexico, but also from Italy, Canada, Russia, Germany and England. Even more damaging, however, Bunker Hill housed a very large number of elderly retired people. This became the crux of the debate: where to relocate the aged – who claimed that the community was intact, and quite charming still – isolated above downtown. By 1957, the Department of Building and Safety identified 60 per cent of the buildings as hazardous, meaning worse than simply substandard. Police reports indicated high crime, and also considerable trade in narcotics, particularly just north of the old funicular cable car, Angel's Flight.

In the novel *Ask the Dust* (1939), John Fante remembered Bunker Hill as it had looked ten years earlier:

> I went up to my room, up the dusty stairs of Bunker Hill, past the soot-covered frame buildings along that dark street, sand and oil and grease choking the futile palm trees standing like dying prisoners, chained to a little plot of ground with black pavement hiding their feet. Dust and old buildings and old people sitting at windows, old people tottering out of doors, old people moving painfully along the dark street.[87]

In another novel of the Depression, *Fast One* (1932), by Paul Cain (the first major hard-boiled crime novel set in L.A.), Bunker Hill is the first neighborhood the criminal outsider visits, a world of molls, gangster dialogue, and professional crooks. Scheming losers live there. In Paul Cain's description of buildings downtown, mixed use and blight take on the Gothic spirit of Dickensian byways:

> Ansel's turned out to be a dark, three-story business block set flush with the sidewalk. There were big For Rent signs in the plate-glass windows and there was a dark stairway at one side.[88]

However glamorous the crime novel, or well-intentioned its "realism," the myth of Bunker Hill was virtually always presented through the eyes of the tourist; in this case, the beleaguered, disillusioned tourist, not unlike Nathanael West's vision of how fantasies were destroyed in Depression Los Angeles:

> Once (tourists get) there, they discover that sunshine isn't enough. They get tired of oranges, even of avocado pears and passion fruit. Nothing happens... The sun is a joke. Oranges can't titillate their jaded palates. Nothing can ever be violent enough to make taut their slack minds and bodies. They have slaved and saved for nothing.[89]

Fante called these battered tourists

> the uprooted ones, the empty sad folks, the old and the young folks, the folks from back home... [Retirees] came here by train and by automobile ... with just enough money to live until their last days... And when they got here they found that other and greater thieves had already taken possession, that even the sun belonged to others.[90]

But, Fante adds, these disgruntled locust people were still better off than the poor in flop houses downtown, who could not afford a fancy polo shirt and sunglasses.

The examples above are among the most famous literary descriptions of the downtown myth. The reader has probably encountered them before, or variations. Dozens of crime films from the forties and fifties worked off this myth and its cognates. By the forties, the image of failing to make a go in Hollywood, with its various scandals and "boulevards of broken dreams" became synonymous with the Depression fantasies of urban blight, and with gangster fiction. By the sixties, crime novelists like Jim Thompson set the downtown myth along the Sunset Strip, another swanky area gone downhill, now a vice district (tacitly permitted by the police), with massage parlors, nudie bars, and a chance for new arrivals to watch live sex acts for the price of a $5 drink.[91]

In brief, as a structuralist paradigm based on dozens of examples, the downtown fable works this way. The outsider arrives (or lives insecurely) in Los Angeles, to find a world peopled by other outsiders. Among the rich, if he rises that far, mostly to mop up their crimes, he finds a perverse ruling class. They are debauched, new rich; they send out false messages about success, schemes that cheat the hopeless multitudes who want a shot at celebrity, or life in the sunshine. Downtown becomes a ruined abbey in a Victorian guidebook. Finally, the abbey is torn down. Meanwhile, the downtown manse is peopled by hundreds of thousands, who serve the story mostly as "local color." They are ornamental, to enhance the glamour of the journey. The gothic crime novel may comment with compassion about "local color," but it never quite enters the spirit of social relationships. It suggests that local color has no community, only transient souls beyond redemption. Better for the honest man to move on.

In that sense, the very popular *dark* side of L.A. tourism, using images of urban blight, has also sold real estate. The "noir image" has glamorized, quite unintentionally, the need to destroy downtown communities. That is the ironic genius of social imaginaries as cities, either of the sunshine variety or the shady: they always wind up selling products, in a culture well adapted to promotion – and I speak not only of Los Angeles, of course.

The downtown myth also stands in for the segregated nature of the city, as indeed any tourist town tends to be segregated carefully, through commercial zoning, housing covenants, careful promotion, and the way police patrols operate from one area to the next. Cities for tourists often have twin images: one for families, one for the underground weekend. L.A. was famous for its underground world, including red-light districts set up by the city itself during the boom of the 1880s. But these shady services had to be isolated carefully from the real estate promoted to white, prosperous tourists. The raunchy businesses were best left in, or near, non-white areas that tended to be permitted in the north and east of downtown, away from residential real-estate expansion, if at all possible.

As the city kept expanding, the myth of an underground downtown came to be associated also with crooked vice cops, gambling tenderloins, exotic pleasures for sale, and finally with Mexican and Chinese neighborhoods, located downtown in particular (and in other areas as well, of course, like East Hollywood). In the publicity sanctioned by the city leaders, the underground image was neither denied nor repressed, so much as walled off. The Balloon Route Tour of old Chinatown (*c.* 1912) promised a family guide who also knew about the opium trade.

This dark or noir mystique of the city was intensified during the thirties – or revived – during the scandals of the Shaw administration. By then, the downtown myth had become linked with police campaigns against vagrancy, with professional crime, with drug use, with losers living on the edge of oblivion downtown. It also had its high bourgeois corollary:

detectives like Chandler's Marlowe meet decadent rich women slumming with gangsters on gambling ships, or doing drugs in seedy back alleys (*Farewell My Lovely* is the obvious example). One might call these fantasy stories urban primitivism, like the classic image of young English women getting a tan among brown-skinned races, then committing crimes un-imaginable in the Protestant normalcy of the Anglo-Saxon family.

After 1948, with the newly authorized Community Redevelopment Agency, and the support of powerful downtown interests, plans for Bunker Hill began again in earnest. The 1949 federal Housing Act strengthened the power of eminent domain. Forced sale of housing was given the strength of law; the seller could be forced to accept terms or have the building condemned, if the site was required for civic redevelopment, or for freeway construction. A battle of nerves began. Local residents resisted redevelopment through law suits, letter campaigns, and handbills.[92]

A related battle took place at the same time. During the housing shortage after World War II, there was a brief flurry of interest in adding low-income apartments downtown. Promises were made by civic leaders to reserve Bunker Hill and Chavez Ravine for public housing. These commitments had to be washed away, through a red-baiting campaign where public housing was labeled as communist. Once that succeeded at the polls in 1953, a much more corporate, upscale program for Bunker Hill was approved by City Council.

The newspapers covered the story mostly as a matter of nostalgia – the old-timers versus the modernizers. In 1954, news of the upcoming Fourth Street "cut" sparked a few nostalgia pieces, about how "ghosts walk on Bunker Hill."[93] To make room for "a graceful 687 foot viaduct to soar eastward from the harbor Freeway ... the old 4th St. neighborhood, with its stately homes and mansions of the gaslight era will be no more."[94] There was already a gaping hole on First Street, awaiting a new County Courthouse.[95] Only the elderly are left to remember who lived where. Of course, memory in the aged is often symbolized by ghosts – old houses as white-bearded men. Art Hewett, reporter for the *Herald*, wrote:

> Bunker Hill is a land that Los Angeles forgot. A strange place the city moved around, chipped at, went under and through, but hardly ever over.[96]

I am leafing through xeroxes from the CRA campaigns of the fifties against keeping Bunker Hill. One has a pie chart showing only 66 owner occupied houses left there, out of 7,244 units. Even more telling (and highly exaggerated), a graph has the arrest rate as almost ten times the city average. Presumably there was nothing left to save. If there are only low-income renters, a neighborhood must be dead already, a crook town.

After eight months of hearings in 1959, the City Council voted for the Bunker Hill Renewal project, "the largest and most dramatic in the United States." It would "keep our city from slipping backward, like San Francisco and New York in the population race." And, more pointedly, it would reverse the "drift" to the suburbs.[97] The opposition was led by Councilman Edward Roybal, who claimed that the hearings had failed to reveal a dangerous level of urban "blight" there, nor an inordinate amount of crime or disease.[98] I am also struck by the tone of many newspaper descriptions of Bunker Hill in the fifties: "a tranquil island of faded elegance in the heart of this bustling city;" "the other quiet streets of Bunker Hill"[99] – hardly the angle I'd expect for a cesspool of crime and tuberculosis.

By the mid sixties, Bunker Hill had been stripped entirely of houses. The planners decided to level the hill but to keep two tunnels, which remain to this day, as monuments to urban erasure. They also seal access for pedestrians going in or out. There is no comfortable way to walk east/west inside the Second or the Third Street Tunnels, except perhaps as a ceremonial dance of death.[100] A few of the old Victorian mansions from Bunker Hill were moved to a site along the Pasadena Freeway, a fitting place: the building of that freeway had initiated the planning that made residential life in the old downtown practically extinct.

During the nineties, in an attempt to develop "communities" downtown, another quixotic master plan has been devised.[101] These maps utterly ignore neighborhoods damaged around downtown, and concentrate more on stop-gap measures to control the problems of homelessness. But neighborhoods are like necklaces. When the clasp is removed (Bunker Hill as the key access from all directions), the necklace is as good as lost. It will take many years for a balance to be restored, if ever.

Also in the 1980s, another Bunker Hill was torn down: at least 850 units, with thousands more to follow, in an old area that is being called Center City West (west of the Harbor Freeway downtown). Clearly, some efforts are being made to avoid another Bunker Hill syndrome. The architects' plans for this new imaginary downtown adjunct are glamorous, calling for a mixed-use, pedestrian-oriented district, with rich and poor reasonably close together, with high-rise hotels, medium-sized office buildings, apartments and even possibly small parks, with a small trolley over the Harbor Freeway. It is a fantasy community, as early plans for Bunker Hill were, but beneath the elegant prospects there is also the death of a neighborhood, and the struggle to split up the financial pie (between developers, council people, the school board, Cal-Trans and slumlords). Twenty thousand people had once lived in this general area, now growing bald, and so erratically that wildcat oil wells have opened in some of the empty lots where houses used to be. Later in this book, I will examine its history, another version of the scorched-earth policy of the industri-opolis.

Struggles to force developers to add low-income housing stalled the bargaining for five years, while tenants, understandably exasperated, even formed alliances with slum landlords to stay in their apartments. Meanwhile, the same landlords cut deals with developers to sell out, because for a while a full city lot sold for as much as $500,000. The sadness, the good intentions, the brokering for power and profit continued, until the final plan was approved in 1991, just in time for the recession, guaranteeing that the area will stay unbuilt, simply forgotten, for another ten years, or perhaps never be built.

Second Myth: Chinatown, 1887–1973 – The Social History of a Tourist and Movie Metaphor

According to legend, there was once a Chinese underground city beneath downtown Los Angeles – a nest of catacombs where inscrutable sins were committed. Presumably it was located underneath the Garnier Building, south of the old Plaza, but the basement there was used mostly for storage, from bins of rice to live chickens, for the restaurants above. Rumors described secret entrances and "hatchetmen high binders" dressed in purple silks, who killed to win "slave" women, like the famous Helen of Chinatown.[102] However, the myth of a Chinese underground came primarily out of white civic policies, as tourism, like the continual references in guidebooks to "whispering" streets with "all the wickedness of its old civilization."[103] From 1887 to 1909, the streets assigned for legalized prostitution were situated officially in Chinatown – and very much above ground, without any approval from residents there.[104] The same was true for the opium trade (where dealers who signed the "poison book" for police could operate, free from arrest). It was felt that Chinese were used to opium and whores, so the seedier aspects of tourism could be isolated there, away from the other areas of downtown. Meanwhile, the cribs for whores and the dens for drugs were run, and frequented, mostly by whites.[105] As a result, white gangs, and addicts, would mug Chinese regularly on the street. In 1887, the center of Chinatown was burnt down, probably by arson, while the Fire Department nearby refused to answer the call.[106] Chinese businesses complained constantly, but had little recourse. For generations, particularly following the Alien Exclusion Act (1883), Chinese were not permitted to give testimony in court. News articles with titles like "Trace Plot to Chink Student" warned of "coolie smuggling" through an underground railway, clearly exaggerated, as if immigration there were run by deviant subterranean abolitionists.[107]

By the thirties, the image of a vice-ridden downtown had been linked clearly with Chinatown, particularly in reports about Fan Tan clubs by the vice cops who worked in the Chinese district: "The Chinese employ intricate ways of hiding their gambling ... cunning ways of stationing lookouts... To the average caucasian, all Chinese look alike... Officers sent to Chinatown are completely out of their element."[108]

Chinatown was also identified with the Mexican *barrio* nearby, known as the Sonora or "Dogtown;" and with the old vaudeville district on Main Street, which John Fante remembered as "neon tubes and a light fog [at midnight], honky tonks and all night picture houses ... secondhand stores and Filipino dance hall, cocktails 15c, continuous entertainment."[109] With Chinatown at its heart, this was indeed a blighted place, still popular for tourists, but also the home to a very stable Chinese community that had been there for over fifty years. The novelist and critic Louis Adamic described the Mexican part of the Plaza in 1928:

[Even] as it is, the Plaza district is the most interesting part of Los Angeles. It consists, for the most part, of cheap wooden tenements occupied by Mexicans and Chinks [Chinese], of various camouflaged bawdy houses, dance halls, forlorn-looking bootleg dives, hop joints, movie shows, tamale stands, peep shows, shooting galleries, and stores selling rosaries and holy pictures. Main Street North, the principal thoroughfare of the district is a moron stream, muddy, filthy, unpleasant to the nose ... an awful stew of human life...

But just as I write this, the doom of the Plaza is sounding. A few millionaire realtors had got together with the railroads running into Los Angeles and cooked up a scheme to build a Union Station on the Plaza, which would give a tremendous boost to the land values in that vicinity.[110]

Adamic goes on to describe the Mexican church of Our Lady at the Plaza. He watches an old toothless woman praying there, then a few blocks away visits a cheap dance hall with a "crowd of young Mexicans, frail-bodied, foppish, decadent-looking boys and girls, the sweat of their bodies mingling with the scents of cheap perfumes and talc; their deep-sunk black eyes aglow with a desperate passion for joy; humming American ragtime."

The news was already on the street about $1.4 million of state funds and much private donation, from the likes of Harry Chandler and the powerful O'Melveny law firm downtown, designated to redesign the plaza area into a pueblo for tourists.[111] Chief of Police Ed Davis even promised prison labor for free.[112] To clean up the area, Chinese were evacuated from the Plaza, perhaps 3,000 residents gone within twenty years.[113] In the thirties, the eastern end of Chinatown was torn down, to make way at last for the Union Station, while the site of the old cribs was allowed to burn down (for fear of contamination by bubonic plague; a new central post office was built there a few years later). Still, in the forties, around the Union Station, picturesque blight dominated, with some of old Chinatown left, much of Main Street, the Sonora, and farther northwest, up hills, along dirt roads, part of Chavez Ravine looked to some like a failing chicken farm.[114] And presiding over the entire area, what some called the "acropolis," Bunker Hill. By 1949, all that was slated to go, as *Times* columnist Lee Shippey explained:

> The one hundred million dollar grant for slum clearance which the city has secured from the federal government should turn Chavez Ravine and other breeding places for delinquency and disease into pleasant, sanitary and well-serviced areas for low-income families. [Finally, of course, Chavez Ravine was turned over to the Dodgers for a baseball stadium] ... The thirty-five million dollar additions to the freeway system are resulting in the clearing away of ugliness which used to face the Union Station, and whatever new structures arise there will give persons arriving by train a wholly new first glimpse of the city.[115]

Within fifteen years, every eyesore visible from the train station would be gone entirely. Of course, by then the Union Station itself had begun to look blighted, the victim of freeway expansion and the decline of rail travel. Nevertheless, the cleanup campaign persisted into the eighties.

Today, the L.A. subway has begun to establish itself at the Union Station, overlooking a new Chinatown,[116] essentially where the old Sonora used to be, beside the great freeway cloverleaf, where the old Chinatown used to be, in what has come to be called Downtown North. Southwest of there, near the precise spot where the exorcism of ethnicity had begun, directly over part of the cloverleaf, are the empty lots on Sunset Boulevard that I describe in the Introduction.

Speaking of the social imaginary turning on itself, Olvera Street itself became a political stewpot in the early nineties.[117] From 1930 on, it was officially promoted as the "fiesta" pueblo (not the miserable slum), a place for Americans to eat "Spanish" food and get a touch of history – see where the Camino Real had started in 1786. But now, Olvera Street is not simply a tourist imaginary anymore, not primarily an excuse to push the Chinese out. The Plaza has grown back a community, its Hispanic support system. It is now seen as a genuine piece of Mexican identity, even with its own Siquieros mural – *America Tropical* – formerly white-washed, being restored. Throughout the eighties, Mexican-American activists tried to get a formal museum space there, but with no luck. Then, late in the eighties, planners offered instead to Europeanize the place altogether, give it some "class," add a museum honoring Italians (not Mexicans) in L.A., then add a French restaurant in the old Pico Hotel. The arguments were fierce for a time. All of that is still in a spin.

A small Chinese museum will also be built south of the Plaza, as well as offices behind Union Station, and a de-Hispanicized theater district on Broadway north of Third Street, all part of what is called Downtown North, a crescent of multi-ethnic tourism, from Little Tokyo to Olvera Street. Downtown "blight" is now being aestheticized. Even Angel's Flight will be restored, as an elevated funicular up an invisible hill, near the Museum of Contemporary Art.

In 1973, the legend of the underground downtown resurfaced in the film *Chinatown*, based on Robert Towne's extraordinary screenplay. This movie, more than any other ever made, has fixed in the public mind what the downtown myth looked like, updating the old film-noir images of Los Angeles, providing an allegory about land speculation and corruption here, and adding a hot desert light to the myth of L.A. on film. (Generally, in forties crime films, it rains a lot, or long shadows cross dark alleys.)

Towne explains that he learned about Chinatown from a retired Hungarian vice cop: "that police were better off in Chinatown doing nothing, because you could never tell what went on there."[118] Thus Chinatown – and the downtown myth – are deepened into a metaphor for the ambiguity of modern life, for "the futility of good intentions." It is a powerful reminder of the glamour that exists for all of us in the

downtown myth, of its buried secrets, of the contradictions between promotion and urban policies here in Los Angeles. We believe the romance;
we need the romance. But we must realize that the myths, whether of
tinsel town, of the sunny village, or of the downtown Babylon, have
never represented the city accurately. They have always systematically
ignored the life of communities in the city; as if the smaller stores, fragile
rituals, mix of classes together in a neighborhood could not exist in our
imagination when we think of Los Angeles. Indeed, these imaginary cities
reveal the futility of our good intentions.

EPILOG: BUILDING THE WHITE WHALE

In 1933, as part of what was then called the "7" parkway, a freeway was
planned down the western end of the San Gabriel Valley, from Pasadena
ten miles south into downtown. Finally, in 1960, the hearings began for
what was then the 710. However, the litigious Republican town of South
Pasadena,[119] still smarting from the builders of the Arroyo Seco Freeway
(1940) not fulfilling their promise to protect the old arroyo, simply refused
to knuckle under; and forced the California Transit Authority to undergo
twenty new plans, and at least seven environmental reports, some taking as
long as six years apiece. The 710, if built, would destroy hundreds of
historically significant houses, and endanger at least five historic districts;
it would also have a profound impact on the largely Hispanic town of El
Sereno.

The battle over the 710 has gone on for over thirty years now, and
involves thousands of pages of legal documents; it is the longest running
dispute over a freeway in American history. Some South Pasadena families
are into their third generation of resistance, selling tee shirts, holding
rallies, maintaining their own legal counsel. The hundred-year-old library
still has a map showing the "heart" of the town eradicated. Over the past
ten years, the town itself has transformed a bit; it is no longer Nixon
headquarters, and much less white Protestant, having far more Asians,
even a Democratic voting history. But, on the matter of 710, the town
council and the voters will not relent. The freeway up to South Pasadena
has a sign reminding drivers that South Pasadena is an "endangered"
historic town. The weekly *South Pasadena Review* runs a column on the
710 in practically every issue.

Among transportation specialists, there are now grave doubts that the
configuration of the L.A. area today would be able to accommodate the

710, or whether it would significantly liberate traffic for more than five years, at a cost of $1.4 billion and very likely much more.[120] There are numerous alternative "low impact" plans; the most recent, paid for by South Pasadena, would cost 92 per cent less. By widening and rerouting existing roads, it would have much the same effect – achieve over 90 per cent of what the freeway would do – but save 700 houses (some say over 1,000), and at least 3,000 very mature trees.[121] The head of planning at Cal Trans dismissed it as the work of "beautifiers," not transportation "engineers."[122] Mile for mile, the 710 promises to be the most expensive freeway ever built, averaging $500 for every licensed driver in the entire county.

Yet, as of New Year in 1995, Cal Trans and the federal authorities were still determined to persevere no matter what. On 28 December, they released the map of yet another route, to avoid another designated historic district; this is the twenty-first new plan, each conceived at a staggering cost.[123] Tens of millions of dollars have been spent already. Cal Trans owns over six hundred houses bought since 1960, generally craftsman cottages over eighty years old, in neighborhoods that have also been historically designated. Many cottages have been allowed to rot, for fear that if they were maintained properly, with their long setbacks and large trees, the freeway might seem less "friendly." In the new route, eighty-eight more structures will be purchased under eminent domain.

Recently, a transportation historian asked one of the executives at Cal Trans whether she had ever heard of Captain Ahab. The term "culture of denial" is used to describe their pursuit of this great whale. But, most likely, before 2010, the leviathan will be finished, come what may. The dehumanization that comes with industri-opolis takes on a Kremlinesque rigidity.[124] It simply goes forward, even if that means backward. The logic of rational investment will be forgotten. Like an office buried inside the CIA even after the Cold War is over, the campaign to fund the 710 knows its mission, and does not need to keep track of time, incidental losses – houses, neighborhoods, trees, historic continuities – or money.

NOTES

1. Charles D. Willard, *A History of the Chamber of Commerce of Los Angeles, California, 1888–1900* (Los Angeles: Kingsley-Barnes and Neuner, 1899), p. 12. Among the many sources on the boom, the most thorough is: Glenn S. Dumke, "Boom of the Eighties in Southern California," dissertation, UCLA, 1942, chapters 4 and 5 in particular.

2. Willard, *A History*, p. 47.

3. These highly ephemeral brochures can be found in libraries and private collections throughout the city. The L.A. Museum of Natural History and UCLA Special Collections have an enormous number of them.

4. For a summary of "the Los Angeles School of Urban Studies," see Marco Cenzatti, *Los Angeles and the L.A. School: Postmodernism and Urban Studies* (West Hollywood: Los Angeles Forum for Architecture and Urban Design, 1993). See also 1900–1930 travel non-fiction describing the effects of boosterism; for example, Sara White Isaman, *Tourist Tales of California* (Chicago: The Reilly and Britton Company, 1967).

5. Gregory Holmes Singleton, "Religion in the City of Angels: American Protestant Culture and Urbanization in Los Angeles, 1850–1930," dissertation, UCLA, 1976, p. 227.

6. *Since You Were Here Before* (Los Angeles: Security Trust, 1926), pp. 49–50 (promo for water power/electric), p. 60 (L.A. oil: 151 mm. barrels/year, 20% of national output). "Smokeless City:" Don J. Kinsey, *The Romance of Water and Power* (Los Angeles: Department of Water and Power, 1926), pp. 19ff.

7. For studying the linkage between social imaginaries and urban power blocs, Ernesto Laclau seems applicable: *New Reflections on the Revolution of Our Time* (London: Verso, 1990). See also Michael Keith and Steve Pile, eds, *Place and the Politics of Identity* (London: Routledge, 1993), particularly the essay by Doreen Massey, "Politics and Space/Time." Massey's review of the debate between spatiality and historicity (Lefebvre, Laclau, Soja, etc.) certainly fits this evidence as well – that the politics of space is very much linked to the politics of identity, is just as fluid.

8. C.B. Glasscock, *Lucky Baldwin, The Story of An Unconventional Success* (Indianapolis: Bobbs-Merrill, 1933), p. 222.

9. Aldous Huxley, *After Many A Summer Dies The Swan* (New York: Harper & Row/Perennial, 1965; orig. 1939), p. 5, early in the first chapter.

10. Nordhoff was published by Harpers, the most powerful press of the day (1870s) (Willard, *A History*, p. 30). Also, he is frequently cited in Carey McWilliams's classic study: *Southern California: An Island on the Land* (Santa Barbara: Peregrine Smith, 1973; orig. 1946). Nordhoff started out as a reader for Fletcher Harper, founder of the press, and remained an extremely influential force in editorial policy there, as well as one of its most popular writers on politics and travel. Also, he was the father of Charles Nordhoff who co-wrote the Bounty trilogy. Eugene Exman, *The House of Harper, 150 Years of Publishing* (New York: Harper & Row), pp. 77, 99, 132.

11. John E. Baur, *The Health Seekers of Southern California, 1870–1900* (San Marino, 1959), pp. 16ff.

12. George H. Napheys, *The Physical Life of Woman* (Toronto, n.d.; orig. 1890s, many editions throughout the English-speaking world), p. 75 (early in chapter entitled "The Wife").

13. Some details were taken from talks with William Mason (in 1986 and 1989), the very informative curator of history at the Museum of Natural History in L.A.

14. William R. Bigger, "Flood Control in Metropolitan Los Angeles," dissertation, UCLA, 1954.

15. Charles Lockwood and Christopher B. Leinberger, "Los Angeles Comes of Age," *The Atlantic Monthly*, Jan. 1988: pp. 31–62.

16. Marvin Brienes, "Smog Comes to Los Angeles," *Southern California Journal*, Winter 1976: pp. 515–32.

17. Laurance L. Hill, *La Reina: Los Angeles in Three Centuries* (Los Angeles: Security-First Bank, 1931 [4th edn]), pp. 169–71.

18. Morrow Mayo, *Los Angeles* (New York: Knopf, 1933), p. 319.

19. McWilliams, *Southern California*, p. 137.

20. Roger Butterfield, "Los Angeles is the Damndest Place," *Life Magazine*, 22 November 1943, pp. 102ff.

21. This becomes the bane of downtown planning for generations – the continual references to Mexicans downtown, even in very upbeat articles on Los Angeles. More on this issue, its links to riots and anti-Mexican hysteria, as well as to planning, will be found in Chapter 6.

22. Joseph P. Beaton, "A Hollywood Case Study of District Issues," dissertation, UCLA, 1981, p. 117. Also Bruce Torrence, *Hollywood: The First Hundred Years* (Hollywood: Hollywood Chamber of Commerce and Fisk Enterprises, 1979), pp. 34–8.

23. William Fulton, "'Those Were Her Best Days:' The Streetcar and the Development of Hollywood Before 1910," *Southern California Journal*, Fall 1984: pp. 242–52.

24. *Miniatures of the Sunny Southland* (Los Angeles: Pacific Electric brochure, *c.* 1907).

25. Robert C. Post, "The Fair Fare Fight: An episode in Los Angeles History," *Southern California Journal*, September 1970, pp. 275–97.

26. See Norman M. Klein, "*Roger Rabbit* Then and Now," Chapter 19 in *Seven Minutes: The Life and Death of the American Animated Cartoon* (London: Verso, 1993).

27. Often cited is the 1907 plan for elevated subways, on to the struggles about the trolleys in the twenties, when the system clearly was in need of new investment. Also, various reroutings, cutbacks, the shift toward buses, were evident as early as the twenties.

28. An autophilic summary of many of the key documents on this matter: Scott L. Bottles, *Los Angeles and the Automobile: The Making of the Modern City* (Berkeley: University of California Press, 1987), chs 2, 4, 5, 6. Summaries that defend the streetcars, while reviewing the old animosity toward the traction companies, include: *The Metropolitan Transit Authority (MTA) Newsletter*, particularly numbers 1–19, 1959–63, following the public debates after a report hinted at in 1959, then released in 1960; preliminary reports by the Assembly Fact-Finding Committee on Highways, Streets and Bridges (1949), by Assembly-Interim Committee on Public Utilities and Corporations (1950, one of the members was then assemblyman Sam Yorty); records of public hearings in 1963; news stories in 1938, on the debt problems of the traction companies. In short, plans for new transit were delivered regularly, even while the existing system was being dismantled. Elements of old Progressive resentment continued long after the traction companies had begun to collapse. A useful summary is *Runaway Train*, special issue of *L.A. Weekly*, 26 July–3 August, 1995, e.g. Mike Davis, "The Subway That's Eating Los Angeles." Also, for charming anecdotes on the twenties resentment of traction companies, see Bruce Henstell, *Sunshine and Wealth: Los Angeles in the Twenties and Thirties* (San Francisco: Chronicle Books, 1984), pp. 25–6.

29. *L.A. Times*, 31 July 1906.

30. Interview with transportation specialist Mathew Roth, 1995.

31. Among various news items on subway and elevated plans is *L.A. Railways*, 27 January 1907, suggesting elevated trams along L.A. Street north from 6th (essentially the same route as the subway that will be completed in the 1990s). As early as 1904, plans for subways in L.A. were presented to civic leaders.

32. Ainsworth went on to become one of the littérateurs on Los Angeles. After his

publishing retirement from the *Times* a decade later, he published personal histories of
L.A. (e.g. *California*, 1951).

33. Ed Ainsworth, *Out of the Noose* (Los Angeles: Automobile Club of Southern
California, 1937), opening page. This brochure was reprinted from a series in the *L.A.
Times*, 12–18 June 1937.

34. Mel Scott, *Cities are for People: The Los Angeles Region Plans for Living* (Los Angeles, Pacific Southwest Academy, 1942), pp. 71, 73. This study accompanied a show
(1941) sponsored by the Regional Planning Commission, and by architects from the
L.A. branch of Telesis. The later edition of the study, revised and much expanded, is
entitled *Metropolitan Los Angeles: One Community* (Los Angeles: The Haynes Foundation, 1949). Consider what seven years had wrought. The earlier version (1942) has
much more material (with photos) on urban blight, to reinforce the plans for a new
city in the exhibition of 1941. The rewritten edition (1949) has considerably more on
the outreach of freeways, much less on the threat of blight; it indicates, in fact, that
blight has begun to be removed.

35. Scott, *Metropolitan Los Angeles*, p. 98.

36. *Planning Is With You* (New York: *Architectural Forum*, 1943), which was reprinted
and apparently delivered free to various planning organizations in Los Angeles.

37. *Planning Is With You.*

38. John Anson Ford, *Thirty Years in Los Angeles County* (San Marino, California:
Untington Library, 1961), pp. 108–9.

39. Summary in Lester D. Estrin, "The Miracle Mile: An Example of Decentralization in Los Angeles," dissertation, UCLA, 1955, pp. 2–17. Numerous pamphlets and
speeches on decentralization were released throughout the forties.

40. David Gebhard and Harriet Van Breton, *L.A. in the Thirties, 1931–1941* (Santa
Barbara: Peregrine Smith, 1975), p. 34. This study accompanied an exhibition of the
same title, in Santa Barbara (1975).

41. I was given these statistics by older residents, but they match other figures I have
seen. Retail sales downtown dropped from 29.6% of the county in 1929 to 17% in
1939, a much larger economy than the city alone. Sales at downtown department stores
dropped from $74.8 of the county total to $47.4 in 1941. Richard Longstreth, *Markets
in the Meadows: Los Angeles, the Automobile and the Transformation of the Modern Retail
Development, 1920–1950* (manuscript, 1994, p. 639, publication forthcoming).

42. Catherine Bauer, "Cities in Flux: A Challenge to the Postwar Planners," *Ameri-
can Studies*, Winter 1943–44, p. 70. The Statement for the Greater Los Angeles Citizens
Committee can be found among the Haynes Foundation Papers, Box 240, in Special
Collections at UCLA. Bauer, housing activist, former book editor, lived in Los Ange-
les. She was a close friend of Lewis Mumford (Donald L. Miller, *Lewis Mumford, A Life*
(New York: Weidenfeld & Nicolson, 1989), pp. 288ff, 312ff.

43. Bauer, "Cities in Flux," p. 72.

44. Singleton, "Religion in the City of Angels."

45. Term mentioned by Henstell, *Sunshine and Wealth*, p. 21.

46. Letter to the Editor, *Nation*, 4 March 1936, p. 295: "Los Angeles Border Patrol,"
by Rose Marie Packard, traveling back to Pasadena. Mrs Packard and her husband
"interviewed" a policeman at the blockade, who specified that he was "only finger-
printing the ones who looked like criminals." When reminded that this might be un-
constitutional, he answered: "What do you mean? We are down here at the orders of
the chief of police of Los Angeles."

47. Bauer, "Cities in Flux," p. 78.

48. Ibid., p. 82.

49. Bauer coined the term "decentrist," defined in Charles Abrams' *Language of Cities* (New York: Viking, 1971: p. 82) as follows: "A group of urban theorists who believe in thinning out the dense cities and dispersing businesses and people to smaller places." Other decentrists were Lewis Mumford, Clarence Stein and Henry Wright. Mumford used the term "poly-nucleation:" satellite cities around a central city. The key problem for decentrists was urban density (ibid., p. 85), as in the phrase from Sir Raymond Unwin: "nothing gained by overcrowding."

50. David L. Clark, *Los Angeles, A City Apart* (Woodland Hills, California: Windsor Publications, sponsored by L.A. Historical Society, 1981), p. 79.

51. "City Council Holds Down Proposed Tall Buildings," *Los Angeles Times*, 12/21/1910, Part II, p. 2, apparently from H.J. Goudge, a developer on Broadway.

52. *Ibid.*

53. Raymond A. Mohl, "Race and Space in the Modern City: Interstate-95 and the Black Community in Miami," in Arnold R. Hirsh and Raymond A. Mohl, eds, *Urban Policy in Twentieth-Century America* (New Brunswick: Rutgers University Press, 1993), p. 106 (contains a useful introduction by Mohl).

54. Ibid., p. 107.

55. For a thorough review of the fearsome impact of decentralization on the mood of urban planners throughout the USA, see Robert A. Beauregard, *Voices of Decline: The Postwar Fate of U.S. Cities* (London: Blackwell, 1993).

56. John Anson Ford, *Forty Explosive Years in Los Angeles County* (San Marino: The Huntington Library, 1961), p. 109.

57. *Los Angeles Citizens Housing Council Conference on Housing*, 18 January 1947, III, p. 5.

58. Neutra, of course, was a leading architect in L.A., involved as well in downtown planning. This comment completed a speech made at the Columbia Bicentennial Conference in 1953, and cited favorably by those in charge (Richard Neutra, "The Adaptation of Design to the Metropolis," in Robert Moore Fisher (chairman of conference), ed., *The Metropolis in Modern Life* (New York: Russell & Russell, 1953), p. 267.

59. Pat Adler, *The Bunker Hill Story* (Glendale: La Siesta Press, 1963), p. 5.

60. See note 49.

61. Gebhard and Van Breton, *L.A. in the Thirties*, pp. 34, 35. In the early forties, sketches of this imaginary downtown were widely disseminated, to builders and civic organizations alike. For example, *Plans for Downtown Los Angeles' Four Pressing Needs* appeared in *Southwest Builder and Contractor*, 7 January 1944; then was reprinted as a promotional brochure. Sketches show virtually all of downtown north from Pershing Square gone and replaced, particularly Bunker Hill, already drawn as leveled, located west of an imaginary cloverleaf.

62. Clark, *Los Angeles, A City Apart*, p. 79.

63. For a look at downtown as of 1940–41, see *Los Angeles*, compiled by Writers of Work Projects Administration (New York: Hastings House, 1941).

64. Longstreth, *Markets in the Meadows*, p. 642.

65. Chapters 5 and 6 of Beauregard's *Voices of Decline*.

66. See Marshall Berman, *All that is Solid Melts into Air* (London: Verso, 1983; orig. 1982) part V, ch. 1, pp. 290-312.

67. Gavin Lambert, "The Slide Area," in *The Slide Area: Scenes of Hollywood Life* (New York: Berkeley Medallion Books, 1960; orig. 1959), p. 10. In the introduction, Lambert writes: "The action starts just before Christmas, 1956." Compare this to a description by the same author in 1971 (of the areas west of downtown, probably as far as Vermont): "East of Hollywood you reach a dead, flat no man's land. The surrounding hills are far away and often masked in smog... Paint peels in the jumble of buildings... The boulevards are lined with seedy delicatessens, tailors' shops, used car lots, hamburger and taco stalls... People walk along the street with a lost gray air, as if no one has told them the set was struck many years ago. The day seems to end a little sooner here, and the first lights come on a little earlier" (*The Goodby People* [New York: Pocket Books, 1972; orig. 1971], p. 67).

68. Victor Gruen ("father" of the shopping mall), *The Heart of Our Cities, The Urban Crisis: Diagnosis and Cure* (New York: Simon & Schuster, 1967), p. 79. Gruen offers this fact as proof of the following: "The city core of Los Angeles is not only small but void of true urban life as well." Also, this same fact − 2/3 of downtown devoted to cars − is used in Banham's study, which appeared a few years later (see note 41). Urban life was described in terms that made no reference to neighborhood institutions (i.e. community shopping; mixed use; ratio by class, race and home ownership; community centers; balance of streets to buildings; sites crucial to integrated experience within a neighborhood; power vis-à-vis city authorities). Again, communities were defined by the industrial act of driving through, like a tourist (industri-opolis).

69. For example: Reyner Banham, *Theory and Design in the First Machine Age* (New York: Praeger, 1967), pp. 116–19, pp. 127ff. The second edition of this book was completed very soon before Banham began work on his study of Los Angeles.

70. Racial and economic problems still unresolved after the Watts Rebellion in 1965 were discussed often during the eighties. In other words, the potential for 1992 was hardly a secret. For example, Mike Davis, "Chinatown, Part Two? The 'Internationalization' of Downtown Los Angeles," *New Left Review* 164, July–August 1987, pp. 65–90. Also, lectures he delivered on Los Angeles in 1989, and very informative discussions; and finally, the appearance of *City of Quartz: Excavating the Future in Los Angeles* (London: Verso, 1990).

71. Mike Davis, *City of Quartz*, ch. 4. See also by Davis: "The Infinite Game, Redeveloping Downtown L.A.," in Diane Ghirardo, ed., *Out of Site: A Social Criticism of Architecture* (Seattle: Bay Press, 1991).

72. Reyner Banham, *Los Angeles: The Architecture of Four Ecologies* (New York: Penguin Books, 1976; orig. 1971), Ch. 11 ("Ecology IV: Autopia), pp. 215 ff. Autopia was the last "ecology" presented, essentially the crowning achievement of the city. Banham opens with quotes by various literary tourists of the sixties − on Los Angeles. The only quote from L.A. itself is "Burn, Baby, Burn," from the Watts rioters, 1965.

73. Banham, *Los Angeles*, p. 201.

74. On national models for industri-opolis, see Bernard J. Friedan and Llyn B. Sagalyn, *Downtown, Inc.: How America Rebuilds Cities* (Cambridge: MIT Press, 1989); Carl Abbott, "Through Fight to Tokyo: Sunbelt Cities and the New World Economy, 1960–1990" (useful summary and bibl.), in Hirsch and Mohl, *Urban Policy*.

75. Roland Barthes, *Empire of Signs*, trans. R. Howard (New York: Hill & Wang, 1982), p. 30: "Quadrangular, reticulated cities (Los Angeles, for instance) are said to produce a profound uneasiness; they offend our synesthetic sentiment of the City, which requires that any urban place have a center to go to, return to, return from, a

complete site to dream of and in relation to which to advance or retreat; in a word, to invent oneself." Barthes goes on to debunk those urbo-centric assumptions, and even lists various institutions linked in the popular imagination to downtown areas, and the myth of downtowns representing a "social truth."

76. Raymond Chandler, *The High Window* (New York: Vintage, 1976; orig. 1942), opening to ch. 8, p. 53. This description was cannibalized from the opening to ch. 3 in his thirties novella, *The King in Yellow*:

> Court Street was old town, wop town, crook town, arty town. It lays across the top of Bunker Hill and you could find anything there from down-at-the-heels ex-Greenwich-villagers to crooks on the lam, from ladies of anybody's evening to County Relief clients brawling with haggard landladies in grand old houses with scrolled porches...

The earlier version makes less reference to urban blight, and more to eccentric (transient) street life, closer perhaps to Chandler's mood during his own years of professional transience; or as part of the "beleaguered neighborhood" fantasies of the thirties (i.e. gangster films, 1930–39), clearly different from the grimmer fantasies about urban blight during the forties (i.e. film noir). The location, however, remains the same for the most part; only the fantasy changes.

77. Chandler, *The High Window*, p. 50.

78. On the city and Chandler, see Philip Durham, *Down These Mean Streets A Man Must Go: Raymond Chandler's Knight* (Chapel Hill: University of North Carolina Press, 1963), pp. 48–60. In the thirties and forties, Chandler rode a lot through Wilshire and Sunset Boulevards, and L.A. west of Hollywood. His account of why he got to hate L.A. has a curious ring: "[Before] Los Angeles was just a big dry sunny place with ugly homes and no style, but good-hearted and peaceful"; a "big hardboiled city with no more personality than a paper cup"; a city without the "individual bony structure" (ibid., p. 51) a real city must have. What Chandler meant precisely by "individual bony structure" is certainly interesting to imagine.

79. Ibid., p. 60.

80. Bunker Hill was bounded by Broadway on the east, Figueroa on the west, Temple Street on the north, and 5th Street on the south. See Arnold Hylen, *Bunker Hill, A Los Angeles Landmark* (Los Angeles, Dawson's Bookshop, 1976).

81. Bradbury Mansion was at Broadway and Third; the Melrose was at Second and Olive; the Armour House, a twenty room mansion, was said to be haunted. See Leo Politi, *Bunker Hill Los Angeles, Reminiscences of Bygone Days* (Palm Desert: Desert-Southwest, 1964). Politi was famous as a children's book illustrator specializing in the downtown and Bunker Hill area. After Bunker Hill was gone, he moved to East Edgeware Road in Angelino Heights.

82. Adler, *The Bunker Hill Story*, pp. 29–31.

83. *L.A. Times*, 10 November 1912, II, p. 1.

84. The earliest reference I found to Bunker Hill as acropolis came from Bertram Goodhue, the architect for the downtown library, which in turn influenced the design for City Hall. Goodhue was essentially a New York architect commissioned to design the library in 1922. He was equally famous for the 1915 Panama-California in San Diego. Some time in the twenties, he is reputed to have said that "Bunker Hill should be your acropolis," then provided a drawing (Art Hewett, "Story of Bunker Hill: Coming of Auto, Rise of West Adams Spell Doom," *Los Angeles Herald*, 7 December 1954). In

the early forties, Neutra also used the term "acropolis" to describe his plan for Bunker Hill, which was never adapted. Many plans were part of the mix in the final redevelopment, though that of course was fundamentally corporate and residential.

85. Art Hewett, "Story of Bunker Hill: Seek to Save Historic Mound from Modern Age" (third in series), *Los Angeles Herald*, 8 December 1954.

86. That meant a population ranging from a high of 14,000 to a low of 6,500, depending on how many buildings had been torn down; and whether that included the lower hills nearby.

87. John Fante, *Ask the Dust* (Santa Barbara: Black Sparrow Press, 1984; orig. 1939), p. 45. Fante revisited the same settings, with a much gentler memory of the dynamic of the downtown community, and more nostalgic obviously (with very little reference to blight at all, ironically enough), in the novel *Dreams From Bunker Hill* (Santa Rosa: Black Sparrow Press, 1988; orig. 1982); for example, from Bunker Hill, "the city was in a tumult of radiant sunset colors" (p. 132); "From the trolley, [the hotel on Bunker Hill] was magic, like a castle in a book of fairy tales" (p. 145). After the resurrection of his work in the seventies (not long before his death), Fante became one of the most admired and influential L.A. novelists.

88. Paul Cain, *Fast One* (Berkeley: Black Lizard, 1987; orig. 1932), p. 62. Cain's real name was George Sims (he also wrote for movies as Eric Rurik), 1902–1966.

89. Nathanael West, *The Day of the Locust* (New York: New Directions, 1962; orig. 1939), p. 177. West's vision of mass violence coming out of the broken promises made by consumer promotion was shared, ironically enough, by Max Horkheimer and Theodor Adorno, whose book *Dialectic of Enlightenment* (1944) had an introduction dated Los Angeles 1947. A relevant line is: "The culture industry perpetually cheats its consumers of what it perpetually promises" (London: Verso, 1979, p. 139).

90. Fante, *Ask the Dust*, p. 45.

91. Jim Thompson, "Sunrise at Midnight" (*c.* 1963), in *Fire-Works: The Lost Writings*, edited by Polito and McCauley (New York: The Mysterious Press, 1988), p. 145. The Strip is also featured in Thompson's novel *The Grifters* (Berkeley: Creative Arts/Black Lizard, 1985; orig. 1963), pp. 92–107.

92. Don Parson, "'This Modern Marvel:' Bunker Hill, Chavez Ravine, and the Politics of Modernism in Los Angeles," *Southern California Quarterly*, Fall/Winter 1993, p. 339.

93. Marjorie Driscoll, "Steam Shovels Cut where Stately Mansions Stood," *Los Angeles Examiner*, 22 August 1954, section 1, part A, p. 12.

94. Ray Parker, "Faded Elegance Amid Bustle of City Recalls Color of Early Days Here," *New York Examiner*, 26 September 1954.

95. Art Hewett, "Story of Bunker Hill: Seek to Save Historic Mound from Modern Age," *Los Angeles Herald*, 8 December 1954.

96. Art Hewett, "Bunker Hill Days as L.A. Social Center Told," *Los Angeles Herald*, 6 December 1954.

97. Les Wagner, "Rejuvenation of Bunker Hill to Start Oct. 1," *Mirror News*, 22 June 1960, p. 8.

98. Ibid. One statistic of the sort that Roybal was answering: on Bunker Hill, the rate of active tuberculosis was twice the average in the rest of the city (Art Hewett, "Story of Bunker Hill: Bigger Tax Take Told in Death Knell of Famed Area," *Los Angeles Herald*, 9 December 1954).

99. Ray Parker, "Faded Elegance." Also, the various film records of neighborhood

life on Bunker Hill in the fifties (in the USC collection) indicate pockets at least of great stability.

100. The film *The Exiles* (1961) does exactly that. I discuss the film briefly in Part IV. A number of crime films use these tunnels for chases or moody criminal monologues, with their soft-filtered light, in an arc of cracked white tile.

101. Maps of the plan were on display for a show at the Museum of Contemporary Art in 1993, directly on the site of what used to be Bunker Hill. I mention some of these in the discussion of the Temple-Beaudry district in Chapter 6.

102. Marshall Stimson, *Fun, Fights, and Fiestas in Old Los Angeles: An Autobiography*, private edition, 1966, pp. 66–8; Harry Carr, *Los Angeles: City of Dreams* (New York: Grossett & Dunlap, 1935), pp. 236–9. Stimson, a leading real-estate investor downtown, remembers his high-school years near Chinatown (*c.* 1895), as a friend of Homer Lea, the "hunchback" American who spoke Chinese, and who later became a general in China during the revolution. Carr was an influential reporter for the L.A. Times, and considered something of a China Hand (an entrance to Chinatown was eventually renamed in his honor).

103. *Travelers Handbook to Southern California* (Pasadena: n.p., 1904), p. 150. The term "whispering" streets also appears in Carr's descriptions, to suggest the density of residential housing. It was also said that the Chinese required less oxygen than Caucasians.

104. Special Collections, El Pueblo Museum, L.A. Also Hector Tobar, "Evidence of Seamy Past is Dug up in Downtown L.A.," *L.A. Times*, May 31, 1996, A1.

105. A typical ad – Mme. Bolanger (438 N. Alameda) – features octoroons and oriental hula-hula dancers, "sport enough to last for a year to come." Other ads are for men "seeking the Chinese girls" in the Plaza. (*Tarnished Angels: Paradisial Turpitude in Los Angeles Revealed*, pamphlet [Los Angeles: Ward Ritchie Press, 1964]).

106. Special Collections, El Pueblo Museum, L.A.

107. "Trace Plot to Chink Student," *L.A. Times*, 16 December 1910, I. p. 5.

108. Charles Stoker, *Thicker 'n Thieves* (Santa Monica: Sidereal Company, 1951), p. 343.

109. Fante, *Ask the Dust*, p. 22.

110. Louis Adamic, *The Truth About Los Angeles* (Girard, Kansas: Haldeman-Julius Publications, 1927), pp. 10–11. Adamic is a much neglected literary figure. For more material on his attitudes toward L.A., see Carey McWilliams, *Louis Adamic and Shadow America* (Los Angeles: Arthur Whipple, 1935), p. 79 and *passim*. Adamic is discussed at length by Mike Davis in *City of Quartz*.

111. John Anson Ford, *Forty Explosive Years*, p. 103.

112. Christina Sterling, *Olvera Street: Its History and Restoration* (Los Angeles: n.p., 1937), p. 16. Sterling was the society activist who fought to save Olvera Street, went on to play the duenna for many of the shopkeepers there, and even tried to initiate a Sino-fantasy plan for a China City after World War II.

113. The precise location of old Chinatown is directly east of the Plaza, from Sunset Boulevard down to Aliso Street. There was also a Chinese Market district from East Ninth to Eleventh Street, between Wall and San Pedro, with Chinese restaurants and residences due east. See Garding Lui, *Inside Los Angeles Chinatown* (Los Angeles: n.p., 1948).

114. The photo entitled "Inconvenience" in Scott's *Cities Are for People* (p. 55) is of Chavez Ravine, though it looks a bit like rural West Virginia; see also the photo by Max Yavno in Lee Shippey, *The Los Angeles Book* (Boston: Houghton-Mifflin, 1950), p. 64.

115. Shippey, *The Los Angeles Book*, p. 105. The photos in this book, by Max Yavno, are remarkable, and unique among the most clearly "neighborhood-centered" of any photographic record from the late forties.

116. By 1946, there were two new Chinatowns actually. The first, China City, was set up by Christina Sterling as a tourist twin to Olvera Street, on a site that was already used by Hollywood studios and had a coterie of Chinese actors, as well as exhibits with props from MGM's *The Good Earth*. The other version, far more successful for the Chinese themselves, was located further north and called New Chinatown, set up by Chinese businessmen. See Garding Lui, *Inside Los Angeles Chinatown*, chs II, IV and V.

117. See Rodolfo Acuna, *Anything But Mexican: Chicanos in Contemporary Los Angeles* (London: Verso, 1996), ch. 2.

118. Conversations with Robert Towne, 1985–86.

119. South Pasadena has a long history of fighting legal battles. Even at its founding in 1887, it incorporated mostly to force Pasadena to stop building saloons there, to make "them" stop messing with their town. In 1912, they were pressured to join the city of Los Angeles, or lose their water. Once again they refused, and waited six years for a stable water supply rather than accommodate. They have also bucked the super-wealthy San Marino just to the east, and are notorious for fussy permitting, if a business seems too noisy or otherwise inappropriate.

120. Traditionally, the overruns in projects like this can double the cost. In a lucky season, expenses will grow only 10 or 20 per cent.

121. There are rumors, however, that the low impact plan would force one-way traffic down key streets, inhibiting business.

122. *Pasadena Star-News*, 8 January 1996, A1.

123. Richard Winton, "Freeway Route Shifted to Spare Historic District," *L.A. Times*, 28 December 1995, B1, 3.

124. Apparently, the new capital for industri-opolis is China. Both Guangdong and Beijing are home of the bulldozer, and what a Chinese designer described to me as "instantly bad Bauhaus" (*L.A. Times*, 8 January 1996, p. A1).

CHAPTER TWO

L.A. NOIR AND FORGETTING

Downtown is Nighttown, where memory is haunted continually by its own erasure. In 1981, William Gibson's Johnny Mnemonic explains:

> I'd never spent much time in Nighttown. Nobody there had anything to pay me to remember, and most of all they paid regularly to forget. Generations of sharpshooters had chipped away at the neon until the maintenance crews gave up. Even at noon the arcs were soot-black against the faintest pearl.[1]

Neon, of course, is a double signifier: first, the sour nightlife in crime movies from the forties, the insomnia of urban decay; and second, the act of shopping as insomnia, as a *frisson*. What results when the two are combined is a noir vision of Los Angeles. Consumer memory is set at night, when the uneasy loner strikes out violently inside poor districts where no community is left at all. The result is a social imaginary about the city vanishing. Consumer promotion no longer merely erases slums; it afflicts the consumer as well.

According to noir novels and films since 1930, L.A. is supposed to die by fire, earthquake, suffocation, amnesia, in the dark, in a movie theater, or in some way seen from a distance, perhaps through the window of a car. The distance often suggests a kind of tourism rather than social realism. That distancing is a vital clue, about voyeurism turning toward self-destruction. Long before the bladerunner nightmares, L.A. seemed to inspire stories about enraged tourists taking their revenge, the most famous being Nathanael West's novel *The Day of the Locust* (1939).

73

Above all, the nightmare is compared to the experience of wandering through consumer-driven spaces, a tourist's guide to hell, in a world built by promotion and set loose like a gyro. Tourism promises righteousness with a taste of sin not far away. First, it promotes a self-contained, sunny Protestant Jerusalem, and second, an amoral yearning, a tantalizing, prurient Babylon. The first generates investment, the other a fast weekend. From the late nineteenth century on, both had to be easy to find, right off the train, in plain view, often literally through the same window. Boosters hoped that new housing tracts would distract attention away from the prurient Babylon many came to find, but it never did entirely. Babylon and the real-estate Jerusalem could be found so close to each other, a commodification of the same desire – to escape into a sunny Arcadia.

Imagine the midwestern tourist arriving by rail to Los Angeles at the turn of the century. The train makes a slow, wide turn at Alameda. From across the street, out of "cribs" in a red-light district,[2] prostitutes wave to make eye contact with prospective customers (not unlike illustrations of whores in New York waving from tenement windows at men in subways).

The tourist consumer is supposed to be well armed against such blasphemies. Even on the train, brochures have been handed out. They were paid for by the L.A. Chamber of Commerce, the Santa Fe Railroad, the Pacific Electric streetcar company, even by realtors. From Chicago to Saint Louis and points west, ads in newspapers and magazines have directed tourists toward the Protestant Eden. Even on the fancy P.E. streetcar maps, there are addresses of realtors to visit immediately after disembarking at the downtown station. But not far from the realtors is the gamblers' Tenderloin, on Spring Street. And, while riding the streetcars, one could see Mexican hod carriers at work on new trunk lines – the inhabitants of the lower rings, living out of sight. In 1903, Mexican track workers became a particular nuisance, walking out during La Fiesta, just when the city leaders wanted to show off the Balloon Route to the visiting President Roosevelt.[3] A struggle that eventually broke their union continued below eye level. As the *Times* insisted for decades, L.A. was a city of racial harmony, "with a minimum of social complexities."[4]

Similarly, in 1904, voters nearly passed Prohibition, even while First and Main downtown was lined with saloons shuttling drunks out into the street. In 1917, a referendum against hard liquor was approved, but whiskey remained easy to buy just north of downtown.[5] During Prohibition, the *Times* claimed that L.A. was only 30 per cent "wet," while arrests for intoxication were nearly twice those in San Francisco, which was supposed to be 80 per cent wet. Smuggling by truck caravan across the border from Mexicali was wide open. L.A. had more moonshine distilleries than anywhere else in California. The "millionaire dry squad" was busy, though often it apologized to the wealthy whom it arrested, and did not press for trial. Among the big fish it caught (and let go), advertising playboy J. Lanford Stack was found to be warehousing over 730 quarts of practically anything drinkable, even seven quarts of absinthe.[6] In 1924, the *Times* declared that crime had doubled that year. There were now more murders in L.A. than in all of Great Britain.[7]

From 1921 to 1924, the booster camouflage began to fail, and tourist literature found a secondary, wicked voice. Beside promotional ads, even on the front pages of the newspapers, were scandals about the film industry: boy-next-door star Wallace Reid collapses with drug addiction; director William Desmond Taylor murdered, his illicit affair with actress Mary Miles Minter revealed; Fatty Arbuckle on trial for raping and murdering a starlet. And, regularly, conservative women's groups organized against vamps: lewd actresses. By 1924, film leaders felt threatened enough to set up the Hays Commission, a morals code.

And even more prominent were headlines on scandals in the oil industry. Speculative balloons from the Julian Corporation had bilked tens of thousands of Angelinos out of millions of dollars.[8] And, finally, as the steamiest indiscretion of all, Sister Aimee Semple McPherson's disappearance and dubious sexual entanglements made the front page more than any other news story of the twenties or thirties.

All these scandals came out of tourist or promotional industries started by "newcomers." By 1923, a spate of articles appeared in the national press on the evils of tourism in Los Angeles; as a metonym for the seamy underbelly of all consumer activities, about idle hands and the devil's workshop. The phrasing already presaged noir, and probably lured even more thrill seekers out west, described by the *New Yorker* as "a huge aimless, idle mob, milling about in search of amusement."[9]

All this sizzle terrorized civic boosters. They were struggling to launch the All-Year-Round Club through dozens of other promotional groups like the Advertising Club of Los Angeles; and gearing up for the 1932 Olympics in L.A. But many of the public works for these were very close to tourist bordellos or speakeasies, which were often only a few blocks away – literally the breath of scandal. For example, there were plans to widen two key streets, Wilshire (through the lake) and Alvarado Boulevards.

Both improvements would mobilize shopping westward, and grow toward what became the mid-city district around the Bullocks Wilshire and the Ambassador Hotel. However, they were also growing too close to Union Street, a red-light district filled with "ladies of the night." So, as a civic service, the vice squad essentially oversaw prostitution as a business on Union; they kept it brisk, and even took their cut, but most of all were expected to keep it from soiling the new Wilshire Corridor.

But the sex industry was only one sin among many that offended the boosters. However, each sin was a business, and each business provided vast revenues for a city built firmly on consumer amusement and tourism. Thus it was throughout America during Prohibition. The Church Federation railed against race-track gambling, but admitted that it was a tax bonanza no one was ready to give up. The Women's National Committee for Law Enforcement fought for better policing of Prohibition laws, which were lax indeed. However, in many respectable homes, empty whiskey bottles were buried in the basement, so that the garbage pickup would not reveal to neighbors precisely how much "medicine" Dr Smith was guzzling every week.

Then, as the equivalent of godlessness in many white Angelinos' minds, there were more of the "Mex," even the "Negro." But noted most anxiously was the growing Mexican population downtown, in the wake of the Mexican Revolution. Around the Plaza (particularly Calle de Negro, translated as Nigger Alley) the non-white presence was extremely evident; it was only a few blocks north of major offices for insurance, real estate, oil and banking. The Plaza district was described in practically every guide book as the hub of non-white L.A. Sonoratown, Chinatown, and Little Tokyo crossed the Plaza, as did the bawdy ten to fifteen vaudeville and burlesque houses along Main. After 1930, the Plaza area was emptied in stages, then converted into a tourist imaginary about Mexican crafts. The master erasure of downtown had begun.

As a related distraction, boosters considered staging a multi-ethnic L.A. crafts carnival in 1926. A local dentist was sent around the country to study *mardi gras* and carnivals elsewhere. But the advice he came up with must have sounded too tame, I suspect: Chrysanthemum animals by the Japanese; "small displays" by "local people [of ability]."[10] So instead, there were plans for a Parade of Nations from the film industry, preferably in Hollywood, with a fruit parade, a motion-picture parade, tableaux (*vivants* no doubt) of Hollywood as "she" was, now that Hollywood had grown tenfold in only ten years.

One imagines how Nathanael West might have described such events. Like so many of the critics, he liked to set the transients of Los Angeles against a background of consumer images – Todd's life among movie sets compared to life at the San Berdoo Apartments (*Day of the Locust*). It has become a standard observation that L.A. noir was written by novelists who also worked as screenwriters, who felt the contrast most vividly between the information tycoons (real estate, film glamour, newspaper promotion, advertising) and what Louis Adamic called "Shadow America (1929)"

> Los Angeles is America. A jungle. Los Angeles grew up suddenly, *planlessly*, under the stimuli of the adventurous spirit of millions of people and the profit motive. It is still growing. Here everything has a chance to thrive – for a while – as a rule only a brief while. Inferior as well as superior plants and trees flourish for a time, then both succumb to chaos and decay. They must give way to new plants pushing up from below and so on. This is freedom under democracy. Jungle Democracy.[11]

Adamic is referring to the hopefuls who were getting lost inside the boom cycle of the twenties. Beyond their vast numbers (over 300 arriving every day), they were treated as ghosts by the newspapers and movie moguls who worked closely with boosters. 1923 was the premium year, with more than 100,000 tourists "pouring in" every month.[12] In the novel condemning L.A. Babbitry, *The Boosters* (1923) by Mark Lee Luther, this tourism generates architectural amnesia, like a hangover from a Forty-Niner Gold Rush.[13]

The "rootlessness" of roadside bricolage was criticized often: the storefront psychics and evangelists, the shoestring fast-food joints, the canary farms and quirky hobby shops. Carey McWilliams called it an "improvised economy" due to the slower growth of manufacturing compared to population, even in the twenties. As a result, "in no city in America has there been such a proliferation of wasteful and meaningless service occupations."[14] "'The thing simply won't add up,' complained James Cain in 1933. 'Life takes on a dreadful vacuity here. I don't know what I miss.'"[15]

Standardly in noir literature, that vacuity (the overhyped but evacuated promise) is precisely what induces the nightmare. In *Angel's Flight* (1927), probably the first L.A. novel that could be called "noir," Don Ryan writes what is now the customary two-page garble about blowing into town – a hymn to quick money and suckers.[16] At first, the hero (a writer from Brooklyn) resists the lies at the newspaper, the fix at court, then decides to hell with it. "March to the cult of the Booster." Skin the peasants. L.A., he declares, is "the Jazz Baby of the Golden West," a city stuffing its windpipe to bursting. Join the swamis, bunco artists and Nazarenes hawking postcards – the "religious farago" preying on tourists lured by Boom and Bloom.

In the twenties, L.A. was the Saudi Arabia for American oil.[17] Its population doubled to 2.2 million, filling in many of the vacant boundaries between townships that once were simply lined with pepper trees, or with summer flowers rising up into the hills unchecked. But many who came found high prices, and severe competition for jobs, at low wages. Workers from the midwest felt in direct competition with Mexican immigrants – tensions that led, in part, to the Zoot Suit Riots during World War II. The white Protestant leadership feared they might "lose" downtown – a familiar theme, repeated by planners in the forties, and onward to the panic of the nineties among Anglos. In the twenties, this rampant growth required vast numbers of cheap labor, which in turn nourished the racist underside of the L.A. dream.

Finally by 1930, the visible contradictions were remarked upon almost standardly. While L.A. was being hyped as "the playground of the world," the "all-year-round city," it also was described by preachers like Sister Aimee as the city of transience, of the last chance.

In print, increasingly, the first wave of anti-tourist literature appeared, in articles about beauty queens getting their hopes undone in the film industry. And then came novels about tourists turning into corrupt screenwriters: first, Harry Leon Wilson's whimsical *Merton of the Movies* (1922), followed by the somewhat darker Carl Van Vechten's *Spider Boy* (1927), the same year as *Angel's Flight*, and finally the bestseller *Queer People* by Carroll and Garrett Graham (1930).[18] *Queer People* is a particularly pivotal novel, an influence on Budd Schulberg and Nathanael West, about the "Hollywood G's – girls, gin and gynecology;" a garden of unearthly delights peopled also by "confidence men, coon shouters, pimps, press agents, song writers, sadists, bootleggers, bandits, Babbits, remittance men, radio annnouncers, realtors."[19]

During the Depression, anti-tourist novels get more viciously exotic, more about consumers involved in murder or suicide. For example, the Hollywood premiere leads to murder in *Day of the Locust*; the dance marathon becomes a *danse macabre* in McCoy's *They Shoot Horses, Don't They?*; the movie mogul is spun into reductive hopelessness, a victim of consumer planning, in Fitzgerald's *The Last Tycoon*, and in Schulberg's *What*

Makes Sammy Run? Restaurants become sites for murder in Cain's *The Postman Always Rings Twice,* and *Mildred Pierce.*

The formulas often involved victims with amnesia brought on by the consumer-driven experience. Their numbing lapses of memory were induced by the extremes that tourism hype produce here, as in this passage from Eric Knight's *You Play the Black and Red Comes Up* (1938):

> The minute you crossed into California you went crazy... I could remember everything about California, but I couldn't feel it. I tried to get my mind to remember something that it could feel, too, but it was no use. It was all gone. All of it. The pink stucco houses and the palm trees and the stores built like cats and dogs and frogs and ice cream freezers and the neon lights round everything...
>
> I thought about coming over the Santa Monica mountains and seeing Hollywood all lighted up like a fairy city; and the way the men in yellow smocks stood on Sunset Boulevard waving bags of Krispy-Korn and trying to sell movie guides to the homes of the stars and how I never saw anyone ever stop to buy one.[20]

In Evelyn Waugh's *The Loved One* (1948), Forest Lawn cemetery is allegorized into a dropsy about mortuary salesmen driving their workers insane. By the time Jim Thompson presents his grifter's whorehouse vision of the Sunset Strip in the late sixties, the dens of noir iniquity may have shifted neighborhoods, but they remain linked to that central theme: how consumer hype erases the sense of place, and invades the self.

The theme is buried inside *The Woman Chaser* by Charles Willeford (1960). Richard Hudson, a sleazoid used-car dealer, lives literally in "the mythical boundary between Los Angeles and Hollywood,"[21] in a continual state of adolescent unease. He watches his overripe, mildly incestuous mother (a retired actress) display her youngish breasts for him. He sleeps near her, in "Lumpy Grits," a Craftsman mansion that reminds him of the quick-cash twenties, but is only a block away from the local shopping center.

My point here is obvious but essential. As much as I love noir, and find it exotically compelling, it is nevertheless often utterly false in its visions of the poor, of the non-white in particular. It is essentially a mythos about white male panic – the white knight in a cesspool of urban decay; about desire turned into a slot machine. Despite its origins as social realism in Hammett, the hard-boiled story cannot help but operate, very fundamentally, as white males building a social imaginary. The booster myths (sunshine, climate, Protestant Eden) generate an emptiness that leads to violence and despair, in the form of urban fables. The crime on dark streets stands in for the fears about foreigners, jobs, speculation, and cheap hype. It pits the white, usually Protestant, shamus against a world that is utterly transient, as if no poor communities exist except as a hangout for crooks and addicts. What results is a pose really; it distracts the memory away from community life as it existed inside the city. It is the dark side of tourism, a roller-coaster ride through "mean" streets (often poor neighborhoods).

In noir pseudo-realism, it is difficult not to imagine entire neighborhoods surviving merely as hangouts for crooks. A good case in point is a lecture Robert Towne gave on what he left out about L.A in writing the screenplay for *Chinatown*. Every question in the packed auditorium came from fans who presumed that his film images of evil in *Chinatown* were truth incarnate, that it all happened as in a Raymond Chandler novel. Noir is that exotically compelling. Its phantasms consume our own memory of the crises of the city. As Davis writes: "Noir was like the transformational grammar turning each charming ingredient of the boosters arcadia into a sinister equivalent."[22]

HEARING VOICES: IMAGINARY DEATH KNELLS

This transformational grammar also operates directly in the mind of the resident here. L.A. is whimsically gothic because the "secured" spaces are designed so often to emphasize the spirit of buyer's impulse, you alone in the shopping mode – in a state of distraction, feeling coddled and swindled at the same time, overstimulated and desensitized, gated in, but under surveillance. Behind all the violence and fury in the fiction, noir refers to inaction, to spaces haunted mostly by consumer passivity – about being lost in the wrong neighborhood without change for a phone call, a mindless unease; or walking through the drab Seven-Eleven after twelve hours of straight television watching. I remember being stuck once for days at a package holiday in La Paz, where it was so ferociously cold that no one could get served food. Meanwhile, sour mariachis sang American Christmas carols that funneled up the building for hours. Then, on the last day, teams of heavily armed soldiers appeared in paper party hats. They were taking over the hotel for the general's birthday. Sometimes, noir consumerism is so embalmed that it exceeds the ridiculous. I remember thinking: this could make a murder story. Remember the tourist spot that made you feel really slimy and lonely? How exactly did I wind up here, you asked, laughing at yourself? You feel stupidly *maudit*, a noir tourist cursed with absolutely nothing to do.

In such settings, perverse fantasies take over, about paranoid brushes with death of the sort one reads in pulp magazines. For example, some people have said to me that when they walk on empty L.A. streets, in the old industrial district downtown, they can feel – imagine they feel – the sights of an infra-red rifle, blocks away: as if a lunatic with nothing much to do were monitoring them, instead of the police, who circle the area like shepherds.

These imaginary nightmares often involve savage reversals of the consumer act. In the late seventies, a myth emerged about supermarket parking lots, a *grand peur* for the shopper loading groceries. As the story went, a man, described by many in precise detail – usually in his early twenties, dark hair, obsequiously helpful, soft-spoken – would walk behind old ladies while they leaned over with bags of groceries, the trunk of the car wide open. One way or another, he would ingratiate himself, look needy. The lady would agree to drive him somewhere. He would murder her *en route*. I am told that the crime described was imaginary – it never took place, a shopper's folktale. However, many people were convinced that they had been following the story in the *Times* or the *Herald*, or knew a family this had happened to. (Even stranger, the bad wish finally "came true" much later, in 1991, with the series of "mall" killings in Covina.[23])

Like these consumer folkmares, there are noir and apocalyptic scenarios that continually repeat in literature, film and the visual arts from Los Angeles. By the mid sixties, they take on an increasingly disengaged spirit, like a nightmare one watches through the windshield of a car. They are myths inspired increasingly by consumer erasure. They become less about losing place, and more about losing the ability to remember altogether – a topology of forgetfulness. In Chris Burden's *Medusa's Head* (1991),[24] an inchoate mass is surrounded by the twisted rails of toy trains, ever circling, never locating a center. Here are a few of the most common dark myths since the mid sixties.

THE CITY BURNING

Summers are fire season in L.A., a stillness and apprehension that can suggest bizarre connections between nature and urban collapse. As in *Day of the Locust*: in the midst of a riot, brought on by consumer ennui,

Nathanael West has Todd Hackett remember his painting of "The Burning of Los Angeles." While watching the riot and the fire in the Hollywood district, Todd is "clinging desperately to the iron rail," thinking of details in his painting:

> ...the burning city, a great bonfire of architectural styles, ranging from Egyptian to Cape Cod colonial. Through the center, winding from left to right, was a long hill street and down it, spilling into the middle foreground, came the mob carrying baseball bats and torches. For the faces of its members, he was using the innumerable sketches he had made of the people who came to California to die.[25]

Similarly, in August 1965 the Watts Rebellion became the fire that altered the culture of the city. Afterward, a flock of apocalyptic books appeared. They tend to describe a world dying by long distance. Joan Didion remembered the Watts Riot as a summer fire seen from the freeway:

> The city burning is Los Angeles' deepest image of itself: Nathanael West perceived that, in *Day of the Locust*; and at the time of the 1965 Watts riots what struck the imagination most indelibly were the fires. For days one could drive the Harbor Freeway and see the city on fire, just as we had always known it would be in the end. Los Angeles weather is the weather of catastrophe, of apocalypse.[26]

Notice how peculiarly disengaged the description is. Obviously, since the mid sixties, there are many more dark stories using the freeway, but that is simply a measure of a much broader distancing device. Social conflict is roped off, like a museum display, or like ashes blown from a fire. Is this mess finally getting out of hand, the driver wonders, uneasy about "sig alerts" that make all problems sound like innocent acts of nature?

The floating disquiet seems quite a contrast to the highly coordinated crisis management that has shaped the look of Los Angeles since – in public services, police, planning, zoning, in the cautious, fortified look of the new downtown; in Operation Hammer by police against L.A. gangs, and the intensity of the war on drugs that led to the most apocalyptic public video of all, the Rodney King tape – all in a trajectory that proceeded after the shock of the Watts Riot. Urban planning was refashioned afterward, as was city politics. Many other forces came into play as well, of course, from Vietnam to white backlash. Together, they appear increasingly in descriptions of nature taking its revenge on the city.

The fire stands in for helplessness before a monumental natural disaster, a world that suddenly has lost its monitor, and gone out of control, as in novelist Thomas Sanchez's description of a fire in the Santa Barbara mountains:

> It was time to evacuate. We piled personal belongings in the cars. I ran through the darkened house locking windows and tying doors together so advancing flames couldn't suck them open. Minutes became hours, hours became lifetimes. There was nothing to do except wait and watch which way the fickle winds of fate would blow. The curtain of flame rose higher around us, the fiery opera in full force, a hundred houses already burned.[27]

Fire meant the end of immunity, the window of advantage gone, the biosphere so essential to Southern California taking revenge, or the non-white hidden world claiming its place. The mood after 1965 sparked national bestsellers about the end of L.A., like Richard Lillard's remarkable *Eden in Jeopardy* (1966),[28] or Curt Gentry's *The Last Days of the Late, Great State of California* (1968). Journalist Lawrence Powell wrote this about a fire in Malibu:

> What next? Cliff slippage? Earthquake? Drought? Plague? War? All have visited the earth at some time in history. Southern Californians should not expect immunity forever.[29]

Speaking of not knowing which immunity is which: landscape specialists[30] tell me that even the horrific Malibu fire of 1994, gruesome as it was, will fertilize the soil and clear the land for chaparral, which is the basis of the entire food chain. However, developers often level the native brown and purple chaparral anyway, on the grounds that it is not green enough. Then plants and trees from other climates are inserted as ornamental exotica, which also inhibit the natural growth.

Similarly, developers selling the "belle-vue" tend to overbuild flood plains and slide areas; while master planners during the thirties had the L.A. River cemented over. The sum effect has nearly eradicated what once were massive *underground* lakes, very abundant aquifers. Water tables continue to drop immensely. Innumerable species have disappeared.

THE INVISIBLE CITY: FREEWAYS

The freeway network was finished essentially by the mid sixties, and ran at high efficiency for about ten years. Architecturally speaking, it completed a process whereby the point that one entered public spaces was narrowed considerably, while the privacy within the auto was enhanced.

This fits into a broader, long-standing policy from the twenties on. Instead of Griffith Park, Elysian Park, or the lush bamboo in Pershing Square, more of the landscape was privatized: fewer new parks and more backyards; eventually a transition to the shopping mall, to the theme park (not to mention the fantasy architecture so common to L.A.). Of course, even as early as 1905, the city was already refusing offers for donations of park land, as if this seemed beside the point.

The political culture behind this growing denial of public space has fascinated scholars for a generation now. Studies on the subject range from Ed Soja on postmodern geographies, to Michael Sorkin on the amusement park as urban paradigm,[31] to Mike Davis on the militancy of the fortified privatized space,[32] to Margaret Crawford on the reclaiming of public spaces by the marginalized poor.[33] They describe a multi-level transformation: classes increasingly isolated physically; industry sprawling into former farm areas; the maturation into cities of what once were simply suburban bedroom communities; the panic in real-estate patterns brought on by non-white immigration; the effects of declining public services, for a city that always relied on smaller budgets per capita, and is about to undergo historic, devastating cutbacks in 1996; and, of course, the continual restructuring of the built environment in response to the automobile, which brings with it the steady loss of green space.

When farms and orchards get ploughed under to make way for housing, there is no coherent vision for replacing their green presence. And none seems necessary – at first. Until the drought of 1915, watermelon patches were plainly visible off Riverside Drive in Echo Park. Legend has it that children used to steal watermelons and sail them down the L.A. River. All that was gone by 1920. A similar transition struck Hollywood in the twenties, the San Fernando and San Gabriel Valleys after World War II, Orange County in the sixties, and now Ventura County in decades to come (though the cost of adding infrastructure there will slow that down considerably).

The way this green space disappears can be very deceptive as well. Hollywood remained half citrus for years. Orchards looked like private parks inside the city. Their bouquet seemed to make parks irrelevant. Then the last orchards went very quickly, in less than two years. But a phantom of which trees grew where has remained. Farms and orchards were boundaries between townships really. Well into the twenties, an extraordinary isolation existed between the three original urban circuits of the city – downtown, the west side, and the San Fernando Valley. Between downtown and Hollywood were pepper trees, mentioned often by old-timers and in diaries. West Los Angeles was identified on the south by truck farmers who would sell on Washington Boulevard.

Each zone developed very separate identities. White flight has made these distinctions even stronger, particularly as suburbs and beach towns matured into alternative downtowns. If you live on the west side, you may never travel east of La Brea, except occasionally to go to MOCA, or the symphony. The habit is well fixed, like the freeway to work. One literally passes through to arrive, but rarely stops.

To outsiders, almost none of this variety seems visible now. However, L.A. remains far more a city of neighborhoods than appearances suggest, with local haunts along what was once the southern gate of an orchard, or the junction of trolley lines. In fact, tourists tend to go precisely where such haunts have been erased. The result can be disquieting. The Bona-venture Hotel, made famous as critical theory by Fredric Jameson,[34] was built specifically in a zone wiped out, then sealed from the east by tunnels and huge parking structures – to the point where nearby residents were almost impossible to find. The entrance, in fact, was so inaccessible to anyone other than guests that an extra entrance had to be added on the eastern face in the late eighties, simply to allow the businesses inside to find *some* street traffic (though there is virtually none except for business lunches). That is consumer-built isolation indeed. Self-alienation might be more like it.

What, then, is the final effect of this architectural evasion, this intro-version of public spaces, already quite evident by the late sixties? In the novel *Invisible Cities* (1972), Italo Calvino finds Los Angeles unapproachable by freeway, as so many visiting writers do. After the forms of cities exhaust their variety, he writes, "and come apart, the end of cities begins."[35] "In the last pages of the atlas there is an outpouring of networks without beginning or end, cities in the shape of Los Angeles ... without shape." Calvino is suggesting a city incapable of holding a memory, or a shape, rather like a bad battery unable to hold a charge, a city after the death of cities.

While this critique, very frequently made, has the charm of a ghost tale, it still tends to obscure vital historical evidence, much as the earlier noir literature often exoticized the chaos. I should summarize these. First, L.A. has never been simply a sprawl. As mad as some of the results may look, more than fifty years of planning went into the freeway basin we see today. Second, L.A. is not without boundary; its boundaries are clearly defined by its transportation outreach, and segregated real-estate planning. Third, L.A. is not suddenly looking like a "real city." There was always massive poverty here, a large pool of cheap labor, usually shut off from the tourist (Balloon) route, and made invisible, until occasional bursts of violence suddenly make the public take notice, as in April 1992, when the worst possible nightmare occurred – the social cost spread into middle-class neighborhoods as well.

Even despite the shocks since 1992, however, one can easily live a lifetime here as a tourist, see mostly what the smoke sends, by way of promotion, never visit what is left out, except by way of crime movies. That is why L.A. begins to resemble a nether world. When Kathryn Bigelow, the director of *Strange Days* (1995), was asked why Los Angeles made an ideal setting for apocalyptic movies, she answered: "Perhaps because there's so little history here." "It's not a city," she added. "There is no center." And no identity except a "poly-identity" suitable for "whatever you project onto it, a faceless place ... blurred into one."[36] Among noir filmmakers, it is almost a credo to talk about L.A. like a bus driver giving a guided tour through a parking lot.

SMOG

On 26 July 1943, the city of L.A. underwent a gas attack: four hours of thick, noxious misery, brought on by the industrial buildup during the war effort. Others followed, one in September. After blaming a rubber factory in East L.A., home incinerators, oil refineries, and automobiles, and asking numerous experts, by 1948 an Air Pollution Control district was set up.[37] From that point forth, the issue of smog has been unmistakably a part of L.A. lore. In the fifties, the *New York Times* carried numerous articles about L.A. air, much as Ed Ruscha would use smog as a chiaroscuro in various paintings in the sixties, or weathercasters on fifties radio describe the air as "neurotic."[38] Even the modest "improvements" in air quality since the seventies (now up to 50 per cent less pollution) are barely noted, beneath the apocalyptic associations – and realities. Just as the racial crises after 1965 encouraged even more white flight, and more segregation, so the myth emerged that smog was worse in non-white areas of the city. Smog as urban blight. Smog as nature's revenge, yet again.

Since the mid sixties, the aurora of smog has become a governing symbol of Los Angeles, the emblem of avoidance and self-reflection, and of white flight. One drives into it with the same expectations as driving into a city skyline – for the city out of control. Along the San Bernardino mountains, toward Lake Arrowhead and Big Bear, the smog can rise up to a mile high, like a mysterious erasure, like the top of an Ed Ruscha painting, but no longer as visceral as Film Noir. We have a new auto-noir, based on a different system of memories, no longer about decaying downtowns. Novelist John Rechy writes:

> Driving out of Los Angeles after a ten-day visit, I looked in my rearview mirror as the freeways that knot within the city untie into a straight highway; and I saw reflected a gray amorphous "dome," a cloud created by entrapped smoke and lingering fog enclosing the "city of lost angels," the city of daily apocalypse.
> At that moment crowded memories of that visit full of sex and revelation seemed to be contained within that mirrored reflection.[39]

This is literally a "telling" quote about voyeuristic inversion in Los Angeles in freeway Los Angeles. The emotional impact of the city suggests tourism, a cloudy mirror, but a mirror nonetheless. We are supposed to watch, or be watched, in the privacy of our vehicle.

> If you approach Los Angeles on the highway turned freeway…, you're aware perhaps as far as a hundred miles away, of the Cloud. It enshrouds the city. In the daytime and from that distance, the Cloud, which is fog and smoke, creates a spectral city: a gray mass floating on the horizon. At night, lit by the millions of colored lights with which the city attempts futilely to smother the dark, it becomes an incandescent, smoking halo; dull orange: as though the city were on fire.[40]

Finally, the smog, like traffic itself, becomes a single, blind organism – a floating, shimmering aminoid swarm. In the novel *Snow Crash* (1992) by Neil Stephenson, an organic haze of amino acids encircles Los Angeles in a hazy sprawl, "ringed and netted like hot wires in a toaster." Traffic "throbs" like "streams of red and white corpuscles," guided by "the fuzzy logic of intelligent traffic lights." "Farther away, spreading across the basin, a million sprightly logos smear into solid arc, like geometric points merging into curves … into a surrounding dimness that is burst here and there by the blaze of a security spotlight in someone's backyard."[41]

This is very much the spirit of L.A. apocalyptic writing from the mid sixties until the Uprising of 1992 – about smogs, fires, and disengaged sensory madness, different in a very essential way from the white mob starting the fire that Nathanael West describes at the end of *Day of the Locust*. Rechy's first novel, *City of Night*, came out of an earlier inspiration; it could serve as a good example of transition, a bit closer to what West evoked in those final scenes – the picaresque into urban blight, as in Jim Thompson or Bukowski novels, or John Fante's *Ask the Dust* (1939). The roman noir in Los Angeles (1927 to the 1960s) kept a record of urban decentralization, from Ryan's description of "groaning" Angel's Flight,[42] to Philip Marlowe's office at the seedy Belfont building, near Hollywood, or Chandler's visions of Bunker Hill. Rechy's *City of Night* (1963) uses Pershing Square downtown as a nexus, of what he called "Outcast America." Pershing Square, formerly L.A. Bughouse Square once lush with overgrown bamboo and banana palms, and "generally crowded until the late hours of the night,"[43] was turned into a cement parking structure during the sixties; then given back some green space in the early nineties. Bukowski mentions Pershing Square a lot. He lived downtown often, and locates his stories along the path of its steady demise – its demolition and its depopulation, leaving wino bars and flophouses where only the desperately marginalized stayed.

Artist Llyn Foulkes lived near Bunker Hill downtown in the early sixties, and watched it get bulldozed to clear a path for what eventually became California Plaza and MOCA, among other puzzle pieces of the new steel and glass downtown that stands alongside the Harbor Freeway today. As I mentioned in Chapter 1, a few of the best of the gingerbread, tall Victorians from Bunker Hill were moved for display at Heritage Square, four miles north, off the Pasadena Freeway, near the old Lummis house – a monument to Protestant high culture during the first quarter of the century, now a museum. Then, two of the Victorians on blocks at Heritage Square burned down one day in the early sixties – apparently arson. Foulkes visited the ashes, much the way photographer William Reagh[44] photographed each gash the cranes made while ripping apart Bunker Hill (thousands of pictures, like frames from a time-lapse film about the erasure of downtown). While Foulkes stood examining the corpse of the buildings, a tourist (or someone from another part of town) came by. The visitor asked what had happened. Foulkes said "The city did it." He felt they did it to make sure that the best of these buildings were not around as evidence for the future.[45]

By car, Heritage Square looks inscrutable, like Victorian fence posts in the middle of nowhere. When I teach classes in Pasadena (not far from

Heritage Square), I am asked regularly what those uninhabited mansions are doing there. They don't relate to what's around them, a mishmash of stucco dingbats and uninspired frame houses. Very few onlookers seem to have the slightest clue as to what these mansions originally were. A fragment of lost cityscape operates as floating signifier, a string of buildings without a street. It is very much like the empty lot I mention in my introduction – too much missing to provoke much more than a mnemonic ache (phantom limb).

When Bunker Hill was being razed, a wrecker downtown found a sack of gold dust worth $4,647 in the rubble. "Beyond the dust ... the City Hall Tower was barely visible."[46] In the fading remnants, kids used to rummage as well. One resident remembers interiors that were "vast and dank and huge with Victorian spaces to hide in, alcoves, seating areas by big windows, huge staircases. No furnishings. But I remember letters on the floors, people's effects. It was exciting to steal into them."[47]

By the seventies, with Bunker Hill unrecognizable – new upscale condos – only neo-noir films like *Chinatown* suggest the erasure of downtown; or occasionally a reference in a crime novel to the "Angel's Flight cop's bar" imagined for Echo Park in Gerald Petievich's *To Live and Die in L.A.* (1984).[48] The erased Chinatown itself becomes purely a state of mind, best forgotten. *The Two Jakes* (1990) could be retitled "How I Learned to Become an Amnesiac after the War." In films like *To Live and Die in L.A.* (1985), or *The Grifters* (1990), the characters operate as if their motivational centers had been burnt away; they have family routines, but no family memory, no intimacy, no remorse.

Helter Skelter (L.A. noir since the late sixties), the term associated with the Manson trial and with a Beatles song, is in many ways an introduction to another version of darkness and forgetting: murders in random sequence, the POV of Manson's eyes, with a swastika carved into his forehead, as if to inscribe a memory. In the decades since the Manson hysteria, after the Hillside Strangler case, among many others, and finally the O.J. Simpson story, a new variety of noir has developed – the *danse macabre* by way of media. Underneath the towering impact of global consumer marketing and its electronic non-communities, the apocalyptic vision became even more about the invaded self, and fantasies of self-immolating revenge against anonymous faces, as in serial murder.

Crime and place vanish behind the freeway city. In Dennis Cooper's fiction, acts of sadism are presented bluntly alongside L.A. consumer life, all of it held together with fantasies about serial killers hiding corpses, or the phony theater in televison coverage of the Simpson trials, like a shopping network about murder. I am reminded of Bataille's sense that the act of consumption can feel so dehumanized that it evokes fantasies of great brutality.[49] In J.G. Ballard's writings, high-rises and concrete islands between traffic devolve into a brutalizing stone age. Promotion and tourism generate a consumer ennui that turns paranoic; media fantasies about random crimes sell this paranoia, the way crime films sell serial killers. Random murder stands in for random politics. The killer acts like a bored shopper stalking blindly, carelessly.

In Cooper's short story "A Herd" (1981),[50] a serial killer cruises the streets for a victim. He finds Jay, and kills him by injecting a drug overdose. He puts Jay's body in his car. It is 4 a.m. Ray drives up the San Diego Freeway, to a cluster of trees, and parks; he then claws through the brush for a place to leave the body. "He was surprised the earth felt warm. Like skin, he realized, just after death when there was no hint of the sentence passed over it." He drops the body, as if it had been "stolen from some art museum and broken." Then, after pushing it down a slope, he "thought how the corpse might stay hidden, a distant white blur to the hurrying drivers, like their expressions in choppy pond water. It was a sight which would smear his mind, be erased by the long straight freeway, grow vague as the date, as the night would become, then the month and everything not photographed in it." As in films and novels about cyborgs in futuristic *barrios*, these images present a barbaric amnesia replacing white civilization, in a city whose sky is the "color of television tuned to a dead channel."[51]

In Steve Erickson's futuristic novel *Rubicon Beach* (1986), downtown is hidden in a lagoon at the edge of swampland. The river echoes through empty buildings, and along the "Weeping Storefronts" in Chinatown, as ghostly ships like black mountains bring Chinese and Mexican immigrants into downtown, or help police remove criminals "informed of their own murder." Immigration has been translated into Foucauldian nightmare, a great containment that is just beginning to take shape:

> The boat had the same blind Asians and Latinos; as before, they were still standing on deck staring in the direction of the spray… They didn't even know they'd been there for weeks. Nobody called them from the shore; in Los Angeles you have to figure out for yourself when you're there, nobody calls you from the shore.[52]

NOTES

1. William Gibson, "Johnny Mnemonic" (1981), in *Burning Chrome* (New York: Ace Books, 1987; orig. 1986), p. 8.

2. Rumor and memory play tricks with the location assigned to the cribs. Old-timers I interviewed said the cribs were just northeast of Olvera Street, and were allowed to burn down in the twenties, when cases of smallpox were found there; the site then was replaced by the Terminal Annex post office. However, archaeologiests have dug red brick "cribs" elsewhere, farther southeast, beyond Union Station (*L.A. Times*, 31 May 1996, A1). See also W.W. Robinson, *Tarnished Angels: Paradisiacal Turpitude in Los Angeles* (Los Angeles: Ward Ritchie Press, 1964) p. 18.

3. Luis Leobardo Arroyo, "Mexican Workers and American Unions: The Los Angeles AFL, 1800–1933," *Chicano Political Economy Collective, Working Paper Series*, No. 107, 1981, pp. 10, 16, 17.

4. Kenneth D. Rose, "Dry Los Angeles and Its Liquor Problems in 1924," *Journal of the Historical Society of Southern California*, 1979, p. 53. From *L.A. Times* article by Timothy Turner, 9 September 1924.

5. Bruce Henstell, *Sunshine and Wealth: Los Angeles in the Twenties and Thirties* (San Francisco: Chronicle Books, 1984), p. 57.

6. Ibid., p. 67. This scandal was covered in the *L.A. Examiner*, a paper with enough of the old Republican moral Progressivism left in its editorial policy to ignore the pressures of boosterism a bit more than the *Times* during the twenties.

7. Rose, "Dry Los Angeles," pp. 59–61.

8. Jules Tygiel studies these scandals magnificently in *The Great Los Angeles Swindle* (New York: Oxford University Press, 1994).

9. Albert W. Atwood, "Money from Everywhere," *Saturday Evening Post*, 12 May 1923, pp. 10–11.

10. Letter to Edward A. Dickson, editor of the *L.A. Examiner* and high in the promotional network; founder of the Westwood campus of UCLA. UCLA Research Library, Special Coll. #663. Dentist (Edward Irvin): Box 5.

11. Carey McWilliams, *Louis Adamic and Shadow America* (Los Angeles: Arthur Whipple, 1935), p. 79. Mike Davis introduced me to this rare volume from one of the many small presses that have come and gone, with barely a ripple, in Los Angeles.

12. "From All Quarters They Come to Us: Tourists Pour into Los Angeles and the Southland at the Rate of More than 100,000 a Month. Many of them to Remain Here." *Southern California Business*, February 1923, p. 21.

13. David Fine, "Introduction," *Los Angeles in Fiction: A Collection of Original Essays* (Albuquerque: University of New Mexico Press, 1984), p. 5.

14. Carey McWilliams, *Southern California: An Island on the Land* (Santa Barbara: Peregrine Smith, 1979; orig. 1946), p. 237.

15. Ibid.

16. Don Ryan, *Angel's Flight* (New York: Livright & Sons, 1927), pp. 62–3.

17. The standard figure, repeated in numerous sources, is 20 per cent of American oil produced in Los Angeles.

18. Carroll and Garrett Graham, *Queer People* (New York: Grossett & Dunlap, 1930). This novel went through at least eleven editions in its first year. It was reprinted in the eighties.

19. Ibid., pp. 79–80.

20. Eric Knight, *You Play the Black and Red Comes Up* (Berkeley: Black Lizard Books, 1986; orig. 1938), pp. 131–2. See also an analysis of the opening lines of Cornell Woolrich's novel *The Black Curtain* (1941), about the fragmented perceptions of amnesiac Frank Townshend: David Reid and Jayne L. Walker, "Strange Pursuit: Cornell Woolrich and the Abandoned City of the Forties," in Joan Copjec, ed., *Shades of Noir* (London: Verso, 1993), p. 75. The trope of erasure of face or memory – of identity – is fundamental to many noir openings, e.g. the flashback in *Flashbacks in Film* by Maureen Turim (London: Routledge, 1989).

21. Charles Willeford, *The Woman Chaser* (New York: Carroll & Graf, 1990; orig. 1960), p. 23. Lumpy Grits would probably be in Las Feliz, based on the description.

22. Mike Davis, "*Chinatown*, Part Two? The 'Internationalization' of Downtown Los Angeles," *New Left Review* 165, July–August 1987, republished in David Read, ed., *Sex, Death and God in L.A.* (New York: Random House, 1992).

23. Laurie Becklund, "Rage and Alienation Marks Suspects in Mall Murders," *Los Angeles Times*, 22 September 1991. The tone of the article even reads like a noir novel.

24. *Medusa's Head* was featured at the show in January 1992, *Helter Skelter* at the L.A. Museum of Contemporary Art. Some of the text for this chapter comes from my catalogue essay: *Helter Skelter: L.A. Art in the 1990s*, edited by Catherine Gudis (Los Angeles: The Museum of Contemporary Art, 1992).

25. Nathanael West, *Day of the Locust* (New York: New Directions, 1969; orig. 1939), pp. 184–5.

26. Joan Didion, *Slouching Toward Bethlehem* (New York: Dell Publishing, 1968), p. 65.

27. Thomas Sanchez, *Angels Burning: Native Notes From the Land of Earthquake and Fire* (Santa Barbara: Capra Press, 1987), p. 33.

28. Lillard's work has become a classic study on how ecology erases. Much of what it warned might happen has since taken place.

29. Lawrence Clark Powell, *Ocean in View: The Malibu* (Santa Barbara: Capra Press, 1987; orig. 1968), p. 57.

30. Meetings for Southern California Environment and History Conference, 1996. Nasty land policies resemble urban policies downtown – tarred by almost the same brush.

31. Edward W. Soja, *Postmodern Geographies: The Reassertion of Space in Critical Social Theory* (Verso: London, 1988). Michael Sorkin, ed., *Variations on a Theme Park* (New York: Hill & Wang, 1992): quite an influential anthology, though probably each author has shifted position since then. See also Denise Scott Brown, ed., *Urban Concepts* (New York: St Martin's Press, 1990; issue of *Architectural Design*). And the debate over "porosity" – whether enclaved spaces are less "fortified" than their image suggests: Steven Flusty, *Building Paranoia* (Los Angeles For Architecture and Urban Design, 1994); and forthcoming book by Edward Blakely III, entitled *Fortress America*.

32. An ongoing theme in most of Davis's writings from 1989 to 1991, the time that he was working on *City of Quartz*.

33. Margaret Crawford, "The Architecture of Everyday Life," Work in Progress Series, Getty Center for the History of Art and the Humanities, February 1995. This argument is developed in *Everyday Urbanism* (New York: Manocelli Press, 1997).

34. Fredric Jameson, "Postmodernism, or the Cultural Logic of Late Capitalism," *New Left Review* 146, July–August 1984, subsequently incorporated into his book of the same title (London: Verso, 1991). See also Mike Davis, "Urban Renaissance and the

Spirit of Postmodernism," *New Left Review* 151, May–June 1985, which is also published in the anthology edited by E. Ann Kaplan, *Postmodernism and Its Discontents: Theories, Practice* (London: Verso, 1988); and, finally, the article by Alex Callinicos reviewing the debate, "Reactionary Postmodernism," in Roy Boyne and Ali Rattansi, eds, *Postmodernism and Society* (London: Macmillan, 1990).

35. Italo Calvino, *Invisible Cities*, trans. W. Weaver (New York: Harcourt Brace Jovanovich, 1972), p. 139. Barthes suggests much the same in his comparison between L.A. and Tokyo as cities without centers, in *The Empire of Signs*, trans. R. Howard (New York: Hill & Wang, 1982). Among earlier novels about this sense of absence/presence in freeway L.A., see Christopher Isherwood, *A Single Man* (1964); Alison Lurie, *The Nowhere City* (1965).

36. "Reality Bytes: Andrew Hultkrans Talks with Kathryn Bigelow," *Artforum*, November 1995, p. 80.

37. Richard G. Lillard, *Eden in Jeopardy* (New York: Alfred A. Knopf, 1966), p. 235.

38. Gavin Lambert, *The Slide Area: Scenes of Hollywood Life* (New York: Berkeley Publishing, 1960; orig. 1959), p. 9.

39. John Rechy, *Numbers* (New York: Grove Press, 1984), in the Foreword.

40. Ibid., p. 19. This passage was probably written within a year of the Watts Rebellion.

41. Neil Stephenson, *Snow Crash* (New York: Bantam Books, 1992), p. 190.

42. Ryan, *Angel's Flight*, p. 62. In the twenties, Angel's Flight averaged about 12,000 rides a day; by 1941, only 3,000, even before it was slated for removal: *Los Angeles*, Works Progress Administration, p. 157.

43. Ibid.

44. From 1939 to 1990, William Reagh produced 40,000 photographs of Los Angeles, in considerable architectural detail, primarily of the downtown area. See two calendars of photos by William Reagh, *The Changing Face of L.A.* (Los Angeles: Photoventures Publishing, 1989, 1990).

45. Interview with Llyn Foulkes in 1991. His paintings often contain references to the dismantling of downtown L.A.

46. Newspaper clipping file, Downtown Public Library.

47. Interview at Echo Park Library, 1995.

48. Gerald Petievich, *To Live and Die in L.A.* (New York: Pinnacle Books, 1984), p. 53.

49. Norman O. Brown, *Apocalypse and/or Metamorphosis* (Berkeley: University of California Press, 1971), p. 192.

50. Dennis Cooper, "A Herd," *The Tenderness of the Wolves* (Trumansburg, NY: The Crossing Press, 1982), pp. 69–70.

51. From the opening line of William Gibson's novel *Neuromancer* (London: Gollancz, 1984). Quite a few cyberpunk novels are set in L.A., including Norman Spinrad's *Little Heroes* (New York: Bantam, 1988) and Mick Farren's *The Armageddon Crazy* (New York: Bantam Books, 1987).

52. Steve Erickson, *Rubicon Beach* (New York: Vintage Books, 1987; orig. 1986), p. 8.

CHAPTER THREE

BUILDING BLADE RUNNER

In February 1990, at a public lecture series on art in Los Angeles, three out of five leading urban planners agreed that they hoped L.A. would someday look like the film *Blade Runner*.[1] The audience, safe and comfortable in the Pacific Design Center, buzzed audibly with concern. One could practically hear rumors starting – that it was time to sell that condo by the beach, and move to Seattle. Two of the designers gave specific examples. They loved Santee Alley, a bustling outdoor market in the downtown garment center, also not far from the homeless district. Of course, that general area is slated (or sleighted) for urban renewal anyway, so this was a safe comment. It is easy to root for the horse once it is off to the glue factory.

Another planner, architect for the powerful Community Redevelopment Agency, praised the Interstate Savings and Loan logo atop the new eighty-storey office building on the main library grounds downtown. It reminded him favorably of *Blade Runner*. That drew an audible hiss, so he added that in thirty years that bank would be out of business anyway and the logo would be gone. Then he admitted that he had approved the logo because there was no way to stop a business from obtaining permission to put one on a building downtown (the governing rule, set up by the downtown redevelopment agency, allows for logos, though the full title of a company is considered invasive – ambience over advertising). He was saying, in effect: why not allow free enterprise to show its face honestly, without the seamless camouflage? We need more than cityscapes and skylines, he and the others were suggesting. Apparently, we need the rude aesthetics of an immigrant market, but imagine it safely barricaded between buildings hundreds of feet high. We want to return to a fanciful version of the urban ghetto, back to cluttered industrial imagery, away from the simplified urban grid. We need *Blade Runner* – or do we?

By 1990, Frank Gehry's architecture is praised in a mainstream review as "post-apocalyptic," having a "Blade Runner inventiveness." The term "Blade Runner" is also applied to police tactics – Operation Hammer, the gang "sweeps" of 1991, and the watchful waiting (promotional campaign by LAPD) after the Rodney King beating. And, most of all, by 1994, it is applied to the widening gulf in real-estate values – "Blade Runner neighborhoods" – the middle-class panic about crime that is helping to spin many poor communities in Los Angeles further into the problems that this fantasy suggests. One myth builds another.

The film *Blade Runner* has indeed achieved something rare in the history of cinema. It has become a paradigm for the future of cities, for artists across the disciplines. It is undoubtedly the film most requested in art and film classes I teach, whether to environmental designers, illustrators, fine artists, photographers or filmmakers. When it came out in 1982, many critics called it the success of style over substance, or style over story. But the hum of that Vangelis score against the skyline of L.A. in 2019, as the film opens, continues to leave a strange impact on artists and filmmakers.

When they are asked why, very little is said about the forties nasal drip in the film, the drone of the voice-over, the smoky forties lighting, or the Promethean androids, particularly Rutger Hauer, dying balletically. Most of the discussion is about that breathtaking pan, from the stoking fires into the brooding skyline, across to the pyramid of the Tyrrel Corporation, back to the horizontal loops of flying pods, and finally down into the morass of Asian fast-food stalls on the street level. That same pan reappears in the Japanese cyber-noir animated film, *Akira* – most of all, the signature shot in *Blade Runner* most repeated in other films, controlled fire. With faint roars like a giant kitchen range igniting from half a mile away, syncopated exhaust rises in bright flames across the dark cityscape. In the nineties, this image reminds us simultaneously of how the media present disasters from a great distance: comets bouncing off Jupiter; a replay of burning buildings during the Uprising; or of the Malibu fires of 1993. But in *Blade Runner*, the explosions are as preplanned as in an industrial plant: geysers erupting on cue; a cross between a brewery, a refinery and film animation; more like the volcano in front of the Mirage on the Vegas Strip, or an overhead video in 1991 of smart bombs taking out encampments during the Gulf War.

Essentially, the first four minutes – the Blade Runner Ride – have become the movie. In terms of the special effects, these four minutes represent layers of nostalgia, each built by a different technology from a different era. The bottom layer is old-fashioned movie set, out of the thirties and forties. The climate was enhanced through a mixture of old glycerine effects from the late thirties (hurricanes inside movie sets) with a kind of eighties film xerography. The flying pods are enhanced through computer controlled effects, similar to those in Spielberg's *Close Encounters* (remember the arrival of the space ship at the end?). There are old mattes with new forms of mattes (now, of course, they would be digitalized). The 700-storey Tyrrel pyramid, so similar to the monoliths in *Metropolis* (1926), looks like a cathedral radio, like a ziggurat (thirties moderne), and also like a copper computer board. It was the last model finished, based on earlier sketches by miniatures specialist David Stewart, and reflects the final architectural statement of the film – a feast of audience memories turned into an amusement park about urban decay. We remember the old thirties neighborhoods long since destroyed, and imagine them as primeval sources for immigrant nightmares after the apocalypse, after the decline of continental American civilization.

In terms of the aesthetics of special effects, *Blade Runner* is a transitional film. It contains the forties memorabilia of Lucas and Spielberg films (from *Star Wars* to *Raiders of the Lost Ark*). It also points toward the post-apocalyptic look of *Aliens* (biotech nightmare), of *Batman* (a softcore version taken from *The Dark Knight* graphic novel, which was influenced by the look of *Blade Runner*), and clearly of Japanese cyberpunk *animé*, the New Tokyo series, and dozens more.

The physical construction of the *Blade Runner* look is very revealing. The bottom layer, with all its street hubbub, was built partially in the Warners Burbank studios, literally on the so-called "New York Street" so familiar to us all from gangster films of the thirties and forties. The intent is to aestheticize poverty; not to look like a safe white boulevard, but rather like an explosive Lower East Side from the twenties, elbow to elbow. Americans, or at least Angelinos, want that old community sensation back, now that the density in L.A. must grow, particularly given that the immigrant population is expanding massively. Ironically enough, those old neighborhoods, the *Blade Runner* streets as they looked in the forties, were precisely the ones that were torn down as part of the massive

restructuring of downtown L.A. that I return to throughout this book –
when old Chinatown, the old Mexican Sonora, the old burlesque district,
the old Victorian slum district, and other *barrios* west of downtown were
leveled, virtually without a trace.

And the reality of such street life today in Los Angeles takes us to
what Mike Davis calls the "proletarian hunter-gatherer" existence in Pico
Union, a stricken Mexican and Central American area that is not only on
the edge of the urban erasures downtown but also in the midst of vast
unemployment during the nineties recession. A similar process can be
seen in parts of Hollywood, in poorer areas of the San Fernando Valley, as
rug vendors, food vendors, and homeless set up shop against the cinder-
block walls of rapidly decaying strip malls – in fact dress them up, hang
their wares against them.[2] I have heard Angelinos call these "Blade
Runner" enclaves. The popular sociology of the urban poor has been
invested by this film. Chat lines and web pages on *Blade Runner* continue
to grow.[3] But special effects are primarily a nostalgia machine, even when
the subject is the future. As I explained in the introduction, nostalgia
only works when the original experience has been forgotten, so that the
container is empty enough to fill with wide-ranging anxieties about what
we have lost. So it seems on the street level of *Blade Runner* city.

The upper levels are a mix of L.A. with Tokyo (a look that director
Ridley Scott continued, as a kind of background-effects sequel, in *Black
Rain*). The video billboards are clearly Japanese. The flying pods were
designed by trans specialist Syd Mead, in the spirit of acrobats without a
net, because in America and Europe the idea of high spiralling loops for
mass transit has been a designer fantasy since the second decade of the
century. In this case, there is no track, only the craft in the air.

The endless rain, presumably very acid and a signal of a climate gone
industrially mad, looks at first glance as if it was easy to do, but in fact it
took considerable effort. The rain and smoke have a depth of field quite
different from earlier films, where audiences sense a "curtain," as one of
the special-effects advisors David Dryer explained. Usually the rain is
double exposed, but then none of the set behind it would have appeared
wet. In the *Blade Runner* rains, crews set up "little sprinkle spurts to make
water drops in puddles when the live action shot was done without full
rain," and backlit them. Afterward, to add these effects to shots where no
rain was used (the "clean" shots), a new technique was devised; it allowed
the final print to show the rain only where the water was backlit (along
with extra puddles). In order to manage this effect, however, the

composited scene had to be shot in low contrast black and white, as if the film were being returned to a forties black-and-white movie. After all, the thirties and forties gangster or later noir look often used rain as a symptom of the dark streets and dark souls inhabiting the inner city. It has become standard to think of forties detectives in their raincoats; so standard, in fact, that the raincoat itself was parodied in Columbo shows. The *Blade Runner* rain becomes the mark of the devil, in this case a devil of man's own making – the smog finally destroying the desert climate itself.

I don't know what climate Scott and his effects people might imagine for Los Angeles today, with all the debates on the greenhouse effect (and severe drought throughout the late eighties in southern California). In the early eighties, they decided upon dank rain, like a sticky night in old Havana, by way of Singapore, while the man in the Bogart haircut talks to us about his divorced wife, and his taste for clammy raw fish. (Of course, in the director's cut, one of five[4] versions of the film that have been released, there is practically no voice-over at all.)

Interestingly enough, audiences in L.A. often remember this fast-food scene fondly – Harrison Ford at lunch – at a Farmers' Market outdoor eaterie that might have possibilities. Indeed, there is nothing of the shopping-mall bistro here. It looks random, alive. My memory, having grown up in immigrant neighborhoods in south Brooklyn, is somewhat different. I see a world where no one has time or place to sit longer than a few minutes, where the streets are endlessly milling. I see the high urban decay of Coney Island in the early fifties, horny businessmen at Nathan's coming on to men and women alike, luckily not young boys. It was unsafe, a place to watch one's back. It was not homey, not a site very essential to community coherence. I suspect that was the look Scott was going for. But in this age of nostalgia for fantasy tourist downtowns, he may have achieved the ultimate light show: a sizzling night with Bogart at a commissary from hell on a forties movie set.

Up in the zones of power, toward the Tyrrel pyramid, the shopping-mall overview really takes hold. The optical camera that blended all the effects together tended to airbrush the edges – to "blend, soften and add," to "rephotograph something that has already been built and photographed and make it even better." The spirit of the theme park *circa* 1982 is very much alive here. We enter the space, and sense that the air conditioning is designed to fit the mood. It is a fantasy that we see in deep focus, with each piece (climate, miniatures, movie flats) as a soothing reminder that this world is entirely under control – ominous, but clearly under control. We are tourists off the bus, in Orlando Florida, visiting a film noir ride. No matter how realistic the depth of field, we sense the artifice. We realize that many media have been put to work simultaneously, to serve us. We know in the way movie-goers of the forties knew that hurricanes were being presented inside movie sets – a faintly simulated edge, a varnish. There is no level of realistic special effects that does not leave us feeling safe; we have somehow gentrified our worst nightmares, rephotographed them at our leisure. The *Blade Runner* city, therefore, is comforting in a strange way. We won't live there. It is not our future. It is *their* future – particularly the ethnic future after the great vanishing that brings us to 2019. But we will be allowed to visit. It makes for an interesting quiz actually. Ask the viewer: in terms of the future, do you see yourself as one of the dispossessed in *Blade Runner*, or as one of the visitors?

One student has told me that *Blade Runner* feels very much like downtown L.A. where she lives, not because of the density but because of the artificially controlled political chaos. Perhaps that is part of the *Blade Runner* appeal. It looks like decay in the hypermall, complete with transfer vehicles out. And many artists today, whatever their politics, however leftist their intentions, feel themselves slowly being forced into an elitist outland, into the hypersphere of an isolated scholarly class pretending to understand the great vanishing that is underway somewhere else, very close by and growing but behind a wall. Increasingly, one is facing the theory of socialism without the working class, of noir art strategies that get snarled between upscale marketing and the increasing separation between the classes.

We wish for the old mom-and-pop stores in the old mixed neighborhoods that no longer fit well in the electronic, transnational world we live in today. *Blade Runner* helps us remember – and forget – high urban decay at the moment before downtown L.A. sank like a stone, an urban-planned island trapped by its own policies.

Therefore, for the moment, until Los Angeles planning is forced to turn around, as it will have to long before 2019, *Blade Runner* is still a tourist imago, like a movie still – a frontier outpost, a wetlands preserve. It reminds the viewer that the non-white poor may reclaim the momentum of urban life eventually, but for the immediate future, the old mixed community is gone except as a theme park, as an interactive movie set.

The *Blade Runner* imagery is drawing us farther away. At the same time, themed environments grow more tangible. Clearly, between now and 2019, almost no public spaces will be built, or even renovated, except as privatized malls. We watch the future emerging like an air-conditioning unit designed to obscure the poverty and confusion that lie only a few blocks away. We do not want to be isolated, but we do not want to be singled out for misery either.

In 1979, William Burroughs wrote a screen treatment for *Blade Runner*, about New York engulfed in a medical crisis after the Riots of 1984, where "derelict skyscrapers, without elevator service since the riots, have been taken over by hang-glider and autogyro gangs, mountaineers and steeple jacks," a city where "any treatment, any drug, any vice can be found ... for a price."[5] How strange to watch our culture achieve that perverse bedlam, but in a deodorized form, or, so the shopping-mall city suggests, a polite blade runner labyrinth. All in all, we would rather eat off the street, mix with the locals, but not too much, just enough to let the crisis provide us with a visual symphony. As Baudelaire explained: "Anywhere, anywhere, just out of this world."

Rumors persist that in a lost version of *Blade Runner*, Deckard drives Rachel out to a snowbound road, up in a futuristic Big Bear. Rachel suddenly exits the car, and starts to build a figure in the snow – a unicorn. When the unicorn is finished, she tells Deckard that every replicant has a trigger inside. When their cycle toward elimination begins, a designated shape will initiate a program that writes over their existing memory. The files installed by Tyrrel Corporation, the family photographs and childhood vacations, will corrupt. Suddenly you remember precisely how and when you were constructed. Your trigger, she explains, is the unicorn. And with that she dies, and he falls beside her on the side of the road.

In the early drafts of the screenplay, Deckard was supposed to be a replicant constructed to eliminate other "skinjobs." The dandified policeman, Gaff, knows this, and continually makes origami unicorns to prepare him for the shock. In the closing scenes of the film, Roy does not kill Deckard because – except for blade runners – replicants are programmed never to kill their own. In another draft, the unicorn is Gaff's "gauntlet," his signal that he will have to hunt them down. In yet another, Deckard dreams of a unicorn, the symbol of the extinction of all "beasts of the earth and fowls of the air, except in replicant form."

And finally, one draft has Tyrrel himself, the inventor, as a replicant, while the real Tyrrel is frozen in a cryocrypt. Clearly, the impulse to imagine a much more extended community of replicants was considered bad for marketing the film, though fans of *Blade Runner* seem to be fascinated by the censorship at Warners[6] that removed this trope from the script. The designed environment was supposed to extend literally to the body itself.

NOTES

1. This chapter is adapted from an article published in *Social Text*, no. 28, 1989. The body of criticism on *Blade Runner* is immense. A few of the most useful, chronologically are: *American Cinematographer*, July 1982; *Cinemafantastique*, nos 5–6, July–August, 1982; *Cinefex*, no. 9, July 1982; David Scroggy et al., *The Bladerunner Sketchbook* (also includes screenplay) (San Diego: Blue Dolphin Enterprises, 1982); Douglas Kellner, Flo Leibowitz and Michael Kellner, "*Blade Runner*: A Diagnostic Critique," *Jumpcut* 29, 1984; David Dresser, "*Blade Runner*, Science Fiction and Transcendence," *Literature/Film Quarterly* 13, no. 3, 1985; Giuliana Bruno, "Ramble City: Postmodernism and *Blade Runner*," *October*, no. 41, 1987; Vivian Sobchack, *Screening Spaces* (New York: Ungar, 1987); Judith Kerman, ed. *Retrofitting Blade Runner* (Bowling Green: Bowling Green University Press, 1991); Frances Bonner, "Separate Development: Cyberpunk in Film and TV," in George Slusser and Tom Shippey, eds, *Fiction 2000: Cyberpunk and the Future of Narrative* (Athens, Ga.: University of Georgia Press, 1992; Scott Bukatman, *Terminal Identity: The Virtual Subject in Postmodern Science Fiction* (Durham, N.C.: Duke University Press, 1993); Michael J. Shapiro, "'Manning the Frontiers: The Politics of (Human) Nature in *Blade Runner*," in Jane Bennett and William Chaloupka, eds, *The Nature of Things: Language, Politics and the Environment* (Minneapolis: University of Minnesota Press, 1993). And finally, the number of interviews with director Ridley Scott, and principal screenwriter David Peoples (after the release of *Unforgiven*, another of his scripts); also the screen treatment for *Blade Runner* by William Burroughs, set in New York, during a plague (*Blade Runner, A Movie* [Berkeley: Blue Wind Press, 1986]).

2. Margaret Crawford has begun examining the role these vendors play in the overall cityscape emerging in Los Angeles.

3. cis.ohio-state.edu/hypertext/faq/usenet/movies/bladerunner-faq/faq.html. Also: http://www.cm.cf.ac.uk/M/title-more?locations%203BE3E. Also: http://www.ifi.uio.no/-gorme/Bladerunner/Blade.html.

4. There are at least five different version of *Blade Runner* (as listed at: cis.ohio-state.edu/hypertext/faq/usenet/movies/bladerunner-faq/faq.html):

(1) The work print in sneak preview in Denver and Dallas, 1982, including a Webster's 2012 definition of a replicant in the opening crawl, and no voice-over, except in the scene where the replicant Battey dies. Also ends with elevator door closing, and no salvation clear for Deckard and Rachel; this was considered too depressing, and the Burbank into-the-sunset ending was added. I have seen this work print at a special showing in 1991, and thought the dictionary opening was fine; however, this version does not exist on video or laser.

(2) San Diego sneak preview in 1982 (without voice-over); European theatrical release; the Director's Cut (1992): scenes added of Battey on the phone, Deckard reloading his weapon, nothing very different.

(3) European theatrical release: more blood; Tyrrel dies more miserably; Pris lifts Deckard by his nostrils; Deckard shoots Pris a third time; Roy pushes nail through his hand. This is the tenth anniversary video edition.

(4) Director's Cut: voice-overs completely gone; a few added shots: e.g. twelve seconds more of the unicorn beside Deckard as he plays the piano; ending at elevator doors.

(5) Cable television: extra line of dialogue.

(6) Video before 1993: violence in European version included.

On laser, seven variations have been released, some with supplements, all with differences in sound mix.

5. Burroughs, *Blade Runner, A Movie.*

6. The active rumor on the ending: Ridley Scott was told by Warners executives that the ending where Deckard and Rachel go to the elevator is ominous, and incomplete. Since she will die soon, he has no future really, and might still get caught for breaking the Samurai code of the blade runner. Instead, the studio pressured for an ending where Rachel turns out to have been programmed for a long life. They drive toward the sun together, as safe as newlyweds heading toward Palm Springs 2019. However, presumably director Scott had the last laugh – more like a faint chuckle really. He used a shot from *The Shining* to suggest horror lurking beneath the bucolic exterior. However, he proved once again what Kuleshov had demonstrated in the early 1920s: no shot stands alone; it receives its meaning from what is synchronized beside it. It could have been Hitler and Eva off on a drive to a Nuremberg Rally.

CHAPTER FOUR

MOVIE LOCATIONS

A nest of movie vans parked on a residential street is a common sight in Los Angeles. The crew rarely look pleased. The waits are interminable. It is hard to believe that any of this will make an impact except on available parking. And yet, the imaginary maps that these movies generate are repeated throughout the world. In downtown alone, on any given day, at least ten film crews will be working. One sees copies – and parodies – of imaginary L.A. streets in Hong Kong gangster films (John Woo's *Hardboiled*) and in French noir (Godard's *Breathless*, or Melville's *Bob the Gambler*).

Three examples of cinematic maps that manage to replace the city, particularly the general downtown area, for tourists and residents alike are: Spring Street; *Falling Down*; City of Lights. The first is the history of a frequently used street; the second is concerned with the public response to a film; the third refers to a lighting technique in film that operates as an ideological map. I would call them "machines for forgetting," a phrase coined by critic Thomas Frank, though he was writing about promotion in Kansas City, "the city of the booster, the speculator, the developer, the responsible businessman," and its noir opposites: the saloons on State Line Avenue, the jazz clubs, what Composer Virgil Thomson called "a joyous lowlife."[1] Indeed, the marketing obsessions of Southern California had close cognates across the country; even in the very city along the Santa Fe line – Kansas City – that brought thousands of tourists to L.A. in 1885, to launch the boosterism that finally attracted film producers after 1908. Cinema merely took this imaginary Santa Fe line one step further.

Instead of luring people to Southern California, it exported Southern California back to Kansas City, and everywhere else.

UNSPRUNG

The shortest route between Heaven and Hell in contemporary America is probably Fifth Street in Downtown L.A. West of the refurbished Biltmore Hotel, and spilling across the moat of the Harbor Freeway, a post-1970 glass and steel skyscape advertises the landrush of Pacific Rim capital to the central city.[2]

This is one of the more remembered allegories of Los Angeles: downtown as Hell, here captured by Mike Davis in an article about the corruptions of downtown urban planning. Much of the division is evident where Fifth bisects Spring, another street of grave extremes. Even eighty years ago,[3] Spring Street had specialized in contrasts, in big business and illegal high-stakes poker parlours side by side. It had been the home of legalized gambling at the turn of the century. Every fourth address housed a card room, saloon or cigar counter for dice, until a series of crackdowns in the thirties. Lavish floor shows helped attract gamblers, who met at the Jeffries Bar, near the Alexandria Hotel where D.W. Griffith and other film pioneers held court.[4] It had many of the fanciest speakeasies in the twenties. But, most of all, it was touted in the twenties as "the Wall Street of the West," with more "skyscrapers" than any other street.

The dividing line was Main Street. Everything east was proletarian and honky tonk, filled with workmen wearing little round black felt railway boomers' hats, or big tan ranchers' hats. In 1942, essayist Timothy G. Turner describes "cheap-john stores, pawnshops, restaurants with fifteen-cent meals, and saloons, some with pathetic attempts at floor shows," also with B girls (barmaids), and "sloppers" behind the bar.[5] An arrogant young "copper" in a tight black leather jacket drops by to beat an old bum, and leaves "satisfied with having performed a civic duty." As the bartender said, bums belonged near the missions, to "howl [sing] for a meal."[6]

Up along Main Street were burlesque shows, and "big stores catering to ranchmen and workingmen." "The racial mix was a league of nations: Mexican, Japanese, Chinese, American ranchmen and longshoremen, little dandified Filipinos, a few Hindus and Sikhs from the cotton country down in the Imperial Valley [Greek restaurants around the corner]." A local saloon had a job blackboard, for day work at the wholesale district nearby: jobs driving delivery trucks with groceries, or for a soap plant.

On the west end of Fifth, and along Spring, were the headquarters for Title Insurance,[7] and for swank lawyers' offices. Every week, someone from O'Melveny and Meyers, the stellar law firm, would wipe the dust off the fire hydrants, and polish the brass at the entrance.[8] Even in the fifties, the two worlds would collide. Polite secretaries would overhear prostitutes complaining loudly to well-dressed johns who tried to leave without paying.

Since the Second World War, Spring Street in particular has been the site of many key scenes in crime films. It appears briefly, as part of the descent of a building contractor with a hidden past, in *Act of Violence* (he had consorted with Nazis while incarcerated during the war, and was now being hunted down by one of the survivors of his folly). He is hunted by his past, brought down from the polite suburban subdivision he opens to the darkest corners of downtown Los Angeles, where he dies amidst windswept, muddy newspapers.

Spring Street remained a favorite for film noir as late as 1980, when one critic called it "the spiritual home of urban gothic film." On the same day in 1979, three noir revivals were shot there on location simultaneously, shuttling north and south, between First and Seventh Street: *True Confessions*, *The Postman Always Rings Twice*, and *Honky Tonk*. Apparently, the film crews were practically bumping heads.

Michael Barlow, Associate Producer of *Postman* felt in 1980 that Spring Street was "ideal" for filming because it was virtually uninhabited, due to construction for L.A.'s bicentennial (1981); and at the same time so utterly neglected over the past thirty years that many of the older structures were still standing.

Across the western boundary, past Figueroa a few blocks farther on, one could still see the Thomas Cadillac location back in 1980, a brownstone remnant near a famous auto dealership, about six buildings long, where scenes of thirties Chicago had been staged for *The Sting*.

However many pseudo-forties movie crimes are committed in Angelino Heights, or up along Franklin in Hollywood (a site for part of *Blade Runner*),[9] Spring Street still remains the most identified source of downtown L.A. gothic entropy in high key lighting.[10] The *Los Angeles Times* is located at one end, near the banking district, which empties of business like an eclipse after dark. In the mornings, reporters claim they are asked for money regularly by what seem like franchises of panhandlers, just in the walk from the parking structure to the office. (Plans to move the *Times* entirely into Burbank are underway.)

The attempt at reviving Spring Street has fizzled as if it had been hit by an iceberg. With three million square feet of commercial space, and 65,000[11] passing by it every day, its renaissance was promoted heavily in the seventies. A theater district was initiated there, then finally abandoned at a cost of tens of millions, and considerable loss to the theater community in L.A. There was simply no way to repair what had already been done: the unsightly open parking lots between major buildings; the loss of major tenants like Crocker, Bank of America, Security Pacific, and the many import-export firms that relied on these banks. The Stock Exchange Nightclub opened in 1987, and closed down two years later. The condo owners at the Premiere Towers lodged a series of complaints that reached the *L.A. Times* in 1991. One banker living at the Towers said: "Just the other evening I saw a guy on the corner by the state office building wearing a hospital gown with an IV hanging out of his arm. He was just out of the hospital. That kind of topped it."[12] On television that year, the Alexandria Hotel was officially designated the "capital" of the downtown drug trade.

The wave of failures in urban planning since the fifties left a brooding scar there. While its nine blocks are listed on the national register, there is no pearl if the necklace has no clasp. With so much of downtown depopulated – by intent, through urban "revitalizations" – pedestrians are too nervous after the offices go dark. So many key walking streets heading west have been blocked off, and turned into DMZ zones, with habitable buildings replaced by office towers. There is simply no active flow of street life left to support it at night. The massive skid row has moved in, from the east and from the south.

This should be a vast enough transition to leave a formal record on film. We look at the movies using this street over the years, in the midst of these astonishing decisions, as it slipped from mixed-use district to international banking district, under the flood of steady decay and depopulation, to become a massive contradiction of desolation and power, inside the global Pacific economy. There were some documentaries about the street life there, but obviously no record in commercial cinema. It remains a faded movie location, less usable now since it is inhabited increasingly by too many homeless. Only the extremes were now visible to outsiders. The muscle that held it together, the neighborhoods around it and hidden inside it, were never media-genic material. They remained unnoticed when they were viable (the dark side of Main), and unnoticed when they disappeared.

The emptied downtown has begun to find its new cinematic imaginary, a variation of Fortress L.A. Since 1989, the Hollywood Location Company has leased 39 downtown sites – "the vertical backlot" they call it – mostly new high-rises, particularly as interiors in *Virtuosity*, *Primal Fear*, and *Batman Forever*.[13] Beginning in 1996, "HLC" occupies all the "filmic assets" of the empty 450,000 square feet of the former Unocal Tower just west of the Harbor Freeway. Now the Unocal entrance can double as the Parker Center (Police Headquarters); its driveway as an ambulance arrival point. While many of the older moderne buildings downtown are still used (The Los Angeles Theater Center on Spring; the Herald Examiner Building on Broadway, for *Usual Suspects*), the shock to downtown real estate in the nineties has recoded its location, more as sites for "die-hard" disasters, and the birth of civil wars (*Strange Days*). The Bonaventure has been anointed twice as suitable for assassinating a president or vice-president (*Line of Fire* and *Nick of Time*). And with *Escape from L.A.*, downtown finally becomes an island prison.

FALLING DOWN: WHEN EAST L.A. CONQUERED THE PACIFIC

The movie *Falling Down* had to interrupt shooting during the L.A. Uprising. Ironically enough, this film became the first remapping of the new Los Angeles myth – the city as Hispanic hell. The story is essentially about white male panic and revenge. An unemployed engineer known as D-FENS (Michael Douglas) goes berserk while walking across Los Angeles on the way to his daughter's birthday party. The city he finds is ruthless and apocalyptic, as dark in spirit as he is.

Audiences in Los Angeles responded very oddly to the film. Many cheered the pathological anti-hero as he cracked heads, or shot at annoyances on his way across town, attacking a Korean grocery store, a Chicano gang, a "Whammy" Burger fast-food outlet, a neo-Nazi owner of an army/navy store, threatening the rich, assaulting the city. Others felt grievously insulted, like the film reviewer for the *L.A. Times*, Kenneth Turan. The reactions became a news event for weeks. Various talk radio shows ran long segments on D-FENS, where callers expressed their horror, and argued with the screenwriter or the director. One man claimed to have walked precisely the same route through L.A. that the Douglas character did, without encountering any problems at all.

The route that D-FENS takes emphasized the fact of an increasingly non-Anglo city; and also revealed many areas hurt by the recession, or by weak urban planning. He begins by clubbing gangbangers in Temple-Beaudry, on precisely the same hill used in *Predator* and *Colors*. Then he survives an imaginary driveby in what is supposed to be East L.A., but is actually 56th and Figueroa in the Monte Vista neighborhood of Highland Park, four miles north of downtown. Another frequently used location, its business street looks "more Hispanic" than East L.A.; and its railroad tracks very "fifties" industrial (used for scenes in Tarantino's *Reservoir Dogs*).

Next D-FENS, with his bag of assault weapons, bypasses downtown and winds up near the new Metro Station at MacArthur Park, which he blows up. Then he reappears much farther west, in West Hollywood, at Whammy Burgers. At last, he meets his end by the ocean at Venice, presumably the only poorer neighborhood still white, but also, as in dozens of crime films since *Touch of Evil* in 1958, a carnival of human debris (it also features in comedies about suicide like *I Love You Alice B. Toklas* and *Mixed Nuts*).

Not only has he left the impression that East L.A. has stormed the gates of the Pacific, he accidentally traces the failure of urban planning west of downtown as well. Below Temple-Beaudry, he passes through the Pico Union area, a Central American *barrio* that may be the most profoundly neglected Hispanic area in the city. Equally troubled is the area around Sixth and Alvarado (the MacArthur Park station), which he studies then hits with an anti-tank missile. (Urban planners imply that they would like to de-Hispanicize MacArthur Park – which is most unlikely unless "social" investment accompanies the ornamental trim around the station.)

At Sixth and Alvarado, D-FENS stood only two blocks away from another favorite movie location – the Park Plaza,[14] with its Egyptian motif gargoyles, its deeply tattered "original" rugs, and very grand ballroom. The Park Plaza is ideal if the script calls for a spicy "rundown" hotel, a "last hope" thirties place to die. On the upper floors, where rooms still rent for only $300 a month, Barton Fink went frantic staring at a blank page in his typewriter, while the jovial but psychotic salesman next door set fire to the hotel. Downstairs, David Lynch shot key scenes for *Wild at Heart*. Out in the parking lot, the attendant Frankie, a gravel-voiced, tap-dancing gnome-and-bookie has charmed enough film crews to do walk-ons in various films.

Further west, where the conditions are getting equally grim, the so-called Hancock Park[15] "adjacent" keeps losing its appeal, since the Ambassador Hotel and Bullocks Wilshire potentially face the wrecking ball, barely surviving except as movie locations;[16] and another anchor, Otis-Parsons Art School, is about to move. Finally, MacArthur Park Lake was dredged, as if new water for the ducks would gentrify the entire neighborhood.

D-FENS next heads west past La Brea, where the shocks of the Uprising were still remembered (this was the spring of 1992). The neo-Nazi's store was set in the Silver Lake district, less than half a mile from looting along Sunset Boulevard, a street also neglected by urban planners. However, if that stretch of Sunset had been restored, it would easily have linked up the emptied downtown with five established communities nearby – as many as 200,000 people now shut off from convivial access to the "Center City."

In short, the actual path D-FENS takes is through mis-management, fear, poverty and neglect – which is not flattering even as fantasy, particularly for a city that, at the time the film opened, was bracing itself for a second Rodney King trial. For those not personally familiar with D-FENS' path, it suggests that no neighborhood is safe enough, that L.A. is *barrio* and little else; as if the entire city were stricken by random gunfire and bad attitudes.

The film makes the hyper-*barrio* seem infinitely larger than it really is, just as some correspondents in Europe thought that "South Central" in Los Angeles was five times its actual size. Such racial simplification ignores the polyglot, the hybrid that is L.A., but it makes for better suspense thrillers, is better for dirty kills. A city that is adapting to non-white immigration at breakneck speed will always look, from the Anglo point of view, as if it is falling down.

CITY OF LIGHTS

How the lights of Los Angeles are represented from overhead is an index of its glamour, if not of its neighborhoods. In the fifties, many films showed the Hollywood grid at night from a smart-looking car up in the hills. In the sixties, helicopter shots circled the cloverleaf in rush hour. In the nineties, the grid of lights are denser, to suggest an older sovereign city, particularly the canopy of neon along the high-rises downtown.

Heat (1995) is clearly a homage to the denser Los Angeles, "something of a valentine to a city that's experienced racial uneasiness and tabloid-style criminal trials."[17] The director, Michael Mann had decided to use the "techno industrial feel" in a more operatic way, more like his home in Chicago, the modernist encryption of skyscrapers at night along Michigan Boulevard.

The sprawl and deadly haze of the L.A. cloverleaf was ignored. Mann was particularly struck instead by the look of L.A. from the top of a tall building, near midnight during the smog-free season in January or February: "[If] you're not moved a little bit by what you're seeing – the blinking lights and the 16 or 17 airplanes on approach to LAX – there's some emotional deficit going on there."[18]

That response is beginning to repeat in a number of sources: treating Los Angeles as an older city, not as easily divided between sunshine suburbs and inner-city noir. It shows L.A. as more corporatized, Manhattanized, with fewer smog pastels, fewer overheads of freeways humming in gaseous midday traffic, where the only light comes from an "infected" sky. Instead, most of *Heat* is shot at night: The veteran thief Neil McCauley (Robert de Niro) peers through the window of his luxurious but unfurnished apartment in the Palisades, and calls Los Angeles the "city of lights." In one scene after the other, the downtown skyline is glowing in the background, like a pole star directing the action. Never has industri-opolis looked this majestic.

Apparently, the director, Michael Mann traveled from one end of the city to the other, in "countless rides along with undercover cops, and [his] own midnight rambles throughout South Central and East Los Angeles ... [or] at Pico-Union around 2 a.m."[19] In many, he recreated the sensation of his tourist research. Over 85 locations were used, in what is described as the most striking revision of how to light a crime film in L.A. in decades. The only comparison that comes to mind is John Boorman's *Point Blank* (1968), but for a different era: an ironic, mod fragmentary style suitable to the late sixties; the interiors straight out of a decorator's catalogue; so recently carpeted, and without furniture, that the paint on the drywall seems barely dry, painted in pastel latex flat.

Only the master thief's apartment in *Heat* has that transient latex-flat identity. The rest is much more contoured, rather traditional film, in the genre of *Asphalt Jungle*, and *The Killing*, about a team of thieves synchronized as if on a business trip. They behave like moody tourists on a tight schedule, first with an armored car robbery at the Convention Center. Then – after mishaps and moral encounters – by the conclusion, McCauley prepares to fly out of LAX, wrung out like any traveler, with the woman who can save him alongside. But he is found out, and dies on the landing strip in a shower of lights.

The locations for crimes are traditional as well. Murders look best on the western fringes of downtown. Actually, the location map is Dante-esque, in two rings essentially. The flatlands are lit for violence near downtown. The safe houses are always up on hills, facing the lights of Hollywood.

Night is a vital motif in *Escape from L.A.*, which is lit more like *Blade Runner* (carceral, somnolent and grimy) – in this case, the absence or death of light. "One of the movie's big plot points is that most of the story takes place at night, because in post-nuclear-holocaust/earthquake-destroyed L.A., ultraviolet rays have become almost instantly deadly."[20]

Light downtown triggers the fading of memory in some of the new crime fiction as well. In Alex Abella's *The Killing of the Saints* (1991), a Cuban detective enters by way of Broadway, the dense Hispanic shopping district:

I walked around downtown for the two hours we had for lunch that day. Restless, half-formed feelings and vague memories assaulted me in the brassy light that winter afternoon. A block west, on Broadway, a river of Hispanics surged and flowed on the sidewalks, from First to Olympic, past the grandiose movie theaters built like Aztec temples and the concrete and masonry buildings with money-changing offices and *farmacias* and Spanish-language newsstands and discount electronic stores on the first floor, past Pershing Square and the Japanese owned Biltmore Hotel and the bloodied Jewelry Mart where this tragedy had struck on a winter's morning almost three years before.[21]

And Jean Baudrillard, despite his highly detached mystification of Los Angeles, has an eloquent passage on lights at night, the oneiric sprawl as a plane descends over the basin, the glyphs of streets and infrastructure. These lights suggest a matured, dense city, as layered with lost memories as cities in Europe, but in a geometric grid. The memory left by decades of freeway building, as well as streetlights tracing the patterns of vanished orchards turned into suburbs, could be compared to the mother board in a computer:

There is nothing to match flying over Los Angeles by night. A sort of luminous, geometric, incandescent immensity, stretching as far as the eye can see, bursting out from the cracks in the clouds. Only Hieronymous Bosch's hell can match this inferno effect. The muted fluorescence of all the diagonals: Wilshire, Sunset, Santa Monica. Already, flying over San Fernando Valley, you come upon the horizontal infinite in every direction. But, once you are beyond the mountain, a city ten times larger hits you. You will never have encountered anything that stretches as far as this before. Even the sea cannot match it, since it is not divided up geometrically. The irregular, scattered flickering of European cities does not produce the same parallel lines, the same vanishing points, the same aerial perspectives either. They are medieval cities. This one condenses by night the entire future geometry of the networks of human relations, gleaming in their abstraction, luminous in their extension, astral in their reproduction to infinity.[22]

NOTES

1. Thomas Frank, "A Machine for Forgetting: Kansas City and the Declining Significance of Place," *The Baffler*, no. 7, 1995, p. 115. Also: "Like other cities [Kansas City] has experienced the trauma of the conventional variety of civic forgetting: its old downtown is a study in vacant lots; the river banks from which it initially sprang are now inaccessible to civilians" (p. 114).

I would interpret "machine" in three ways: first as "machinic," Deleuze and Guattari's term — a language-based abstract machine that "conjugates" an assemblage, a process of deterritorialization (*A Thousand Plateaus: Capitalism and Schizophrenia*, trans. B. Massumi [Minneapolis: University of Minnesota Press, 1987; orig. 1980], pp. 140); second, "machine" suggests the industrial nature of this tourist imaginary, the fact that it was linked to the railroad lines, to mass publishing; and third, the ironic use of "machine" as in "machine politics," to suggest the cronyism always involved in building a social imaginary, and the bizarre ideology about place that emerges.

2. Mike Davis, "*Chinatown*, Part Two? The Internationalization of Downtown Los Angeles," *New Left Review* 164, July–August 1989, p. 65.

3. The banking district shifted to Spring Street from Main in 1901, when First National Bank moved. Despite a few scandals, like the All Night and Day Bank that was closed in 1910 due to unrestricted hours, more "skyscrapers" were added (none was allowed legally to go higher than twelve stories): the Hellman Building; Citizens National Trust; the new Stock Market in 1921; the Title Exchange in 1928.

4. Research provided by Spring Street young resident Barbara Koch, 1991.

5. Timothy G. Turner, *Turn Off the Sunshine: Tales of Los Angeles on the Wrong Side of the Tracks* (Caldwell, Idaho: The Caxton Printers, Ltd, 1942), p. 23. Also, William Russell Swigart, *Biography of Spring Street* (Los Angeles: Pader and Co., 1946), biographies of local luminaries, and so forth.

6. Ibid., p. 26.

7. Cost $4 million (1928), at the height of confidence in Spring Street as the "Wall Street of the West."

8. Interviews with old residents, 1993.

9. The Ennis House by Wright (on Franklin) was used as Deckard's apartment entrance in *Blade Runner*.

10. Another candidate might be *Blade Runner* sites: Bradbury Building (Broadway; also in the original *DOA* (1949); and Union Station. *Variety* (19 December 1995, p. 12) lists the most popular downtown locations: Queen Anne Hospital (187 shooting days in 1994); Union Station; City Hall; Park Plaza (see next section, "Falling Down"); Wilshire Ebell Theater.

11. Dr Robert A. Sigafoos, "Spring Street Faces Uncertain Future," *L.A. Times*, 20 December 1970, p. G14.

12. Elaine Woo, "Condo Pioneers Bitter as Spring Street Rebirth Fails," *L.A. Times*, 1 April 1991, p. A1. Another tenant said: "You need a lot of insight to make this a vibrant area. I am real angry with the CRA." Despite adding some middle-class housing downtown, the CRA reduced access for poor neighborhoods outside, thus essentially starving the area for practically any pedestrian who might consider staying after dark.

13. John Regardie, "Location, Location, Location," *Los Angeles Downtown News*, 13 May 1996, p. 1.

14. Park Plaza (built 1925): 607 South Parkview, across from MacArthur Park. Other films shot there include: *The Phantom*, *Tango and Cash*, *The Bodyguard*, *Chaplin*, and *Bugsy* (see "I Checked in for One Day and I've Been There Ever Since," *L.A. Times*, 1 January 1993, p. E1). Also Connie Benesch, "L.A. Hosts Hot Spots Aplenty," *Daily Variety*, 19 December 1995, pp. 12ff; William A. Gordon *Shot on This Site*.

15. Hancock Park itself is wealthy (but not its adjacent); it receives 30,000 requests a year for location information. *Outbreak*, *Higher Learning*, *Speechless* had scenes shot there.

16. The Ambassador (built 1921) closed in 1989, and is used "just for filming," 80–100 productions a year (Benesch, "L.A. Hosts Hot Spots Aplenty," p. 16), including parts of *Forrest Gump*, *True Lies*, *Devil in a Blue Dress*, *Apollo 13*, *Seven*, *True Romance*, *Sister Act*. It may be occupied, finally, by a law school.

17. Scott Collins, "Mann's Best Friend: L.A.," *Los Angeles Times*, 16 December 1995, pp. F1, 16.

18. Ibid., p. F16.

19. Ibid.

20. "Russell's Banking on L.A." (Liz Smith's column), *Los Angeles Times*, 21 July 1995, p. F2.

21. Alex Abella, *The Killing of the Saints* (New York: Penguin Books, 1993; orig. 1991), p. 276.

22. Jean Baudrillard, "Ideal Cosy Nook, Los Angeles by Night," from *America* (London: Verso, 1988).

CHAPTER FIVE

THE PANIC:
IMAGINED FEARS
AFTER APRIL 1992

1978: While eating breakfast at a hotel in Paris, I mention having lived in Chicago. Suddenly, a Parisian stands up, and pretends to fire a tommy gun, as if newsreels of Al Capone were still loose in the world, or more likely gangster films from Warners or Roger Corman. I encountered this gesture two other times during the seventies, while being told by Parisians that Chicago was "obviously" very dangerous to visit. Los Angeles, by extreme contrast, was well known to be extremely safe and hospitable.

1992: That outlook has been utterly reversed. Los Angeles has traded places with "Depression-era" Chicago as the social imaginary of America's most dangerous city. From the European press, the news on L.A. is consistently about disintegration and civil collapse, with imagery as familiar as a hip-hop video: a bleached ghetto street, burnt-out store fronts, perhaps a chain-link fence prominent, signs of women of all ages in mourning.

This is an extreme shift. Only two years before, L.A. was viewed as very peaceable, certainly in the American press, as the burgeoning Pacific Byzantium, a hub for Asian investments, a polyglot city of the future. There were dozens of articles explaining that while L.A. was absorbing up to one-third of all foreign immigration during the eighties, its social problems were more or less under control (they were not). Growing density was seen as a good sign, that L.A. was becoming a "world class city" – one of Mayor Bradley's favorite expressions. The agonizing poverty was usually downplayed, reserved for a paragraph or two at the end of these articles. Massive dislocation and crumbling schools were not ills; they were growing pains.

As a new regional power structure takes shape, (L.A.) faces the urban ills that are often overlooked because of the region's affluence and pleasant climate. (*Atlantic Monthly*, January 1988)

They accompanied foreign capital, and better ethnic restaurants. L.A. is once again giving us a glimpse into our future; in the decades to come, virtually all Americans will feel the dual impact of Asian immigration and investment. (*Time*, 22 February 1988)

Such optimism sounds nostalgic in the nineties. In April 1993, as the second Rodney King trial came to a close, a *Time* magazine cover story asked: "Is L.A. Going to Hell?" This was referring not only to the Uprising: American coverage of L.A. during the nineties has been soured more by the recession/depression here than by civil unrest. Anglo joblessness and business flight are often linked with the dominant imago of rioting and gunplay. In other words, the *random* "drive-by" economy meets the *random* looter. As a result, the city is self-evidently breaking apart into Balkanized pieces. Practically every film, every TV magazine story, every myth that I can locate seems to echo the same fantasy: a tottering imperial mess, a feudal, overfortified, crime-ridden living hell.

So I will not add to the apocalyptic fugue right now – too easy. Besides, if I did, I would not be clarifying how this imaginary operates as of 1997, as the economy shows signs of recovery. Consider the standard photo of mass looting during the Uprising; or video tapes of single men crumpled beneath body blows, either from police or from looters. These videos or movies always spotlight encircling barbarity. The background around the violence tends to be indistinct or faded. At the epicenter, police batons or assault weapons tilt forward as if by centrifugal force. The poor are being sucked into barbarity. Family life has gone down the drain. Drugs descend like a cloud on every street corner. Social problems are depicted as a "black" hole, where every good act is lost. There is no humanist antidote left.

This would seem to be the national, if not the global imaginary for Los Angeles – the collective fiction. However, inside the city itself, the response is more complicated, at least tempered by direct experience. The mood is difficult to describe in any scholarly way, except perhaps as collective post-traumatic memory: collective avoidance. Angelinos have been "politicized," to use old sixties rhetoric, but politicized to little effect. I am genuinely convinced that more people in L.A. are aware of root social causes as a result of the Uprising and the shattering events since, particularly the fires, earthquake and economic shocks – the taste of disaster that can blow in any direction. However, as political action, no significant monies or policies are forthcoming to poor areas. Poverty exists mostly as a media discourse in itself, little more than a face on a Sunday magazine cover, or a human-interest insert between the sports reports. Or as a panic, like a faintly pulsating headache. The radio talk shows are practically the only programs dealing with poverty consistently, and much of this narrows around defenses of free enterprise, or demands that we get tough on crime – the enough-is-enough syndrome. Indeed, what troubles me more than the hours of pious media debate in L.A. is the "Panic"; it has generated a noir imaginary that camouflages existing needs almost as ruthlessly as the upbeat eighties boom cycle did. It continues the "panic" of the forties that played so strangely in downtown planning, the campaign to deracinate the urban core.

Services for non-whites around downtown will be downsized, as the city budget suffers deficits. County USC Medical Center, the busiest hospital in California will be rebuilt, but smaller. The streets around metro stations are being revamped, like the Westlake station on Seventh and Alvarado (again west of downtown), where presumably $120 million will be raised to add more shops; however as yet with little effect, except to help Langers, the famous delicatessen, bring more lunch trade. The new "post-liberal" urban policy assumes that consumerism can solve social ills – more shops, cleaner shopping areas, better flow. It is merely a continuation of tourist policies. The competition to site a $200 million hockey stadium just west of downtown still sounds like boosterism *circa* 1925, "to bring downtown to life after dark [by] injecting more dollars into its hotels, restaurants and shops ... [to] attract 'outsiders.'"

The ineffectually tiny subway system still resembles what I have suggested it was in 1990: a cement contractor's idea of progress – too elitist, too much waste, too many sweetheart deals, too slow, and now diverting attention away from the buses that are infinitely more fundamental. At the moment, the subway/trolley serves mostly a small middle-class market, at a cost per rider of $5 above fares. At that rate, even though the inter-urban line from the San Fernando Valley is succeeding, the city cannot support much more until the system passes five hundred miles of track; and that will take another forty years at least. The old trolley lines were more than 1,200 miles long as of 1912, for a county about one tenth the size in population. So what will 120 miles of track accomplish now – 1 per cent efficiency compared to eighty years ago?

In September 1994, corruption by builders made the news again. Shoddy tunneling led to cave-ins along Hollywood Boulevard, which in turn forced audits and more evidence of padded accounts, along with a need for lavish retrofitting throughout the system. This persuaded federal agencies to withhold over a billion dollars, which will stall the project even more, while the transportation board (MTA) squabbles and squanders. On talk radio, the subway system is being dubbed the "other" disaster beside riots, fires and earthquakes. In December 1995, the CEO of the transportation authority was fired, mostly to avoid the blame spreading to the board. Clearly, the $10 billion dollars needed for the system may never arrive, not in the seven years that the federal government plans to use to balance the budget.

The panic over Mexican immigration – a running theme since the forties – found a new point of gravity when Proposition 187 (SOS – Save Our State) was passed by statewide referendum in 1994. An anti-immigration movement grandstanded by Governor Wilson, it promised to sever many of the fundamental rights of non-legal residents, and force the government ever more directly into a custodial role, to scapegoat non-Americans for what Americans cannot buy, to spend more public money (up to $100 million the first year) merely to find out who is illegal, and essentially none on lifting even a few immigrants out of poverty. At the moment, most of this "amendment" to the constitution is mired in the courts, but the pressure from the US Congress to deny basic civil rights and services to all immigrants became a banner headline during an election year, then draconian welfare "reform" in 1997.

Clearly the isolation by class and the feudal enclaving of the city are steadily taking place. Some federal funds will be used to dress up a few commercial streets in South Central and East Hollywood – add trees, benches, new store fronts; but there will be little or no public funds to improve residential conditions directly – for example, to increase home ownership among the poor, to provide access to new skills or new jobs. A new cultural center at 52nd and Vermont will be sponsored exclusively through private charity, in this case mostly with funds donated by Berry Gordy, founder of Motown Records. There is no overall plan being implemented by government at the federal, state or local level for streets without stores.

The panic against poor neighborhoods and "unfit" housing is worse than at any time I can remember. It is most evident in real estate: almost fanatical concerns about inspections, about "secure" neighborhoods, far beyond what can ever be satisfied realistically. This overreaction – to shut away the problem before it gets loose – is vaguely in keeping with the state-wide support for more prisons, even at the cost of university funding, libraries, public education and basic infrastructure (i.e. that which might reduce crime). A black performance artist, Keith Antar Mason, told me recently that he is now working increasingly in the only public spaces for African-Americans that are supported actively by government – the prisons. In 1995 alone, the state-wide cost overrun for prisons was $300 million, and rising.

For the first time since the thirties, with the debacle in aerospace, the Anglo middle class was hit harder by a downturn than the rest of the country. The resulting anger seemed confirmed by images of white neighborhoods like West Hollywood being looted in 1992. The anger has contributed to a drop in real-estate prices, up to 60 per cent in areas even faintly associated with the "Riots," cavernous drops in neighborhoods that did not participate, and are not necessarily more dangerous than others, but look poor. At the same time, among wealthy homeowners, the fashion for gun ownership expands. Many more couples spend Saturdays at the shooting range, as if it were a golf course. In the Spring of 1994, at the home of a successful lawyer, I entered a conversation that went essentially like this.

A well-dressed man says: "My wife is terrific with a forty-five. At the shooting range, she hits the target better than I can. Of course, I own more than just forty-fives, more than just a handgun." His wife says: "I don't like a forty-five, honey. I want a smaller gun, so I don't make such an immense hole in somebody." Then from another corner of the room, a former Vietnam vet adds: "You got this all wrong. If you use a smaller gun, a thirty-eight or a twenty-two, you have to get closer to the guy. You see the wound up close. Just stick with a forty-five. Trust me on this. You can fire from a greater distance, and not see so much."

The Panic is a noir imaginary about the loss of Anglo sovereignty. As a result, entire belts of the urban core may be laid to waste, particularly the mid-Wilshire area, which had been evolving into a Korean downtown, and is now being abandoned utterly by investors.

Nevertheless, facts suggest a drop in crime, not an increase. Since December 1995, the media regularly announced fewer reported crimes, but the public does not seem to believe it, particularly now that even suburbs are "getting worse." Many of the Valley suburbs established immediately after the Second World War are turning into *barrio*, parts of

Pomona, Reseda, North Hollywood. That should suggest that as the suburbs mature, urban problems will be spread "more evenly." The number of homes lost to bankruptcy is immense in the suburbs, not unlike the inner core. Orange County is reeling under cutbacks and an investment drought after its bankruptcy in 1995. Gang violence is increasing in Santa Ana in Orange County, with signals of wider problems to come. There seems to be no neighborhood that is genuinely safe against crime. In Beverly Hills, some parents do not even let their children leave the house at all, as if kidnapers were circling like chicken hawks.

Realistically, this "democratization of crime" should encourage residents to be less obsessed about looking for whiteness as the most practical guarantee that a neighborhood is safe. Instead the opposite is taking place, particularly after the Northridge earthquake. Nothing seems white enough, now that nature has "looted" the middle class.

However, the feelings of apocalypse do not come out of a death watch for earthquakes – at least, not directly; and not even out of communities that die, like Bunker Hill. They emerge more from the repression of experience by a tourist supraculture – by the vital information that L.A. promotion denies us (whether it is sunny or noir). Our knowledge of the city becomes as segregated as the class structure itself.

SIMU-QUAKE

How does an earthquake alter collective memory? On Sunday, 16 January 1994, after a weekend trip to Las Vegas, where I saw a volcano erupt every night and a warship sink on the hour, along with a casino version of the Fall of Rome and a boat ride through the Egyptian underworld, my family and I drove back to Los Angeles. It was difficult to settle down, but I managed to fall asleep around 2 a.m. Then, two hours later, I was jolted by the Northridge earthquake. The walls twisted. The roar seemed to explode internally, and then the silence was absolute.

Damage to my house was not severe, only plaster cracks. Nothing much even fell off the walls. Other people I talked to were infinitely worse off. Chimneys collapsed, even onto cars. Kitchens were wrecked. A toilet erupted off the wall. For many, the electricity took twelve hours, even days to come back; and when it did, the light seemed unsteady, like an oil lamp inside a tent.

The news on television was totalizing, of course. No other information was available except on the quake. Talk radio sounded like a baptist revival, one caller after the other confessing their moment at the cross. Someone said that his apartment resembled a nervous breakdown. Another decided to witness the entire crisis through television, by never leaving his room – a kind of media agoraphobia. He would erase any distinction between the video shock and the aftershock. That way, he could turn the earthquake into a CD-Rom, and sell it to a company on Pacific Coast Highway.

At Studio City, Universal Tours canceled their earthquake ride, just as they had canceled their Backdraft exhibit after the great fires of 1993. There was no way to simulate the improvidence of a real earthquake for millions of people who had recently felt their real houses and roads smash to bits. Real earthquakes are too random – just the reverse of the control of space and gravity that visitors expect in a theme park.

By Wednesday, many people still admitted to feeling dizzy, and to dozing intermittently from depression. There was a feeling of randomness – the unpredictability of problems in Southern California remained a constant theme, across the media – of uncertainty as to whether the ground would stay still. In a period of less than two years, Southern California had gone through a massive uprising, a week of spectacularly damaging hillside fires, and a devastating earthquake – as well as the worst recession in almost sixty years. No community, rich or poor, had been spared.

On 23 January the Sunday L.A. Times Magazine ran a long feature on new ways to envision real estate in the city, given its problems. First, the article dispelled myths that crime was worse in Mexican East L.A. than in "yuppie" Santa Monica. Crime statistics between the east side of town and the west side (nearer to the beaches) was not all that different, particularly relating to car theft. Even income variations were not that different. And the pollution that struck South Bay, for example, could not register for the public, because beach towns do not fit the paradigm of smog.

This reshuffling of the real-estate valences seemed to fit into the general mood (unspoken, but slowly emerging): to reconsider areas spared by the three demons – uprisings, fires, and earthquakes. One of these areas, Angelino Heights, was highlighted with a photo on the first page of the article, and showed an inner-city white couple playing with their child in front of their clean, hygienic, very Anglo-looking house. I immediately could see the real-estate advertisements: "Victorian classic, 3bd, 1½ bath, view, featured in *Times*." In the interview with the couple, they described how friendly their neighbors were, and how easy the interethnic mix was, and also how much safer the streets were.

That week, on a PBS talk show, *Life and Times*, a real-estate expert said that Los Angeles was getting ready to reurbanize its east side districts; that the era of sprawl and white flight to the suburbs had ended (probably more wishful thinking, since neighborhoods like Angelino Heights are still perceived by perspective home buyers as much more violent anyway, no matter what statistics indicate). The racist fiction is much more powerful than the social fact when real-estate myths are involved.

I called up an editor for the San Fernando Valley edition of the *Los Angeles Times* – who was inundated with details on the quake damage – and asked him what changes he saw around him, in the suburban towns so severely close to the thrust fault. "I hate to say this," he explained, "but lately, news people are playing amateur social critic too much, with an emphasis on the word 'amateur.' Frankly, how many reporters can even compute a statistic? Also, a lot of people in Northridge are not living in tents here. Most people are just going about their business. But that's too boring for a news story. The man says to the camera: 'Well, I put all the pictures back on the wall, as you can see. Now I'm going to the hardware store for some spackle.' The media are clearly partly to blame for what's not remembered. There aren't all that many people in Northridge getting into brawls at Federal relief agencies. But the news on TV goes mostly where the cameras go. I'm sure there are invisible changes taking place, but news people are not trained to look for those."

1996

Dozens of quake-damaged buildings in Northridge remain unrepaired, empty – what locals call "ghost-towns." Some are converting into slums, but are now forgotten by the media, since the economy has begun to improve.

In the spring, *Twister* opened – greenlighted two years earlier at the time of the earthquake. The number of new disaster films has increased, like births nine months after a blackout, including *Independence Day*, *The Trigger Effect*, *Escape from L.A.* (directly inspired by the quake); *Volcano*; *Dante's Peak*. "We're living in Pompeii," Kurt Russell explained, "waiting for the volcano to blow and denying it."[1]

"Everyone gets very excited ... about lava engulfing L.A.," said Mick Jackson, director of *Volcano*. "It's really about the chaos of Los Angeles. We have earth-quakes and mudslides and fires. This city really shouldn't be here – it's built in a silly place, right by a fault line.".... "It's the great thing about [*Volcano*] – you can never exaggerate too much about Los Angeles. You should have seen us on our location scouts, 30 of us tumbling out of a huge van, with a cell phone glued to our ear." Jackson takes out a note pad and scribbles down a reminder, 'A new image for the movie,' he says brightly. "Molten lava oozing over a cell phone."[2]

NOTES

1. Steven Smith, "There's Simply No Escape from L.A. Jokes," *L.A. Times*, 10 August 1996, F1. After the quake, Russell decided to sponsor and star in *Escape from L.A.*

2. Patrick Goldstein, 'Volcanic Convergence,' *L.A. Times*, 19 August 1996, p. F7.

CHAPTER SIX

TWO NEIGHBORHOODS

In the late seventies, I noticed vast stretches west of downtown being torn down, in the area called Temple-Beaudry, part of what was to be renamed Center City West. The project stalled, and nothing was built. In fact by the late seventies, oil wells from 1910 were pumping again in the vacant lots. Meanwhile a long community battle emerged, before the final plan could be approved in 1991. By then, of course, the economy in Southern California had gone sour, so nothing was built. Once a year, the owners were required to level the weeds on huge stretches of empty land, as if these had been caravan cities punished into oblivion by the armies of Genghis Khan. On the north, yet another area was still blank, from failed planning dating back to the late fifties: along Sunset Boulevard, including the garbage heaped on Custer Street, chopped to half a block by the freeway, a forgotten last stand.

Occasionally, through a movie or a newspaper article, there was memory relapse, a reference to "threatened" Temple-Beaudry, even an occasional interview with residents who still lived there; but the reference usually appeared as human interest in the Metro section – a bit of heartfelt irony, too faintly handled to draw much attention. After this momentary flicker, the memory would be closed again, like a bridge for repairs. At the same time, the movie industry, tourist fantasies and Anglo nostalgia moved in.

IMAGINARY CHICANO CITY: TEMPLE-BEAUDRY

The Temple-Beaudry area was settled during the boom of the 1800s, as a western extension of the old Temple Block, the former city hall. Mansions built in the 1870s on Miramar (in what is supposed to become Crown Hill) formed its genteel core. It lay directly north of the Los Angeles oil strike of 1892 (First and Colton), inside the "oil district." At one time (c. 1905), there were over a thousand working wells in the area from downtown to Vermont Avenue, and even special tours for a nickel.[1] Oil companies had to pay for stains left on clothing during laundry days. Legend has it that Echo Park Lake at its northern edge went on fire at least once (1907).[2]

Unlike many neighborhoods, there were essentially no covenants here restricting rentals to Jews, blacks or Mexicans.[3] As a result, by the twenties, an influx of central Mexicans settled in Temple-Beaudry, and founded Our Lady of Holy Rosary Mission. Finally, the area became a predominantly Mexican neighborhood during the thirties; along with a large Russian Jewish community left over from the teens.

In 1925, a new trolley tunnel was cut from downtown to Glendale Boulevard, shifting enough traffic from jammed Spring Street to Temple-Beaudry and its southern extremes, Crown Hill and Beverly Alvarado. As a result, all these neighborhoods enjoyed modest growth as a mixed working-class annex of downtown. At the northern end, it was called "West Temple" as late as World War II; the area was known for cheap apartments, but some of them in classic Victorian architecture. Residents particularly remember the Jewish delicatessens and bakeries along Temple: the pickle barrels outside and the roast turkeys for sale. Shops along Temple Avenue continued a mile west, to the public library at the southern rise of Echo Park.[4]

The thumb of the park formed a hinge into other neighborhoods directly north, which became known in the twenties as a "bohemian" district. More recently, California historian Kevin Starr (1990) also described Echo Park of the twenties as *bohemian*, pointing to the Elysian Hills section (where the hill and the canyon a mile above the park join) as "the closest thing Los Angeles had at the time to an artists' quarter ... the bohemian quarter of the 1920s and 1930s, a pastoral[5] alternative to Bunker Hill in the downtown."[6]

While I have heard the term "bohemian" bandied about by some of the older residents as well, they seem to be describing a neighborhood rhythm more than anything directly about the arts or an avant-garde (or even the Bohemian Club in San Francisco). I suspect the usage may be a hangover from the British (c. 1860–1915), derived from the Parisians in the 1840s, as popularized worldwide in Murger's diaries on bohemian life

(1846). In Paris, "bohemian" referred more to lifestyle and class structure within a specific *quartier*, usually poor, where marginalized (gypsy-like) groups[7] tended to congregate. In the Parisian popular press,[8] bohemians generally were worker identified – transient workers at that, living in forgotten *taudis* ("miserable rooms; hovels"[9]) where artists might reside as well.

This distinction is important for understanding the role of the park itself. After all, despite all the enthusiasms by scholars about Los Angeles culture during the twenties, what managed to survive as an L.A. gallery scene or as modernist literature was slim, and deeply isolated from the power elite, infinitely farther from the drawing rooms of the wealthy than art in New York, or even Chicago. It had very little public support through local museums and national journals, not many collectors (nor do the alternative arts have as much as one might expect today, distracted as they are by the vastness of the film industry). In fact, this "bohemia" passed largely unheralded. It could not compete with the glamour of the movies, where many fine artists worked anyway, as art directors, set designers, illustrators, and animators; and had a powerful impact in the forties[10] – in the movie "crafts."

Craft in film implied a fierce labor identity back then. Many of the largest strikes in the movie business started with animators and set builders. Writers in the bohemian circle, including Carey McWilliams who lived in Echo Park for years, were also deeply involved in leftist politics. As far as image went, the bohemians on the "Hill"[11] were considered socialists, or at least that is how the *L.A. Times* might have branded them. Given how vindictive Harry Chandler was toward the left, and the power he had with police, the Echo Park group was comfortable staying unobserved.

Very little publicity was devoted to Echo Park even in its "glory" years. Daily newspapers barely mentioned it. Nor was it considered relevant by the boosters, certainly not in the preferred way – and not because there weren't churches. There were perhaps too many. The Saint Athanasius Episcopal Church had been founded in 1864; that was suitable. But nearby were what some called "last chance" religions, with soup lines in the thirties stretching three blocks to Sunset Boulevard; and a Ukranian church not far from a synagogue. In other words, when a gentleman in 1930 used the term "bohemian", he also meant – in picturesque euphemism – a place where too many of the wrong religion and the wrong race cohabit. Echo Park looked more like the Lower East Side than Greenwich Village. It attracted groups who found themselves isolated ethnically or culturally from a profoundly midwest "Anglo-Saxon" identified city.

Much of the bookselling world, the film world, many visual artists, even many radical labor activists shared the park with the Mexican and Jewish residents, and also with a few black families living just south of the lake,[12] and various emigres after the shocks of World War I (Poles, Lithuanians).[13] As of 1925, the Russian/Polish Jews would walk up from Temple Street on the sabbath, and notice the baptist faithful gathering at the Foursquare Gospel Church built by diva evangelist Aimee Semple McPherson. Sister Aimee, of course, warrants a book in herself. Other than Garbo or Harlow, she was far and away the most famous American woman in media (radio), but also something of an embarrassment. In 1926, she disappeared for a month with her lover, then claimed, like Botticelli's Venus, to have risen from the sea after being kidnaped. As one of the locals recalls: "Sister Aimee had great entrances."

Only a quarter of a mile north of the park, the emerging film industry was headquartered in Edendale, along Glendale Boulevard. Moviemaking there began in 1909 with the Bison Studios (one-reeler westerns), followed by Mack Sennett in 1912.[14] In what was called "northern" Edendale, cowboy star Tom Mix built a studio ranch in the late teens, or rather it was built for him by Bison/Selig: 12 acres including a complete frontier town, a "saloon," corrals, a desert and an Indian village.[15] Locals remember seeing Chaplin, Pickford, Swanson and Fairbanks in the park. On one occasion, Fairbanks opened the window of his limousine to flag down a newsboy named John Dukitch, who was struggling on a bicycle up the hill, the so-called Movie Hill back then. Fairbanks told the exhausted ten-year-old to stow his bike in the back seat, and ride with a star instead. The incident left an indelible mark on Dukitch even fifty years later. I must have heard him tell the same story five times. He also remembered being hired to work as a child extra in a Chaplin comedy, paid $10 to dress as an altar boy. When he asked the "movie folks" what to do, they told him "just try and catch Charlie." Another resident recalls that Chaplin built a two-storey house a little farther north, in the Berkeley Hills, part of 38 fancy acres[16] developed for gentry who wanted a view, but away from *hoi polloi* in Echo Park.[17]

Many of the cheaper court complexes on either end of the park became rentals for movie extras and crew. And all of this remained easily accessible by subway to downtown; to the bookstore row along Sixth Street; to the circle of printers, artists and writers meeting the bookseller

Jake Zeitlin, who lived on Allesandro Street, a stone's throw from Sennett's Studios, in view of Keystone Comedies being shot along Glendale. At the southernmost point of the Sennett lot on Glendale, the "revolving drum background" for slapstick chase scenes was plainly visible, a local landmark.[18]

Kids used to break into where film was stored, and make stink bombs of the flammable celluloid.[19] Older residents also remember war pictures being shot on the hill, only a few hundred yards from dairies and a horse ranch, and a few blocks west of the small Angona winery[20] on Portia Street.

After 1916, the film industry started to drift away from Edendale, moving west to where newer suburbs were growing fast, like Silver Lake, Las Feliz, and East Hollywood; also toward expansions of existing studios in Culver City, or in the San Fernando Valley. Finally, by the thirties, during the Depression, new housing construction practically ceased throughout the Echo Park area. In the forties, there was a fear that it might "turn negro" in the area near Alvarado and Sunset. That undoubtedly scared off investors as well. Only 13 per cent more housing has been added to Temple-Beaudry since 1933.[21]

Then, in the fifties, buildings began to be systematically removed. The new Hollywood Freeway cut right through the lower third of the park from east to west (what used to be California Street). That isolated Temple from the grassy knoll that was the easiest path to the rest of Echo Park. Also, looking east, overpasses removed any comfortable walking access from Temple Street to downtown. So instead of pedestrians meeting easily, the freeway roared overhead, two hundred thousand cars a day. What remained of the knoll became detached. Shut off from its life lines, business along Temple began to dissolve.

In 1954, the first redevelopment plan was proposed for Temple-Beaudry, and many more since, mostly to turn it into a new financial and legal district, to offset the decline of banking along Spring Street downtown. At the same time, however, making problems worse, the subway tunnel that fed north to Glendale Boulevard was canceled in the fifties. Every neighborhood formerly supported by Glendale Boulevard fell in value.

Bargain hunters scoured for cheap real-estate deals, generating extreme mood swings throughout the area, but no new construction. For example, from the forties into the sixties, on the corner of Temple and Figueroa, a nest of Victorian cottages served as a gay arts complex for silkscreening, pottery and other crafts. The owner, Grant Beach, very much a beloved local character, ran classes for residents, for artists in the general area, even for a core group of Native Americans. The complex had pottery wheels, kilns and other equipment. Then, in the sixties, Grant Beach was pressured to sell. At a party, he announced to students and friends that he was holding out for the penthouse in the high-rise that he was told "they" would build on his site. A few years later, after he died, ownership passed to others. The cottages were knocked down to make way for a parking lot facing an overpass.[22] Beach's house was converted into a restaurant called Itchy Foot, specializing in business lunches, and attempts at generating dinner theater at night. The property is for lease now. Since 1960, only 4 per cent new housing has been added throughout Temple-Beaudry.

During the 1971 earthquake, the Temple library on the isolated knoll was damaged, then removed rather than repaired. The remains of the knoll were converted into public tennis courts. A few blocks east, a temporary building shaped like an oversized boxcar became the interim library, near the deafening freeway and beside a dangerous, often unlit, tunnel. Then, nothing was done. Promises for a new library remained in limbo for twenty-five years. Monies were designated through a bond issue in the mid eighties, but no one could agree on a site, so the matter floated for another ten years. Finally, in 1995, construction for the library began on Temple Street, to accompany two new public housing projects, each with a theme about old neighborhoods. The first has a rancho dome, in mission revival stucco (named Castle Gloria, after former Councilwoman Gloria Molina). The second sprawls down Edgeware Road, in pseudo Victorian with mock turrets, similar to the Victorians that had been knocked down twenty years before. It stands across the street from a late-modernist Japanese motel that went up in the eighties during the Pacific realty boom that failed. Other than that, nothing much has been built after forty years of fierce speculation.

No home improvement was allowed through city loans either, not while the arguments raged about whether any residential housing should be allowed to survive at all. One faction wanted downtown to extend further west, into Temple-Beaudry; another wanted it to stay densely packed, east of Beaudry. During these forty years of ambivalence, only two uncertain steps were taken: a nine-storey windowless computer center for the Bank of America, and the truncated Pacific Stock Exchange, both on Beaudry. Meanwhile, insurance companies also redlined the neighborhood, making mortgages for residents very tough, but much easier for large commercial investors who wanted to flatten ten acres at a time.

By the eighties, the district had become a point of entry for Central Americans, who lived in miserable rentals that were overlooked by the city, thinking it was cheaper than public housing (besides, the HUD money had vanished during the Reagan years). Some streets began to take on the ambience of a Tijuana weigh station in an abandoned corn field, particularly once the demolitions left massive blanks. Apartment owners stayed pat rather than repair anything – waiting to make a killing with developers.

Even though ceilings caved in from leaking roofs, and plumbing rotted, some investors were paying as much as $100,000 per square foot for the land itself. For example, downtown investor Richard Riordan entered a consortium in 1981 that bought a city block near Beaudry, on Angelina Street – 21 acres for $4.3 million – then sold to another group in 1988, who in turn sold a large section to the L.A. School District in 1993, for upwards of $650,000 for each lot – almost three times its 1981 value. In 1992, of course, Riordan was elected mayor. Whether he had profit participation in this wondrous deal is not known. I heard a resident in Temple-Beaudry joke that everything under the ground may be worth millions, but anyone living above the ground was worth nothing.

Official statistics increasingly favored demolition, just as they had when Bunker Hill was going down. The misery was supposed to look beyond saving. In 1980, police warned me that Temple-Beaudry had the lowest per-capita income of any neighborhood in the state of California. The CRA trumpeted the same data: a median family income of $7,825.[23] How officials arrived at this certainty seemed very dubious to me. The census was unreliable. I knew Vietnamese as well as Salvadoran families who were not counted in 1980. The few census workers I met in 1980 had not a clue about the inner workings of the area, about street vending or illegal sweatshops. They had been hired seasonally, for the rush, not as specialists in immigrant life. They seemed far too polite and uncertain to interfere with immigrants who did not want to be noticed: families hiding in garages; day workers sleeping in beds that dropped like ironing boards from closets. I heard stories about as many as five itinerant workers sharing a single bedroom, at least until they could save some money.

One condescending document admitted that "in actuality, overcrowding may exist."[24] What an evasive understatement! Clearly the bleak housing shortage was getting much worse; over 30 per cent of the buildings had been eliminated from 1970 to 1986, while the population continued to grow.[25] That meant an average of two families living in each housing "unit," though the *Times* ran a story about as many as three families in a tiny, halved apartment.[26]

On the condition of the houses themselves, reports were even more overweening in their contempt. Nevertheless, as in the census, their data was dubious. Based on very short visits, perhaps a dozen in a day, inspectors could not possibly be that certain. Reports described only 5 to 10 per cent of the buildings as sound. Most structures were called "deteriorated and warrant[ing] clearance."[27] I know this is preposterous.[28] In Angelino Heights, every antique house I walked through, and watched being restored, had been cited by inspectors as "in serious disrepair," often followed by advice (off the record): "It would be cheaper to knock it down and start over again." One such "disaster" was transplanted from Temple-Beaudry to a lot next door to me, and now stands in gleaming renewal as a historic monument. In fact I knew one slumlord in Angelino Heights who had been an inspector; he used to buy houses at auction that he himself had helped condemn, then rent them out for years, and finally sell them to Anglos, who fixed them up.

Many of the demolitions in Temple-Beaudry were a bit hard to spot anyway. On Crown Hill, where the most intense removal took place, the streets are cantilevered, leaving many corners easy to miss. I used to drive through the area every month or so, but never had the patience to make all the snaking turns that a full check required. Then, from the corner of my eye, as if finding a back molar suddenly missing, I would notice a new clearing down a slope. Invariably, I never quite remembered what building had stood there.

The demolition stopped in 1988, under an "interim control ordinance" by the City Council, with promises that a new plan was less than a year away. By 1988, however, the damage had been done. One displaced former resident said: "[Whatever the plan does] no one can replace the community we lost."[29] In one 100 acre corridor, ten developers had removed 47 per cent of the housing.[30] Even that represents less than 20 per cent of the affected area. Meanwhile, most of the structures left standing are legally "beyond saving." At the same time, however, code violations have been ignored as standard practice. Nothing was done to improve many of them. Today, seven years later, another dozen buildings remain boarded up, while developers wait for the moratorium to lift. Some investors have folded altogether, with the economy going sour after

1990.[31] So, while no more buildings have succumbed recently, less than 5 per cent of what is empty has been rebuilt.

One of my students grew up in Temple-Beaudry. After his block was simply excised altogether, the gang he belonged to lost its territory, and finally vanished. And his street remained blank ten years later. It probably will stay emptied of houses, on barren hills, for another ten years at least, because the owner had planned a master high-rise complex for "Center City West," and has since gone effectively bankrupt.

In the meantime, the site was discovered by location scouts for the movies. It was overgrown but close by, and just needed a few ethnic touches. Since this young man was a former "tagger" (graffitist), he was hired regularly to paint gang insignia for movie sets there – to erase his own identity. He added graffiti on the walls of what used to be his neighborhood, but had now become a war zone used for combat films like *Predator*, or gang movies like *Colors*, or middle-class backlash movies like *Falling Down*. He was literally making a graphocentric version of local color, in the nineteenth-century sense of the term – to distract poverty with the picturesque.

Looking for safe versions of poverty, location scouts preferred these hills precisely because they were so decimated, a gritty (instead of a clean) slate that could be dressed up very easily for post-apocalyptic fantasies. There was even an unobstructed view of the downtown skyline at night – to provide an inaccurate map of hell, but very powerful as movie language. Hell looks better just a few blocks west of a wealthy skyline; however, downtown is neither wealthy nor inhabited after 5 o'clock. Downtown lit at night is clearly a movie set of sorts.[32]

This movie staging of Temple-Beaudry, like noir films set in Bunker Hill years before, is now a chronicle of evasions; it validates further the death of a neighborhood. And for residents hired to work on these movies, the effect must feel like a mild case of paramnesia. To the young tagger, this very faint whiff of movie celebrity became a socializing agent that continued to confuse him a bit. He wondered whether he had aestheticized his own disappearance or whether he simply had started a career. He began oil paintings of the sites that the movies used, trying a metaphysical style reminiscent of de Chirico, because the hills are so empty of people but carry an echo of who used to live there. Partly as a result of making graffiti for the movies, he found more courage to sell some of his work, had a few gallery shows, then applied to an art school and was accepted; that is where he met me, in a class on the poetics of crime movies, and passed this story along for yet another mutation. Recently, he was one of a group asked to graffiti a show at MOCA about the history of urban planning. His work appears precisely where Temple-Beaudry would have been, if the show had bothered to include it on the map.

ZOOT SUIT IMAGINARY

In speaking of Temple-Beaudry as an "Imaginary Chicano City," I should emphasize that, except for Chinatown, every neighborhood erased by urban planning in and around downtown was Mexican, or was perceived that way (generally, they were mixed, often no more than 30 per cent Mexican). The fear of a Mexican horde surrounding downtown has much to do with what historian Mauricio Mazon calls "the psychology of symbolic annihilation."[33] Urban plans for neighborhoods like Bunker Hill or even Temple-Beaudry remained under the spell left by the anti-Mexican hysteria during the Second World War. The fear was very grave after the Sleepy Lagoon murder trial of fourteen Mexican youths in 1942, but most of all after the Zoot Suit Riots downtown a year later, where Anglo soldiers attacked pachuco[34] youth. Miguel Duran devotes a chapter in his novel *Don't Spit On My Corner* to personal reminiscences of that feverish week:

> all hell broke loose. Servicemen acted like vigilantes. They would roam up and down Spring, Main, Broadway and Hill Streets. In the beginning, they jumped any young person who looked Mexican and Black and dressed in drapes [zoot suits]. Later, they went after anyone that was brown or black. White America cheered [the national press, *Life* magazine, etc.] and the police stood by and watched the action. The servicemen got real brave, they got into taxi cabs and drove around barrios like Alpine, Temple, Califa and Macy [all on the western edges of downtown]. Man, they spit on our corners! They went into movie theaters, jumped guys, beat them up and ripped their clothes off. They were treated like heroes by the Paddys [cops, identified as Irish]. All of this was reported in those two rags, the *Times* and the *Herald Express*. They wrote some inflammatory stories about how the Zoot Suit hoodlums were going to be cleaned out by servicemen and good riddance and all that shit.[35]

The problem boils down to location. While East L.A. may *today* seem the singular capital of Mexican-American life in the city, the mental map was different in the forties. The heartland of Mexican-American Los Angeles was identified as sprawling west, directly past downtown, from north to south. Bunker Hill was identified as "Mexican" by 1940, like Sonoratown just north of it (essentially in what is "China City" Chinatown today; and particularly Chavez Ravine (originally called Palo Verde) – venerable youth gangs started near there. The White Fence Gang extended west in the thirties from what is now the Lincoln Heights District, a mile north of the Sonora, off Broadway. The southern boundary of this "pachuco" zone (as Anglos perceived it) proceeded south another four miles, down toward Thirty-Eight street, the site of the Sleepy Lagoon swimming hole where the body of José Diaz was found, leading to a police sweep of up to six hundred Mexican youths – including the fourteen put on trial for murder, and nearly railroaded into the gas chamber.[36] Even ten years later, the general area west of downtown remained in the public imagination as the site of the Zoot Suit Riots, of the collective action against Mexicans. This unquestionably helps explain the severely anti-Mexican bias in urban plans for the center city, many of which were initiated precisely during the years when the zoot-suit hysteria was fiercest.

Temple-Beaudry was at least half a mile from the heart of all this, more like the western perimeter. And Echo Park was even farther west, where many Mexicans had moved in the late thirties, often to buy a first home. But Chavez Ravine immediately became vulnerable, closer in, and ragged, with very cheap rents, and many unpaved roads. The rickety cottages looked almost rural, beside tiny cornfields, even goats in some back yards, certainly chickens, and even a few cows, I am told. The quaint grocery stores, and long-term stable tenants, like the old Arechiga family, were ignored.[37] The area was labeled as transient and hopeless, and was owned mostly by the Department of Water and Power anyway, making it easier to redevelop. So Chavez Ravine went first: 7,500 displaced by 1953, after considerable resistance that led all the way to the Supreme Court. At the end, some residents threatened to throw themselves in front of bulldozers.

Public indignation over Chavez Ravine made headlines by the early fifties, particularly the 10,000-unit housing project planned there, and others elsewhere, even as far east as Broadway. A conservative smear campaign declared that public housing was a communist-inspired plot. Billboards read: "Stop this multi-million dollar housing scheme. Why pay someone else to rent?" Finally, under the new Mayor Poulson, the emptied Chavez Ravine was given to the Dodgers for a stadium. The scandal of Chavez Ravine remains a scarred memory to practically everyone I meet who lived west of downtown through the fifties, even Angelinos through-out the city. The "public housing war" made headlines. Forty years later, novelist James Ellroy fictionalized the political background in *White Jazz* (1992): "Dirt roads, shacks. Hills trapping smog – Chavez Ravine."[38]

The next Mexican neighborhood slated to go was Bunker Hill in the sixties. And finally, by the seventies, Temple-Beaudry was targeted, imme-diately after the new upscale Bunker Hill Towers went up, with advertis-ing for top rents. However, erasing Temple-Beaudry proved a bit thornier than the investors had expected – indeed, almost as tough as Chavez Ravine had been. Nonetheless, by 1980 every one of the westerly "zoot-suit" districts of the forties was gone, many even from the map itself, as if no one had ever lived there. The popular play *Zoot Suit* became essen-tially a rallying call for East L.A.

WHITE DECAY

Until the recent film *Mi Vida Loca* (1993), about Chicano gangbangers in Echo Park, the movie images of this district have not in fact been Mexican at all; quite the contrary. They are unrelentingly white, usually about impoverished white con men and sleazoids, not unlike the anti-tourist novels of the twenties. *Chinatown* has a typical cameo: the false Mrs Mulwray, an actress who will take any job, is found dead in "Echo Park," in a court apartment, set back where murders never get noticed. Earlier in the film, the wealthy Mr Mulwray is caught boating on the lake with a suspiciously young blonde.

The source of this white noir identity is not immediately clear, but probably is linked in popular memory to the dark reading of "bohemian," about the "Hebes, Mex and lefties," up the hill; and about marginal types in the "flats" by the park. The opening monologue of *Mi Vida Loca* says that the park was "built" in the twenties. I suppose in some ways its image was.

However, I haven't found much historic evidence of noir criminality on the flats of Echo Park, only penny ante along Sunset Boulevard in the forties, or earlier. Barber shops on the 1500 block took bets on the horses – what was called "speed;" but so did barber shops everywhere. There might have been a few lively stories about Jensen's Rec Center a block west. It had a seedy reputation, in contrast to its neon sign above the roof, of a man bowling a strike. Jensen's was a mecca for boxers and their dubious connections. "If you knew who to ask at Jensen's, you could play dice, buy drugs and find prostitutes."[39] By the fifties, drugs were apparently sold openly there, as the neighborhood continued to sink.

During the fifties, the hills of Echo Park were called Red Gulch, or Red Hill, because so many who were blacklisted lived up there, particularly "reds and pinkos" in the film crafts or in screenwriting, and also various political activists who lingered through the seventies, until many resettled in Venice. Anna Louise Strong, a leading communist, lived in a Tower House in Angelino Heights during the fifties. I am told that locals were shocked mostly because "she wore no underpants."

One rumor says that movie stars used to keep hidden rooms for trysts with starlets living up in the Elysian hills. From another angle, the young John Huston is rumored to have lodged up on Cerro Gordo, overlooking the freight yards. Finally, Charlie Manson lived up there for a time as well, so they say.

And in 1927, a psychotic college student named Edward Hickman tried to raise $1,500 in tuition money by kidnaping a 12-year-old girl named Marion Parker. After trying to ransom her, he finally cut her corpse into pieces at the Bellevue Arms in Angelino Heights.[40] An interstate manhunt ensued after he escaped, not once but twice, from police. However, none of that grisly story seemed to register much with old residents. I asked why not. One neighbor theorized: "Probably because Hickman wouldn't be caught dead in Echo Park, not even during the manhunt." That merits a response: has Echo Park been remembered as a perfect hideout for white criminals? In the novel *The Blue Knight* (1972), Joseph Wambaugh writes: "'If I ever see you downtown scoring pills again, I'll make sure you go to the Hall.' The kid took a deep breath. 'You'll never see me again. Unless you come out around Echo Park.'"[41] Perhaps Echo Park simply looks unexplored enough to hide a crime. An old reporter at the *Times* used to say: "If it's bad, we say it happened in Echo Park. If it's good, it happened in Silver Lake [a wealthier district nearby]."[42]

Anglo residents love to describe Echo Park as a hill trapped in an earlier state of decay, with 70-year-old shrubs and odd canyon housing from the twenties — the charm of phantoms just beneath its surface. The poet Eloise Healy Klein writes: "[Echo Park] is a trail, even under asphalt. Every downtown street cuts through adobe... The life before cement is ghosting up..."[43]

Not much of the twenties' ghost is immediately visible though: there are no plaques, no stores intact, no major buildings, no museums; very few books have been written about Echo Park – only a few pamphlets. I suspect that most of the noir image has to do more with cheap rents than any memories of old crimes. Elysian Heights remains the most affordable canyon in L.A. It has taken on the imaginary of marginal whites in the film industry or the drug world – what used to be called "Hollyweirds," like the lovably hopeless ensemble in the movie *Echo Park* (1984). Except for a few Asian college students, every face in that film in every direction is Anglo.[44] They all dream of consumer glamour, but each is going nowhere – delivering pizza, stripping for parties. Similarly, in the screenplay for *Pulp Fiction* the nearly brain-dead white drug dealer is described as living in Echo Park, not unlike a similar character in the Tarantino script for *True Romance*. In *Pulp Fiction*, the killers pass into oblivion under a bridge at Silver Lake Boulevard, by the boundary at Echo Park. Like Temple-Beaudry, these sites find a noir identity because they suggest absence, an access to no memory at all, a good place to dump a body.

The Sonora just north of downtown is gone. The Moctezuma nightclub on Sunset, its last toehold, was torn down in the eighties to make room for a new shopping center that is the entry to the Vietnamese section of Chinatown. The owner of the Dodgers has announced that he wants to turn the rest of Chavez Ravine (a parking lot) into a hockey rink or a football stadium. The Jensen Building was subdivided into a flea market for discount stores. No one but oldtimers and dedicated neighborhood historians[45] have the slightest memory of what used to stand where.

While the Latino population from Temple-Beaudry and points north remains huge, its points of reference within a built environment have been largely removed. The Holy Rosary Mission, once the core of Mexican life in Temple-Beaudry, had its last mass in 1993; it is to be torn down for a new middle school, despite neighborhood complaints.[46] At first, when a crucial but homely landmark is taken down, from the outsider's point of view very little seems at stake. And often, by the time the structure itself is removed, so much invisible damage has already taken place that the actual bulldozing seems trivial.

IMAGINARY ANGLO CITY: ANGELINO HEIGHTS

If the Temple-Beaudry District has become a movie set for Chicano film stories, then just north of the Hollywood Freeway, in Angelino Heights, quite the reverse was being built – or restored – after 1975. Houses in

Angelino Heights have been used frequently in films about old Anglo Los Angeles, including *Chinatown*, *Winds of War*, and the mini-series *East of Eden*. The neighborhood has survived practically intact; 75 per cent looks as it did fifty years ago. Virtually no buildings have been lost, except through fire; and it is undergoing a variety of restorations, since it contains the highest concentration of Victorian homes in Los Angeles, and another three hundred architecturally significant Craftsman woodframes, all within only six square blocks.

It had once been home to mayoral officials, the first Cedars-Sinai Hospital, as well as Jewish, Italian and Protestant entrepreneurial families. That protected it at first. Its Improvement Association even protected Temple Street below and the rest of Echo Park against excesses by "oil men," and fought for improved water bonds. As late as 1921, Angeleno Heights, as it was spelled back then, was still powerful enough to bring all oil drilling nearby utterly to a halt:

> The residents [of Angeleno Heights] who don't want the well say that the oil men are crude. The oil men admit they are crude because that's the kind of oil they are after... Citizens desiring to see some slapstick amusement are urged to stand in front of the City Hall and watch the oil men as they hit the sidewalk. The only regret the Angelenoites have is that the Council Chamber is on the second floor.[47]

The decline came when the blue-book families began to leave a decade later, and was quite evident by the Second World War, when some of the fanciest Victorian homes were turned into rooming houses. Not until the mid sixties did the local shops slip, and the level of crime begin to soar. By the early seventies, prostitution and drug dealing were out in the open along Douglas, the principal street cutting north to Sunset. However, some of the old wealthy residents stayed anyway, preventing a few key mansions from being turned into rooming houses. Also, the mansions large enough to serve as dense tenements were generally not torn down even by slumlords who bought them.

On the western edge of downtown, even prize architecture survived only through benign — or racist — neglect. This ragged enclave of Victorian and Craftsman homes was considered too isolated by developers to be torn down, and too Mexican to be built up. Then, beginning in the mid seventies, dozens of the Victorian and Craftsman houses were restored, mostly by Anglos, though also by a few Latino and Vietnamese families. One street, Carroll Avenue, even has Victorian streetlights again, and most of the wires have been taken underground, as well as three older Victorians added – an "old-town" Los Angeles one block long that is ideal for movie crews. (None of the improvements, incidentally, came through city money. Funds were raised privately, through house tours, with neighbors as docents.)

The area remains racially and economically mixed, with a cityscape that looks on film like Los Angeles *circa* 1920–45, but in fact has pockets of enormous poverty. New owners in 1978 found as many as fifty people holed in the shell of a Victorian building. The tenants were generally forced out as quickly as possible, often with cash inducements. In some cases, however, they have been allowed to stay, even at specially reduced rents. This is a mixed blessing by any measure. Fights break out between the Anglo and the Hispanic children. One Mexican father, very poor, upon seeing an Anglo woman walking her dog, said "I wish I was your dog." And yet, quite by accident, Angelino Heights has become one of the most integrated communities in Southern California, not at all what most of the homeowners had expected. There is some shared sacrifice between the haves and the have-nots, and many examples of interracial cooperation – community watches against crime, and strong friendships between children across class lines. There are also Anglo families who ship their kids to private schools, and stay clear of the "locals" as much as possible.

Finally, the shocks of the nineties brought more homeowner flight for the first time in decades. Panic about crime and schools drove out six more Anglo families who have children. At the same time, more middle-class Mexican-Americans are buying in, and restoring houses. Also, increasingly, the district is turning into a rental area for single artists, actors and movie personnel, or for professional couples who do not plan to raise families.

With economic crisis closing in, the cityscape itself – the "old-timey" look of the five hundred houses that compose the district – is more than ever the community's only protection against utter collapse. City Hall cannot, and realtors will not, provide any meaningful support, unless the neighborhood "looks" more upscale. So the old-fashioned appearance is guarded very carefully by a few devoted homeowners, who fight city policies regularly, have meetings when threats from developers arise, set up house tours to raise support money, and have continuing connections with zoning agencies and the police. One restorationist has even become a small land baron, buying seven houses, upgrading and renting them out.

To guarantee that empty lots are filled with "compatible architecture," investors have been encouraged to ship in antique houses. Since 1978, six old Victorian homes have been brought by truck, like a weirdly shifting cul-de-sac sliding down the street, then set on blocks, before new foundations are laid. One relocated mansion (1870) and one cottage (1872) are actually older than the neighborhood itself (1887). These two houses came from the very streets in Temple-Beaudry where my student had grown up. The others were moved from Boyle Heights in East Los Angeles (another Hispanic district) or were houses stranded by freeway construction around downtown. Such houses are plucked from slums where the housing stock is continually being depleted through neglect or by racist urban planning. In the Hispanic east side, for example, street crews have even been known to remove most of the sidewalk, to add a lane for traffic to zoom through, while violating the public spaces.

By contrast, in Angelino Heights, design control was instituted in 1983. This came as part of a "deal" that let a city councilman's "crony" use a dubious bond to erect a 42-unit apartment complex too dense for normal fire lanes (there were three fires at the site while it was being built; one suspicious fire in the middle of rainstorm, with witnesses spotting the arsonists, but no action taken). Like a great beached whale, this condo giant remains utterly out of scale beside the old houses; it is now already so worn down that it will never be anything but apartments. As part of the deal to keep "complainers" quiet, the neighborhood was quickly rewarded a "historic overlay zone" weeks *after* documents were found of the illegal bond issue that might implicate the councilman.

After the new zoning was in place, the restorationists were allowed to select their own committee to approve building permits. Now Craftsman touches are generally required in new construction (Victorian touches are too expensive). Old frame houses cannot be stuccoed over, or have aluminum windows added. Most of all, large developers in the booming eighties were not allowed illegal variances to build any more chock-a-block housing. However, in 1996, city planning threatened to replace all Angelino Heights zoning members with appointees from City Hall.

The fear among residents is that Angelino Heights may be swallowed into what is around it. Downtown planned developments, left over from the fifties to the eighties, have led to the wholesale strip mining of square miles into oblivias of derelict, barely occupied mini-malls, or cheap lop-sided unusable complexes, as well as half-built or unbuilt projects – in short, what a poor "Mexican" neighborhood seems to "deserve," its meager share of the pie.

The general area, Echo Park, is 60 per cent occupied by newly arrived immigrants, mostly from Latin America, as well as some overflow from the poorer sections of Chinatown a mile west. Therefore the small core of Anglos are accidentally protecting the living space of a widely diverse population, even though their private agenda is quite different.

Over the past decade however, many of the Anglos have developed strong friendships with immigrant families, have become much more comfortable with the racial mix, while at the same time more horrified by the frightful decay that remains, by the collapsing school system, and by the lack of city services. Having adjusted their sights enormously, most will say now that they are restoring (even using the term "urban pioneers") in the hopes that this might become a balanced neighborhood, of solidly middle class and "stable" working class together. The community has developed a surprising degree of solidarity. Often renters and the poor will literally stand guard over a restored house, and even copy down the license plates of strange cars, simply as an act of friendship (and mutual survival). So while the film industry is reinforcing the stereotypes of racial violence in beleagered neighborhoods like Angelino Heights, the street-level version is far more complicated. There is less crime there than outsiders would imagine; in fact, the lowest in the police district, approximately the same ratio of robberies as in much wealthier (whiter) areas further west.

The façades of these houses are more than simply a case of naive postmodern. They are also a piece of urban politics: how a neighborhood survives while it is forgotten. Postmodern theory has probably devoted too much energy to looking at corporate simulation – engaged in too much disengaged gawking at expensive hyper-real spaces, and not done enough digging into the political contradictions of local culture step by step. Focusing on Vegas and Orlando tends to confuse the corporate with the communal. On the corporate level, the postmodern label is easy: we can barely avoid noticing hyper-real spectacles about popular memory – in theme parks, in mall planning, in suburban gated townhouse sub-divisions, with deco and mission revival façades. These pluralist quotations cost tens and hundreds of millions of dollars to assemble. They more than announce their artifice; they have to scream gentility like a circus barker. They are monumentalized corporate boosterism, designed to be noticed, built at fabulous expense – money that has to be earned back. However, in the older inner cities many architectural decisions taken street by street reveal the culture just as directly, as in the case above of two dozen

Anglos restoring buildings in a *barrio*, while hoping to erase the last eighty years – as literally as possible.

One couple in Angelino Heights installed a 1910 kitchen, complete with old stove and icebox/condenser; they even dressed like turn-of-the-century gardeners when they worked on the lawn. Others tore down rooms or fronts that were not "original," like a 1900 addition to an 1893 cottage, in order to make the houses look essentially as if no one had moved in yet. The theory is that houses are "original" only at the moment they are built. There is little interest in how they were adapted, or improved after about 1920. Houses become formal texts, stripped of the memory of those who lived there. Imagine if the wings of the Louvre that were added in the seventeenth century had to be bulldozed away, in order to return to the façade that Catherine de Medici saw on the day she first took possession in 1562.

INSTANT ARCHAEOLOGY: THEATRES OF MEMORY

In 1978, an interior decorator bought a craftsman house in Angelino Heights. He was dreadfully disappointed with it. The boxed beams in the living room creaked. The wainscoting looked inferior (only Douglas fir). And the façade was unfortunately nothing like a façade. A façade was a statement; this was merely a wood-frame house. It spoke only of middle-income housing in 1915: a little parlour; a room upstairs in the back for the grandmother. It needed an image. In the summer, during a trip to England, he took an excursion out of London, to a few smaller villages. The damp old brick houses and tidy gardens fascinated him. He decided to remake his little craftsman house into a photograph of an English cottage. What did it matter that he lived in a semi-arid climate, or that it took five hundred years to make an English village look that way? The Hundred Years War was no more meaningful than a coat of paint.

He returned from his Grand Tour and went to work. After removing all the beams and the wainscoting, he proceeded to stucco over the redwood frame, and apply artificial bricks, in a herringbone pattern, like an English cottage. He was repeating, quite by accident, a fashion at the time in London for restoring old industrial brick buildings that "ten or twenty years ago would have been routinely consigned to the bulldozer."[48] (In lower Manhattan, equally humble warehouses in the TriBeCa district became fashionable enough to attract stockbrokers and lawyers.[49])

Historian Raphael Samuel calls these renovations "theatres of memory," the social imaginary of heritage.

To theatricalize memory, the interior decorator finessed ivy into an instant hedge by growing it around cinderblocks. On the sides of the building, at the roof line, he poured a thinned brown paint, to create the illusion of a weathered house, the stain of time. Finally, he added what Raphael Samuel calls "modernization in disguise."[50] Inside the house, all wood trim and plaster were removed. Unlike diehards who preserve plaster because it looks "fleshier" or "fuller," then "retouch" hairline cracks every few years, he simply dry-walled from top to bottom. That proved that he was starting over, making it newer than new. It now looked as if no one had moved in yet. He made certain, however, to keep at least one bearing wall. According to building codes, that meant the finished product could not be assessed as new housing.

Each Christmas, the decorator's front window was animated with a mechanical Santa and elves, busily at mock work. They swayed like puppets on display at an old shoe store, cobbling imaginary soles with hammers and saws, cutting nothing, hammering nothing. The blinking Christmas lights around the front windows added to the spirit of a toy store in an upscale mall, particularly when the neighborhood had its Victorian Christmas tour. One year, a hired Santa drove by in a Cadillac and waved at the mechanical Santa, who waved back.

By the nineties, the ivy finally covered the false brick altogether. The façade was now obscured enough to look old. At last it blended into the neighborhood, next to bungalows that resembled Iowa in 1915, and Queen Annes that resembled San Francisco in 1887. Each building on the street theatricalizes a different era of false identity, which is forgotten twenty years later.

I walk down to Carroll Avenue. It looks like a zoo for the last Victorian street, with the downtown skyline frowning behind the smog. The mansions encapsulate sixty years of class conflict. Living rooms for musicales in the 1890s became dormitory dining areas for rooming houses by the fifties. "This street has come back," the news copy often reads. However, Carroll Avenue received city-wide press attention only in the seventies, precisely when Bunker Hill was beginning to be missed. That linked it to the racial fears about *barrios*. In other words, antiques near *barrios* remind tourists of faded wealth and continuing poverty. No matter how deodorized or glamorous – or safe – the old mansions get, Angelino Heights will register to visitors generally as a place in decline, for another twenty years I suspect. To most outsiders, except a few young artists, it still looks too Mexican, too risky in the alleys, with too many non-whites in front of buildings that used to be Anglo.

NOTES

1. Norman Dash, *Yesterday's Los Angeles* (Miami: E.A. Seemann Publishing, 1976), p. 79. Dash estimates 1,150 wells; the book includes photos that reveal how dense it was. Tourist excursions to the Oil District left from First and Spring, and cost a nickel: *Newman's Directory and Guide of Los Angeles and Vicinity* (1903), p. 98.

2. Two photos of early L.A. oil wells are in Dolores Hayden's *Power of Place: Urban Landscape as Public History* (Cambridge: MIT Press, 1995), p. 105. Locations: Temple-Beaudry (First and Belmont); at least fourteen wells on the Southern edge of Echo Park Lake. Houses, offices, water lines, and storage tanks are all very close to each other.

3. One black family, named Jones, resided south of Echo Park Lake in 1890; however, I have seen covenants in deeds from that period with blacks restricted.

4. Echo Park had been built around the reservoir that was dammed in 1873 to catch the rivulets that ran down what is now Glendale Boulevard. The gathered water was then routed near the flats of Temple Avenue to Sixth and Figueroa downtown, where it powered the wheel of a woollen mill. Finally, when the mill closed, the reservoir was donated as a park to the city (27 acres in 1891). By 1903, Glendale Boulevard was utterly dry when it was paved for a trolley. The knoll below, to Temple, was a natural extension of what came to be called the largest man-made lake in Los Angeles (from a lecture by William Mason, September 1995). From another resident: the water draining into downtown from Echo Park Lake became part of the *zanja* (Spanish for "ditch") irrigation system, where children played on what was called Zanja Street.

5. Cattle were allowed to graze in Echo Park, but not downtown, which explains the importance of the dairies, as well as the horse ranching in the Echo Park hills, to service downtown, in a "pastoral" setting only a mile from business areas.

6. Kevin Starr, *Material Dreams: Southern California Through the 1920s* (New York: Oxford University Press, 1990), p. 329.

7. The term "bohemian," of course, meant gypsy – those areas in Paris where the transient lived like gypsies, along with a few Romany gypsies I suppose. The exoticism of the gypsy lifestyle is what Murger suggests (1846), when he applies it to artists and impoverished students.

8. Balzac and Dumas both use the term "bohemian" in serial novels from the late 1830s on, again more about lifestyle than art production. Balzac, in his novel *La Raballouilleuse* (*Black Sheep*), calls the loose-living soldier a bohemian, but not his hard-working brother who happens to be an artist. Again, I realize that there was a Bohemian Club in San Francisco, but the broader meaning of the term cannot be ignored.

9. *Harrap's Modern College Dictionary*, 1967 edn. Also: les taudis de Paris (slums of Paris); lutte contre taudis (slum clearance campaign).

10. For example: Rico Lebrun, Jules Engel, and John McLaughlin – painters clearly

involved in the film industry. Also Oskar Fischinger, a key figure, particularly in the opening credits for *Fantasia*. In my book *Seven Minutes*, I review some of the links between abstract art, graphic design and character animation in Los Angeles during the forties and fifties.

11. It seems that practically every hillock that claimed its own identity in Echo Park became to its local residents "the hill," as in Elysian Hills, Berkeley Hills, and Angelino Heights. I believe this is an extension of the memory of genteel Bunker Hill, even while it still stood in decline; even after it was gone. Also, many of the first suburbs in the 1880s, in Pittsburgh or above New York City, were on hills – cooler in summer, away from the rush. Like Bunker Hill, they were often very upscale indeed.

12. By the fifties, a small black neighborhood had emerged along Alvarado, at the western edge of Echo Park. Very likely, the fear of encroaching black slum (not accurate) restricted development along yet another key street, which formerly had linked with Westlake. Both areas suffered, of course; both are severely impoverished now.

13. Llynn Stewart, "History: Silver Lake–Echo Park Plan Area," document for City Council, 1979.

14. Also the Marshal Neilan studio, the Garson Studio, the Selig Studio; and Disney and Griffith, among others, not far away, a few miles west (*Historic Echo Park Neighborhood Guide* [Echo Park Historical Society, 1995]).

15. Ibid. Mixville was 12 acres, compared to about 20 acres at Sennett. It was located in what then was called northern Edendale, now part of Silver Lake. The site today is a strip mall with a Hughes market, near the junction of Glendale and Rowena, a few blocks north of where the architect Neutra had his offices. Rumors suggest that Wyatt Earp consulted for Mix, and lived in a court complex on a hill along Echo Park Boulevard. In the eighties, there were plans for a large Mixville mall across the street, and acres were cleared of houses. An architect's rendering, expensively postmodern, was attached to a post at the corner. For about five years, it read "Coming, Mixville," until the colors faded, and the picture of the mall simply disappeared. A few back hoes and flat-bed trucks were stored behind the sign, but there was no construction at all, until the graded lot was put up for sale, for years.

16. Interview with Walter Sida (September 1995), who grew up in Echo Park during the thirties; and returned after World War II to open a radio repair store on Echo Park Avenue, which he ran for many years.

17. The developer was Frank A. Garbutt. This area is now known as the Hathaway Hills, for the Hathaway House at the center. Cal Trans had bought most of it, awaiting a freeway that was never built, then unloaded houses in the eighties. Some expensive homes were added there, to generate a Hollywood Hills gentry district near Echo Park, with a view of downtown – another interdictory, fortified space.

18. Israel Smith, "Memories of Edendale in the Early Twenties," *Parkside Journal*, 7 May 1984. The drum was located at the "corner where Alvarado angles into Glendale Boulevard." I may be chronologically condensing memories here: Zeitlin arrived in the late twenties, just before the coming of sound. The revolving drum at Sennett obviously continued only as long as silents were shot, but Sennett moved in the twenties.

19. Interview with Walter Sida (September 1995).

20. The winery was contained in two barns behind the house and in a cellar below, until about 1910. According to local stories, the Angonas were the first settlers in Echo Park. Fifteen children of their children were born there, the first in 1890 (Kevin Fitzmaurice, "Echo Park Winery: First Settlers in Area," *Parkside Journal*, 6 January 1977).

21. *Temple-Beaudry Revitalization Report*, Community Redevelopment Agency of the City of Los Angeles, 1981, p. 40.

22. Interviews with artist Peter Shire, 1983–95. While an art student at Chinouard Institute downtown, he bought one of the kilns auctioned off at the property when it was about to be demolished. Shire was born in Echo Park, and still has his home and studio there.

23. A statistic that repeats in numerous documents (neighborhood flyers, etc.). The source is probably the *Temple-Beaudry Revitalization Report*, from the Community Redevelopment Agency in April 1981, responding to a request in 1977 by Councilman John Ferraro. I also have seen income figures for the area as much as $2,000 higher ($9,470 in the late eighties).

24. *Temple-Beaudry Revitalization Report*, Community Redevelopment Agency, April, 1981, p. 71.

25. Ibid.; Richard Good, "Angelino Heights: The Survival of Downtown Growth," unpublished paper; "L.A. Core: Limiting Leaps and Bounds," *L.A. Times*, 3 May 1989.

26. Hector Tobar, "An Urban Ghost Town," *L.A. Times*, 31 October 1988, Metro, p. 1.

27. *Temple-Beaudry Revitalization Report*, p. 5.

28. This exaggerated statistic seems to be culled from a Work Product no. 2 report prepared by the Barrio Planners on 26 July 1988. However, this paper identifies only 12 per cent of the housing as beyond saving.

29. Tobar, "An Urban Ghost Town," p. 6.

30. Ibid. And in a report (December 1988) from the Echo Park Renters and Home-owners Association (primarily in the hills farther north, and away from Temple-Beaudry), and from the Inner City Alliance: seven developers were cited as major players in the Center City West Alliance – Bank of America; Union Oil (Unocal); 1st Interstate; Ray Watt (bought Thomas Cadillac, an old staple near downtown); Good Samaritan Hospital; American Express; and UIG. Soon after, Unocal pulled out, and American Express tried to sell. The Watt Center failed to find enough investors and renters for its complex. King Enterprises, a major player, also fizzled out. A Filipino investor, who razed two antique apartment complexes along Temple Street, vanished after Marcos lost power. A Chinese investor held on, leaving his buildings unoccupied for years, or so the rumors went. Very little leadership remains to get Center City West going, leaving even more doubt about its future. In the new downtown plan, CCW is increasingly ignored, not even mentioned much in the downtown weekly any more.

31. See note 30 above.

32. See the section headed "City of Lights" in Chapter 4.

33. Mauricio Mazon, *The Zoot-Suit Riots: The Psychology of Symbolic Annihilation* (Austin: University of Texas Press, 1984). See also the writings of Joan W. Moore; and Beatrice Griffith, *American Me* (Boston: Houghton-Mifflin, 1947).

34. In the late forties, Mexican poet Octavio Paz wrote a curious description of the *pachuco* as subculture, and *their* memory of the Zoot Suit Riots: "What distinguishes them is their furtive, restless air: they act like persons who are wearing disguises, who are afraid of a stranger's look because it could strip them and leave them stark naked." He admires their defiance before extraordinarily racist isolation; he also calls it "artificial," the antics of the "impassive or sinister clown." He considers Mexicanism as "floating" in Los Angeles, lacking "spirit." Even for this grand master of Mexican literature, the hybrid Mexican-American culture was considered degenerative; some of

that condescension still exists between Mexican high culture and the Mexican American (*The Labyrinth of Solitude: Life and Thought in Mexico*, trans. L. Kemp [New York: Grove Press, 1961; orig. 1950], pp. 13–17).

35. Miguel Duran, *Don't Spit on My Corner* (Houston: Arte Publico Press, 1992), p. 59.

36. Mazon, *The Zoot-Suit Riots*, p. 26. Diaz died during a party-crashing that brought violence.

37. The Arrechiga family owned various houses in Chavez Ravine, and are remembered as leaders in the community. They resisted demolition to the very end, and even set up a tent near their lost house to bring public attention to the problem. Television and newspapers made a fuss. Then someone discovered that the Arrichegas could have stayed at the vacant house their son-in-law owned. Public interest in the story faded, along with support against the evictions in Chavez Ravine. The "sneaky" Arrichegas suited Poulson's campaign against sneaky communists, despite complaints in their defense by Councilman Roybal (see Neil Sullivan, *The Dodgers Move West* [New York: Oxford University Press, 1987], pp. 178–9).

38. James Ellroy, *White Jazz* (New York: Fawcett Gold Medal/Ballantine, 1992), p. 135. See also pp. 80, 308.

39. Interview with Walter Sida (September 1995); and interviews with Peter Shire.

40. Marvin J. Wolf and Katherine Mader, *Fallen Angels: Chronicles of L.A. Crime and Mystery* (New York: Ballantine Books, 1986), ch. 13.

41. Joseph Wambaugh, *The Blue Knight* (New York: Dell Publishing, 1972), p. 300.

42. Interview with William Mason, September 1995.

43. Eloise Klein Healy, *Artemis in Echo Park* (Ithaca, N.Y.: Firebrand Books, 1991), p. 13. See also her poem about the year that Echo Park Lake was dredged (*c.* 1985): "Only the Moonlight Matters," "how the moon came out and blued out the scars" (p. 15) – very much about urban forgetting; also the poem "The City Beneath the City" (p. 21), about the Californio and nineteenth-century Chinese.

44. The location for the film *Echo Park* is a dome house on the 1400 block of Carroll Avenue in Angelino Heights, close to Mexican, Salvadoran and Chinese neighbors – and at the time, very few Anglos.

45. Campaign in 1996 to get the Jensen neon working again; also to establish a local archive for Echo Park.

46. Leslie Berestein, "Group Works to Save Church; Holy Rosary Mission has Historic Emotional Ties to Temple-Beaudry Area," *L.A. Times*, City Times, 13 November 1994, pp. 3ff.

47. "Angel Falls From Heights," *L.A Times*, 1 August 1921, Pt. II, p. 7. From the personal archive of Daniel Munoz.

48. Raphael Samuel, "The Philosophy of Brick," *New Formations*, Summer 1990, pp. 45–55. The rest of this issue concentrated on what guest editor Dick Hebdige called "the space of fantasy and the role and significance of place in fantasy (as screen for projections, as invented or imagined or figurative 'site')" (p. viii).

49. Robert Fitch, *The Assassination of New York* (London: Verso, 1994), p. 44.

50. Raphael Samuel, *Theatres of Memory, Vol. I: Past and Present in Contemporary Culture* (London: Verso, 1994), p. 75. An exceptional study on the political culture of retrochic, retrofitting and heritage-baiting, beginning with reference to Camillo's memory theaters of the sixteenth century.

PART II

IMAGINARY VIETNAMESE
IN LOS ANGELES

Now that the United States has officially recognized Vietnam an era of neglect is ending. Vietnam is being "upstreamed" into global capitalism as "the next economic tiger" in Asia. Billboards promoting Visa cards in English can be seen along major roads into Ho Chi Minh City. The interviews for this book began much earlier, in 1979, while Vietnamese "boat people" were still arriving – "the new diaspora" some called it. At that time, the only intimate Vietnam that had appeared consistently in the media was what American GIs took home from the war. As one veteran told me: "We died there, but we were only tourists."

This militarized memory of Vietnam – a sinister noir if ever there was one – came in sharp contrast, of course, to my Vietnamese neighbors in Angelino Heights, who were family friends. By 1980, it became apparent that they were revealing details to me that I could not find in print anywhere. I asked them if I might convert some of this into a story.

I began interviewing two families in particular, and continued over a thirteen-year period, while speaking also to their friends, to local businesses, and then to Vietnamese from other parts of Southern California. They often warned me that English was an invader to their telling, a second filter that kept their eloquence out. They also advised me that certain things had to be said "differently" to Americans, but never that way to friends (which was I, from day to day, year to year?).

Selective memory operated at all times. Details often contradicted each other or were simply forgotten over the years. Since the evidence was partly fictional, the outcome was something close to a short novel. There seemed no other way to be honest. I was not Vietnamese, and did not speak the language. I even reviewed story points and characters with them, to be certain that I was seeing through their point of view, not mine. Despite my best efforts, my English invaded anyway. I kept transposing memories from my own upbringing in immigrant Brooklyn.[1] So I decided that the reader should sense my interference, notice my covert Yiddish turn of phrase, or attempts at Balzacian irony.[2] To contextualize the account that follows, I now provide some background notes that I kept during the first interviews and through talks with social workers involved with the Vietnamese community.

SCAR TISSUE

My entry in the margin of an interview: "Stories about the war become a scar, evident to the touch, but faded, the way a language less spoken fades."

In 1975, 145,000 Vietnamese fled to camps mostly in Thailand, to dense barracks. Although they presumably were meant to stay for only 45 days, many endured as long as five years. To enter the United States they needed proof of $4,000 per household; however, most had long since lost their possessions, either to pirates during the flight from Vietnam, or to thieves in the camps themselves. Thus the wait for a sponsor could seem interminable, and remained very unpredictable over the next five years. By 1976, food and shelter were already miserable. And with each year, conditions grew worse for those who remained.

By 1981, despite the hazards, well over 150,000 Vietnamese had emigrated to California alone, where they encountered new problems, often to their great surprise. Initially, unemployment was very high – over 40 per cent for men and about 60 per cent for women. The jobs centered in manufacturing, on assembly lines in electronics, in the food industries, in construction, or in janitorial work. Only 10 per cent owned their own businesses. Another 10 per cent were professionals. There was little necessity to speak English in order to keep a job. As with all "ethnic" immigration into the USA, the newcomers were practically forced into quarantine economically and culturally. They were simply expected to find a way out of quarantine; some would, others wouldn't. In the meantime, neighborhoods quivered under the multiple shocks – the density of housing shared by Vietnamese, Salvadorans, Mexicans and Chicanos; the conflict in routines; and the competition for work.

Beginning in 1981, when I worked on an early draft of this novella, the shocks were very intense within Vietnamese families themselves: the fear of loss of respect, along with survival guilt for those who came first – and for those who stayed behind or had died during the war. Many of the adjustments were very difficult: for example, the loss of filial piety, of religious patterns, and of "obedient" children or wives, or simply the shame of having your children translate into English for you. The loss of place, even of a sexually unequal place, could be devastating; this was compounded by financial insecurity. The divorce rate became considerably higher than in Vietnam; cases of insanity were very numerous, particularly among women.

By the early nineties, however, much of the intensity had begun to slip from view. The process of acculturation had started for many, but not all, Vietnamese. The emphases in their stories had changed. I was told that community had been stronger in Vietnam. Memories of evenings during the shellings took on a strange wistfulness – more about families chatting outdoors, and less about the rocket fire or the camps. The placement of irony had shifted as well. What seemed worth a dark joke in 1980 had become old by 1993. Instead of laughing about a long war whose insanities had become natural, the stories announced how unnatural America remained, and at what price. In 1995, one of the families saw a driveby shooting, a spray of gunfire that missed its target across the street. The shock was immediate: older memories about shellings reappeared, as if the family were fleeing again. They moved literally the next day, to an apartment a mile northeast, closer to Chinatown. When they spoke, the sense of embarrassment before the children – that they had reignited what was best forgotten – was clearly on their faces.

Compare this with crime fantasies in popular fiction about L.A.'s Chinatown, updated to include the "hypothetical Vietnamese"[3] but still fundamentally about Chandleresque white male panic. In Timothy Hallinan's *The Man With No Time*, detective Simeon Grist studies the formica decors in a boring Travelodge up on Hill Street, Chinatown. Soon, he will encounter the labyrinthine Chinese mafiosi. The publisher's blurb on the paperback reads as it might have fifty years ago: "There is another L.A. carefully hidden from Hollywood eyes – a dangerous world of ancient shadows and exotic cultures. Here fear is the teacher and power the law. Here strangers are not welcome."

NOTES

1. During my childhood, my parents decided not to allow me to understand their native languages – Hungarian and Yiddish – so that I would grow up an American. Today, I can identify Hungarian by tone and inflection, but have not the faintest idea what is being said. That experience is comparable to these interviews – absence as presence – a synesthetic effect (to hear a touch, and so on). Similarly, English terms about forgetting seemed tonal/synesthetic (i.e. asterism: a constellation of objects that belong together but fail to invoke a meaning; almost like a tonal scale about unrecognition – to hear the familiar, but not remember its meaning). A note I left while editing the novella reads:

> Memory lapses are either short or long, loose or vague, opaque or seemingly trans-parent. The event that is forgotten could be blocked, inhibited, repressed, sup-pressed, sublimated; or in theatrical terms, masked, or even masqued (like a courtly dance in honor of erasure, their elegant, but changing memories of Vietnam itself). The space evacuated by forgetting might be described as a gap, a slip-up, a slip of the tongue; or simply having the narrator slipping out of time in the text, just lose a few months, perhaps lie about it, perhaps not, perhaps not knowing where the time went, or caring.

2. Though I never structured this specifically as an ethnographic study – I borrowed more from the European novel – in final edits I reread work on diasporic and Holocaust studies, as well as essays by James Clifford and studies on the spatial migration of memory in immigrant communities – e.g. the anthology edited by Michael Keith and Steve Pile, *The Place and the Politics of Identity* (London: Routledge, 1993). The essay by George Revill on "Reading Rosehill" struck me as close to the spirit of the problem in this project, as did Geertz's famous essay on Balinese cockfights. Another defense of fictive erasure that seemed comforting was Deleuze and Guattari's theory of the no-vella, in chapter 8 of *A Thousand Plateaus*: "The novella has little to do with a memory of the past or an act of reflection; quite the contrary, it plays upon a fundamental forgetting" (Minneapolis: University of Minnesota Press, 1987; orig. 1980), p. 193.

3. Timothy Hallinan, *The Man with No Time* (New York: Avon Books, 1993), p. 50; Hill Street, p. 105.

CHAPTER SEVEN

STORIES IN AN ENGLISH
I DON'T SPEAK: A NOVEL

I was born during the Second World War, as a Chinese in Vietnam. I am told that after the Japanese left, and during the war against the French, my family lived in considerable luxury. That continued when the Americans came to my city, Kien-Giang in the far south, though my father lost most of our fortune in 1961. I never had to say one word to Americans until I arrived here in Los Angeles.

Today, three Americans are coming to drag me from my apartment. A young man in my room has destroyed every piece of furniture. He is sitting three feet from me, his body as bloated as a small child. I don't know what I'll say when the medical team arrives. I still barely, if ever, talk to Americans, only imagine stories in an English I don't speak. They're coming at three, expecting me to help; that leaves enough time for me to hatch a plan.

When I was about four years old, someone wrapped me in a soft coverlet, and took me suddenly from Ha Tien to Kien-Giang, because the war had spread. It was not safe outside, but I was comfortable where I was. The rest of it is not all that clear.

The plantations in Ha Tien had become impossible to run. Our bailiffs were crooks (in other words, officers in the army). Then came bad advice, one of those cures that kills the patient. We were told our land was about to drop in value. My father's debts, meanwhile, never dropped in value; nor did his unfailing energy to mount up more debts. Many old families had taken the same advice, I should add, and ran away at the wrong time – what Frenchmen call "grande peur." This much became clear: no peasant was willing to work any of the fields with the war spreading. We had to settle at a miserable price and enter the future landless, no more solvent than I am today – staring at a hole where a window used to be, nursing a mental patient who plays the same Carpenters album ten times running. It sounds like someone sawing at a tree. I have earned a right to enter paradise.

Anyway, broke – "embarrassed" as they say – my family was left with nothing to trade but its name, which we changed from its Chinese, the hated ignorant sound that Vietnamese dislike (among Vietnamese, the Chinese are considered ignorant and foolish). We decided never to go back to Ha Tien (particularly in a soldier's green). My father knew a tradesman in Kien-Giang; they had been together in the war against the French. The families got together, or the fathers did. There were mutual investments to arrange – we with nothing but a family name; they with nothing but hotels and a fish factory.

My father forced me to marry, as *our* part of the investment. If only he had remarried after my mother's death, all this probably never would have happened. We might have put gold in our clothes, and left early for Los Angeles, like some cousins I know. I'd be running a shopping center in Chinatown right now, instead of sneaking home-made *bao* from unauthorized kitchens to the vendors on Hill Street and up New High.

Anyway, I was told that my bride was pretty, with a lively laugh – infectious they said. As my part of the bargain, I had two acts to perform – ablutions you might say (that is, after confirming that I had no venereal diseases). First, I had to ask my father-in-law, on my knees, to let me work for him. Then he could politely refuse, which to my utter dismay he didn't, so I went into the hotel business, like a mouse in a hole. And second, I had to shop for new suits and show myself off like a mannikin with a good family name; put some class into the operation. I never was all that handsome, or rugged. My chest always sank. My shoulders sloped. But in the right suit, I had a kind of sheepish charm, a face so soft that people tended to trust me.

The prize was a downtown hotel with over thirty rooms and a fleet of five fishing boats, along with the famous fish processing plant, from where vats of fish broth went to homes and restaurants throughout the most southern of what was then South Vietnam. I used to watch my father-in-law compute figures in his head, down to the nearest thousand piastres – the price of any downtown property, allowing for 114 per cent inflation. Then, with a gruesome smile, he would convert that number instantly into dollars. Finally, lording over the couch, he would lean over toward me looking for some morsel I could add to the conversation, some financial wizardry, a touch of that style I was expected to bring along with my new suits but always seemed to have left in my other pants.

Still, by taking on his new fortune as my own, I did find my avocation: to behave like a guest wherever I went. In the American era I suffered only a slight decline, but so did the entire country. Runaway inflation, millions of casualties, and more American labels on more products. And yet, Americans or no, I still managed to stay European in my tailoring. I never succumbed to what my father-in-law thought about wash 'n wear. I remembered from my French lycée in Saigon that in France before the Revolution nobility married constantly into families whose fortunes came from commerce, but kept their wigs and shields. Of course, such arrangements vanish in an afternoon.

My wife turned out to be cheerful, but not nearly as infectious when she laughed as I had hoped. She did pass on to the children some of the industriousness that went with her class. Everyone in the family tried to make common sense. Still, now that I think back, there was already a mad panic in the way my wife worked them over – like shoppers at an auction, a suicide's auction. Good behavior was money in the bank, they were told. Competition gave boys courage. The oldest boy – at age three – was left alone regularly, to teach him independence, or to teach him terror – mostly to frighten him into submission, since he was the oldest and the male. Yet, by the age of five it became clear that he was too frail – very clever but extremely thin, with a yellow color around his eyes. To prevent his depressions, she stalked their nursery that much more ferociously. Even worse, she introduced everybody, including my father, to Italian and French movies, and peculiarly to vulgar American romances.

But worst of all, early in our marriage, my wife discovered a version of nobility that revolted me. She began improving her diction, removing the business patois altogether, and generally turning herself into a cross between an actress in a soap opera and a dowager empress. Finally, the more she improved her accent, the more I decided to outdo her. I began to celebrate my ancestors according to the letter of the oldest, deadest law I could find. However, as cultural revenge her way was faster, like nail polish.

By September 1974, I had had enough of her. Except for an occasional Wednesday night, we were rarely completely naked. On those Wednesdays, the race from cock to thighs reminded me of opening mail, to finish up before she sank back to sleep. And yet as mammalian and thoughtless as it was between us, sex remained uncomfortable, unless we spent some of our foreplay talking about our how much we both hated her family. If only her father could have been there to watch us, forced to sit in the corner of the bedroom. That might have lit a fire.

My wife told me about her boyfriend, the man her parents decided she could not marry; then she asked me if I intended to take a *vo be*, an extra wife. After all, I was the son of a *vo be* myself. The tradition is four thousand years old. A Vietnamese man could marry several times, even decree his own divorce – until a boy is produced. As many as seven wives were permitted, and another five mistresses (concubines) if desired. He was allowed to sample as he pleased. My wife accepted this with a slow-boiling rage. I tried to reassure her that I would never have a child by a *vo be*. The rest we left unsaid, in acrid stillness, with flashes of a tolerance that was supposed to become a friendship. We grew together as if we had been planted accidentally by strangers.

She was not allowed to return to her boyfriend, though she would visit him once in a while, now that he was married and still yearning.

My yearning brought muscle cramps. My sleep was interrupted every few hours by a new ache, like a phone wire caught under a door. I had decided never to add another wife. Why duplicate my problem? Some forms of toleration become a slowly advancing arthritis.

My wife said once, at a tender moment, as we sat watching our three children: "Tell me what revenge you plan to take."

"Revenge for what?"

"For the secrets we're expected to keep."

I already had been taking trips to Saigon, to visit school mates from my youth at the lycée, where even the faculty were European. Their creaky French manners helped us show off our contempt for our own race; we even spoke of the old empire as an alternative. Some of us had traveled to Europe to study French. Others lived in Switzerland, and came home once a year to look for grime on the wall, notice the decline of their parents, and leave in great relief. We all, in one way or the other, thought we were monarchists.

I lived a bad pornographic novel, the little pulpy comic-books that businessmen read on trains: about aristocrats – overdressed Europeans waiting in expensive bedrooms, or playing two-handed piano while naked with whores. We went cruising for whores we thought had style (and did not want to be a second wife), that is, whores who could congratulate us

Sunset Boulevard at Echo Park Avenue, 1929
(*Automobile Club of Southern California, corporate archives*)

Sunset Boulevard at Echo Park Avenue, 1996 (*Paul Forrer*)

Bunker Hill: Angel's Flight,
c. 1957 (*Huntington Library*)

Formerly Bunker Hill:
Fourth Street Tunnel, 1996
(*Paul Forrer*)

Walking up
Bunker Hill, 1950s
(*Huntington Library*)

Up Bunker Hill, 1950s (*Huntington Library*)

Victorian Bunker Hill:
Rooming House, 1950s
(*Huntington Library*)

Victorian Bunker Hill:
Demolition, 1950s
(*Huntington Library*)

Angelino Heights: View South toward Temple-Beaudry and Downtown
(*Benjamin Jay Klein*)

Angelino Heights, 1996 (*Benjamin Jay Klein*)

Temple-Beaudry: One Block West of Downtown (*Paul Forrer*)

Temple-Beaudry: Two Blocks West of Downtown (*Paul Forrer*)

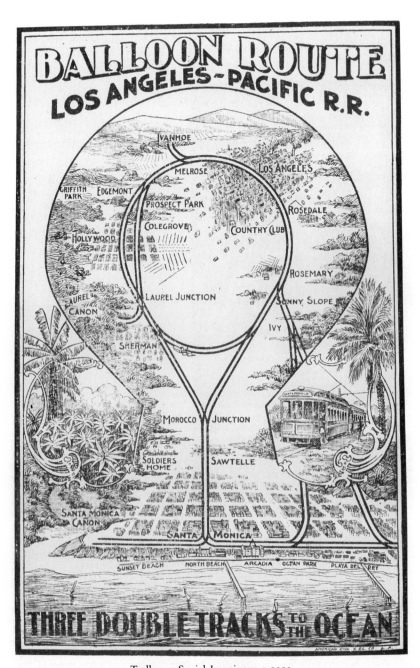

Trolley as Social Imaginary, *c.* 1910

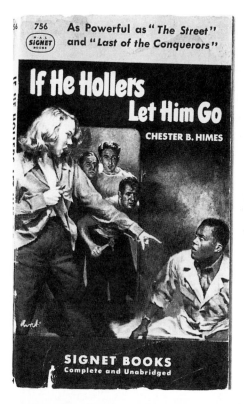

Cover of 1949 Signet edition of
If He Hollers Let Him Go
(*artwork: James Avati*)

Filming *Volcano*, West Hollywood, 1996 (*Allan Sekula*)

for our worldly tastes. Or we ate erotic fish, and fucked extremely young pubescent girls (that last shocked me, I must add, and the shock still stays with me, reminds me of my son, and the stories I knew of men marrying their wives' nieces, even with the wives' consent). I developed a certain taste for my fantasy of the *demi-mondaine*, in this case, *demi-asiatique* as well. Something of the mix between Chinese, Vietnamese, and the European excited me ferociously. The body type, the mystery of miscegenation, of imperial conquest – I couldn't entirely explain it; only the way it affected me, and finally damaged me.

These whorehouses were too expensive to simply be called brothels – these were for the old noblesse, and a few wealthy Chinese. I know that Americans think only of five-dollar whores rifling bars, living off GIs. But Americans were not part of this European Vietnam, no American I can think of really. And very little of it survived the war. They say some of it still exists in Taiwan, near the big hotels – elsewhere too I'm sure. I watched it fading in Saigon month by month, through to death or illness – seraglios getting worse at a hotel by an abandoned road.

The face of a European/Vietnamese woman crosses my mind, like a stab wound. I met her originally in 1974, soon after it suddenly dawned on me that if services for the wealthy were collapsing then the war, our only reliable system of manners and politics, must be ending; that we were all waiting like overdressed Nazis in bunkers underneath exploding cities. A germ of purpose emerged in my head. I absolutely did not want to repeat my father's wasted life, so instead, I managed to do him one step worse, in the sour melodrama of a dying civil war.

I gave up going to nightclubs for the rich, where European educated people danced to blends of French music and Vietnamese opera, or American big-band music. A drunken rich Vietnamese, with his friends on Catina Street threatened me, told me to go back to the *cholon*, the Chinatown, to the whores near the Catholic Church there (our version of lorette), to shop for groceries in the markets there. "Leave little Paris monzoor," he warned me, and tried to kick me like a little Chinee, but he was too drunk to reach me. After that, wealthy Saigon looked foreign, an enclave of French buildings set aside like special silverware for mock noblesse in the fancy Ngwyen Hue district (Whin Way), surrounded by a world of children's gangs, and an army of security that kept the city strangely isolated – a few American high-rises beside the new highway; the blur of people hiding in the city; the copies of French buildings, stone faces on their façades, like mummies from a dead empire. Guards sleeping in the basement of the suburban airport Tan Son Nhiet, beneath bombing that could be heard twenty miles away. There were better places to hide. I preferred a world far away from Saigon – wanted to go where soldiers in the provinces went; to see the widows abandoned by the war. Like the old king who watched his servants murder all his livestock and wives before the invading army came in, I needed to witness the last gunshot of the war – hopefully to escape, like one of those characters from my wife's favorite movies, through a back door to a waiting car, to speed to the border, ducking gunfire with the microfilm sewn into my coat.

Two days before I left Saigon for the last time, I stayed at the rooms of a visiting provincial mayor, a man who had fought with Ho Chi Minh until 1954, then left the party after it turned communist. At that time, his town was less than a kilometer from the war itself. His children slept surrounded by sandbags, and had learned to curl under them when the whistle of rockets was approaching. My Lai – where the American Calley had thrown six year olds down a well – was nearby. Last year, the mayor's daughter had been yanked angrily by her hair, almost lifted off the ground by a marine in a convoy truck, who thought all Vietnamese children were there as props. Other children inside the disputed territories saw their own parents decapitated. Very few in the town doubted that the VC had the will to win, and would; and that the *linh*, or Vietnamese soldier, was a meal for the two wolves who circled – one with purpose, and one unsure of purpose. In that spirit, the mayor and his son (one of my friends) were arguing about the maid, a woman who was clearly a VC, and high up in the communist army.

"Why are you letting her stay on?" the son asked.

"Last year she asked for two weeks' holiday," the father said, "to bring supplies to the Ho Chi Minh trail. She had done her work in the house. There was no point ruining her morale."

"*Her* morale?"

"We don't have a morale to ruin here in the south. We only talk over lunch with our friends in the daytime, and let them fight the war against us at night. It's a matter of civilized retreat."

The mayor went on about the open secrets of the war – that his wife was sneaking rice at night to the VC, that she was starting to have her doubts about the government. All this was said calmly, as if he were sorting out pencils at the Paris peace talks. I could see that he had suffered internally – the king who dies when the land dies – but this suffering had produced a kindly hauteur, a serenity.

They went on about his daughter's friend, an eleven-year-old girl who probably made bombs for the VC and may have blown up a local theater hall where South Vietnamese *linh* stayed, but he called her a "sweet-tempered child." Then he detailed how the north would eventually unify the country, as surely as the seasons. Unfortunately his specifics for the future were almost completely wrong – the wrong year, the wrong sense of a final cataclysmic battle with Americans; every factor clearly understood except what would happen even ten minutes after he spoke.

"We must prepare for our graceful disappearance," he said, "provide for our country. I am polishing the silver for the new tenants."

I never saw him again. I understand that he died the next year, but never was arrested. His daughter wound up a boat person floating into Hong Kong.

KIEN-GIANG, VIETNAM, 1974

Increasingly, I was seen at coffee bars. Crowds at these tiny cafés would spill out on to the street. Women there serviced troops from Korea, Australia, Vietnam, but most of all, Americans – and most of all on American paydays every first and fifteenth.

They were called coffee bars after the French, and if you squinted, the French brasserie might look familiar: French coffee served, wine, that "33" beer made by a French brewery still in Vietnam, a few tables outside hugging the street. Indoors, they were rarely more than fifteen feet across, with tiny tables and seats often no taller than two feet high, cut from tree trunks.

This was, in a sense, the theater of war – or simply theater *as* war. Kien-Giang was a seaport two hundred miles from Saigon, closer to Thailand than the fighting ("two hours" from the fighting). Even news from the north barely penetrated the city.

The August rains ended late that year. Vietnamese celebrated Tet Trung Thu, a Chinese holiday, with paper dragons and cakes, and lights strung out over many houses. Under the full moon, children marched through the city carrying thin staffs, lit by tapers, covered by paper stars or fish. The wooden houses with grass roofs of the poor had changed very little; a few had white tile roofs instead, in simple nests of blue, white and yellow buildings, with an occasional cement mansion or store. The doors stayed open in the moist heat, and neighbors ran into each other's homes regularly. At five, after dinner, the women gathered on the curbs to chat and watch the almost continual flow of people. Little Hyundai 650 two-seater motorbikes puffed along, with only the occasional car. The rare GI walked a head taller, in an invisible tunnel, speaking to no one, trained to look straight ahead, as if the muscles of his eyes were impaired. Many of the wealthier mothers took their children on 650s to the beach in the daytime. At night, women and families knew to stay inside, often listening for strange sounds. That was when the rattle of guns, and symptoms of the war became unavoidable.

On the sixteenth, a girl alone without family named Hue, who worked as a bar whore, was warned that an American named Mitchell was out to kill her, to get his money back. On the seventeenth, she came to me for advice, to beg for my support. That same day, a twelve year old boy tossed hand bombs into a bus, killing two Vietnamese soldiers. A few weeks later the boy was caught, and threatened with a beating. He was taken to a small room. The arresting sergeant promised to keep him from harm; soothed him, manipulated him. The boy confided in the man, and two more children were caught the next day.

The war against the enemy was actually fought a few hours northwest, at the older port of Ha Tien, or so one supposed. With the rains over, the mountains waited as placidly as a silk painting; they made a good calendar picture – a rich peacock green, with mounds of undergrowth. Inside, the Viet Cong were stationed. Daily, South Vietnamese soldiers marched into the mountains, always reluctantly. A few days later, many would return, swearing they had gone to the assigned position. The lieutenant would smile, and write it all down. Paper grew into mountains also.

Only the man who had no family left alive, or was too poor to protect himself, might actually find himself shooting at a Communist in the mountains. After thirty years, one had to try to be sensible.

Everyone in Kien-Giang would agree that few tried harder to be sensible than I did. As nature's nobleman, from a Chinese family considered equal to the old Vietnamese aristocrats, I felt safe enough to dabble, you might say. Like a manorial overlord, I decided, naïvely of course, to protect some of the lower life in the city, at the coffee bars. When the unprotected woman Hue asked for my help I was flattered, completely taken in.

I gave the girl 500 piastres, and told her not to feel obligated in return. Then, I warned her to stay in her house, and consider herself "on leave" for a few days. You can imagine how contritely she thanked me – strange to consider now, with all that came out of that, even years later.

On the fifteenth of September, Hue had left the Lan Quan Thuy bar with a GI, who was probably nervously gesturing to her, because she understood little or no English. His name was Mitchell, and he was white, which made him even more vulnerable somehow. She took Mitchell to her room, and neglected to tell him about the men in her family who had died over the past thirty years of war.

She let the night move like simplicity itself, like a magazine story on the will of Americans to fight for Asia. While he slept, she took his clothing and his money.

In the morning, she waited across the street, to see Mitchell's response. She saw her window slam open. The GI was roaring mad, in his shorts, screaming at everyone who looked up at him from the street. He waved frantically for an MP. A Vietnamese QC came, then left smiling.

Of course, there was an investigation, limited to a single sheet sent to the Vietnamese FBI at Kien-Giang. Another GI had been rolled by another tiny Vietnamese prostitute, from another coffee bar. The widow Lan, who owned the bar, had nothing to say to QC or Vietnamese FBI except that a wealthy Chinese was protecting her, and they should be polite.

The paper was filed by the chief of staff of the Vietnamese FBI. Another report was being buried with full honors by a ranking officer. Then, the chief of staff had to swallow a lecture by a peasant field officer, saying that Vietnamese should let Americans drink whiskey in Vietnamese homes. Imagine that. Simply because Americans owned the telephone company, and were still building military roads.

I heard it said that "Dai is blessed. He has more than a man could hope for." And generally I agreed with them, but what was I getting out of it? I could sense their eyes punching holes through the walls as I, a lowly Chinaman, left for lunch with the chief of staff; or when a car came to take me home. And what a home it was: many homes, even venerable ones, as venerable as the family, arriving rich from China a hundred years ago, and working hand-in-glove with the old families and the French.

I prided myself on never speaking to an American. It was assumed that I would never have to be indulged in that way. My family had bought (through bribery) one of the greatest honors possible for a man of esteemed family, who also happened to be recruited into the army. Not only did I avoid twenty-four hour details, I rarely left a downtown office. Every morning, at 7.30, I went to work as a janitor for the Vietnamese FBI. I would arrange the papers on the chief of staff's desk, usually into utter incoherency, but this was forgivable. At lunch, he and I would joke about how badly I worked – and argue about bribes. But he never got past the guarded language, and implied threats.

"Give me your opinion," he asked. "Do we let Americans drink whiskey with us? I still remember them swimming nude at Ha Tien." His mind went back to families in 1966 leaning over a bridge while American sailors, unaware that we were sensitive to such bizarre behavior, took plunges naked into the water directly at the entrance to the harbor – "waving hello with their cocks" some called it.

"Hardly," I answered. "Only my in-laws drink with Americans. I think our solution is to keep fatter files. That's always the solution."

"On the matter of fatter files, I shouldn't be mentioning this, but I've been told you protect widows in coffee bars."

"Are you short the money to protect a widow vo be of your own?"

"The Americans will ask for reports on the coffee bars."

"Tell them the reports are in Vietnamese. Put the folders in the Chinese alphabet. We've lost files before."

"The case has gone to the war office [he was lying]. Do you know the GI's plan to kill that little girl who took their money?"

I let that go. A day later, he pushed a little farther:

"I've never been very good at living in the present," he confessed, more than once actually, and always while he was eating. "But you, on the other hand, live as if the present were paid in full... The privilege of birth..." (an approving smile, then an added military stare that tried to suggest how tough he was).

"Is something missing? Something I owe?"

"I can't say for sure what's missing, not yet. Something has to be requested first, and not turn up, about a woman at a coffee bar as a VC. Something has been missing from my desk, something not put in my hand."

I stared at his hand, at the missing information, and came up blank. His eyes quivered strangely. He was slowly going crazy.

"Let's guess then." I said. "I pay you a bonus every month. I remember your family on special holidays, so special no one celebrates them but you. What else is missing today?"

"You don't see what I'm getting at?"

"No."

"You're embarrassing me."

"Embarrassing you? Tell me what you want?"

No response. I felt like an embezzler with amnesia. What could embarrass a man like that? There were rules set up for me to ignore, just for show. And then there were rules that everyone ignored. Failing that, there were rules we all pretended existed, like those files that kept getting lost. That was my theory of diplomacy and surveillance. It was madness at a slow boil, never a rolling boil. Still, I sensed – rightly – that from that day forth, I could not be assured of his help, no matter how many bribes I gave.

That was my first "official" verbal warning, that VC were in the night air where I went (they were wrong about where they were, but that hardly mattered). Afterward, I began to lose sleep over an unnamable sense that something in the mail was coming to get me, a letter, or a bomb, or children with hand bombs.

I went to *quan thuy* at night, where I could feel the opera of the war more directly. At the Lan Quan Thuy, near a parking lot, as so many *quan thuy* were, I could watch the Americans spend their money desperately every first and fifteenth of the month.

Americans would try to get my attention. They thought I might speak English because I wore linen suits from Italy. They gestured, and expected me to understand. They huddled together like a herd grazing. The sound of English speech was harsh, like fortifications thrown up to dam a stream, like old siege machines. It was built mostly with consonants, and came at you like cannon fire, or axes through the leaves of a tree.

I suddenly got more religious as well (the more useless the ritual, the better) – tradition to the letter, every prayer, every holiday, every ceremony to ancestors done with monkish severity. I imagined myself part of a dying dynasty, in my ceremonial smock (*ao dai*), black, worn long, down to my shoes like an elder. At Lan Quan Thuy, the women wore the peasant smock instead (*ao ba ba*), in white silk if they had some money, cut very short and smooth to their hips, with black stockings. Showing the lower thighs in black became part of their serf's uniform, as if even a breath from the man could be felt against their skin.

The widow who owned Lan Quan Thuy would not dress in black stockings. She wore her hair chopped to one side, like a penance, or a warning. Nonetheless, she had the miraculous blend I preferred, a long-legged mixture of French and Vietnamese. She preferred to dress in versions of European clothing – very inexpensive local versions – and never, but never, in the short white smock, the whore's uniform, where the hem made a shadow like a vagina along the legs. Not that she didn't dress to show herself off. In the wet heat, she wore sheer blouses cut quite low, like a moth's wings across her chest. But that did not change the facts: the widow Lan refused to show her legs, in stockings or otherwise, and when I noticed them, she invited me to stare at my drink instead. Her eyes were pouchy, exhausted. She was about to turn old, somewhere near forty; and yet, the more I watched her, night after night, the more I noticed her hands, her breasts, until she seemed to grow younger. Every night she left ten years younger.

She became a theater for me, along with the five women working for her, who knew my connections, and treated me like a sun king.

"I won't touch Hue," I said to Lan. "I'll protect her for you."

"For me? What does 'for me' mean?" She never permitted direct eye contact. She never suggested that I approach her.

Women who worked in *quan thuy* were already protected by the *dudeng* (pronounced "yudang" – from the slang for gangster). Like a deadly insurance assessor, the *dudeng* arrived each night at one o'clock. He was the only man who was considered more dangerous than the army.

I found out his name was Quy, and I studied the costume of his trade. He never wore any uniform. He tended not to beat the women. He set a fee, presumably fixed, but he could raise it as he pleased. Like Darwin's turtles, he was a creature of evolution, a twisted adaptation. Tens of thousands of widows had been stranded by the war. Millions of soldiers needed whores. There was no one to keep the game working smoothly.

Police never risked cruising the *quan thuy* – not the civilian nor the military police. According to records, presumably no crimes and no war went on there. *Dudengs* grew in the shade, between rocks. No Vietnamese soldier dared cross them, or even look at them. Everyone knew that Quy had a cousin who was a lieutenant colonel in the army; and could transfer offenders into the war. If you killed Quy, his cousin (who invested in Quy's business) would send someone after you.

Quy was the son of a sharecropper, like those who used to work my family's land, now lost. I was his class enemy, simple as that. I don't remember precisely what either of us said. I was that unconscious of how his rules went, until gradually I realized that he was staring at me every time he came to the *quan thuy*. He began to arrive wearing a Colt 45.

I could have left before he arrived each night. I tried avoiding him for weeks. But with no one to advise me, and no one who cared one way or the other, I finally decided to stop worrying, *dudeng* or no.

If this was a battle of wills, its subtleties were lost on me. Does a blink mean something, or a sudden grin? At the same time, the widow Lan avoided me even more than usual. And yet she seemed to flirt in the way she moved across the bar, stop with her back to me, position the sails of her dress for me to admire. The line of her leg made a fine arch – remarkably youthful, like a colt; much younger than her face.

I began to follow her during the mornings. It took two weeks for us to start talking. I should remember our dialogue here, I know, but it's drifting away. American movies always show couples talking before they act. I'd prefer to forget what I said at first, because it wouldn't help me much now. The charm of sexual encounters, skin and heat, helps me more – my memory at least. But even there, I get confused. She remained so composed, like the time she warned me: "I want a friendly business arrangement. With guarantees."

I vaguely remember how I talked my way past that, something like: "I guarantee a life with me as quiet and safe as a boat ride in a private lake. We'll watch from our lake to see if the world explodes, or wait some-where even farther away." Most of all I cannot visualize what in my face or my manner convinced someone like her to get interested, so experi-enced as she was; to let me protect her. Today, no matter what I do to spruce up, no matter how much I shave, or put on a youthful smirk, I can't imagine a smart woman taking me seriously. That option vanished with the war. I was invulnerable only when the world was collapsing.

I prefer to remember myself suddenly inside her, that initial astonish-ment, the skin first meeting, and skip my theories about whether I impres-sed her, how I deepened my voice to sound important, or made jokes about myself until I made her laugh (or feel a bit of pain for me). I invite Americans reading in English to write their favorite dialogue in the margins, about my technique (the easy smile, well-practiced, the light catching my hair, over-oiled) and her growing commitment, the change in her expression as she watched me – always watching for signs.

"I can pretend only for maybe two months that we're paddling down a river," she would say. "I'm just a soldier's widow paying for her clothing."

Before long, even before she let me have her, we were mistaken for a married couple by old women on the street; I gave it away simply by doting on her in public. I wasn't even aware that I was so obvious. In private I promised her too much, in long insinuating speeches, expensive speeches. I fed her, clothed her, finally became her lover. Yet the more I sweated inside her during the day, the more she avoided me at work.

In the nights when I was home with my wife, I still imagined the Widow Lan's shoulders in the corner of the room, as clearly as if she were there. She was a work of sculpture to me, particularly her hands and wrists, the curve of her neck, and the childlike narrower curve of her thighs, as if she were a young boy or a twelve-year-old girl. She always made me feel as if I were committing incest with her.

I am embarrassed to say that even the time I spent traveling to meet her often gave me a strong erection, before I even saw her. Do Americans discuss erections in public? One day she said:

"I was crying again about you. [What brought that on?] Maybe it wasn't you. Maybe I decided to make it you. I kept your shirt alone with me in bed, to sleep with your body smells near me. That may be a warning that it's time to get over you."

She acted as if it was a pleasure to cry about how bitter I made her; she discussed our misery about me with every living soul she could find, in the *quan thuy*, on the streets; and yet she kept us entirely a secret (so she said). Once she offered this plan:

"Let me find a boyfriend to go out with in public at night, so we can meet and fuck alone in the afternoons. That would satisfy you, and keep me safe."

I should have agreed, but instead I felt guilty. I sensed that the *dudeng* might be fucking her as well. She never would tell me precisely what favors she granted to keep him feeling in control, to balance the score with him. Since I was a married man in bondage to a hotel and five fishing boats, I couldn't, in good conscience, complain when she told me that the *dudeng* visited her too, though the image – his face beside hers – stayed with me constantly. She insisted that they were not lovers, quite sincerely repeated that the *dudeng* did not fuck her; but right after saying that, she asked me how much precisely I wanted to know – how much "really" – about what she did on the weekends by herself, and on nights when I was away? I kept silent, like losing a game of tiles (*au san*). She claimed that the *dudeng* had never wanted her physically until I came along, which meant that he was jealous of me; he became part of my drama, my opera about the end of the dynasty. He was paying me a strange but exciting compliment, a sickly bit of envy and denial. I accepted her story that they were not having sex. In fact, as I think on it now, I was preposterous.

Anyway, on 15 September 1975, a GI named Mitchell was rolled by the child Hue; that you know already. The GI stewed over it longer than most, and found his way back to Lan Quan Thuy, asking for a Leena or Lisa or Lucy, an English name that Hue gave only to Americans, to help them remember her; but of no meaning to Vietnamese.

"Hoa?" the Vietnamese at the bar replied, a bit slyly, knowing this word was improper. The word *hoa* – pronounced "Hh-Whaa" – translates as flower, bar slang for the vagina. What word this sounds like in English I cannot fathom, from the little I know. Perhaps "what," or "why." Mitchell was boiling.

"Hoa Phuong?" they added, to calm him down. That meant "red flower", Hue's nickname. Each *hoa* had its color.

Mitchell then brought Viet MPs along, who did not help either. They explained to him what *hoa* meant, in confusing English, and merely smirked their way through a report, until he stormed out.

The next night Mitchell came back. This time he found the *dudeng* waiting, leaning across the doorway, arms crossed. This usually was warning enough, but not in the American version of a war to save the world against communism. As if on patrol, Mitchell had brought friends to stand beside him, American "buddies."

After a few minutes of anxious quiet, the Americans started pounding their fists on the little tables at the coffee bar. It struck me how much like bulls fighting for grazing rights all this was, without a common language except growling and posturing. The *dudeng* gestured and screamed back, hopping like a grasshopper or a monkey prince.

The Widow Lan looked toward me, as Hue's wealthy supporter. She was *chi hai* – slang for women's protector, or "older sister," the one responsible. A Vietnamese soldier said something about me in English. I stood up reluctantly, as if to play the conciliator, never strong enough. I creep to my feet shyly whenever I speak to Americans. I go rigid, look weighed down with responsibility, and always with the same result: I get jumped on. Almost immediately after I stood up, I felt the crush of heavy bodies falling upon me. My head bounced off the linoleum floor as if I were just waking up. I'd been unconscious for a minute. Mitchell and his friends forced me up, and into the street, to find Hue for them. The stores around me looked vapory, while one American butted me on the forehead, like an ox butting a rail. They regularly beat me as we went, mostly slapping my face, and made gestures about the size of my body. Their uniforms looked like the skins of animals. I remember my ears bursting with blood when they shoved me forward, as if I were a little street boy to smack around. I had no control of my arms. I quivered when I felt their fingers, even their nails, pressing into the back of my neck.

Meanwhile, or so I learned later on, the *dudeng* was following them from a few blocks away. With him was a husky Vietnamese soldier who moonlighted as a hired gun of sorts (to pay for his wife's grocery store, he claimed). I can imagine him talking all the time, in a half whisper, about the war in the jungle. The man never stopped talking.

Storage sheds might be larger than Hue's tiny house. The water, brought in large canisters, took up most of one corner. An old wooden stove was kept shined and scrubbed in a tiny alcove that served as the kitchen.

Hue's family had moved away to Saigon, where it was safer, or so they believed. She had disgraced them by fucking soldiers. They now considered her dead to the family. Whenever I mentioned anything about her parents she literally spat with fury, about their greed, particularly now that there was no work on farms. They had been impoverished by the Communists, she claimed, because the great estates near Kien-Giang where they used to work had been threatened regularly by Viet Cong coming at night from the jungle, to forage, trade for weapons, or frighten off the great landlords. Rumor had it though that some of Hue's family, listed as missing in action, had in fact joined the Communists, even burned their own fields.

Hue tried spasmodically to tell the GIs about her life and sorrows, but her English was quite hopeless. I thought they might kill her. Instead, they looked for money, and began tearing apart the room. Then they kicked her, as close to her crotch as they could.

We were both forced to take off our clothes, and stand bloodied, our mouths twisted with pain as they watched, perhaps in erotic fascination. I remember wondering if they were masturbating, or planning to rape us. They stared at her breasts and my cock. Maybe they were considering what punishment was best. That sounds most likely. They barked, to let me understand the idea that I was "naked like a dog." Mitchell also had been left naked like a dog. An eye for an eye; now we would be naked the same way, and worse. They tossed both her clothes and mine out of the window, and took my wallet, while they ripped into shreds every bit of cloth they could find that looked like clothing. Finally, they marched out the door. As they left, I could see them headed nervously toward the department store lights and traffic of Nguyen Trunc Truc.

On an alley nearby, the *dudeng* followed them. They might easily have noticed him. I suspect they felt invulnerable once they were out among crowds. I can imagine them with boyish grins (they were still children after all, cubs with guns). I know they hired a three-wheeled bicycle taxi at Nguyen Trunc Truc. The drivers often puff and sweat at the pedals. I can visualize the light from the stores against the driver's wet face, while the GIs leaned over the side, long legs brushing the heels of their boots against the street, in a magisterial fantasy. The bicycle was certainly exposed: no windows, no roof.

As the bicycle stalled at a major intersection, there was faint backfire. One of the GIs was killed; shot through the chest. I've never seen someone shot, and only heard about it later. I suppose he slumped over, or tumbled sideways, because he fell out onto the street. Crowds gathered around the body. In the confusion, the taxi drivers left the GIs standing there. Belatedly, MPs arrived, like exhausted mailmen. Then ambulances struggled through the snarled traffic.

Once the body was taken away, the night swallowed the rest: witnesses, shootings. Traffic returned, as if it had been a rowboat overturned, now righted again. The GIs had been warned. Their childlike game was over.

I'd rather not explain how I managed to get back that night, huddled naked in a blanket. I was too embarrassed to go to work from then on. The news afterward was impossible to fix by bribes. In addition, the *dudeng* seemed to have a strange notion of how I fit into what he did. After ranging through the city all night looking for Lan, who'd disappeared, terrified that he might kill her next, he began to threaten me and demand money from me; but I was afraid to start paying him, especially after he tried to find me at the family hotel.

She was terrified. "You cannot ever let him make me wear the short *ao ba ba* in the street, or I will send someone after you."

Lan Quan Thuy was shut down, because I had hidden Lan, making me her sole support. There's a nice moment for an old man to remember, Lan growing even younger to me. The warmth of her back and shoulders under the blanket reminded me of one of my children. I needed her naked walking through a room, to watch the jiggle of her hips, each muscle alone. I can't explain how aware of each other's movements we became. "I'm getting lost here," she said. "The more you cut yourself off from everyone, the more confused I get." I grew frightened to walk in the street without her. And then, just as suddenly, no one assassinated us, as if the threatening weather stopped. *Dudeng* disappeared. But more than him, I worried about the army. I imagined them sending me into the jungle to fight, to bleed to death without helicopter cover (those *linh* without helicopters in the jungle were essentially sentenced to die, often as punishment without trial). But the army never went after me. The gears had stalled, as so often happens, particularly when a war is collapsing. I had no idea how chaotic the collapse had become. Soldiers were being executed merely as an empty drill. Others were not even noticed at all, no matter how close to the war they were – an erasure, like waves on an empty beach, rules and penalties back and forth, leaving no trace but wet sand.

A few weeks later, my father-in-law announced, quite suddenly: "We are going up to Dalat to avoid all this gangster business."

This was mostly to stall discussion of my sweaty afternoons with my flower – or with other *quan thuy hoa* they thought I was taking in (even though I'd sneak home at night, like a dog coming back after prowling through the back of a butcher shop).

"I'm lonely," my wife explained. "the more you show up, the lonelier I feel."

"You were lonely when you claimed we were happy," I replied.

I cried with her, grieving for our lost years together, and began to caress her back, uncertain whether I wanted her to get moist or not. I caught a glimpse of my sheepish look in the mirror. For two days, we were reconciled, but the impulse to leave returned the next afternoon, a fear that suddenly Lan would have had enough of me. I also couldn't stand my son's hostility to me, as if his anger were taking energy away that he needed just to go through the day.

Dalat was a mountain resort only a few miles from the North Vietnamese border. No more than five kilometers from heavy shooting, Dalat still remained fashionable, its roads in and out quite safe, as if tourism had antibodies against the war.

With imperial nearsightedness, the family packed for days. One servant was to be brought along. My wife began screaming that I was a Communist, that I was destroying her chance to present our family to General Thieu's relatives. I told her the general was probably getting ready to open a liquor store in California, which turned out to be literally true.

That did it. I'd spat on the flag. Members of General Thieu's family were expected at Dalat. With a severe heat wave in September, the exodus to cool places had stirred even President Thieu himself. My wife, bearing up well, was frighteningly low-key, while she had decided to make an effort to present herself glamorously to the Thieu family, as if Dalat were a summer palace, and the season were starting there. Did she think Dalat was Switzerland, I thought to myself?

"You haven't been to Switzerland any more than I have," she said, showing me her back.

"Meaning that you and that pig Thieu are more dignified than I am?" I answered.

We parried insults, most of which neither of us remember, just emptying our anger. How do Americans write in shorthand about fights that last for years, between people who never belonged together in the first place? She was reduced to saying, in three or four variations: "Who cares where you stick your cock? All it brings is loneliness. Like an insect spray. Stick it in *her* face. Give your dignity to her."

The family elders were planning to rewrite the marriage of our estates, make me pay where it hurts, by reducing my share of the hotel and the fish factory. So I moved first.

"I want to make a family announcement," I said. "I have decided to install a mistress."

"A what?" my father-in-law screamed, surprised even that I would call Lan a mistress.

"Say what you please," I added.

"I certainly will. Do you plan to install her here at the hotel?"

"The rooms really aren't up to my standard."

My father woke up after that comment, like an insulted maître d'. He seemed to snap out of a lizardlike or syphilitic doldrum. "You want me dead too?" he asked, staring me down pathetically. "Never exceed your father," he reminded me.

For the moment, he forgot the mistress he had brought home when I was six, to my mother the second wife, who in turn had to appease the sour sisters my grandfather had taken in as concubines – aunts tearing at each other's throats while the lords complained.

"Go give the Viet Cong our hotel while you're at it," he added. "Give them *our* hotel."

A new use of the possessive case: "*our*" hotel. To him business ownership was a part of speech, the mercenary case. How bizarre, I thought: My father had become more bourgeois; my wife had become more genteel. And both in the worst possible way, and in the worst possible clothing.

I said they all looked like tourists from Hong Kong.

"Hong Kong? Hong Kong?" my father-in-law was sarcastic. "You swinging a business deal for us now?" He gave me a rude pinch on the cheek. "Ah leave him be. A few days in Dalat, he'll be fine."

"But I'm dead serious," I kept insisting. My eyes must have stretched as wide as cooking pans.

"Listen," my father-in-law added, rather gently, "I try to swallow all this screwing around, the old families, your father's whores. But really, my own daughter; my own flesh and blood. I could have you murdered."

"You too? A *dudeng* wants me murdered."

"That's the one. He offered to kill you for a thousand piastres. Listen to what I say. A thousand."

"A month's groceries. Take it out of the dowry if you're short."

"He's gone mad. Look at those eyes rolling in his head."

"Clearly, and maybe dangerous."

"What's the point of all this?" I asked. "The Communists are going to win in a matter of weeks. You might find yourself under a bomb in Dalat. With Thieu. Especially with Thieu."

The war was as reliable as an endless drought or a long-term investment. That the war might dissolve away was unthinkable. Where was the evidence that it was shutting down? Just because Americans had reduced their troop strength a little? No American president could give up Vietnam. My father-in-law was finally forced to sum up: "He doesn't even understand business."

The family howled at me, circled viciously. My father, the bloodshot roué, cried foul. My father-in-law, the real-estate dragon, wounded like a cuckolded husband. His daughter, my wife, fainted in the daintiest way she knew – head into her knees, down into a chair, based on movies she liked. Her mother observed me tragically. She had long since vanished into a world of cooking noodle dishes with the servants. Her mother yapped an insult once she had the strength, rotating her teeth in her mouth. She was senile, with occasional lucid moments of cruelty – mostly connected to the way her new teeth fit. And there were cousins I barely knew who had things to say.

I was abandoned, to destroy myself in a heatwave. The family left the next day without me on a bus to Dalat. Surprisingly, the family attorney went as well. Even as the transmission ground along (low in fluid), and the bus bounced past the humps in the road, the family was making legal arrangements to fortify itself against my mistress, my mountebank.

Between the women moaning, and waves of hatred mixed with flashes of tolerance, I can hear my father-in-law asking "Where is that boy living: what planet?"

"We have investments," he would say, "a future in Vietnam. This is the new Korea. Fifteen per cent growth annually for the next twenty years."

"But for the time being," my father jumped in, "we must invest in the bear economy, isn't that so, brother?" He was protecting himself (he thought) by using business jargon, like a man forced to order in a foreign language.

He knew that eventually the venom would turn toward him too – that much was inevitable – to complaints about his own earlier indiscretions. He would have to chafe under a flood of moralists, and half-forgiveness, and to insults about his own son like "The boy is an asshole, if you pardon my frankness."

"You noblesse confuse me," my father-in-law finally had to declare. "I'm getting a little sick of this 'Tho Ong Ba' (ancestor ceremonies). Do we need a twelve-thousand-piastre wedding feast every time some anniversary for the dead comes along? Does that wash away the sins of the children? Hypocrites. Don't expect us to forget this."

In return, my father would argue for patience. He feared that he might be thrown out along with me. He even tried to protect me, asking for a last shred of kindness, his own version of playing the bear economy. Meanwhile, up in Saigon, among the creaky remains of the military government, plans for complete evacuation were being made, but details withheld from the rest of the country, in a last attempt to save face at the expense of the body.

There was a universal hrrumph, as the bus finally reached the mountains near Dalat, under a cooling mist.

By the time they came back, I was already local gossip back in Kien-Giang. Had there been gossip columnists allowed, they would have dogged my steps I suppose, described my mistress's choice of makeup – overdone – or how I preferred to wear linen suits when I took her bathing – perhaps to blend in with the white paint on the buildings, in case someone took a shot at me in the daytime.

I certainly avoided taking carriages through any streets where I might get shot. And I knew that my mistress would be offered a bribe to leave me. Formality required. And I could see her concern for both of us, in the way she stacked a single bundle of our clothes in a closet, to speed our escape.

I would brush her cheek gently, then flop carelessly on the modern couch in the sun room. I admired the line of studs propping the window frame. With the best feigned boredom I could muster, I would open the casement that looked out into the country garden. I spent the daylight mostly in the garden, vertical and still, as if I were another fruit tree pruned by gardeners for generations. I saw no one socially any more, and enjoyed what I thought was the sunset of Vietnam, planning how I might leave for America, or for Hong Kong, if I could release any money from my frozen accounts.

Lan had become an expert on my strange mood. She adored me as a mother does an older child, when the child is ignorantly discussing the world, getting the facts upside down. I do believe that momentarily at least, she stopped thinking of our arrangement as financial, and showed a faint interest in our welfare as a couple. That involved some self-control, given her history. Her husband had died in his twenties in 1969. He had left her childless, with three years of marriage to erase, and no family to protect her.

Now she had thirty dresses, each more impossible than the next, ridiculously assembled according to the green in her eyes, the slice of European, the wonder of long legs, the insubstantiality of our time together.

She was shrewd enough not to be frightened away too soon, even after my family cut me off, forcing me to live off a pale inheritance. She knew the *dudeng* might be parked a block away, like a frog waiting on a leaf.

One day, six weeks into my idyllic breakdown (my favorite of at least three breakdowns), my wife suddenly appeared at my door. She looked squat and tired, in too much pink, but clearly more forgiving than I might expect. This took some courage, and I believe I sent the wrong messages to Lan by welcoming my wife, noticing her earrings, and eating from her basket of U cakes, even while we fought and worried each other, particularly about how I might stay alive.

"You should go to Hong Kong or Thailand," my wife suggested. "Change your name the way *nha du* have." I have to explain this: It was illegal for a soldier to leave Vietnam, except under an alias, "*nha du,*" which made them impossible to track. So great was the confusion of false identities that erasing someone's existence was not very expensive. Many families helped their children acquire aliases.

I asked my wife to try to arrange a new name for me, with thanks, and reminded her that the war was ending in a month anyway, a friendly warning, though I could sense her doubt on that score. "Your first son has been screaming for you in his sleep," she said.

I realize that I have said very little about my children, particularly about my oldest son, who was eleven at the time. I was still allowed to see him occasionally, and we would talk about the world he thought he was entering. A nightmarish sensation was overtaking him, but he always protected himself, by forgetting what he dreamt at night.

"Are you having nightmares?"

"Yes."

"About what?"

"About... faces. I can't remember."

"What are the faces like."

"I know how they look at me."

"Do they talk to you?"

"I can't remember."

He started to have dreams of me dead; then he asked to see the enemy corpses who were deposited at the hospital, probably to convince himself that there was a tangible body as object left behind, beyond a smell like mulch, from cut grass.

This request of his bothered me for days, but he asked more than once. Finally, I took him to the street of the army hospital. The bodies of dead Viet Cong were placed on display out at the entrance, like a Wednesday market, to prove that the war was being won. He walked up to one of the corpses of a fourteen year old, the face sunken, the eyes deep in their sockets.

"I thought they were jungle people," he said suddenly – meaning ape-like I guess, not the body he saw, who looked like him but in a crooked sleep; the head thrown back like a sack held together by string, and jaundiced.

"His hair isn't braided," he noticed, then moved his face closer, as if to jam his foot inside an imaginary door. The dead boy's hair was short, also like his own. This panicked him, I could see. He would not survive easily what was coming.

I was responsible for this weakness, for the weak back that doctors diagnosed, for that clumsy colt-like movement, the uncertainty that enclosed him, the nervous peeks he took at his scrawny reflection when he passed store windows.

The next month I went into penance, without realizing it. I removed every pleasure that came free, changed my diet, away from anything

French, no wine, no morning coffee. I withdrew steadily from Lan, first by consuming her with attention, out of guilt, until all we talked about was my feelings toward her – a sure sign of the collapse of what little we had. We began to strangle together. I started to talk constantly of the image of my son sleeping badly at night, tossing and turning. I had lost my chance to learn what my son was dreaming about while he slept.

News spread that I was offering one of the family fishing boats for trade in contraband with Viet Cong – tribute I thought to the men who would be running my world soon. I even arranged a meeting between a VC and my family, to convince my father-in-law, suddenly a patriot, wearing everything but gloves and medals. Consider, I explained, what an opportunity we were missing, money sitting like unclaimed mail on the street. It was well known that at least a tenth of all American supplies found its way to the Viet Cong, usually at discounted (stolen) prices, but still for high profit. Better to invest in the winners, I went on, rather than in cement and fish soup. Why give even more loans to friends in the army, who stop paying, and send their money to America? Losing the war was a growing industry, but you cannot invest in the wrong side. My father-in-law asked me what I meant by "losing." How could incurring a loss be a good investment? There the conversation stopped. I think I meant "losing" as in "fading," a recision, like paper fading in sunlight, or the shoreline retreating. That's how the daily normalcy of *losing* the war felt.

Crews of port thieves were a familiar institution. Woman made a living as *shils* to seduce the guards at the docks, while the warehouses were plundered. Sabotage was legitimate tithe for the war. I went through the facts to my father-in-law, then looked up to see that he was studying my face instead of my argument – my state of mind, the shadows under my eyes, not the state of the war – or the clean and nervous VC I brought from the barber shop. I told my father-in-law that here in this young man was a bear market if ever there was one.

I would visit the barber shops where information from Viet Cong was passed very openly. I used to see agents from my office there, listening as FBI counter-intelligence, for whatever feeble good that did. The FBI were more interested in locating faces than in learning military secrets. There weren't military secrets left any more anyway, only erasures, comments in pencil rubbed out, and new bits scribbled in. The secrets were open; the obvious was hidden. My trips to the barber were very open, and were added to reports, then crossed out or simply drowned under a pile of paper.

Hints about my subversion did reach the army brass eventually; not all that quickly, even though I was easy enough to find. I spoke about what (in military terms) must be called subversion to agent Do Huong (my wife's second cousin); I spoke at least twice that I remember, while we were both having a haircut; he wrote down what I said in what he considered a favorable light (though I was talking treason), then forwarded it to our FBI. Even after that, no one came after me for weeks. There was hardly time at the FBI even to count up how many subversive leaks were flooding their office. The elite corps of army spies, the insiders called "*an-ninh*" were themselves beginning to collapse; eager career *an-ninh* from small villages began escaping in all directions like the rest of us.

Finally, one of the last loyal *an-ninh*, his uniform sewn to his body, did arrive at the family hotel. He carried some of my file, like a hot lunch from home, and asked for a bribe. I wasn't there, or anywhere to be found. I had been kicked out of the hotel, out of the shipyards; and was in hiding – eating badly and without a change of clothes – in a narrow, sweaty room provided by Lan. But apparently my relatives at the hotel paid him off anyway, a tender act of mercy, or tribute again, to keep my problems from spreading to someone else. Afterward, officially my papers were lost, for the second time. I was formally scribbled out, an invisible statistic, one of the uncounted.

Meanwhile, in Saigon, the news of the end of the war had reached everyone who had the money to leave. But no final reports came for weeks to the most southerly towns like Kien-Giang. Nonetheless, I still tried to convince my family, slim as the evidence was. But the more I struggled, the more they seemed convinced that I was ruining their financial plans. After a while they started to convince me that the facts were missing. I began to doubt whether I had ever understood the war at all.

On 9 January 1975 Lan was offered a bribe through a go-between hired by my family. It was a sloppy business. The go-between was fat from an illness. One corner of his mouth seemed paralyzed, perhaps from a stroke. The more he sat up straight, the worse he looked in his suit. He tried to impress her with a rich man's accent but spoke with too much patois, and in a slushy voice because of that half-frozen mouth. Even his gold watch was too polished, too much like a shiny button on a waiter's uniform. And his compliments cut the wrong way:

"Your hair looks elegant tied up," he said. But her hair was knotted because she hadn't washed it. She had decided to look like a poor *chi hai*. Who blames the poor? He complimented her incorrectly about her shoes.

Those were her old pair, again *chi hai*. She was determined to impress him by her destitution, to show that she was not spending all my money. He didn't give up paying her compliments though. The worse they got, the harder he tried. He told her she walked as easily as a bird, which she did, but in his slang "bird" could also mean a man's penis.

When it came to bargaining, however, he was a changed man, smooth as glass, so graceful he soon looked almost handsome, fat as he was. He started his pitch when Lan asked: "Will the family give me money enough to start over in Hong Kong?" He answered as if he were a salesman who knew her family. He pretended to level with her, his eyes straight ahead, never blinking:

"I'm supposed to lie to you about money. Everybody lies to you. They sent me to lie. The family claims they're totally broke. Do we believe that?"

"We?" Was he a relative suddenly? He planted his shoulders in a straight angle to the table. He squeezed her hand as if he were slipping her a theater ticket, and added: "They claim all their money is in cement."

"In cement?"

"I can't promise you much that isn't made with cement. Do you want an acre of concrete poured over anyone?"

He laughed, eyes squinting and wide apart like a pie. Then he checked her expression, and settled into the smile of a relative, pausing between words:

"They don't care about either of us. We have to find our own way to deal with them."

All this talk was background music, buying time to study her movements carefully. He kept his stare pinned to her eyes like an electronic alarm system. She in turn studied him too, *chi hai*, judging what he intended by how he advanced his body against hers. She watched the movement of his arms when he leaned toward her. His stomach rolled like a barrel in water. After they bickered in a friendly way over price, about how little my family would pay, he gave her a reassuring rub, one of those pretended accidents, faintly near her thigh, followed by another earnest squeeze of her hand. Then came more background talk, more speechifying in that slushy voice, about how he hated being put in this situation, hated it just as much as she did.

"I want only one thing from you," she said, "a fair exchange. A favor to a woman who leaves in poverty, as we both know."

"Yes."

"I want to be guaranteed that I can leave the country on the same plane you do, as safe as you are. I am convinced that the war has only a matter of hours left."

Whenever I think of her shoulder to belly with him, I get sexually aroused – pathetic to admit at my age. I see myself in a pornographic illustration, as a Biedermeier silhouette of an old man with a hard-on. I'm in profile staring through a keyhole.

Lan often used to talk to me about her taste in young men, to prove she had someone exciting on the side when I was away, as a balance to my marriage – not that she had sex with them, but that she had offers from twenty-five year olds, "remarkably mature." Her smile went sour as she spoke, but her stories about young men, even naked young men, taking advantage of her excited me. Then she would turn her misadventures into a compliment to me, by saying that I was still young enough to compete, stroke for stroke, that maybe she would take an older boyfriend for show, and we could fuck together in secret all afternoon. When she spoke, she would arch her neck, to keep her chin looking slim, like a cut flower wobbling in an oversized vase, trying to stay fresh a little longer, knowing my imagination would do the rest, find something in the curve of her mouth (a tiny heartshaped mouth) or the soft turn of her arm. Her hands were extremely small but muscular, already a bit veiny with clawlike fingers, clearly aging. Sex with her was a brilliant necrophilia. Every moment was almost the last. You stayed inside as long as you could, to watch her beauty vanish while she held on. Her legs were still extremely youthful, and the turn of her hips a bit veiny, even flabby. She was a requiem, but she grasped my back with a firm, thrilling touch.

I can see those long fingers, and tiny wrist, but I see them buried inside the fat palm of that go-between, on his lap, round as a well-made bed, near his cock. I remember what she told me about him later on. She said she never accepted my family's bribe, because the "timing was wrong." The phases of the moon warned her to stay with me a bit longer, or was it the direction of the wind that day? That excuse about the moon worked on me like a sour cough. And yet, illogical as it was, I was still profoundly, even melodramatically, grateful. She had sacrificed money to give us a few more good weeks together. Then, like a rip you suddenly notice in the lining of a coat, it became clear that she expected something in return – action from me, a plan for leaving at least. That's a guess; precisely what she wanted I couldn't be certain. It was never clear whether she wanted only a flight out, or simply a narcotic final month, or just to have me sleep with my mouth closed and stop snoring. I offered to take her as a second wife, and she bluntly refused. She never made it clear whether she wanted me to treat her less like a wife, or more like a wife. Her eyes would narrow, as if she were reading the small print on a contract. I hadn't seen her eyes show so much doubt before. "You're sinking in your own bathtub," she would say. Me sinking? I started to dress for breakfast. I romanced her more lavishly, so theatrically it gave me mild chest pains. I began to feel awkward with her, even though for once I meant every kind word I said. Finally she grew very cool. "You're six weeks too late with that," she told me. "And you know why, don't you?"

"Of course I do," I said, "I've known for months," though I had no idea what improvidence she was talking about. Was it a young boy she knew, or a fight we had? Perhaps some other romance altogether. The distance couldn't be made up. Now, sitting here more than fifteen years later, I suddenly realize what shit I made of her. She wasn't interested in mothering any more. I can't explain my problem any better than that. We broke off in that civilized way when the woman is glad to be done with you, but enjoys watching you suffer a little longer.

That's when she insisted – in tears – that she never let the fat man give her money, that she had refused fifty thousand piastres. She had asked for ten times that, to break it off with him. However – and this brings me back to my Biedermeier memory – on the day I gave her up, this go-between was waiting to drive her away. I saw his fat Oldsmobile nearby, as upholstered as he was, with fenders as polished as his watch.

I don't see the point in telling you what happened next. I prefer erasing that image of her leaving. I'd rather leave a space for the blank that followed, when I returned to the bosom of my family, like a marsupial animal into the pouch. There was contempt waiting for me there, as you would expect, so much contempt that even argument seemed impossible, only a knifelike silence. My wife stared at me the way a nurse checks a patient, to see if I was developing a cough, or looked ready to leave the room. But I wasn't ready, and didn't know why. I would spend hours talking with my son, trying to calm him down. In spite of all that had happened, I still remained a mystery to myself.

However, I kept my manners, like a man who slept with a crease in his pants. I was a polite hotel guest. Rather than be grilled like a teenage boy I stayed clear of the mess, learned to walk along the walls. I became as neutral as furniture. Let them invest until they drown in cement, I thought to myself. But doubts creep in when all you do is listen. I began to wonder if my father-in-law might be right; that this twilight of the war might go on another twenty years. My doubts were exhausting me. It got me so sleepy I nearly dozed with food in my mouth while I ate. This seemed to encourage my wife, who thought my blank expression meant that I was healing. Meanwhile, the family continued to sink their cash deeper into real estate and fish processing, part of a five-year plan. More money was added for buildings not built yet.

"Why not buy up land to invest in more cemeteries for the war dead?" I suggested.

We did not know this at the time, but we were simplifying our own burial at sea. We were going to be buried in a sea of cement. Capital was supposed to free up by 1977. Vietnam was on its way to becoming another Taiwan or Korea.

In a muffled voice from another room, I heard myself reconsider: "On second thoughts, never underestimate the power of a business rebound." Heads turned. Good thought. Yes, Vietnam might make a rebound. I even had an investment dream that same night, filled with prophesies about a business upswing: cement buildings rose like the gates to an emperor's house; fish jumped into our boats, and all were wrapped in towels signed, like checks, from our hotel. I may have misremembered the last part, embroidered the towels a bit; still, I was impressed that I remembered any of the dream at all. I repeated it to my wife, who started to trust me, slowly, like a houseplant bending toward the window. I was encouraged, and inside of two weeks (with my usual bad sense of timing) I stopped reminding them that the war was just about over, and that we should leave with whatever we could get our hands on. I lost track, and joined the faithful. With everyone else, I drifted unprepared toward late April.

The war ended only days after the family had tied the last of its assets into building futures, then waited like pilgrims for a business rebound, for the business buddha. Instead the war succumbed like a sick patient; it ceased. The patient died in the late afternoon of 30 April. At least that was the day it stopped for us (a day earlier for those in Saigon). News came in all directions, about people fleeing south from one ant hole after another. I left the city that evening, and tried to remain one step ahead of the Communist government. While I was away, my family decided to hold on even longer, to try to keep their businesses going.

Two weeks after the war, by mid May, the new government was taking shape. My father-in-law met an old friend he had known as a child, a man who had fled thirty years ago to join the Communist army up north. After the war stopped, every VC officer who had roots in the south was ordered to return to the town where he grew up, to organize the local government there. This was the new beginning. My father-in-law, trying furiously to remember details about this man who was from his childhood, set up a lunch with his old friend, who said, rather graciously:

"From Hanoi, I just received a message from my son. He told me that he and friends captured two American flyers after a B52 raid. My son, with other children did this. They packed up the Americans, and drove them in secret to where the bombs had hit, to show them what a B52 does on the ground. But suddenly the villagers saw the GIs, and began to rush them, to beat them to death. My son and the other children saved the American flyers from being torn apart. That is the new order. That is how we make government in Hanoi, and down here. There are no enemies."

At the meeting, the friend explained that very soon all the wealthy families would be stripped of their fortunes, even put into prison, for past crimes. At least that is the version my father-in-law took home. "The blue has turned brown," he said, of the brown colors worn in the north, and the sky blues popular everywhere. "We leave before it's too late." And my father-in-law's word was final. Everyone seemed convinced, but me.

"I know we've disagreed before," I said, "but was I entirely wrong? They're still outsiders in Kien-Giang. The new government has no one to run our factories, no one left. This is definitely not the time to drop everything we have, and run."

My wife nodded. That night, she and I argued, cried, and almost had sex again.

"I have some relations with these people," I said. "We can make deals."

"We?" she screamed back. "Which we? Am I part of we?"

I philosophized for ten minutes about "we," as opposed to "us," with one hand on her stomach, and another lightly fingering her breasts.

"Weren't we always we?" I said. "Like a rope knotted?"

"To hang us."

"You think they'll hang us? The Communists won't hang me. I'm guessing, of course. (My penis hardened, which I took to be a sign of my political shrewdness.) You seem to be lubricated. (I entered. She snorted, I grunted.) My connections say we can wait. They told me so yesterday, at the barber shop."

Only minutes later, I repeated this theory about VC at the barber shop, after waking up all the elders, now gathered in bathrobes. My father-in-law moved his head inches from mine, as if he were looking inside a mouse hole, into my skull. "I see nothing in what he says," he declared. His word was still final, as always. The family would be leaving by boat – with or without me.

I still pursued the matter. After some persuading, I got my wife to risk staying behind a few more days. And with her on my side, our first son stayed also. He clung to my shirt, while I looked boldly toward where I imagined the future lay, or the end of all futures. I felt prepared for the eclipse all around me; the end of laws, of schools, of marriages. I could live with dignity inside this chaos. I could donate my last few piastres to the widows, before they were re-educated. Afterward, if the chaos turned vicious, I would retire with my wife and children into modest exile in a small house; the last scrap left to me by the revolution (after I helped them dismantle the rest). Occasionally, when operations at our former factories might go sour, I could offer my modest services on behalf of the revolution, on call when needed. But otherwise, I would stay in seclusion at my diminished estate, which would be in ruins but still standing, a monument to the faded intelligentsia, like Gorky's farm (or was his farm faded?). Islands of safety around me would disappear, of course, but I had converted early enough to the VC. I only had to cut a deal with the four I knew from the barber shop.

Of course, my plan might fail. I considered the down-side, and imagined theatrical ways to die, rather ugly daydreams. For a time, I began to think that I was under arrest, subtly on trial, then secretly convicted. I saw myself tortured by VC children in my own lobby, while I tried to explain to them that I really had made every effort humanly possible to stop my father-in-law from investing in real estate; it wasn't my fault that he believed in the wrong kind of equity. Then I daydreamed that my first son was thrown into prison with me: I heard myself blubber out loud, all alone in the empty lobby, until I nearly woke up the neighborhood, now so suddenly quiet, with no clients, no hotel guests, traffic dead.

My wife came to stand by me, like the good Chinese woman in old sepia photographs, a bit of stylized family heroism. I imagined us posing for a photo. My hand was planted on her beefy shoulder. She stared submissively at the camera. My descendants a hundred years from now would say: thanks to me, her luck finally ran out.

The next morning, an hour before sunrise, my father-in-law left without us, even took my own father along (always the first out, the first mosquito through the door), and invited various cousins, until altogether the family was a group of eleven, with more that they met at the boat.

Our goodbyes were appropriately tearful. I remember thinking how much like a bad opera we must look. Then, with everyone gone, in that sudden vacuum, my wife and son and I found ourselves alone. They looked toward me, poor souls, while I prepared to take charge. But I stopped in mid sentence, like a crooked door unable to shut. I clasped my wife's shoulder. I told her what *noblesse oblige* meant, actually explained the French to her. By her terrified reaction, she was plainly already worrying about me.

My father-in-law had left with only a little money in his pockets, no gold. The rest was still sunk in Vietnamese futures, sunk as deep as a well. My mother in-law had taken only a few jewels along, the minimum; what little she could muster without looking too conspicuous, to avoid getting arrested. They took to the sea two hours before the sun, eighteen people altogether, on one of our fishing boats, to Thailand. They brought deep-sea nets along, hoping to build a new fortune once they arrived: steamed fish over Thai noodles. Everything else, even personal diaries and extra sets of clothing were left behind.

Their timing wasn't bad. Communists burst into our hotel literally at sunrise, two hours after the family took to sea. The front lock was removed by a soldier, and a sentry planted at the door. They motioned with rifle barrels.

"That was quick," I said to my wife. "If matters get out of hand, we can go into hiding. I know how to go into hiding. But first we collect what gold we can."

The weeks that followed were not as deadly as they looked from the outside, in newspapers I saw later. I was partly right about the early stages. The Communists were anxious to let the first thousands of us leave, so they kept the way out by sea fairly open. But I stayed on. That led to misunderstandings. The VC mistakenly thought that I knew precisely where the liquid assets of the family fortune were hidden. Otherwise, why was I there? However, financial secrets are hard to give up. My father-in-law was clever enough *not* to tell me where all his money was put. He told my wife, his daughter, but she grew afraid to let me find it. So began another circus of omissions.

A lieutenant with a badly tailored uniform, Soviet-made I suspect (or Chinese, definitely not Italian) interrogated me, relatively politely at first. "With your support," he explained, while he inspected the dishes for chips, "we can run those factories better than ever, with enough profit to repay all your debts."

Debts? Which debts I wondered? I tried to return a knowing glance, look as alert as I could.

"Who in your family will stay on to cover these debts?" he added.

I bargained as best I could, in complete ignorance of details; a true executive, relying on style. My friends among the VC, my advisors at the barber shops, were suddenly not around to help. They could not be found. To a man, they had been shipped back to Ho Chi Minh City to be troubleshooters; sent somewhere new every other month, everywhere but Kien-Giang. Telephones were down. Everything from beer to meat was rounded up.

At last it became clear that we were under house arrest, until a trial date could be set. That raised my doubts to full hysteria, twisting the muscles across my chest. That lieutenant stayed ignominiously polite, as if he were saving me for something, perhaps for last. They seemed more involved at this stage in rounding up dentists and automobiles than in imprisoning hotel owners who kept nodding at everything they said.

The food supplies in town sank, until we all ate like peasants with lice, sharing our best rooms with soldiers who mustered every morning and expected to be fed. This went on for two months. The lieutenant, prompt if not informed, came by every morning for a second breakfast – "the better breakfast" he always explained, giving me a complimentary pat on my back, the kind you reserve for head waiters. Then he proceeded with our chat. He was "helping me" (in his words) liquidate our family's hold-ings. My sense of it was that he was checking with me as each new article of the family wealth was found, to see if any coins had rolled under the moldings somewhere. The controls only tightened later on. But even later on, there were still boats available for escape in the dark (for a hefty price), and still ways to avoid the Vietnamese navy until you were far enough out to sea. My money to leave came from America, from family again.

I escaped by sea late in the summer, if escape is the right word, because this was the first time in my life I clearly could not escape. Each ship was a floating coffin, holding more than three hundred people; the hull itself felt like the shell of a giant lobster, with everyone frozen into a single body. The boat was terribly low in the water. It tumbled along as if it were about to crack in two, rising with the waves, and crashing flat against the sea. It circled in distress until there was no more fuel, until there was no sound except the moans of the timbers, the purl of deep water, and the breathing of three hundred bodies.

Like salvage, we were gathered up as we floated, and robbed by pirates – actually Thai fishermen doubling as patrols, working with the Thai coast guard. No one was raped, though I've heard stories of such things.

In the boat, I hallucinated, and the vapors of that instant have been with me ever since. I thought I saw my first son fall into the water and disappear. Then, just as suddenly I felt him return – a trifle wet, but quite warm – sitting beside me. However, his body was heavier, my younger son Binh. The older boy was simply lost.

In the months that followed, I heard so many grim tales about the pirates that I wonder if these who boarded us were imposters, only ushers at a theater; just as I wonder if I dreamt of my son drowning. I'm talking nonsense here: I know in fact that he died that afternoon. The stillness of his leaving was very plain. It left me amazed, more than anything else, until my chest began to burn as if he were screaming for air inside me.

The pirates took the boat, and every bit of jewelry or money sewn into jackets, jammed into stockings, even bits of gold hidden under tongues, or up the buttocks or vagina. Our boat was towed alongside, until we were deposited on shore, not exactly like tuna in nets, but more or less in the same spirit. Instead of nets, there were camps.

Our camp had grown from tents to makeshift shacks, a stew of people, nearly four thousand. Very quickly, we were devoting every minute to the most basic survival, like dogs waiting behind a butcher shop. The world shrank to a few meters, to gathering any scrap that could serve as toilet paper, much less food, to worrying about the drinking water, because it tasted either rusty or rancid.

I was surely hallucinating that my wife near me was imaginary in some way. The sensation is difficult to describe. For a time I could barely recognize her face. And my sleeping! I grew almost cataleptic, sleeping most of the day, staying close to our daughters, who never forgave me for my son drowning. It seemed a sensible adjustment to sleep, like hibernation. Around me, I saw the old men grow very feeble; the children paler, like leaves browning.

Over a period of two weeks, I forced my younger son to tell me what expressions my drowned son would have used about one thing or the other. I needed my son Binh to stay next to me continuously. I clung to him to avoid speaking too much. Meanwhile, Binh kept talking about his aunt, my wife's sister, who ran a grocery store in Saigon, where he had stayed for a few months, and about being sent back to us by bus alone. In stages, he grew terrified of falling asleep, imagining always that he might be robbed or attacked. He was much fatter than my first son, but moved with an awkwardness that kept reminding me of the other's face, as if one were still buried inside the other. To help Binh sleep I pretended that I knew stories about the old Chinese, and we played together, without much sadness.

Binh told me his version of a folk tale – *Tam Cam*, an old fable about "tam" the lovely sister, and "cam," the nasty sister. It was a story that kept us together for days, like a diary. Once in a forgotten time, he said, a good sister was murdered by her evil sister, who then by trickery, married the Prince. The Prince missed loving the good sister, but for that reason, could be fooled. To help him enjoy being fooled, once the evil Cam was queen she actually took her dead sister's clothes, and dressed up that way to confuse and excite him at night. However, in time the spirit of the dead sister came back, first as a bird. The evil queen went into a rage, and had the bird killed. Seasons passed. The good sister's spirit came back again, this time as a tree. But the evil queen had it cut down, the branches burned, and the ashes spread. The erasure was still not thorough enough. Tam's spirit survived. Her ashes fertilized another tree. And this tree bore fruit, whose rind was burned and mashed into a preserve which was kept a secret from the evil queen, stored in jars, and sold by an old woman, who prospered.

By this time, in fact, the evil sister had died, and was little missed. People lost track. And with no one left to remember, the good spirit of the lost sister – inside those jars – remained a secret, and in a few years was forgotten altogether. As a salty preserve, it finally was eaten by the good prince himself, who still grieved for his childhood sweetheart, and was strangely refreshed. So all ended well for Tam, if a little too late.

Binh stopped suddenly. His version sounded wrong. He had run astray. I tried to correct the story, but I myself wasn't quite sure how it went, which rind and which ashes, except that somehow the prince had to resurrect Tam in person, in her young body, and marry her, or at least keep her in a jar by his bed, and whisper to her for advice. A soothing dizziness took me over; the surrounding light poured over me like an underwater green, or a very misty dark blue.

Later, the tent was rained through, and we all had to sleep standing up. In the dry months, snakes climbed in with us under the blankets. The floor was grass, with sleeping pallets so thin that every stone bruised you as you lay, between dozing. Lines for water at the rusty pump – barely pouring – went on for hours. The camp finally revealed to me what the war had been like for thirty years – a delayed impact, but just as devastating.

I saw Lan there. I think I saw her, much thinner, with her hair tied back. That was when I first began to think about Lan again. I waited at the same spot for her, without luck, until I had to stop. Just standing still too long among the milling people was an invitation to get punched or kicked to the ground, mostly by former Vietnamese soldiers. Without orders, or a war, they were trying to invent a new pecking order, based on who gave pain to others. If you looked blank and stopped in the wrong place, eventually one of a small cadre of angry soldiers might release his frustrations on you. Only a few dozen did the damage, mostly on days before food arrived, when the hunger literally tore inside to the bone. It made many of us faint, and left some soldiers strangely energized but disoriented, as if on a drug.

While we lingered between meals, Binh would always complain that families near us were screaming too loud. They were reading their mail, and the news was grievous. He asked me to speak to them: I heard from them about other children who drowned, were swallowed *en route* to Thailand; and began to realize I was listening to them talk about me. Gradually, it became absolutely clear that they were speaking directly to me – that my son had drowned, just tumbled off the boat into foam. I decided not to go over to speak to them again, but was surprised that I did not feel insulted. It is difficult to describe the hollow clarity that such places generate.

With each year, even I forget the physical miseries inside those camps. I have a mind like a sieve, probably in my best interest. I only remember my middle years, like a middle dynasty, from the months before the war ended in 1975. I was thirty-four years old in 1977, when I arrived in Los Angeles.

CALIFORNIA

To be humbled in the official way before your family takes on the agony of surgery without anesthetic, what we call "*mat mac*" (penance). As my *mat mac*, I stood before my father-in-law again, who had found the money through cousins to pay my way on the boat from Vietnam, and now stood in judgment over me. And yet there was no judgment really. He looked frail. The loss of everything had broken him, even though his trip had been much easier than mine — too early for the pirates to trouble them; certainly no one drowning; a camp that was not overcrowded, where cookies and bread were available every day. They stayed for only two-and-a-half months at Song Ka. Then a B52 took them to Bangkok, five hundred Vietnamese and four hundred and fifty Cambodians. From there, they were transported by 747 to Camp Pendleton, at the Oceanside Airport, treated to American breakfast (ham, sausage and fruit), and American lunch, with Hawaiian Punch, coffee and tea.

And now they were in a garden spot near the ocean, a place called Oxnard. Their sponsor was a woman who owned a farm there, and was paid by the US government to keep us. They had been put to work the day after they arrived. But they never received any money. It all went to her, to pay for keeping us.

"No one keeps money in their pocket here," she told us. "We have banks."

"Where is our money then?" I had to ask.

"I have an account for you."

"Where? Which bank?"

"You're too new to all this."

"You think we're horses who never saw a bank?"

"What?"

"You think we don't know about banks?"

She started to wheeze like a broken toilet. She swelled up with anger; and then just as suddenly, she spoke softly, about how everything we need is here for us, in her house.

My family had worked at the seafood company cutting fish for four months now. I joined them riding the bus, always on the same seats in the front; seats that never were taken, no matter how crowded. Each time I plumped myself down on these seats, I noticed sour looks from Americans, a chilling silence. Finally, one of the Vietnamese women working at the seafood factory told me that these were reserved for the handicapped.

"You may be new and stupid," she said, "but you're not handicapped." Then she laughed. We spoke at work. The rooms smelled of ice chips mixed with rotting fish.

"At first, every American looks like a genius," she said. "Then gradually, human nature looks the same. You cash a check by signing the back, and taking it to the bank, starting an account. A horse could do it."

With her support, I persuaded my family to confront the sponsor about our checks. She grew even angrier, and threw us out that night, into a howl of traffic. Bad advice. I had miscued again, more grounds for *mat mac*. This time, however, luck served me, though later on the same luck hurt me. My friend at work, Thanh, learned about our disaster, and served as angel of mercy. After our family spent a few desperate days on the street (that was the absolute bottom for me), she helped us get money for an apartment – and then disappeared; simply left without a word, moved up to San Jose.

But we had begun. In time we saved enough to buy a 1976 Pinto, which I learned later was a car that was known to kill people. Luckily, if statistics can be trusted, someone else's Pinto must have killed double its share, because our car was only cranky; it never blew up or lost a wheel. The Pinto put us on the road, rather than beside it. And with the first taste of upward mobility, I ended my *mat mac*, the end of my first stage of humility. Suddenly, for lack of anyone better to lead, I became our prophet through the American maze. I had taken my family from a cruel sponsor who took our checks, into savings and a Pinto. My father-in-law gave me grudging support, while he drifted farther from work, and into gardening, and visits with cronies (as befits an elder who has passed sixty). "Dai has been struck by common sense, like a tree with lightning," he would say, nodding for emphasis, or nodding because he was ready to take a nap. I became an interim elder, between dynasties, the stupid general on horseback. Until the family knew better, they believed I had learned the tricks for living in America.

I had a job at $2.50 an hour working for a Vietnamese electrician, who explained building codes very quickly to me (too quickly for any-one to understand what he meant), and laughed sadistically when I shocked myself into a severe burn, from my knuckles to my elbow. Still, in time, even Dai, who barely turned on a light, figured out that every wire is either blue or red. The woman Thanh had been right. A barnyard animal could do it.

Our family (fathers, wives and teenaged children) spent a few months assembling radio parts and welding computer boards up in San Jose, then came back to Los Angeles, to live near downtown. We bundled into a house in an area known as Angelino Heights, a neighborhood of tottering wooden mansions and wider cracked streets, of Mexicans and a few Americans, where the skyscrapers downtown floated into view through the smog, and a strange cool wind managed to arrive from the ocean.

The electrician's job stopped. That left too much time to review myself. For about a month, I even became hospitable to Americans – truly my idiot's stage, as if I had memorized a few lines from a very bad script. Every morning from nine to eleven, I practiced saying "Hi Vietnam" to whoever seemed faintly interested. They generally looked at me as if I were out of costume, then started very primitive conversations with me.

For support, since I was risking speaking English to my heathen superiors, I clung like a cripple to my Binh, who rarely slept. I still started to call him my double son. My wife, meanwhile, was terrified at the way I kept him no more than six feet away. Binh was twice as wide as my first son had been, as if he ate for two; but he was just as troubled, with very clouded judgment. We were characters out of a television comedy, I realize now, chained together on an empty path, like pantomime artists – faintly laughable, utterly harmless, too harmless to look trustworthy. I think the problem was English: once I was determined to learn to speak the language, the effort haunted me. I opened my mouth, but the sound came from somewhere else. And what's worse, I always would twitch like an illiterate while I stood there in stony silence.

"I feel required to introduce us to America," I told Binh.

"Even in the camps," he said, "you could ask neighbors you didn't know for money, as if they were family. In America, you're not supposed to ask them anything. You can't even leave your doors open for visitors."

"That's because they don't want to lose the air conditioning, and because Americans never carry cash, only credit cards." I simply made up theories like this for the sound of it, and felt my feet grow wider, my sandals feel like cheaper plastic, my pants more inelegant than I had ever imagined.

The champion moment in my campaign to meet Americans came on a Sunday – the first time I lost track of Binh. I was walking with as much dignity as possible, saying "Hi Vietnam" to any two-legged mammal who couldn't speak my language, following that with a congenial wave, similar to what I saw at the end of dating shows on TV. Then I would try to control my twitching.

Today, however, was slightly different. It stirred me. A congestion of Americans from somewhere else presented itself. They were blocking my path – a mob of extremely white Americans, shuttling in and out of huge vans. They were assembling equipment, mostly lights, setting up tables for food, camping out in the middle of the street.

One man seemed to get special attention, a darker-skinned actor named Eric Estrada (his name Eric Estrada was written on a little chair reserved for him, which I read out loud, but in an accent that no one understood). Eric Estrada was dressed in excellently tailored pants and shirt, but appeared to be only a traffic cop, on a sparkling new motorcycle. His hair was sculpted down to the smallest whisker. Nothing on my dressing table from my wealthy days could have matched it.

But why were there so many very white Americans around him dressed up as poor Mexican children, in baggy pants and baseball caps? Clearly they were not really Mexicans, much less gangsters. Nearby, a group of actual Mexican boys watched; they were shocked to see white copies of themselves pretend to get arrested on TV. But they admired the shiny motorcycles.

I saw my opportunity to be a diplomat, and decided this once to leave Binh who was trying to meet either the false or the real Mexican children, by himself, but they sensed that he was wrong in the head. They almost looked frightened when he moved his arms strangely. They pushed him aside, like an infection. I watched, but didn't step in this time. Binh had daydreams over it later on, pretending he was hitting them.

Perhaps I wanted to agree with him, and wanted to stay clear; take a brief holiday from him. I relieved myself of Binh for a moment. I went from one blond American to the other (the men in charge), saying "Hi Vietnam." But the sound came from six feet away. I was a ventriloquist without a dummy. The more distressed they became, the more affable I tried to be, between some twitching. I laughed at one sour face I saw, then cursed him in Mandarin and Chinese.

I decided to adjust my phrasing of English a little, add a third word to "Hi Vietnam," say "Hi Vietnam – *again*." I locked my arms as if I were waiting for a waiter, pointed my toes in an aristocratic manner, and tried to be an actor playing myself as I was. They gestured even more hysterically for me to stay away. One man yanked electrical cables on the ground, and pointed to water hoses to show me what they were doing. Another pointed to Eric Estrada, who sat with manicured fingers gripping the controls of his motorcycle. Wherever I went, I was in someone's way.

That is what becomes of trying to be affable in bad English. Binh suddenly, without warning, tried to knock some sense in me, almost punched me; but he was too clumsy, and the Mexicans simply teased him, as children do. Binh told me finally that the Americans were shooting a TV show called *CHIPs*; an episode – I learned later, when I finally saw the show – about racially inferior Mexican drug lords. To keep matters white, they used white Americans whom they thought looked like angry gangchild Mexicans. Eric Estrada, boots gleaming, practiced skidding his tires for the chase scene with the white Mexicans.

Then all the crew ate donuts with coffee. For them I was a possum caught in their headlights, blocking the road. I was what insurance assessors call an act of nature, a leak somewhere, a defective camera. From that point on, I decided how I should act with Americans. I would pretend they were bailiffs at my plantation, and never speak English unless money was involved.

This English problem never ceased to make me look foolish. For a time, I tried to learn American music, but in those early months neither Binh nor I could quite translate the lyrics of songs. At the store on Sunset I bought what we assumed was American music, but it turned out to be in Spanish, a lot of tenors and warbling, and guitars that sounded American. Everything here except me is adjusted to sound like English.

Slightly down the hill, looking at a house just south of ours, I noticed a scruffy, bearded American struggling furiously to turn over the barren hard soil in front of his house. He kept trying to stab the soil with a pickax, then slumping in dismay.

I mentioned to farmers in our family that this American had problems turning over the soil on his parkway. That innocuous comment, without a plan, marked the beginning of my end. I advised them to see an opportunity here to connect with an American directly, to win a place. But I refused to be part of it. I was not ready to hyperventilate again trying to pronounce those bricks in English.

On my advice, they sent Do Huong, a cousin, to help. Do Huong was recently arrived from re-education in Vietnam, where, as a former FBI, he had been forced to farm for three years. The re-education had made him boring to listen to, always repeating the same stories about the war. In early May 1975, he'd escaped from Kien-Giang by moving to Saigon, thinking he could catch a diplomatic flight to Guam, but no one would let him leave. He found himself hiding instead at one of the stores that faced an air strip. To prevent arrest, he had his wife throw his government-issued rifle and uniform into the street, to remove anything that might identify him as a South Vietnamese soldier. "The streets looked like an army and navy store, jackets and weapons everywhere. The easiest

way to avoid arrest was to go naked." But Do Huong did not stay undis-
covered for long. He was questioned finally by Communists, and in his
words "stupidly admitted" he was a sergeant. For that moment of hon-
esty, he spent thirty months fighting the mud and the fleas, training for
the future of the proletariat. Most of all he learned a new skill: how to
keep crops alive.

The moment he met the American, Henry, the two seemed to hit it
off. In almost no time, about a week, with help from his children who
served as interpreters, Do Huong turned Henry's front yard into a miniature
re-education garden. Saint Augustine grass was taken in cuttings from the
yard of Billy the Mexican, who had dug it out of the grounds at Echo Park
Lake. Billy worked as a magician, and lived two blocks down at Kellam;
he worked in Canada, Mexico City and occasionally Las Vegas. He kept
doves in the back, and built his own trick boxes for sawing women apart;
he even practiced sawing his daughter apart in the backyard, in a lascivious
way that infuriated his wife, though he also would be seen throwing a
football with his son. Billy always combed his hair to make it bigger,
fluffed like a pigeon, and spent too much money when he traveled on tour
– if there was any money when he traveled on tour, if there was a tour.
He kept his front windows wide open at all times, for his two Doberman
dogs to watch for burglars and glare. But most of the time at home, Billy
was on a holy mission to improve Angelino Heights, to make it as delicate
as he imagined himself, like a landscaped boulevard for the rich in Mexico
City. He traded for stacks of old wall sconces and door knobs from old
houses. With his advice, Do Huong planted swatches or plugs of drought-
resistent grass every two feet, like a quilt.

The American, Henry, was deeply appreciative, though he acted sometimes like a kindly loan shark. He had a habit of waving his arms too
much, and explaining himself too much, that he came from back east. He
told Do that he was "recovering," from what no one quite knew; it
wasn't alcohol, but he sometimes he went off whatever wagon it was, a
small wagon I think. Henry was a teacher of some sort, and a writer for
a newspaper that didn't pay much money. We took his position in the
world the wrong way. We mistakenly thought that American teachers had
some influence on government, could help us, or knew ways to protect
our family.

Do Huong continued to work for Henry, started something of a business as a contractor. In front of the yard, he built a white picket fence
from scraps, which we all agreed were sub-standard, would warp and

collapse in ten years, but showed that Do Huong might have a knack for carpentry eventually. Then Do began stripping away paint from the wood walls inside Henry's house, using a noxious orange glue that was scraped off the wall in lumps and dropped onto newspaper, and onto the rugs throughout Henry's living room and den.

Our family thought they had found a lucky house with Henry, though, and could leave their doors open now. To show their respect, they invited Henry for a Vietnamese meal, he and his wife. I still cannot pronounce her first name, but she seemed very tall and calmer than he was, calmer than anyone I'd ever seen really, perhaps not really calm.

As in Vietnam, a whiskey bottle was left in the center of the dining table, and everyone tried to speak gruffly, as if they were laughing like soldiers, in the way American GIs prefer. Clearly, this wasn't working for Henry. He rarely drank, rarely smoked, and seemed more interested in our stone fireplace ("too bad it's painted, you can't get paint off sand-stone") than in our whiskey. Then he started asking about Binh, offering names where medical care might be possible. I grew anxious, and had to go into the kitchen to control my anger, while Henry apparently started to sing praises about Do Huong's work, how reliable Do was.

I screamed to Do Huong: "You are stealing from me." What I meant was that he was stealing my chance to protect my son, by making him too American too soon. But I looked foolish, and was noticed even by Henry, who invited his own children to jump off the roof in a rainstorm, no rules.

My interim period as elder stopped quite abruptly that week, and Do Huong's star emerged in place of mine. Demoted, I developed physical symptoms. My feet swelled, and I felt unprotected in the household; my best shirt tore in the wash. I spent days afterward being glum. Thus began my metaphysical stage, a return to my breakdown at the camps, but in a more studious way. I studied the relationship of the sun to the line of Henry's house, because I sensed bad luck might be hidden there. The last breath of daylight, after the sun set on his roof, did not enter his upstairs window properly. I squatted patiently from across the street, staring at the roof for ten minutes at a time, sensing weather patterns. I looked as if I were waiting for a helicopter to land. And when I crossed to Henry's side of the street, no matter how peaceful the traffic, I took Binh along and forced him to lead. We walked in line, as if on an imaginary leash.

At one point, I tried to speak to Henry, after preparing a speech for days, reciting to myself carefully in English. To set the right mood, since

I was dressed in very cheap rayon, I pretended that Henry was a *dudeng*, and that I owed him money. I learned to tilt my head like an American when they cannot understand but think they mean well. Finally, showing some style beneath the ashes, I caught his attention. Then I explained, in one surprisingly good English paragraph, that I had just arrived, that I'd been a doctor in Vietnam. To which he answered in a buttery English, swallowing his words too quickly; and I was sunk. My relatives heard about what I had said, and ran over to correct the mistaken image I had presented. They told Henry that I had lost my son during the boat ride to Thailand after the war — and that they needed Henry to help with doctors for my second son, Binh, who was pretending to be an American singer in his room. After that, Henry's expression changed, clouded, when he saw me. A few weeks are lost: I was sinking, and lost track of time. As a last resort, I decided to pretend that I had never existed, and that helped me get some better paying jobs, but I never quite knew why.

About six months later, I was working for the local Pioneer Supermarket, gathering shopping carts that had been wheeled away into the neighborhood. I looked confident, animated, like an American. From my used pickup truck, I smiled broadly at Henry, showing off a new set of false teeth that were much too large (soon after, I bought teeth that fit).

Henry asked me questions through a child interpreter, but not Binh, who was refusing to speak English suddenly, and went into a gloomy period of only playing guitar in his room. Henry asked me if I wanted to do some carpentry, build shelves, because Do Huong was getting too busy, and had medical problems with his chest. I felt my luck changing, and spent four weekends squatting inside Henry's house as I measured and cut shelves, studying every centimeter as if it were algebra, or a missile program. Henry was clearly amazed at my diligence, and my incredible slowness.

During that time, I studied Henry's patterns hour by hour, and Henry's children ripping the handle off the refrigerator, as well as Henry's wife, who spoke German and was also a teacher. I began to look for clues again, seeds for planning the future, so I could prepare my support system for my next breakdown, at least get Binh off to a professional start.

Binh was getting worse, but seemed happier. My sister-in-law in Saigon had a first son almost as crazy as he, so crazy that even the Communists did not recruit him. He refused to work, and the entire family managed with less to keep him secure in her house, as a sacred act, but a form of martyrdom I certainly couldn't handle. A good god was needed to put a hand in and protect him.

Unfortunately, I drifted for a week or so. Something must have happened with Binh while I was away, because Henry and his wife seemed to make a point of not mentioning him any more. His absence in their conversation made a big hole. In the meantime, an older American woman, Henry's wife's lady friend, came to live with them for a while. For the first time in years, I felt a vague sexual attraction to a woman who looked European – with suicidal reminder of how I failed with Lan. So with adolescent anxiety, I began to iron my best shirt, and to speak to her in French and Mandarin, patiently waiting for any response while I delicately sanded the shelves yet again. I watched her eyes glisten, a good sign.

Her face was very soft, and she had eyes like a peaceful rat, but suddenly, when she smiled, her face took on a youthfulness, almost a shy girlishness, that made her quite exciting to me. Gradually, I learned that she had made quite a few mistakes in her life; foolish marriages, but no children – which was encouraging.

I decided to act sorry about my past offenses, *noblesse oblige*, a new age. I told her that I had been, in my youth, a cruel man; that I had been unfair to women, and probably couldn't change. She agreed that I probably couldn't, and stopped smiling as much.

My family stopped smiling at me as well. I had failed to get Binh a doctor. Clearly he was not going to be a professional man. Over my objections, they sent him to a clinic after he began screaming Chinese obscenities at the other children. Actually he wasn't quite screaming. He had begun a series of theatricals. In a series of impersonations of famous men in history, he would repeat, rather loudly, encounters by Chinese leaders with American soldiers. He even had songs to go with key scenes. Gradually, he included Henry in the drama, even began to mimic the way Henry spoke, but in Vietnamese.

At last I mentioned something of my problem to Henry, who offered to call someone. We must have gone through six different names. But there was a fracture somewhere in Henry's children too, a broken promise or a loss. To explain why, I returned to my metaphysics, listening to the hum of termites in the walls. The fracture felt like the termites had gone half way down the house, sending the faintest heat, a fraction of a degree, into the old wooden panels in the living room. But there was no sensible way to explain that in English. His wife and her lady friend used to hide from Henry anyway. They huddled and spoke softly in the corners of rooms, a sure sign that he was partly the subject.

I don't remember the months after this, except that I traveled, but came back.

Henry saw me again two years later, after my next collapse. I'm certain that I looked very broken, after traveling as much as I did, but I knew better than to discuss details with him. I had left my family, but came back for Binh, or so I thought.

Henry's window needed paint. But more obviously, his wife was ready to leave him. It was obvious in the way she dressed. She must have been a good twenty pounds lighter, and was clearly leading a life that did not include him.

I noticed her lady friend visiting one day. She now had her own apartment. When she saw me, a twig of what I had once been, I apologized that my barrel chest had shrunk because I had been under treatment, which made me feel less cruel about what I have done, more frail. She smiled very broadly, and her face broke into that girlish expression again. "You don't look worse at all," she said. "Just leaner. In fact, you look more dashing than you did. You seem to be dressing up more."

"This is living proof," I said, "that based on how I am seen in your eyes, I'll never know how I look. Which is good. In Vietnam I enjoyed being a mystery even to myself. Sometimes, I would pretend I didn't know my own face. It helped me be more objective."

Of course, I said this in such terrible English that I could see that barely a fraction was making any sense to her. I wondered what my words actually meant, while she placed her hand on top of mine, and simply returned a look of amazement, as if I were delivering a story about skinning dogs for cooking. She disappeared like a fragrance that was never quite strong enough to leave the bottle. I was sad for two weeks.

Binh meanwhile had grown interested in the decors of our grotesque apartment. He studied the flaking along the window sill. I said that flaking paint reminded me of the way I spoke English. That sounded funny to Binh. I was lifted somewhat, though I wondered if he was sane enough to get my point. For a time, he began to improve.

I know my relatives began to complain to Americans who came to ask about me. But most of what my family said, and still say, has grown more confused, fainter each year. My cousins became more prosperous, and many of their children are professionals, but they are convinced that

Americans think, underneath it all, that all Vietnamese are communists. But I think Americans believe all Vietnamese were capitalists, except me. I soil my hands, but never start my own business.

Here is my sense of it, thinking American for a moment: In the late seventies and early eighties, many more came from Saigon and arrived by way of Guam (during the war against Cambodia), then made money in clothing, or in stores or real estate, while others bought used BMWs, sent their children to tutors, then had the eldest child teach the younger, gave their children American names, particularly the lucky women's letters L or C. In a few years, more colonies of Vietnamese settled in Orange County, mostly Westminster; and L.A. Chinatown; or San Jose. They arrive in what Americans think are pajamas, and spent months carrying great pails of food from one apartment to the next. Then they filter quickly into business, like coffee into water, and find the secret of overworking and underbidding in America. Others never get filtered – particularly the women, who don't want to leave the house or to go to jobs; or simply split into pieces, go mad, as if they were trapped in a hole somewhere, drowning. And stories float everywhere. The Hmongh in Minnesota didn't know what kitchens were for when they arrived; they would cook by digging large holes in the basements. Now, according to Do, they "practically own Minnesota." I don't know if I can trust what Do says, particularly about me.

I noticed how the untruths my family gave Americans multiplied. I once had too many wives, they told Henry's male friend, but now all my wives are gone. I was born rich, though another cousin says I was born broke. I am considered very hard-working, but apparently never show up at a job site after the first few days.

And I'm only half married, but which half is that? One night, after almost six years of gradual recovery, my wife and I found a measure of friendship again, and I moved back in with her – without Binh, who was still working on his theatricals in the apartment diagonal from Henry's bedroom actually. The world I remembered from the end of the war, where Lan was my mistress, were barely photographs of myself looking very young. I even became prosperous, two years later, when I had $800 squirreled away from the family, but my feet swelled up again, so I took a break from staying with my wife. After the $800 was spent, I decided to go back to my wife, to recover on our living room couch, have the television all to myself when everyone was asleep. By now we were all in cultural re-education. Since our daughter wanted to be a professional, my wife instructed the entire family to speak to me only in English, to speed my recovery by making me uncomfortable. During my hiatus on the couch, however, I cooked up a plan to make Binh a professional after all; save him from all those doctors. He was practically a medical business all by himself – pills, visits. There must have been two nurses and two doctors, until the county money gave out. But all he really needed to feel like a happy sow was a stack of LP records, and his theatricals, about his father this time.

I would date the first stages of my plan to make Binh a professional to about eight months ago, when I saw Do Huong commandeering a team of Mexicans to tear down a building two houses away. The building was owned by a family of North Vietnamese, who were breeding pigeons up in a grapefruit tree. They also owned a restaurant, which in fact, was not doing too well. You can guess why. Anyway, the North Vietnamese (from very far north, almost like Hmong near the Chinese border) sold the house to Americans, who hired Mexicans to tear it down. But Do had found a way to turn their misery into money. He claimed he had put a bid on their tottering house when it was for sale, but wasn't accepted because the sleazy American real-estate agent wanted another American to co-sign – an unlikely story. So instead, he was taking it down for the new owners, to make room for something else – something that I was sure could help me with Binh, have him study real estate in a correspondence course.

I admire the way Americans take a building down, speaking with some degree of personal experience. I rented a movie about Vietnam just the other day. Chuck Norris was gunning down thousands of small people in straw hats. They made good artillery targets. Then Chuck Norris took the buildings down.

There's a lot of money in it – not for me of course. I don't even have cooking privileges here. I have about an hour at most before the Americans come to arrest me today, and that fleshy presence sitting here, as if he grew out of the couch. (Lately I've been daydreaming of Lan in only a thin rayon robe, bending over an oven, while I hold her ass in my hands, and make jokes: I think I'll stay with that thought for a few minutes, take a short break.)

Binh is as fat as an old pigeon these days, and sits with his neck forward like a male pigeon puffing on a ledge. He continually and solemnly studies his record collection, for new theatricals. There's a hole where he kicked out the window, looking for movement in Henry's house, and quietly mimicking English. I've stayed almost boarded up with him for nearly three weeks now.

As a related issue, about eight months ago, a Mexican with his hair shaved like a movie Indian threw a brick into my wife's living room window. Binh and I had been visiting, and Binh started screaming into the street at the children there. And when the brick came through the window, he acted as if he knew the Mexican, and seemed pleased by the sound it made. All this confirmed my wife's worst fears about Binh. The Mexican began screaming insults, in Spanish or a kind of English, apparently imagining that we were the very Vietnamese who had forced his friends to go to war. I had seen men screaming like that before, and had seen pirates attacking women on a ship – or heard about it anyway; even seen bodies of children on display, like stuffed animals. But I was completely unprepared for this explosion of broken glass through the bad curtains left us by our landlord. I had been trying to enjoy a basketball game on television, watching tall black Americans mostly. I even threw an encouraging look toward my wife, who treats me like luggage she forgot to put away. I was reasonably satisfied with my dinner. I was starting to reminisce peacefully about my childhood, being bundled away, and taken from Ha Tien – until that hail of glass fell on top of me.

It insulted my sense of fair exchange. Someone was committing extortion, but not asking for a bribe. During the family conference afterward, I sat mute, sensing parts of my childhood disappearing again, the safety. I felt like a stone in their shoe, but a strategy was arranged for me, to force me to care for Binh exclusively, and leave the rest to them. They called in a young man, Lo Duc, originally from Kien-Giang. My family mistakenly believed he had made good here. He worked as an actor in Chinese karate movies produced in Los Angeles (the new Hong Kong of Chinese filmmaking, he claimed). When he walked into my house, I noticed iron weights attached to his ankles, apparently to strengthen his kick.

"I don't make movies as an art form," he explained. "I just pretend to kick ass hour after hour, like a water mill. They add the grunts in post-production."

My family asked him to walk to a telephone pole near the Mexican's house. Then he was to practice death kicks furiously against the pole, as close to the height of someone's throat as possible. He also would grunt on impact, to send terror to the Mexican gang.

It was my father's bright idea. For a few hours, my father thought he had people's attention. It was essentially our last conversation together, before he disappeared into religion, became a regular at Temple. He went so far as to wear country black and the traditional smock (*ao dai*) even in the house, as if every day were a holiday, or as if he were a priest under house arrest. "Remember," he told me, puffing up philosophically "it is an insult to exceed your father's accomplishments."

Now that I was required to watch over Binh, I spent my money on whatever pleased him. With a microphone I bought him, he interviewed me in front of our old hotel in Kien-Giang, which I had inherited in a sweepstake in the mail. What's the Christian expression in English: "from my son's lips to God's ear?" (I learned this saying during my brief fire-and-brimstone conversion to Christianity in 1984, by way of my Salvadoran landlady, who took me to the Four Square Gospel Church, where God enters people's bodies and forces them to speak magically "in tongues," a language only God understands. Legally speaking, no one can stay legally in America, my landlady explained, unless you become a Christian. They may deport you otherwise.)

Anyway, to get back to getting my son to study real estate: a week later, but still about eight months ago, Do Huong was having his erratic heartbeat examined again (a permanent condition, he claims, caused by his re-education in Vietnam). His shirt was off. The doctor was poking his finger against Do Huong's lungs, and listening. At the same time, Do Huong was listening to the doctor breathing for clues about what was wrong (no one seems to know). The doctor looked up and said, in Cantonese I believe: "Your case reminds me of someone else, a woman named Lan, who also came up here from Los Angeles."

The threads were tying together, between Do Huong, and Lan, and the children (maybe gang children) who knew Binh in Angelino Heights, and a few of them who did deliveries for a Vietnamese bakery. Lan works in Echo Park, regularly paints out graffiti, because she runs a business near where I live. How had we missed seeing each other for years? Perhaps it was during my second collapse, when I refused to go near Vietnamese food for over a year. Do Huong, who has never been my friend, kept this information about Lan away from me for weeks. Every day we intentionally ignored each other, as we always do. He jumped into his truck, his pride and joy, fired up the rebuilt ignition. With a glow on his face, he looked at my terrifying old Toyota sitting there in army camouflage, in four different colors, each sanded but never painted. Occasionally, I could see something more than indifference on his face, more like jubilation. That meant he felt superior enough to pity me, and we could talk. I had figured him out. Today, he seemed to want to talk, but why give him the satisfaction?. He had been hiding news about me, but telling everyone else.

I assumed that his secret would be the subject of conversation when I went to the deli and liquor store owned by my old lieutenant colonel, Pharm, from the Vietnamese FBI. I tried to stay unusually alert. Pharm had managed to leave Vietnam early, with more money than he should rightly have had. And with that he bought a convenience market. Lately I always saw him the same way, behind his register: his face was crowned by potato chips and corn chips on the wall, an assortment of yellow plastic bags; and gums, chocolates. All this was for show, ornaments for the real money-makers, the whiskies and vodkas against the far wall.

In bins in front of the counter were Vietnamese packaged goods, various sweets with mung bean; and rice with pork in pandang leaves. The smell of the leaves, like sweet hay, surrounded him.

"I have a surprise for you," he said in his usual staccato way of speaking: six words at a time, then stopping momentarily, like a loose connection.

Finally, during his pauses, I had to fill the void: "A surprise like all the others I've had?"

"Do you see the cakes?"

I nodded.

"They come from a bakery."

I nodded again.

"Run by a woman who married my cousin. Mostly for his new ovens. Certainly not for his looks."

He adjusted the bags of Mexican pork rinds, in such a way that I could tell that he had no idea where they went. (His assistant in the distance was watching him bend and nearly crush each bag. The assistant looked offended, as if the bones of little potatoes were breaking.) However, the lieutenant colonel was merely acting like an army man, trying to look official, putting some bark in his voice:

"This woman knows you. (He slowly inhaled and exhaled.) And she wants you to go work for her, now that you're on your own. Your family advised me to help."

Those were my orders, in six words or less, as if the army were alive and well in a frozen display case. The old soldiers are like celebrities to us now, entertainers who used to sing hit songs. I heard someone compare them to Elvis in America. Or Elvis Phuong, the singing impersonator, who is certainly better known than veterans now.

The lieutenant colonel was sending me a message from Lan. She had somehow joined a paramilitary food network, a reinvention of the Vietnam War. Clans of food wholesalers took with them dreams like the Cubans, of going back to Hanoi or Saigon, and building hotels with mile-long buffets. I don't know how else to describe them; they had maps of potential sites for a marine landing, while in their stores they sold maps showing the assault routes into Disneyland and Sea World. After 1986, many found it much easier to go back to Vietnam on business trips, and spoke more of joint ventures than amphibious assaults.

Lan had taken over a bakery, owned by her new (old to the rest of the world) husband. As a corporal, he had arrived six months before the end of the war, on an extended business trip. He helped set up a money-laundering chain tied to war profits, sorely depleted now; and had settled into food sales as a last resort, after the money-laundering ran out. Next, he opened a fast-food restaurant, but at a stupidly overpriced lease; then he broke the lease, and found a small warehouse in what we now call Little Saigon, with a bakery up in Echo Park, where he kept adding new dishes to his menu, from sweets to U-cakes; moon cakes at Harvest Moon (Tet Trung Thu), and birthday cakes for Vietnamese, Mexicans, and the occasional Anglo. At the same time – as if to dress up his table; like adding lace tablecloth and silver service – he unpacked his best suit, bought new shoes, and found himself a younger wife.

His bakery had signs painted in English and Spanish, but it was really Lan's business by now. He delivered orders by truck, and conspired with old cronies during lunch. She ran the details. When I saw Lan again, she was in the back testing her recipe for salted duck eggs (to avoid those expensive Chinese imports, where the duck yolks are presumably baked under ground). I saw her first from behind, still one of her better angles, though her ass has dropped a bit. And I've mostly seen her back ever since, but I know she senses me even thirty feet behind her. It was around that time that I suffered another collapse: my third, an utter flattening of my memory. However, two facts stand out about her, front and back. She looked younger, astonishingly fit, as if she'd been lacquered, given herself a new paint job. And more robust, a trifle fuller bodied around the hips than in Vietnam, which seemed appropriate, like a well-formed tree taking on a graceful ring or two. She looked better tended. And second, her husband was not interested in a second family, for fear he might have to split his money with a new set of children. I know this distressed her, and somehow she took her pound of flesh.

All this, her gruff but solemn manner, suggested an unhappy house-wife to me – like in soap operas, where American women have affairs with friends of their husbands; the boyfriend then murders the husband (I saw the movie, and thought I was Jack Nicholson in *The Postman Always Rings Twice*). My imagination went to work. I considered sneaking over to Lan in the mornings while her husband made deliveries. In our prime, Lan was at her best in the mornings.

Some days she did let me touch her arm, a possible hint, even let me kiss her on the cheek. Or she would brush her bosom against my shoulder. She even more or less promised me intimate breakfasts, or eve-nings together. She would say "Stop racing your engine," then laugh, clearly flattered. Then she'd say: "Why aren't you visiting me?" On other days she stared blankly, as if I were an uncrated shipment, to be stored away from the light. She'd give me dull chores; have me stack, or pack. Once she asked, mostly to herself: "How does a prince feel dragging forty-pound sacks of flour?" But right after, she rubbed my neck, and scratched her nails a little inside my shirt.

However, my real job came later. Her husband asked me, on behalf of his fellow investors: "How do you feel about bending the law?"

"Which law?" I asked.

"Health codes."

"Does anyone care?"

"Bakers care. The city inspectors care, more or less. Do you know how many unlicensed bakers there are? They undersell the rest of us. And they break the health codes."

"I'd stop them."

"Not exactly."

I thought at first that I was supposed to prevent illegal baking. Instead, I realized soon enough that Pharm was having it both ways. He claimed to be against illegal bakers, while he bought from them, at great discount. Then he'd stick his own labels on their foods.

So instead of being in the bakery FBI, I became a pastry *dudeng*, turning breakfast foods into war profits. I picked up and delivered illegal cakes, dumplings and snacks, mostly in the Chinatown area.

War had turned into parody, like all my wars. There was real pain, though, from Orange County up to San Jose: apartments heavy with grease, enough to stick paper on the wall. I saw thirty people trapped in a single apartment, with peeled paint on the ceilings and hanging plaster; and metal bowls on the floor, making a trail into the barren, narrow kitchen, where they baked in secret – a farcical version of misery, but misery nonetheless. The women squatted like children, and patiently shaped mung bean patties, then sweetened each with coconut milk. I was a bootlegger in snack foods. I sold to street vendors in Chinatown, along New High Street and down Hill Street. Some of them came from Vietnam by way of Guam; others from Indonesia; many from the worst camps in Malaysia.

Near Lan's warehouse, I would stop by the Asia Garden Mall, and stand in our copy of teeming Vietnam, so thick with smokers that the air seems to do everything but cough, in rhythm with music from the cafes, Viet Pop. I saw Vietnamese children – gang members – take extortion from the businesses: *dudengs* in hundred-dollar sneakers.

I brought the money I'd collected to Lan, who ran the war. Publicly, she was opposed to illegal bakeries. Privately, she was a prime distributor. For a time, I forgot that in Vietnam she'd been in the flesh trade and French beer business, not in pastry cakes. I couldn't remember our adventures together any more, except in terms of tapioca or pink bakery cartons.

One woman who made cakes for Lan told me: "To be an American is like forgetting half your life, and never learning half of theirs." I saw divorced families on welfare, many women perched like leased furniture in front of broken TVs (the silliest way yet to go crazy). There were rumors of Vietnamese gangs dressing like blacks and Mexicans in Santa Ana; of young Chinese *dudengs* establishing mafias. Then there were banal changes: Americanized Viet mothers who refused to keep faith by leaving their hair unwashed for the first month after the baby was born – until the baby was officially alive. And every day, I brought snacks to sweatshops (mostly clothing); stores without signs, hiding in half light, identified only by gates blocking the open doors and usually in what had once been business districts, along patchy streets like bombed-out war zones near downtown.

While driving west of Chinatown along Sunset, I used to talk to myself as if I were an American giving a tour to my son Binh, whom I imagined as much thinner. I always slowed to ten miles an hour, to study the cement steps leading up an incline to empty lots. Houses had been torn down perhaps twenty years ago (by the look of the lots, enormous houses), and then left blank and flat; now, Mexicans planted corn among the weeds, like the spirit of a dead sister returning as tortillas – yet another snack.

(Insert shopping coupons here: For a time, all my symbols involved prepared food, even where Binh was concerned. He probably would swallow napalm if it came in chocolate creams.)

Anyway, a demolition war of some kind had taken place in Los Angeles, a war of attrition that, though certainly no Vietnamese understood it first-hand, they could still turn to a profit, by renting what was left. Despite one larger Vietnamese shopping center in southern Chinatown and a few strip malls, Viet shops were mostly in the abandoned walls of the city – in old stores accidentally left standing during the mysterious war of whites against downtown buildings. Steadily Viet businesses spread to warehouses up in Lincoln Park, north of Chinatown, along with a few Vietnamese restaurants, to service the workers as more moved in. In Echo Park, Vietnamese furniture owners met the bakers for coffee (to consider investments), at a cafe that ran its own publishing company: children gold-stamping volumes of poetry printed in Vietnamese while their parents handled the lunch trade. Vietnam in Los Angeles is a series of broken branches caught upstream, circling, and occasionally looking like an orderly community, as in Little Saigon near Long Beach, but actually too mixed with others to be very solid in most places. White areas grow whiter; everywhere else, many races crowd in the same buildings, like twelve different kinds of worker ant. Stores near these apartments, along Western or across Pico, have signs in three or four languages. Some Vietnamese do very well in this dog race, send their well-adjusted children to Cal State Northridge or to Cal State L.A., and pay mortgages on clean new houses. They build larger businesses, and keep buying apartments, as Lan does. Others vanish as I am vanishing. They simply drown in the half light.

About three months ago, the war stopped. Lan told me that I was never to visit illegal bakeries again. "We don't need them. It's bad food."

"Did someone die of coconut poisoning? The war is over then."

"Over. We've gone wholesale."

She had begun to sell direct, and tried to make her pastries taste better. Pandam leaves now came from Thailand, and were soaked carefully, to make that sage-and-vinegar taste for U-cakes. The best tapioca came from Singapore. She paid various old women to teach her the best ways to season and spice. She even went to cooking classes; traveled once to Thailand to learn more recipes. Slowly, the backyard behind her bakery filled with more storage sheds, as she kept extending, by adding new batter machines, and a bigger oven.

I saw her once after five o'clock, testing the food in her sweets labora-
tory. "I go eighteen hours a day," she said, warning me, or possibly welcoming me. "Seven days a week."

"And yet you don't look it. I, of course, never go eighteen hours
straight at anything. The only part of me that goes eighteen hours a day
is my memory, and remembering my son. I'm alone with him now, you
know. My sacred obligation. My wife can't bear me, particularly since I
started to work here. She thinks you're still after me, now that I have my
new teeth."

"Hardly. You've actually found another way to make yourself ridiculous.
I didn't think there was one more way left. (She laughed, as if being
ridiculous were one of my sterling qualities. At first she laughed maternally,
then with some exhaustion, as if she were trying to expel something
from her throat.)

"Don't choke over it."

"Your wife and I meet all the time. We're almost friends. Girlfriends.
Even before I left Kien-Giang we spoke, to arrange things. It's a blessing
to be stupid, Dai, but it makes you unlucky. You could have been luckier
if you'd listened to me. You should listen to me now."

I could have been snotty to her after that, said something like:
"Luckier? Luckier than every man you've ever had? Now that's saying
something." Instead, I leaned close to her, as the only heat source in my
life. Perhaps she sensed this, and let me touch her on the neck, then
caressed me down my arm, not quite as expertly as she used to (she was
spending more time nowadays wrapping spring rolls and bao), but with
enough curiosity to arouse me, until I simply asked her to take me to her
home – in the most direct way I could; no evasions, no more elaborate
compliments.

"I need to be alone with you for a while. Now before the pain sets
in." My subtleties never hit the mark anyway, if there was a mark to hit.

She drove me to her house, strangely empty, with tile everywhere – in
the living room, to the ceiling in the bathroom, into her bedroom –
with no one around, and too much neatly stacked. She clearly had a
separate arrangement with her husband, though she claimed they were
very happy living separately, whatever that meant. It had never occurred
to me that she had been free all this time.

We moved slower in her new house, past glass tiles instead of windows
up the stairs. We rubbed and licked each other with a bit less fire than I
had remembered. Not that we were stalling. What was the point of

stalling? I was simply in shock to be with her again. For an hour, or however long before I managed to get a second erection, I felt like I was catching a glimpse of someone else naked through an open window. The memory being revived was more intense than the fact of me beside her. Her body was older, with a new sag in a new place, though her arms and shoulders looked exquisite. Her age threw me into a tearful fit that was so exciting I barely stayed hard, until we found a rhythm. We were examining our memories primarily, like a commemorative event, a flag day, to celebrate, in her words "with something more solid than telling each other stories about what you used to do."

Later, I began talking about myself, that unlikely and constant subject, always speaking in a distant third person. I reviewed the disasters blow by blow, while rubbing her leg and behind her knee. I discussed the lime still on my hand, left over from my months working for a cement contractor; and the dust from a leaf blower when I worked for a gardener. Most of all, I spent nearly an hour on my fantasies about drowning children, and that I was sharing my room with my "double" son Binh, who never left the house, week after week, and that I needed her help to find Americans who can care for him, because I'm afraid he might turn violent again. Then I lied to convince her. I said that Binh was sure the war in Vietnam had spread to his street, like a latent virus returning. Last month, a Mexican youth, sixteen, had jumped in front of his pregnant girlfriend (nine months pregnant) when a Vietnamese gang fired – retaliating I guess for something. The boy had died immediately. The bullet passed through his chest into her stomach, killed their child in the womb, and exited just below her spine. As the police and ambulances gathered, American and Mexican children came to watch the body being taken away. Binh kept repeating that the corpse looked asleep, like a story his dead brother used to tell, about seeing young Vietnamese dead on display, a certain way the head was bent, the arms and hands twisted, that same restlessness, as if it were just about to move.

He has been returning to that spot for a moment every day, then freezes in thought, and worms away shyly, and stays very still for hours afterward. He has begun to speak in a combination of Vietnamese, Mandarin and English that sometimes I cannot decipher. He claims that Americans plan to send the Vietnamese to camps, that he heard them talking through an open window about this shooting. He couldn't get all the facts in English, except that American little boys also have nightmares about hands with loaded guns under their bed.

"Could he have made some of that up?" Lan asked.

"That's what makes me think I can persuade an American to help; that we have a common problem. But I need a woman to intervene."

Lan stopped me before I started to unravel again. She wanted to tell me her nasty epic, how she made her way out of a camp in Indonesia, by hooking up with old army officers, to become a baker lady with flour on her hands, la bourgeoise. But I had exhausted her desire to talk at all.

"Let's decide what to do with your son first, the one who is left. Tell Binh to leave you alone. Tell him gently, and send him to the hospital. You have no sacred duty."

"Yes that would be best, to send him to the hospital, and try to make him some kind of professional." I imagined a surgeon carefully separating the dead son from the living son.

A few days later, my son Binh had one of his clearest days in years. I was impressed that he knew *cao gio* (gow yaw), how to "scratch the wind" by rubbing a coin along his spine, muscles, ribs, until the flesh reddens. He worked the coin so long that it left purple marks along his stomach. I watched him slowly apply ointment, as he spoke about the week in Dalat in 1976: "I made a friend there, who used to watch the battles from the hill. You could see the bullets chasing each other, like fireworks. The South had AR and M16. From the North, we heard AK that sounded like frogs, *ka pa*, but creepier, short and crisp, frightening for a child."

I lived in a three bedroom house subdivided for twenty people, and shared the bedroom with Binh, who paid rent directly to me, though he hadn't worked for six months now, but prepared to go to junior college to study real estate, if I coaxed him. For most of those six months, Binh had been hiding in a chair near a stereo. He was supposed to take anti-psychotic drugs, but refused, threatening suicide if anyone tried to make him swallow anything. Regularly, like the phases of the moon, he would spin into a dance where he spoke in English, using his microphone, for Henry's benefit I think. He thought he was in concert, serving as TV cameraman, audience and performer.

When he pretended to be an audience, he applauded with a high shriek, sometimes sneezing loudly enough to wake up the neighbors, while the stereo kept blasting, playing an album by the Carpenters, end-lessly repeating, a woman singing full throated about her bad luck and occasional lovers. When he sang along, the rasp of his voice terrorized me.

A few days ago, Binh went into a particularly loud rage. That brought a response from neighbors. A gate was added outside, to settle a boundary dispute next door, and keep him from threatening neighbors. In response, he ripped the gate from its hinges, then ran upstairs and tossed furniture through his window to the street fifteen feet below. The window frames were butted loose, and shattered on to the cement below, along with couches, tables and TVs, into piles up to five feet deep.

Some of the stucco covering the house quivered loose as well, revealing the original building underneath – an old wooden shell, like the many layers of roof and the dozens of renovations from one generation to the next, each tearing out another built-in or adding a copy of a kitchen they thought looked like the May Company; and then adding texture coat over what was left. I am told that fifty years ago it had been something of a whorehouse, with a bar in the living room, and rooms upstairs. The brass rail from the bar was hauled away eventually, and kept like a trophy in the basement of the house next door until the man who took it went on one drunk too many, and his angry sister cleared out the basement, while he slept on the back steps one morning.

A year later, a very expensive looking young woman (in fine boots and snug jeans) came by to find that old drunk, now too heavily into boozing to do much. She was told that he snored outdoors like a barking dog, to which she replied: "His sister is sick now, but she brought me up in her rooming house, and I love her. I remember him so well. He was gigantic, very honest, and was considered a handsome man, a roofer. The drinking didn't show up on his face, and he worked regularly. You know what is the worst about being old? The real problem is that no one is left to remember how they were in their prime." And then she left without seeing him, perhaps to avoid confusing herself. Soon after, the woman's house was sold, and her drinking brother disappeared into the $10-a-day rooms near Western, near a Guatemalan street I think. Or perhaps he lives on the street itself by now, or was brought back by family to Ohio, where he came from originally; if that's so, he may be sleeping today comfortably in someone's den. His old drinking buddy, a little skinny man with a gut, kept looking for him for months afterward, then got cranky, and eventually disappeared too.

Outside, just south of my house, a star-shaped water fountain still remains from when this was a brothel. The fountain may have been a waiting area, a little watershow for clients waiting their turn, to keep them focused on swift ejaculation, a quick roll and out. At the corners of the fountain, five cement frogs used to spout clear water. At the center, a little cement boy held his tiny cock and continually urinated. After decades now, the plumbing through the frogs' mouths and the boy's cock has rusted solid. The pool itself has washed clear of paint. Two years ago, during a heavy rain, the boy's penis fell off, removing the last clue to the building's former use.

Through my obliterated window, I felt dreadfully exposed to prying eyes, as if I were in Americans' conversations suddenly. Worse than that, my time with Lan had left me close to falling apart. My hearing seemed muffled. I was packed in cotton.

I remember Binh turning all the lights on, which made more available for Americans to see him looking as fat as a large worm. His face had become starchy. His muscle tone had dissolved. He seemed literally evaporating into himself.

Lan had told me that it couldn't be all my problem, that my wife had decided to make this my penance. Besides, officially, the owners of the house were making Binh into a business. They sent me bills, but they received some government money for him I think, and money from my in-laws. So they refused to call the police. And I was afraid what the police would do to him – maybe haul us both away.

Finally neighbors did make a call, in desperation. Two hours later, very late, a squad car pulled up, but the cops looked bored. They wrote the report grudgingly, reminded everyone that the owner still refuses to file charges, and that this is the fifth time they've answered complaints at this address.

But after examining the damage, the police took Binh away. I was chilled with fear. Surprisingly, Binh did not struggle at all. Even more surprisingly, I was quite relieved to see him go, as Lan had predicted. I'd done him no good anyway. They wanted to book him I suppose, or study him while he sang a theatrical in his Sino-Viet private language at the Ramparts Police Station. Then they could file another report. Apparently, there was no legal way to keep him in jail, or anywhere else. He couldn't stay in hospital more than forty-eight hours. So, two days later, like returned mail, he was released, and taken back to the same house he had battered.

He arrived late afternoon. The holes where windows once hung were being boarded up. The landlord's handyman was measuring for replacements. But he stopped in his tracks when the police ushered the poor boy up the steps.

With Americans watching, Binh looked even younger and fatter than before. He walked as if trying to remember how to use his motor reflexes. He seemed to lack an outer layer for the open air. He mumbled politely, in his pigeon Chinese, and asked me whether his record collection had been put back in its place, whether his guitar is still near his bed. Yes, I told him. "Are you hungry?" I asked, flooded with guilt.

"Not especially," I think he answered. He always ate at 5.15 precisely, a ritual feeding, and it was only four o'clock.

He moved like a gas; nodded to me respectfully, then mournfully to the handyman, and shuffled upstairs. The handyman nodded back until the body disappeared from sight, with me following, as if practicing.

Within the hour, as always, with no other recourse, Americans called the police again. They were told simply that the fat "tenant" was under a doctor's care, but the doctor was away that week. Nothing could be done without family approval. So American neighbors began calling up my family.

Two more days passed but no medical team appeared, to no one's surprise. By then, Binh had started an entirely new episode. For three hours, he applauded in a howl so fierce that it seemed to tear his larynx. He sensed my need to withdraw from him, and pushed even harder.

"I'm singing for you, Father," he said. "Don't look away. If you look away, I might forget myself. That's a threat."

We yelled at each other for a few minutes, until I said: "We have to let the Americans treat you for a while." I painted a picture of grateful relatives who would welcome him after he came back. But his face was a mask, flushed.

"Would you die with me if I asked you?" he added, then held my face in his hand, and ran his fingers through what remains of my hair.

I felt parched, and ran out of family stories. Meanwhile, he poked his head out of the window hole, to see if his racket was loud enough to stir up an audience; and if Americans from across the street were sending me orders to put him back in jail.

We embraced, or rehearsed an embrace for a theatrical he had in mind. He looked around him, at the fractured windows, as if awakening, and said: "I never saw this even during the war. I never saw anything blown apart from the inside."

A very acrid shame covered him. He tilted his head, and began to pull out every magazine and correspondence course I had dragged in for him, as if preparing to make a bonfire. I heard him speaking so fast; it was a gibberish of Vietnamese and English. His eyes in particular were foreign. They never told me enough anyway, nothing I could rely on. To cover for his illness, I used to lie that he was a soldier injured in the war.

Then very suddenly, I collapsed – as if struck on the head I thought. I was down probably a few minutes.

I dreamt of food, of fat on the top of a boiling pot on the sea off Vietnam, further out toward Thailand, where my son fell, and never came back. I was floating, and breaking apart, like oil slowly mixing and stretching. The next details escape me, something foolish about forty pounds of batter, rolled and filled, for delivery from the bakery.

The blade had been pulled across my stomach. The incision wasn't as painful as I expected. I saw the faces of three Americans coming toward me, and realized how withered and penitent I must look to them.

"Don't lift me."

I see no point elaborating on how much pain I felt. I can assure you that it felt nothing like the television movie about me. I may as well have died halfway through that show. Once the blade plunges into the actor who plays me, he falls backward out of the frame. At which point my existence in the movie ceases – with thirty minutes left. You never see me again: just my son in treatment, getting a better haircut, speaking better English, thanking his therapist (a hug); romancing his English teacher, she's naked on top, he's naked on top. He suddenly looked like a weightlifter. And as for me, you see my photo once from then on. And the letter I wrote, with all the hearts and flowers? Do I look like someone who just slips his entire life into an envelope? I was supposed to realize what utter shit my life was at exactly the moment of my being stabbed, as if the knife were performing brain surgery. And then, after the surgery, I have no story left.

The pain from the knife crossed my shoulder, and went through my stomach into my legs. But believe me, it was almost a relief compared to the pain I went through for five years before. I still to this day have trouble seeing how the actor playing my son stabs the actor playing me, how he lunged after me with the angle of the knife. And then in the movie, all my son sees right before is the landlord leading the Americans up the stairs. Can you imagine that would be enough reason to stab your father?

While I lay there after being stabbed, the Americans loomed over me as if I were the last stop on the way to the bar and grill. Their expressions copied the look on my face, which means I must have looked terrifying, or they had no expressions left. They said things to suggest calm, while I heard Binh screaming. I wanted to explain that all this must be kept between us. "This is not a crime." But my best attempt at speaking was another embarrassment, after all my preparation, more oil breaking up on water. I was held down almost the way he was, on the floor. A pillow from someone's couch was propped behind my neck. Then I heard my-self howl, and the pillow was replaced by towels.

The grimy slick of the old rug was near my face. I smelled how many footsteps and how much dust it had absorbed. But I was glued to it, not even uncomfortably, more like the blanket I was wrapped in as a child when my family took me from Ha Tien to Kien-Giang.

A Vietnamese who looked vaguely familiar leaned over me, but his complexion looked nothing like the movie, and he wasn't an old drinking buddy. In fact, I couldn't place him. In my delusion from the loss of blood, I guess, I swore that it was Quy, the *dudeng* from Vietnam, transformed into a paramedic, or a lawyer, or a fourth cousin on my wife's side.

I said in Vietnamese: "Every movement on the floor, even the creak of joists deep down the spine of the house hurts me. I feel every ache and crooked nail in this building."

He answered something suitable for the occasion, but nothing I can remember, nothing about the war, as he did in the movie. You think all we talk about all day is the war, even after someone stabs us? I was told to lay still. Then, after floating down the steps, I was strapped in the ambulance, and felt the ache of the motor, especially at turns, through my legs and up my stomach again. All this was too late to fix.

I dreamt about two children in Hanoi, a true story, true enough. In 1970, two children spent days living through a B52 raid, unable to leave their shelter because a bomb nearby failed to go off.

I heard a cluster of gunfire a block or more away, too rhythmic to be dangerous. It is a common sound in Los Angeles. Often people are simply firing into the air, imagining that the bullets will never land. In one apartment I had, I would occasionally hear bullets tap the roof, like a light rain, the faintest reminder, a stain breaking up in the water and gone.

1992: HO CHI MINH CITY, VIETNAM

I saved up some money again, and thought I should look up old faces, but the money didn't go as far as I thought. Saigon's walls and gates are long gone everywhere, the French style of Catina Street long gone, all thrown into a tumbler that is noisier than during the war. Business has taken to the streets, in open stalls between the traffic, vendors selling TVs, washing machines, dishwashers brought in by black market from Thailand, Taiwan, Malaysia, workers earning fifty cents or seventy-five cents a day. They jump in between grumpy twenty-year-old cars spinning across the road. Many of the rich have become poor, even live in what remains of Catina Street. Seventeen-year-old girls still are for sale, even at group rates, now that tourism has started from all over eastern Asia, and the jobs are still scarce. Some of the poor have become rich, particularly those in government. Prices have begun to stabilize, despite the under-ground businesses. Eventually, the black market will cover the buildings themselves, like an ivy.

Wars leave street vendors, not mourners. It's the same in Los Angeles: too many races shoved into the same space. Filipinos, Vietnamese, Salvadorans and Mexicans share the same dismal hallway, where street vendors mix with homeless; ever-lengthening lines of day laborers waiting for handouts at hardware stores. Quite a few street vendors – les enragés – must have taken some revenge last April, when Los Angeles burnt down, as if the Asian war had finally entered America. My son tells me that a cousin of mine was mistaken for a Korean. I won't tell you where my son was when it happened. Someone might make a sequel.

Nevertheless, despite the fires, a few street vendors manage to get rich. Lan has begun to eat too many of her pastries, seems to have ex-panded her five o'clock tasting ritual into dinner, and spread past her waist until her bosom and her belly form more of a mass together. But she covers it well, dresses to her station, and looks like a dumpling I still remember fondly; while I, in turn, become one of those cute, whimsical old uncles in the world, with my lame leg, and the crease I always keep in my pants.

And most surprising, last year in Los Angeles, I finally caught up with Quy the dudeng, who combs his hair back to cover a bald spot. Even an animal adjusts to a new job. Quy sells fruit wholesale at the produce market downtown, hasn't shot an American recently, and drives a Toyota, though he's considering an American car next. I tortured him with descriptions of young Lan naked at sunset, her legs parted, her head swinging in rhythm as she spoke. His eyes narrowed, and for a moment I'm sure he reached involuntarily toward his imaginary Colt 45, the way an amputee senses a lost leg.

I hear the scream of children outside, the same voices common to

Saigon or Los Angeles, nine year olds who have learned to speak in a nearly baritone voice, like an ochre, to practice sounding tough. Street vendors in the making. Three dogs roam the weedy parkway. A few men are repairing cars across the street, a business too fragile to provide enough income to lease a garage. It is all too fragile. But allow me to point out, it is not tragic. Tragedy is best reserved for those who have enough money and luck. Reviewing how you handled problems twenty years ago takes more time than a man with my income can afford. So instead, I remember like paint, which is my Sunday job, by the way: thin layers at a time.

I now speak enough dignified English to operate a cash register at a gas station. I hit the keys with the enthusiasm and ambition of a chicken at a food tray. At the window, I see young men approximately my son's age, and marvel at their grace, and their new cars. I wait for the right woman to come along.

I have quite a speech prepared for her.

PART III

DOCUFABLES

As I explain in the introduction, the docufable is a short essay crossbred between scholarship and the imaginary.

The contrasts between memory and erasure – distraction – are exaggerated. They are *ficciones* about forgetting, set inside social and historical research, rather than character-driven melodrama.

CHAPTER EIGHT

WITNESSES AFTER THE FACT

On 8 December 1991, a sixteen year old was shot dead in a drive-by on Douglas, in Angelino Heights. The car barreled away as if the murderers were simply joyriding. The body lay near where kids ride bicycles and families walk their dogs. A bullet had also entered the tailbone of the victim's girlfriend, who was nine months pregnant; another bullet in the stomach killed her unborn child.

The neighbors' reaction went from shock to panic. It was a quiet Sunday afternoon. Angelino Heights resembles a very peaceful, faded, moderately restored old midwestern town, an unshaved whisker from everything else torn down around it. In 1979, its turn-of-the-century name – "Angelino Heights" – was restored, with two street signs, costing the city a few hundred dollars, the sum of public investment in the area.

Ironically enough, Angelino Heights often gets dressed up for murders in the movies. In *Chinatown*, one scene in particular was shot there: the murder in Echo Park took place on Kensington Avenue up a narrow court building – across the street from where the wounded girl had lived, and where her lover's legend began – one fiction facing another in the making. Michael Jackson's *Thriller* was shot three blocks south, on Carroll Avenue, as were other horror films, and any number of television commercials and movies-of the-week. One house slated for demolition was converted in 1991 into a detective's office for the movie *The Last Boy Scout*; it still has the sleuth's make-believe sign – Hollenbeckis – on the pebbled-glass window, behind a front railing built by a movie crew to match the tumbled, weathered façade, with a wooden medallion painted into a blur up against the roof line. The rail was artificially aged, with newly applied alligator in the paint. Across from the detective's office, an old fallout shelter from the fifties has been permanently locked for generations, a steel door across a bunker, on the lawn of a ten-bedroom Victorian mansion, stuccoed over in the fifties (bunkered in its way), and now owned by a Korean church, and well tended by the faithful.

The signals that led to the two shootings were felt mostly by those on Kensington, in a growing panic as the business of children with guns invaded the lives of strangers. Otherwise, beyond a rash of new graffiti that was painted out twice a week, and one mugging near Kensington, the area continued to look and feel like an old maiden aunt. A teenage girl, perhaps fifteen, had taken up with a member of the Osiri Boys, stationed in the area. After she (and her mother) allowed the business of the gang to take over the house, a rash of OBS graffiti tags appeared, like an ad campaign announcing the opening of an Osiri business. The letters grew to six feet in height along the paver walls, and even on the sidewalk along Kensington. The noise brought complaints at night. One neighbor next door to 833 Kensington noticed bullet holes through his living-room window one morning.

Drug deals on Kensington moved front and center, from an obscured back alley, used by gangs for generations now, behind Edgeware Road, to valet service in the middle of the block, even beside occasional garage sales, where old clothes might be hung along a chain link fence, and old appliances displayed for sale. Drivers stopped very casually to pay for drugs delivered, and to chat, like bootleggers during Prohibition, out in the open, even on weekend afternoons. There may have been other signals that only insiders could spot, like sneakers tied at the shoelaces and thrown over a telephone wire – a way to advertise selectively, a marker only for clients. On Ridge Way, possibly left over from a crack house that had burned down leaving just a grassy meadow, I could see a pair of white socks bound up and tied carefully to electrical wires, near where Fred Halsted's little girl had been shot through the calf in the early seventies. But all that was barely remembered.

Despite community meetings about the shootings, and a hired canine patrol that circled the neighborhood, and occasionally waved from the van, an odd stillness remained, and still does, harboring four blocks of Mexicans, Salvadorans, Anglos, Chicanos, Chinese-Vietnamese, and Japanese.

On the Sunday afternoon when the boy (named Ernesto) was killed, police cordoned off the area. Nine and ten year olds came to study the corpse. For weeks afterward, the boys chattered anxiously about it, and began to invent imaginary crimes, stories about mobs of kids shooting guns. In a few years, they might forget what they saw – bury him inside a displaced nightmare, or confuse him with the face of an actor murdered in a movie.

I can imagine a fictional boy (about ten) who begins to dream the murder. He often dreams in nightmares. At the age of six he used to be haunted in his sleep by three visitors from the dead. First, leaning over his platform bed in his tiny room, near the miniature closet (the dead-space closet, so-called by his parents) was King Arthur, covered with dust from the caves of Avalon. Beside the glowering King Arthur was an equally horrific Jesus covered with blood (as he looked in the church in Oaxaca: ten bleeding Jesuses, each enclosed in glass with realistic blood, depicting scene by scene the journey to Calvary, while statues of the heads of saints stared down from overhead, stuck into the ceiling. Finally, beside Jesus was Dracula after a feast. It took a few months for the boy's father (a fictional surrogate of myself) to realize that all of these resembled a man with a beard – that the father wore a beard.

My fictional son always sleeps vividly, sometimes groaning loud enough to be heard through the house. Otherwise, he seems a cheerful child like my real son, with the usual obsessions, a bit shy with adults and liable to feel hurt suddenly by a cautioning look; but very sturdy in crisis, and generally very optimistic about his future – a perfectionist who ignores the worst of what's around him.

However, at night, particularly on the nights after we fled during the rioting – to Studio City – the terrors grew more intense. Up by the Ventura Freeway, in happy Anglolandia, in the living room set up for us to sleep in, he saw the statue of a child's head on the fireplace – a beloved memento sculpted by a man who had died the year before; a memento mori. One head suggests another.

Now, with us back home, when he goes to sleep, he sees a dense crowd of decapitated ghosts, some with guns. They squeeze into the frame of his movie, while he sits in an elevator of some kind. They wait patiently for the elevator to hit his floor, which is a hundred storeys or more up, atop the Hancock Towers in Chicago, overlooking Lake Michigan. He has never stayed asleep in his dream long enough to find out what happens after the elevator door opens. Any mention of ghosts after four in the afternoon, even of angels, heightens the terror. But once he falls asleep, with me in my thoughts nearby, he dreams like any other child. He won't talk about the shootings day or night. He often walks his dog past where one of the shootings took place. He never rides his bike anymore.

The mood on the street grew much calmer in the summer of 1992. The actor in 833 Kensington (with bullet-ridden windows, since replaced) sold his house; indeed, he put it up for sale the day after the riots, and it sold in a hurry. Anglos and middle-class Mexican Americans, particularly in the arts and in film, find the neighborhood appealing. The real-estate agents know as little as possible about the crimes, so they can lie for the sake of everyone involved. The households where the gangbangers lived seem to have moved to another neighborhood, often through community pressure, and possibly with a hard shove by the police. There was also a private canine patrol added; it was lately fired, to be replaced by an even better patrol, or so the neighborhood watch declares. The area is actually safer than before, probably safer than in decades.

The turn-of-the century fourplex where Ernesto (the boy who died) lived was sold a year later, and restored. After a four-color paint job, the resurrected hotel Craftsman fit comfortably across the street from the turrets and long porches of the gingerbread Victorians along Carroll Avenue. It helps make a better photo for the tour buses that pass by regularly; or a better picture for the Sunday painters who sketch under the massive ficus across the street – seventy feet high, a forest tree planted when the area was so rustic; the notion that this would get too large seemed impossible to conceive.

Recently, the actor who played the cop in *Sunset Boulevard* – the character (without dialogue) who lifted the body of William Holden out of Gloria Swanson's pool, after she shot him – died. The actor, Alan Whitney, had been living in retirement, keeping an eye out for problems while sitting on his porch, beneath his Queen Anne tower – a curmudgeonly presence who liked to share jokes about high urban decay. He was always good for twenty minutes about "hoodlums" he'd seen planning heists in the area; or on Mexicans he caught committing robberies; or on the drug-crazed twelve year olds who, ten years ago, had nearly burnt down his rental carriage house.

Whatever stories we may claim to write about crime, we are all, at best, witnesses after the fact, either because we repress what pain we actually felt, or because we never saw the actual moment when the bullet left the chamber. Rumors about the Uprising continue. We each of us have favorite stories that we tend to repeat. This is a favorite of mine. During the Uprising, at the corner of Hoover and Pico, the owner of the Cali-Mex

Market stood guard with his rifle, against looters. His was practically the only store for blocks that remained untouched. One of his workers carried an Uzi. Another on the roof let looters see his rifle. Finally on Friday, after shootouts and days of looting, and after he had made numerous phone calls to police, one squad car actually arrived. The officer listened to their complaints but was too absorbed in the moment to help. He offered this advice, or observation, as he drove away: "It's open season."[1]

One could write about the Cali-Mex story as if this were a western shootout, or a noir crime story. But neither would capture the heart of the crisis, about a neighborhood slipping into complete erasure, from which it will very likely never recover, because the problems have been forgotten yet again, except for an occasional photo opportunity about an act of charity in a poor neighborhood.

I could invent a few characters to stand in for the Cali-Mex story: a surrogate son, a neglected wife, a "Latino" youth, a cop, and blend them together to make a loaf. But more than urban melodrama, the Uprising struck as a group seizure: hundreds of thousands of people caught in the jaws of a large bird, or in an earthquake – a ground shifting – that had been shifting for fifty years. The Uprising was only a high-profile moment in an ongoing restructuring – neighborhoods in tectonic change; it was not at all like a story built around willful characters who stand in for millions of others. I study the photos of burnt streets: washed away malls, with puddles and broken limbs of buildings, and an occasional palm tree over a collapsed roof. I think that perhaps I am looking at pictures from Thailand, or a corner of Tienanmen Square in 1989, or a Pacific Island after a monsoon (even Florida after Hurricane Andrew). The simple agony, the unbolted fury, nearly make me cry.

However close I come in my own memory, I am still moments away from immediate impact, like the story I heard about a lawyer downtown who had her purse stolen during the demonstrations at Parker Center. Precious photos were taken also, by mistake, along with the manuscript copy of her book on sexual harassment, including all her notes. A few days later, she received a call from strangers, who asked if she would be willing to pay $20 to have her photos back. I can imagine her as a fictional woman, perhaps a single parent in her late thirties, driving to a dense apartment building near King Drive, and going in, finding the contrasts of poverty and normalcy ironic and shocking. According to the story I heard, after she paid a few dollars and was given the photos, she noticed her manuscript in the corner somewhere – they had been using it for toilet paper. I have considered this anecdote as a possible fiction. My source is a homeless person who swears by these facts, but I cannot verify them in any way. It would not even make a strong piece of business in a crime novel – too obvious, too allegorical, and not directly violent enough.

What in fact did most people actually see during this civil disturbance, beyond flourish and smoke? Far fewer fatalities occurred than were originally estimated. The smell of burning wood was so intense that it entered through sealed windows. The cloud of incinerated buildings floated much more heavily than smog. It looked like a thick brandy smoke, blowing eastward, shutting off buildings from view only a hundred yards away. It resembled Stendhal's description of the Battle of Waterloo, in the novel *The Charterhouse of Parma*. Fabricio, the young infantryman, is a bystander. He sees little more than smoke from the margins, the synesthetic smell of artillery; and silence when the battle changes direction.

Throughout the world, the most reprinted photo of the riots was very much like this description of the bystander. It shows a line of dour policemen blocking a street that is burning behind them. The viewer is given the point of view of the spectator pretending to be a rioter; but, actually, it is the POV of outsiders, including one news photographer, rubbernecking after an accident. Critic David Bate observed: "The image of the L.A. police ... confronts the spectator. Either you become a [phantasmatic] hero, pursuing your desire to its ultimate goal, or you become an ordinary citizen giving ground relative to one's desire."[2]

How often do reporters arrive at the scene of the crime after the evidence has already been altered or driven away? And, even if they arrive on time, not much may be visible. Many reporters were close enough to see a rock crash through their windshield, or to interview looters on the spot. However, in an event as massive as this, to be present at one street corner does not make you a reliable source. Nor does it give you enough background to discuss long-term causes, the subtleties of a particular street, its normalcies, its survival. Panic was the story that made this a ratings bonanza. Only the spark of hysteria was required. However, that spark may be all that is remembered.

NOTES

1. The term "open season" is also the title of Darryl Gates' CD-Rom on crime prevention; it is apparently a term commonly used by police to suggest a free-for-all (see section on "B-Rolls: TV Screens" in Chapter 10).

2. David Bate, "The Orgy of Looking: The Construction of the L.A. Rebellion in the British Press," *Afterimage*, October 1994, p. 9.

CHAPTER NINE

FICTIONS

ASI ES LA VIDA

The Rodney King tapes were seen on Spanish-language television. Discussions of the police were common at the South Gate Adult School, and in the South Gate area generally, as in immigrant Hispanic areas throughout Southern California. "Asi es la vida," one student explained; he then told a story about his cousin who had been shot in the head nineteen times by the police. The tone of voice was very factual. His face was entirely neutral, though occasionally he would stop, as if looking out through the window of a car.

A few months ago, another student mentioned a car accident that killed a young mother. The family was on welfare. The neighbors took up contributions, and raised enough for the funeral. There were no elaborate debates about acts of charity. This was a social fabric that requires mending, not a problem that was being solved.

In Angelino Heights, a fourteen-year-old boy goes to a magnet school for business majors, mostly to avoid the violence at King Junior High School, though he finds a great deal of "racism between blacks and Hispanics" outside after class, and not simply knives carried into the room as before. He explains this difference in a tone of voice that he has decided is safest, speaking in very soft vowels with no Spanish expressions. He has learned to be excessively careful about the moments when he laughs out loud, even to cover his face when he laughs – not unlike the way some Asian women do, he has noticed.

His family has been watching the Americans who own a house across the street, to find clues that might be useful, studying them in a friendly way for ten years now. Though he and his younger brother are friends with the Anglo children, a gulf has been growing, as if a target that must be hit never gets any closer, but slowly creeps further away. The boy is proud that he understands the Anglo jokes that the Anglo adults tell, about Nazi history or about local politics. His mother is convinced that a puzzle about success can be deciphered from the way Anglos talk to each other; that the handshake and the precise distance between people when they speak are rituals that bring power to those who act naturally. Anglos are never sudden in their movements.

Last week there was a shooting at the corner just west of the boy's house, in Angelino Heights. A twenty year old who was drunk went on a random spree. No one was hit. The twenty year old drove further north, nearer Sunset, and shot once up in the air when the police drove by. He was too drunk to realize they were actually staring, so they arrested him. The boy loves to repeat the story continuously. His mother watches the way he says it, to look for clues. She wants to be certain that he does not misunderstand what the shooting portends: not that a young man his age nearly died, certainly not that guns are exciting, but the facts of self-control when you present yourself.

The boy has been taught to be the adult male in the house. His father is around, but he drinks too much and gets nasty. His father has always been very slim, and the boy was fat and square from birth, like his brother and sisters – fat enough at eight to throw his drunken father across the room if necessary. So, whenever his father gets brutish, the boy is called over by his mother, and will make a show of force. Afterward, by the next day, the father will usually hide by working ritually on the car into the evening. The children have stopped helping him much, but the car survives.

His mother says that working-class Mexican women have to deal with men who drink – and with their women – but, worst of all, they never receive the bonus for this dishonor that wealthy women get – the freedom to travel a little, a Mexican to help with the cleaning. Her husband rarely disappears for more than a day or two; sometimes to work, other times on a bender. He tries to make it clear that family is like a lion's pride – his place of power. This makes good sense. You may slip the noose, but the family keeps to the same dinner hour every night.

A woman in South Gate has been allowed by her husband to go to adult school, even though she is quite beautiful, with pale skin, very black hair, delicate waist, elegant legs. It is not uncommon for husbands to be afraid that their beautiful wives might attract too much attention at a school. Studying very hard for over a year, she finishes the English program, and is asked by her teachers to be one of two women who will give a speech at graduation. Her husband decides that this is too risky, and she agrees not to show up. Her absence is painful. Her teachers are furious at the husband, even though they never met him. She, in the meantime, has stored her anger. There are more divorces in the USA than in Mexico, she says, because no replacement for the old system in families has emerged yet, except to earn enough money.

The boy in Angelino Heights remembers three years ago spending a weekend up in the mountains with an Anglo friend and family. He had no boots, and fell past his ankles into a sludge hole. But he spent the weekend studying their rules, storing up. One rule is that he does not mention that he is storing his anger. He and his mother are storing together, while she plans for him, but together they sense that she needs more information to plan effectively. "Asi es la vida" is not a big thing, he says. It's just an expression, but he never heard it much anyway. His mother works for a lady in Studio City now; she lives in a dome-shaped house in Topanga. At a party there, he and his mother joke with an Anglo about what a bastard the landlord is. Water drips into their kitchen from a hole upstairs that is never repaired. There is still no heat after fourteen years.

The landlord's son, meanwhile, has taken revenge for them all. He is something of a smart crook, and stole a thousand dollars from the office, spent it on a clothing binge with his friend Poo (who's living in Pasadena now with his father). "It's the only money anyone's got out of him that did any good," the boy says, smiling broadly, then checking himself.

THE PHOENIX TREE

As the son of a businessman in North Vietnam, he felt very well prepared to make a living in the United States. His father had come from China during the Japanese occupation, and made a fortune by wholesaling pastries. But that commercial experience in itself was not the key. The war with Americans taught him more. Whenever the B52s came on a bombing raid, the bunkers afforded no real protection. He saw at least two bunkers take a direct hit. It was statistically less dangerous simply to stay in your house, and wait out the odds.

Generally, in Haiphong where he lived, the Americans warned the populace. First of all, for a few years, the planes came only in the mornings, because of the radar. Then the Americans tried something odd – certainly to the eyes of a ten year old. The bombers dropped filmy sheets of tin foil, thinner than any paper – like large floating wings peeled from shiny insects. Thousands of these silvery sheets drifted downward and caught the light in hot blue flashes, like the center of a butane fire. Afterward, the ground radar did not work: the Americans could bomb at will – about three times a week on average.

As seen from below, the B52s arrived like a nest of flies that show no fear, simply cover a table, then whisk away. The carpet bombing usually involved about three miles by five miles, mostly away from where people lived. At first, the family, particularly the children, would visit the sight after the planes left – to look at the crater. But the damage up close was so difficult to take that it was best not to do that again.

One time in 1972, after three days of bombing, there was enormous mess. The rubble of houses and bodies were blown like rocks and gravel. As for corpses, one found mostly hands and arms, very few heads or full torsos. The impact from the center threw these body parts into the air, where they landed like caterpillars on the Phoenix trees, which had red blossoms at that time of year. Since there were no trucks, the families had to clean up: deposit what they could into plastic bags. This became more common for a while, until there was not much point discussing it.

We were Chinese in the North, so we were not allowed to join the army, or even to attend high school. So we concentrated mostly on setting up small businesses, of the kind that no one would mind, with not too many employees. The Chinese government reminded the Vietnamese to be careful with us; but at the same time, the Maoists were not certain that we could be trusted as Chinese either. At school, we got into fights, and were beaten up as pacifists or outsiders, or even as wealthy hoarders. We in turn did not have much at stake in the war, nothing that sent a clear message to us.

I am convinced that most of those I remember did not really support the Communist government, except those in the army, or those who learned what was at stake first hand. I know my memory doesn't fit what some sources show. One time, there were rumors that the Americans were about to invade. Everyone around me was excited, hoping the war would finally release us. It left me with a sensation that returns in different costume every so often.

As for the death and the general roar of that period, beyond the bombing I remember relatively little, except that since we saw a lot, we developed a way of being numb. I had no trouble sleeping, and do not have nightmares now. I remember seeing my neighbor – not much older than me – when he was told that his father had been blown up. So he went through the rubble where his house had been, and found enough of the corpse to bury it. Then, exhausted, he came home slowly, just in time to see his father, quite alive, arrive from work. You see, very little of what we were told fitted the facts that affected us directly. So we were left to our own devices. Our slang expression for a false fact was "a Hanoi story" or "Beijing radio." I suppose if Ho Chi Minh had lived – for everyone trusted him – that would have been different. But after he died, there was no one I can recall very clearly, no face in my mind.

Luckily for us, after Mao died, the politics between Vietnam and China grew too complicated to classify us. Seventy per cent of Vietnamese imports come from China, which brings resentment and reliance. Our status to travel or stay, or serve as liaisons, could never be settled. We were simply able to leave, with much less suffering than Chinese Vietnamese in the South.

And even now, North and South Vietnam still argue with each other. We in the north presumably have no culture, even though Hanoi is much more beautiful than Ho Chi Minh City – many more French buildings, much cleaner. But these issues will have to fade. When you visit Hanoi today, the duty officers are southerners and the customs officers are northerners. You only have to bribe the northerners, about $20 American. That is simple enough. For the Chinese in my experience, the Tong in any form takes priority over the state on a local level. That is why all business is a Tong. Show me where this is not so.

In Los Angeles, I am more afraid of the Vietnamese gangs, particularly in Garden Grove, than I ever was of the bombing. They will fire without warning. So, in my import/export business, I have no warehouse, no store. I do as much as possible by phone, and by traveling. If you leave no obvious mark, you can come and go.

THE UNRELIABLE NARRATOR

Years ago, I knew a 93-year-old lady named Molly Frankel, who owned a battered Queen Ann Victorian house, about five years older than she was, on what was once a fancy corner lot just north of Carroll Avenue,

in Angelino Heights. She had moved in somewhere between 1919 and
1928; had survived two husbands, one a possible suicide. No one knew
the details for certain; or at least her relatives who might know wouldn't
say. Even Molly didn't seem to have essential facts straight.

"My husband was a sporting man," she used to explain, meaning a
smart dresser, a john for prostitutes, or a gambler. "I came to Los An-
gheles in 1928, right after the war, and got a job as a bookkeeper. His
father saw I was a hard worker, running their business. So he more or
less forced his son to settle down with me. I wasn't much to look at, but
he knew I would help his boy stay at home more."

"Did you?"

Molly laughed, remembering something intimate or embarrassing about
her first husband. Then she added: "Now my second husband I kept
saying no to. He asked me to marry him five times a week. I exaggerate.
He said to me once. He was a lawyer for my business. He says to me:
'We could organize very well together.'"

"So?"

"So he was home continuously."

Molly still ran her shop, located somewhere in the warehouse district
on Main, near the flophouses. She sold "inside felt" that was used for the
collars on suits. "I get my best sleep there," she said.

One Fourth of July, her grand-niece, who now lives in Vegas, came by
to drive her to a party. Molly wore her better wig, had her beaded purse.
But she was confused somehow by the entire event.

The next day, a Sunday, I saw Molly ambling down the hill at dusk,
toward the bus. Then she realized her mistake, and told me: "I must have
overslept. I missed a day somehow."

She was beginning to lose track of the difference between sunrise and
sunset. Having just had her driver's license revoked, she would take the
Temple Street bus into downtown, then get her store ready, waiting for
the sun to come up, until finally it was clear that either there was a solar
eclipse or she'd missed a day somehow.

Molly lived on the second floor and rented out the rest to a large
Mexican family. They seemed desperate to keep Molly around, because
she never raised the rent, and they knew that her family coveted her
property. I was invited to visit Molly once at her house, and found her
seated in the kitchen, making toast over the stove, using a forties vintage
wire toaster that sat on the gas burner. Her built-in cupboards were
bulging with depression glass – pink and rose dishes crammed so tight

that they were about to spring the lock. Up in her attic – some 1,200 square feet of raw space – I found, hidden behind a lateral support beam, a dusty brown bag tied with rope. I asked her what this was, and she shrugged, but said I could have it if I wanted. Inside were four books from the W.E.B. DuBois Club – imprints from the early thirties. Was Molly a thirties Socialist?

"Must have been my sister. She was the reader."

"This has been here for fifty years. Was your sister involved in politics?"

"I don't go up here much."

Later I found out that her husband, apparently the organized one, had hanged himself up in the attic. But no one could say for certain.

Across the street, inside a huge Craftsman house, another of the matrons in the neighborhood had died in her late seventies, and left all her clothing stacked neatly, like fossil sediment, one on top of the other, from 1918 as a Temperance activist to 1983. Apparently, the living room was large enough to hold over three hundred people at her niece's wedding in the early fifties. Now her niece's daughter, a very serious young nurse, had moved in to keep the family interest going – just her and her boyfriend in 7,500 square feet.

The neighbors told her to listen for ghosts. Then after a few weeks, apparently, a rattle developed up in her attic. It would wake her up at night. Finally, out of purely secular desperation for a good night's sleep, she walked up the attic steps and asked her dead aunt for a truce. I'll keep the door closed up here, she offered, if you'll stop waking me up at night. And that was enough apparently.

One early evening I saw Molly on her way to the Temple Street bus again. I stopped her, and insisted that it was sundown. She laughed at me, but agreed to wait long enough to find out. Then, as the sky darkened and the night breezes started, she finally apologized, saying that ever since that Fourth of July party last month she kept getting her days mixed up.

That was about ten years ago. Molly's family took the house, and put her in a senior citizen's home, where she grew enormously fat, and may have been happy for all I know. She died five years later, apparently older than she admitted to, somewhere around a hundred.

It must be strange to live in a world that utterly transforms around you, as if you were an immigrant in your own house. As I explained earlier, from 1928 (or 1919), the area went from mixed Anglo and Jewish bourgeois to prostitutes and drug dealers down the corner in the early seventies. On Sunset Boulevard, there had once been gyms where the young Anthony Quinn trained to be a boxer in the thirties, then thought better of it, and worked on Sundays in the church of Sister Aimee Semple McPherson. Not a whisper of all that remains, except the Jensen center, which had declined into a drug contact by the late fifties, and had long since turned its bowling alleys into discount stores.

There are practically no fragments left of Molly's life, and certainly no memories in the house, which has since been sold and renovated into upscale apartments. I have no idea how I would find out precisely where Molly lied. "I hide a few years," she used to say. I don't even really know if her life was dowdy or melodramatic. Like that of the Vietnamese whom I interviewed, hers is a history of ways to distract information more than erase it.

That is more or less the spirit of unreliable narrator. It is a story based on how we forget or repress memory.[1] Clearly it has a literary tradition behind it: from eighteenth-century fiction in particular (the Münchhausens and Uncle Tobys); in Russian literature after Gogol's short stories;[2] German and Central European fiction after 1880;[3] the Romanticist fascination with demolished historic places as unreliable narrators, the absent presence that in Michelet's words are "obscure and dubious witnesses" (1847).[4] Virginia Woolf's emptied rooms where the remains of memory are displaced;[5] American tall tales that Mark Twain loved; in Roland Barthes' *S/Z*; in noir fiction by Jim Thompson or David Goodis, where the narrator is a criminal who has to repress what he does, and lie to the reader;[6] in the broad crisis of representation in cinema[7] that I discuss in the next section (how film about Los Angeles distracts the real space; the unreliability of television as political memory).

"In old apartments," writes Bruno Schulz, speaking through the voice of a father, "there are rooms which are sometimes forgotten. Unvisited for months on end, they wilt between the walls and ... close in on themselves."[8] The Father went inside one of these collapsed rooms, and found that "slim shoots grow [in the crevices] ... filling the gray air with a scintillating filigree lace of leaves." But by nightfall, they are "gone without a trace." "The whole elusive sight was a fata morgana, an example of the strange make-believe of matter which had created a semblance of life."

NOIR AS THE RUINS OF THE LEFT

Mike Davis has occasionally thought about writing a piece tentatively entitled "Walter Benjamin in Boyle Heights." Benjamin does not commit suicide; instead he takes the boat to New York and winds up among the German émigrés in Los Angeles. Being too much a scholar of the city street, he elects not to live in the Pacific Palisades, not to bow at the feet of Thomas Mann. But he does show up at modified barbecues at Feucht-wanger's[9] estate, chats with Schoenberg, and hopes for some beneficence from Mann, for the phone call that could bring a hefty literary contract perhaps, anything to improve the pittance that the Frankfurt School in Exile provides. (I can feel myself embroidering here.) Benjamin moves instead to Boyle Heights, a Jewish/Mexican/Japanese/Serb enclave just east of downtown, across a bridge that reminds him of bridges in Berlin perhaps. After a somewhat tortured version of a power lunch with Bertolt Brecht, he decides to write a *Chronik* on Hollywood studios, particularly those at Gower Gulch, the marginal ones that produce horse operas and cheesy Flash Gordon serials.

Benjamin takes the Sunset Red Car to Gower, feels his suit in need of pressing under the baking, dry heat, but walks another mile until the Crossroads to the World[10] display catches his eye. A globe of the planet, continents included, spins serenely and idiotically in front of a patch of stores, and what might resemble an arcade (there is also an arcade in downtown Los Angeles). But he feels too far away from all that shopping history to bother anymore. All his notes are crated somewhere in Paris, probably being used as briquettes for heating a flat in the winter.

Years later, a scholar tries to interpret the writings of Walter Benjamin in Los Angeles. Apparently, Benjamin became very interested in meeting Harry Raymond, the detective who had cracked open the Shaw Admin-istration downtown, forced it out of office, to be replaced by the reform mayor Fletcher Bowron. Raymond, who still lived in Boyle Heights just blocks from Benjamin, had survived being blown up by a bomb planted in his car by Earl Kytelle. Later, after continued threats on his life, he "blew the lid off of City Hall" in a very steamy trial.

Benjamin also ate at Clifton's cafeteria downtown, and met the owner, Clifford Clinton, formerly an employer of Harry Raymond, for a very politically explicit radio program back in the thirties. Benjamin spoke with him for a while about radio itself, about the shows each had written (Benjamin had worked in radio in the late twenties in Germany). But, most of all, Benjamin had trouble addressing the ruins, allegories and street energy of Los Angeles, the intricacies of its local politics. Flâneurship took on a disengaged spirit, until he located his subject.

I can see him taking notes in a movie theater, taking in the used book stores on Third Street, working as a tutor, trying once again to position himself within a university. His study on B films as baroque irony took four years to write, while he drifted uneasily inside the margins of the German/noir film community. His descriptions of walking through La Cienaga Boulevard undoubtedly influenced Sartre's visit to L.A. right after the war, and Sartre's essay "American Cities," where he declared in somewhat omniscient fashion that neither New York nor Chicago had neighborhoods in the purer European sense, and that streets in America were generally nothing more than "a piece of highway."

> In certain cities I noticed a real atrophy of the sidewalk. In Los Angeles, for example, on La Cienaga, which is lined with bars, theaters, restaurants, antique dealers and private residences, the sidewalks are scarcely more than side-streets that lead customers and guests from the roadway into the house. Lawns have been planted from the façades to the roadway of this luxurious avenue. I followed a narrow path between the lawns for a time without meeting a living soul, while to my right, cars streaked by on the road; all animation in the street had taken refuge on the high road.[11]

Benjamin actually filed this quotation in 1956, a few months before his death. Beside it, he wrote, in that clipped style he developed later in his life: "A city is a blind courier. It brings nothing. It takes nothing. That is why we grow so fixated on roads. Sartre should have watched the dust settle more."

The scholar found this inside fifty pages of notes for a Los Angeles *Passagenwerk* – nothing as elaborate as what Benjamin planned to write about the Parisian arcades. But on page 14 Benjamin had circled the same quotation from his writing that Davis used, quite coincidentally, as the preface to *City of Quartz*:

> The superficial inducement, the exotic, the picturesque has an effect only on the foreigner. To portray a city, a native must have other, deeper motives – motives of one who travels into the past instead of into the distance. A native's book about his city will always be related to memoirs; the writer has not spent his childhood there in vain.

The term "memoir" is the link; more specifically, the memoir of buildings inhabited by political ghosts. In Benjamin's writings about Berlin and Paris, city streets resemble what he defined as ruin in his first book *The Origins of German Tragic Drama*. Ruins are shells of faded memory recovered as theater – stylized, aestheticized; an exotic memory of distilled torment. No matter how authentic the ruin, it is received, or read, as simulated memory: phantasmagoria, dioramas, arcades. Every building is faintly warped to the eye, as if by glaucoma. The built environment is both political critique and nostalgia. So also is his literary style; the montage of quotations on the surface of the page draws attention to the quotations he finds on the surface of buildings.

The memoir then is a contradiction. It describes actions taken, but in the spirit of lost opportunities – deeds left unfinished, barely desired any longer; moments when the writer was a flâneur. As a somewhat metaphysically inclined Marxist, Benjamin was very aware of how paradoxical this approach was,[12] as is Mike Davis for that matter, by no means a metaphysician, but often, in his own words, a "reteller of the Book of Apocalypse." In that spirit, I can imagine Benjamin inserting this quotation in his archive about Los Angeles:

> Language clearly shows that memory is not an instrument for exploring the past but its theater. It is the medium of past experience, as the ground is the medium in which dead cities lay interred.[13]

Davis was aware when he wrote *City of Quartz* that much in the language of academic history functions as "dead cities interred." Its reliquary function helps distract, rather than spark urban politics. He did not want a style that divided him from deeply held commitments, centrally to the labor movement, but to others as well – the politics that evolved into the gang truce; architectural *charrettes* that occasionally change city policy; more broadly to political journalism for newspapers or for the *Nation*. He therefore chose an activist writing style for *City of Quartz* – the historian using elements of noir fiction and polemical criticism – to build an imaginary lively enough to compete with the sunshine mystique of L.A. promotion. He wanted the book to cut more deeply into muscle tissue, and perhaps make some political difference.

That is not to say that this style is immune to the crisis that Benjamin describes, when history "seize[s] hold of a memory as it flashes up at a moment of danger."[14]. Any critique that uses a noir aesthetic can transform the agonies of the inner city into an exotic descent. On one level at least, that of popular memory, there is no such thing as bad publicity for the crimes of capitalism, any more than there is for pornography.

The popular success of *City of Quartz* has bred an exotic reading that resembles a cyber-noir opera. There seems no way to avoid that. In the minds of many fans of the book – certainly the many students who speak to me – "Fortress L.A." flashes internally like a movie scenario. Despite its effect on local journalism and on urban studies generally, that par-amnesiac imaginary seems impossible to shake. Students describe heli-copters pulsating beneath a huge crane shot. A futuristic swat team crashes through a window, as if from a *Die Hard* scenario.

William Gibson, at the back of his novel *Virtual Light*, cites Davis as a singular influence. "His observations regarding the privatization of public space"[15] can be seen in the character Rydell's life in Los Angeles. Rydell is a renta-cop who works for the IntenSecure company, which also specializes in "gated residential" policing, particularly out in the "edge cities," clearly a term that is part of a much larger debate that includes Davis.[16] I could not say precisely if other cyber novelists have worked directly with Davis's critique. If they have, their stories would seem to merge two contraries that he discusses: upscale enclaving, and the boom in prisons and surveillance. Novels like Stephenson's *Snow Crash* do happen to resemble Davis's version of the panoptical, as expressed in 1990. One can even sense elements of Fortress L.A. in the staging of the movie version of *Johnny Mnemonic*. It is a vision of opportunities shattered, of saving democracy after it has died, in a world twenty years after passages from Davis like the following:

> Anyone who has tried to take a stroll at dusk through a strange neighborhood patrolled by armed security guards and signposted with death threats quickly realizes how merely notional, if not utterly obsolete, is the old idea of the "freedom of the city."[17]

I also see a secondary reading of Fortress L.A., less essential perhaps. In phrases about the "obsolescence of freedom," Davis's text becomes an ironic confession about political activist literature in the 1990s. American politics at the moment leaves a lot to feel nostalgic about. To some degree, the left is also a phantom limb, much as I regret to say it. Conservative promotion has matured much faster than leftist literature. Our political culture has been emulsified by advertising. Policies and politics continue to skew deeply to the right. And the arc has not turned to the left yet. In response, activist literature has begun to take on a baroque theatricality, such that Benjamin used when describing the cultural politics of the twenties and thirties in Western Europe. He sensed, as many in the left do today, that mass promotion had become thorough enough to be a civilization like the Baroque; it delivers its own policies and politics. And while Benjamin was hardly as cynical about this effect as Adorno, he felt its phantoms very personally. They spoke to his own predicament while in exile, an activism distracted, partly erased – like noir literature in yet another way. It is the "detective" describing vagrancy and marginalization, the Jewish Communist intellectual waiting in Paris during an emergent Nazi era.

The linkage in my fictional essay has gone from Benjamin to Davis, and back to noir nostalgia, and finally to cyber-noir. Descriptions of the city street as ruin are at the core of each of these. Benjamin was not deeply involved in noir fiction when he lived in L.A., but he did collect a few quotations from the *Black Mask* school, mostly the moody openings to stories about the climate, particularly the dry winds, driving people to crime. They described for him ruins in the making, similar he noted to "the curling wallpaper in my tiny kitchen." One citation came from the story "Goldfish," written by Raymond Chandler in 1936, who was at a low point financially at the time (perhaps Benjamin empathized):

> I wasn't doing any work that day, just catching up on my foot-dangling. A warm gusty breeze was blowing in at the office window and the soot from the *Mansion House Hotel* oilburners across the alley was rolling across the glass top of my desk in tiny particles, like pollen drifting over a vacant lot.[18]

That is very much the mood of Chandler interiors, memory dissolving at the edges, like old wallpaper. "I'll Be Waiting" appears in the *Saturday Evening Post* on 14 October 1939, only a month after the start of the war in Europe:

> At one in the morning, Carl, the night porter, turned down the last of three table lamps in the main lobby of the Windermere Hotel.[19] The blue carpet darkened a shade or two and the walls drew back into remoteness. The chairs filled with shadowy loungers. In the corners were memories like cobwebs.

The most prescient symbol that Benjamin collected was about the Santa Ana winds, in what probably has now become the most famous Chandler opening, from "Red Wind" (1938):

> There was a desert wind blowing that night. It was one of those hot dry Santa Anas that come down through the mountain passes and curl your hair and make your nerves jump and your skin itch. On nights like that every booze party ends in a fight. Meek little wives feel the edge of the carving knife and study their husbands' necks. Anything can happen. You can even get a full glass of beer at a cocktail lounge.[20]

In the sixties, this passage was made famous in Joan Didion's *Slouching Toward Bethlehem*,[21] a bit of dark flânerie in its own right. But more important to an understanding of what Benjamin sensed, these winds are mentioned by other writers of Chandler's era. Simmering hatreds gather in an uncanny stillness. Ozymandius waits for a dust storm. The dryness is faintly stinging, like a slightly sour amphetamine. (I actually love the Santa Ana sensation, by the way.)

In 1941, Benjamin clipped a section written by Erle Stanley Gardner, then one of the veteran L.A. *Black Mask* writers. It was an extraordinary two pages on santanas. Before they strike, the sky glows with a "startling clarity," "dustless," the air "listless devoid of life." Then the blast of heat "churns up particles of dust so fine they filter between dry lips, grit against the surface of the teeth."[22] The narrator in the story is a writer at work when the dust hits. He has to shutter the windows, but hears the crackle and rattling. His nerves get edgier. The narrative hook has been established, like an undertow. The story begins – in this case about clues to a murder that can be seen in female accessories left on the furniture. A woman appears suddenly in the room, and startles the writer. While the santana continues, she begins to talk about a pair of leather gloves[23] that the writer notices have an inexplicable but telling graphite stain in the corner. (I can't write this without thinking of the gloves in the O.J. Simpson trial being "extra large" but too small, presumably shrunk because they were soaked in blood: another empty trope in that ludicrous trial. Descriptions of trials remain a continual source of threnodic irony in crime books, even parody. Justice is turned into a theatricalized ruin, like the edgy testimony of a hostile witness in a crime film.)

Noir literature emerged in the twenties during many such cases – during the Teapot Domes of the Republican era, during Prohibition, in the vacuum after the Progressive movement was wiped out immediately after the First World War. It was social realism as baroque; leftist activist intentions faintly remembered, then re-enacted with futile results. The crime stories that appeared in *Black Mask* magazine bore out this ambivalence – militant tales about grotesque waste of life, red harvests. The writing generally retains that divided spirit into the thirties, both militant and wistful, despite the enthusiasms of the New Deal – more as a statement about the Depression. It is hard-boiled nostalgia, hinting at periods of moral clarity that have become vestigial in characters like the Continental Op, the Thin Man, or Philip Marlowe. They all booze about a past they cannot entirely forget. And while they have, in Chandler's words, "a disgust for sham and a contempt for pettiness," their world is a withering joke.

> It is not a fragrant world, but it is the world you live in… It is not funny that a man should be killed, but it is sometimes funny that he should be killed for so little.[24]

After they finish with the crooks, and the dust has settled, the crime remains to some degree past the point of no return. The corpse will not be brought back to life.[25] The evil is still in the atmosphere. Often no one seems all that interested in seeing the crime solved anyway. The decisions that could have made for an easy solution were allowed to lapse. The crime scene is also a ruin. The detective suffers a phantom urge for moral correction, like a bout of malaria. It is a nostalgia for activism during deeply treacherous conservative eras.

NOTES

1. Ways of Lying – a few narrative devices involving an unreliable narrator:

(a) Announcing the mental weakness of the character within the first paragraph (usually in the first person) as symptomatic of an affliction, or as the moment after unsettling sleep, when the dream cannot be shaken loose yet. For example, Gogol's Poprischen in *Diary of a Madman* has trouble waking up to get to work, and seems disoriented still as he walks into the dreary Russian cold. In Kafka's *Metamorphosis*, in the third person, of course, the symptom is identified in the first line. The opening of the novel *The Blind Owl* (trans. D. Costello [New York: Grove Weidenfeld, 1957], by Iranian master Sadegh Hedayat (1903–1951): "There are sores which slowly erode the mind in solitude like a kind of canker." And, of course, the model openings in Poe and from Dostoyevsky's *Notes from Underground*.

(b) When the narrator "writes" unreliable entries directly on the imaginary page. The classic example is Gogol's *Diary of a Madman*, where Poprischen loses control of his diary when he can write Spain only as the word China: "China and Spain are really one and the same country… If you don't believe me, then try to write 'Spain,' and you'll end up writing 'China.'" And, of course, the many tricks of misremembering on the page that Sterne performs.

(c) When the narrator clearly refuses to discuss a crucial event that the reader senses. This is very typical of the caricature of the novel of sociability in eighteenth-century literature. In noir fiction, this device allows the murderer to feel morally justified, while the reader senses that this denial will come home to roost. Deleuze and Guattari identify this hiding of events as "fundamental forgetting," "the nothing that makes us say 'whatever could have happened to make me forget where I put my keys, or whether I have mailed that letter?'" The characters have forgotten something that must be fundamental, because they seem lost without it. See also Deleuze and Guattari's chapter on the novella in *A Thousand Plateaus*: the evacuated pre-history that is essential to the novella (the forgotten diegesis); the events that are a phantom presence, but that no character chooses to remember (narrate to us). Kleist's play *Prince Frederick of Homburg* is an interesting case of whether the fundamental forgetting is willful or involuntary. The director of any performance of the play must decide whether the prince is dreaming or not, because the character is never allowed to know.

(d) Hurricane in the eye: once the unreliable parameters are established in the story, no matter how outrageous these are, they must exist in a world of absolute verisimilitude, as in Gregor Samsa's household (*Metamorphosis*), or the responses to the runaway nose in Gogol's story.

(d) Interruptions: as if to suggest something too painful to remember but essential to the story; possibly to shift the blame for something the reader cannot know. In that sense, much stream-of-consciousness fiction uses the unreliable narrator: the deliberately erased story that the narrator wants to explain but will omit.

(e) The matter of degree: obviously these devices appear to some degree in all fiction. In some cases, however, they dominate the structure and the chain of events.

2. Gogol's *Diary of a Madman* and *The Nose* are the classic format – the junction between Romanticist irony and modernist collage – repeated in Dostoyevsky's "The Crocodile," in Kafka's *Metamorphosis*, and in absurdist fiction and theater of the fifties.

3. A particular favorite of mine, gruesome I admit, is the short story "The Autopsy," by Georg Heym (1887–1912) German Expressionist poet/playright and novelist. A dead man is losing memory while the doctor does an autopsy.

4. See Londa Orr, "Intimate Images: Subjectivity and History – Stael, Michelet and Tocqueville," in Frank Ankersmit and Hans Kellner, eds, *A New Philosophy of History* (Chicago: University of Chicago Press, 1995), p. 98. See also in the same anthology: Nancy Partner's critique of historical culture.

5. Woolf's "The Haunted House" is among the most abbreviated examples I know.

6. Also in novels about amnesiacs, like Cornell Woolrich's *Dark Curtain*.

7. From Robert Stam, Robert Burgoyne, and Sandy Flitterman-Lewis, *New Vocabularies in Film Semiotics: Structuralism, Post-Structuralism and Beyond* (London: Routledge, 1992), pp. 97–103: Borrowing from the writings of Genette, the unreliable narrator in film is defined usually as one type of voice-over: the "embedded" narrator – embedded one of the characters who is in the action. The embedded narrator then becomes a subset of the "intra-diegetic" narrator: any form of interior voice-over. For the story to "work," the audience must sense that these voices are "unreliable," that the intra (insider) narrator has a stake in lying, may not "see straight" in the heat of the moment. In opposition to this "intra" variant is the "extra-diegetic." "Extra," as in outside: a voice-over from a character not in the scene, who provides exposition primarily. Among the films usually cited in this discussion are: Hitchcock's *Stage Fright* (the "lying flashback"); Resnais' *Last Year at Marienbad*; Weir's *Breaker Morant*, Kurosawa's *Roshomon*; Altman's *Fool for Love*; Buñuel's *That Obscure Object of Desire*. When *Laura* is cited, that brings to mind another cache of films altogether, to which I would add *Usual Suspects* (1995) – stories where a suspect's memory of a crime is re-enacted from voice-over, but proves to be a red herring, or a lie. Among film theory cited are: Sarah Kozloff *Invisible Storytellers* (1988); Seymour Chatman, *Story and Discourse* (1978); Francesco Casetti, *D'Un Regard L'Autre* (1986); and essays on Hitchcock; Guido Fink on *Laura* and *Mildred Pierce*. However, in this project, I found the omissions by voice-over and flashback

THE HISTORY OF FORGETTING

more appropriate. For example, Barthes in *Image–Music–Text* suggests how props and the gaps between characters imply unreliable memory. Another useful form is how short-term memory operates as montage in experimental cinema – the appropriation or the repetition of familiar texts as loops in films, e.g. Rybzinski's *Tango*. I also would consider Buñuel's "documentary" *Land Without Bread* very much an "unreliable" use of denotation. The "extra-" diegetic voice-over, usually a manly baritone, is "lying." He contradicts with surgical precision what is undeniably real footage by Buñuel's crew – of a truly miserable cluster of towns known as Las Hurdes in Spain.

Finally in this partial list: all forms of "upside-down" animation are unreliable narrators, e.g. the animated cartoon – see my book *Seven Minutes: The Life and Death of the American Animated Cartoon* (London: Verso, 1993). By upside-down, I mean gravity upside down, spatiality upside down, customs upside down (e.g. Tex Avery), as opposed to barely noticed mattes in live action, or heads inserted digitally on another body.

8. Bruno Schulz, *The Street of Crocodiles*, trans. C. Wieniewska (New York: Penguin Books, 1977; orig. 1934), pp. 67–8.

9. Leon Feuchwanger, whose home in Pacific Palisades (at Paseo Robles) was the literary meeting place for the German writers in exile (interview with Richard Hertz, 1995).

10. The actual name was Crossroads *of* the World (Benjamin's problem with English – at first). This was a complex built in 1936–37, along Sunset Boulevard in Hollywood, as "an outstanding landmark and civic attraction as well as a centralized shopping district." It was generally perceived more as a "stage set than most retail facilities of any sort." Each building had a national theme: England, France, the Netherlands, Spain, Persia, Colonial New England, etc. It also had a midway, like a fair or a carny; and the project overall was continuously advertised as the first consumer space to function immediately as a public space as well, however exaggerated the sense of public. Benjamin missed many of these details, but saw it as a composite of "American Surrealist evasion," and found the French simulacrum a bit "terrifying, along with what they thought passed for coffee" (Richard Longstreth, *Markets in the Meadows: Los Angeles, The Automobile and the Transformation of Modern Retail Development, 1920–1950* [manuscript, 1994], pp. 792–4).

11. Jean-Paul Sartre, "American Cities," *Literary and Philosophical Essays*, trans. A. Michelson (New York: Collier Books, 1962; orig. 1955), p. 123.

12. Benjamin describes this contradiction clearly in his oft-cited essay on Surrealists as "profane illuminators." The surrealist use of optical paradox reminds Benjamin of the crisis among revolutionary intelligentsia during the 1920s:

> We penetrate the mystery only to the degree that we recognize it in the everyday world, by virtue of a *dialectical optic* that perceives the everyday as impenetrable, the impenetrable as everyday...
>
> Nowhere do ... metaphor and image collide so drastically and so irreconcilably as in politics... This image sphere, however, can no longer be measured out by contemplation... [That is why] the revolutionary intelligentsia ... has failed almost entirely in making contact with the proletarian masses, because [its imagery] can no longer be performed contemplatively. (*Reflections*, trans. E. Jephcott [New York: Harcourt Brace Jovanovich, 1978], pp. 190–91)

13. Walter Benjamin, *Reflections*, pp. 25–6. *Berliner Chronik* was started in 1932.

14. Walter Benjamin, "Theses on the Philosophy of History," *Illuminations* (New York: Schocken Books, 1969; orig. 1955), p. 255.

15. William Gibson, *Virtual Light* (New York: Bantam Books, 1993) pp. 351–2, 77–9.

16. See above, Chapter 2, footnote 27.

17. Mike Davis, *City of Quartz*, p. 250. Let us examine this image in an innocent way. As a child, I used to wander through Coney Island day and night, watch people knock each other around, hear the groans of prostitutes under the boardwalk, and yet feel immune, as if I had a right to drift through the city. That would seem quite risky for my son, and he instinctively knows it.

18. Raymond Chandler, "Goldfish," opening paragraph, in many editions now (e.g. *Trouble is My Business* [New York: Vintage], originally in *Black Mask* (1936), and reprinted in the Chandler anthology *Red Wind* (Cleveland and New York: The World Publishing Company, 1941).

19. Years ago, a student made a film about this short story. He began by asking for advice about locations, and found a hotel intact from the thirties. He was disappointed though. It wasn't "dark" enough. I told him that a white, neo-classicist look was very trendy in hotel interiors back then. He remained unconvinced. It simply wasn't "real" enough.

20. Raymond Chandler, "Red Wind," *Dime Magazine*, Jan. 1938. See note 19 above. I rarely find an L.A. crime novel that does not mention the Santa Anas somewhere, particularly since 1990 (e.g. Michael Connelly, Alex Abella).

21. Joan Didion, "Los Angeles Notebook," in *Slouching Toward Bethlehem* (New York: Dell Publishing, 1961). The section that mentions Chandler and the winds originally appeared in *The Saturday Evening Post* as "The Santa Ana."

22. A.A. Fair (pseudonym for Erle Stanley Gardner), *Double or Quits* (New York: Dell Publishing, 1960; orig. 1941), pp. 19–20.

23. Also: the photo of gloves in André Breton's surrealist novel, *Nadja* (1927): an aleatory clue to a badly remembered event – in this paramnesiac satire of the gothic. *Nadja* is a prelude to Robbe-Grillet's *The Erasers* (*Les Gommes*, 1953), where American noir is clearly a source. Again, the clues lead to a circle of undetection, then in the final scene mutually eradicate memory of any crime at all. And note Robbe-Grillet's pun – *gomme* as gummy eraser and the gumshoe (as eraser). Both are "a soft crumbly eraser that friction does not twist but reduces to dust" (Alain Robbe-Grillet, *The Erasers*, trans. R. Howard [New York: Grove Press, 1964; orig. 1953], p. 126).

24. Raymond Chandler, *The Simple Art of Murder* (New York: Ballantine Books, 1972; orig. 1950), on the last page of the essay (p. 21). I should add that Chandler's politics did veer to the right, as one might expect for a former oil executive; but always very nostalgically, as if out of disgust for lost chances more than as a commitment to anything resembling the right-wing politics of the forties and fifties, which he generally felt were a pox to the life of the writer. He also found postwar Los Angeles too scrubbed and artificial, even while he is so remorseless in his stories about the decayed districts of prewar Los Angeles. Chandler flourishes in ambience, from the Latin *ambiens*, meaning to "go round," not very far from another Latin root, *ambigere* (as in ambiguity), "to wander."

25. This point brings me to the oddness of the film *Laura* (1944), where the corpse is essentially brought back to life, but the life of the woman who actually was shot to death by mistake, while opening a door, disappears and is barely noted – yet another variation of distraction used as a story hook in crime films, like *Vertigo* (1958), or even *The Third Man* (1949).

PART IV

FORGETTING ON THE SCREEN

CHAPTER TEN

THE MOST PHOTOGRAPHED AND LEAST REMEMBERED CITY IN THE WORLD

The crime film *Criss-Cross* (1949) opens just west of the old downtown. A streetcar with a destination marked "Hollywood" rolls out from the Fourth Street Tunnel. Burt Lancaster gets off and walks up a steep hill, along a hatchwork of wooden steps, into his old neighborhood – Bunker Hill. It has been described as a "dazzling, fresh-air sun-swiped scene," but "all the daylight points up the 'mistake' waiting in the darkness."[1] Later, he plans a heist while in a rooming house in Bunker Hill, not unlike similar scenes a decade later in *Kiss Me Deadly*.

In dozens of feature films set in downtown L.A., there is precious little else to turn to, practically no record of what was erased, and certainly no movie directly on the subject – nothing but an occasional camera angle. *Chinatown* may be the Ur-text for L.A. political history, but it obscures as much as it clarifies. It does chronicle many of the fundamentals – that a coterie of boosters and investors persuaded the public to vote for a bond issue in 1906, to pay for the aqueduct that was finished in 1913. There was indeed an "artificial" drought in 1906, and a conspiracy. It is true that the real power broker, Harry Chandler of the *Times*, does not appear as a character – a powerful omission. The conspirators were more public, less secretive; but then this is noir allegory, about the primal secrets of blind greed. Perhaps John Huston plays an amphibious enough monster to stand in for many. Even the ending reminds the audience that in L.A. the powerful families who "bought" the future in 1906 may still run something like an Albacore Club today (the beach club in the film where the conspiracy is hatched).

247

The actual dates of the water scandal had to be shuffled to make the story more Chandleresque. 1913 would have required stiffer collars and archaic cars. 1937 is more atmospheric. It also places the film inside an imaginary that seems almost Arthurian – the noir of thirties' Los Angeles, the time outside of time for sagas about white male panic. What else indeed can one possibly ask of a film, particularly a great film?

Like Froissart's *Chronicles* in the fourteenth century, even great cinema will record battles and peace treaties as spectacle, and the rest as inspired folklore. I know that there are reels about daily life in L.A. that are being uncovered regularly, and a history of "popular memory" that is adduced by studying films and television. But whose memory really? Producers? Distributors? The gaps remain insurmountable, particularly for a city where the tourist imaginary has been a major export industry.

Documentary films should be a more compelling alternative to *Chinatown*, more about survival without the tourist evasions; but here, too, "the subjective voice"[2] of ethnography often serves as another form of erasure, "the ruins of memory."[3] On the subject of the demolition of downtown, Kent MacKenzies' *The Exiles* is the best documentary fictional film I know. Even the year it was produced fits the problem – 1961, months before Bunker Hill was torn down. In *The Exiles*, Native Americans spend a Joycean night in Bunker Hill, from apartments at the top, down the 280 steps to local bars along Grand and Hill; and into grimy Victorian apartments for low-stakes gambling. They inhabit spaces that mainstream crime films ignore, a post-colonial noir. Instead of being noir vixen, the women are simply forced to sulk at home. It is clearly a film about surviving without a future. At dawn, the men and their girlfriends ghost dance at a familiar spot for necking, in Chavez Ravine – already gone, cleared a few years before, though all that is out of the frame. City Hall hovers in the background, with little else visible.

This amounts to a funeral cortege for Bunker Hill and Chavez Ravine; it is probably the most complete body of imagery that exists of Bunker Hill's daily rhythm.[4] But it is still very much a noir documentary, in high-contrast lighting, buried in shadow. Angel's Flight and the Third Street Tunnel are portentous, almost carceral, trapping the characters inside the frame, shutting out the rest.

To enhance this portrait of isolation, the film ignores the Mexicans and Chinese who were indeed on the same teeming downtown streets late into the night. It even ignores the demolition of Bunker Hill that could be seen a hundred yards from where the film was shot. That was very much the discipline of the film. It heightened the isolation of Native Americans downtown by removing distractions. It left in shadow other cases of isolation down the street. If the director had included these, widened his context, he might have diluted both the mood and statement of the film.

On film, I suppose, the work of Duane Kubo comes closest to a collective history of how downtown L.A. was erased, certainly closer than survivalist films on the homeless like *On the Nickel*; or tapes about family biography, like those of Janice Tanaka, to be discussed later on. Kubo's *Raise the Banner* (1980) is an ambitious melodrama about the eviction of Japanese in Little Tokyo, seen mostly through the agonies of one elderly man, who flashes back to his arrival here as an immigrant, his exploitation by Americans on the job, and the internment camps during World War II.

However, quite innocently, this film reinforces the problem. By presenting downtown as virtually intact until the 1970s, it implies that ethnic neighborhoods had not been dismantled yet. The camera stays within the confines of First Street, narrowly shutting out the nearby banking district, which had already swallowed much of the vitality of downtown neighborhood life. Of course, the subject here was not the general downtown plan; it was about how ethnicity is manipulated on behalf of tourism. Little Tokyo in the 1970s, like Olvera Street in the 1930s, went from being an isolated neighborhood to a tourist magnet. The ethnic label was left intact with even more picturesque street signs, but the streets have been ferociously redesigned to make the walk friendly for outsiders more than for residents. Throughout the eighties, Little Tokyo was lauded as a success story, something to be duplicated by many urban planners who still perceive ethnicity too often as picturesque ornament, a garland to dress up the metro system, and rarely as a community fabric.

And therein lies the problem. The twin beasts that erased much of downtown – racist neglect and ruthless planning – leave only a faint echo in cinema, because generally one will distract the other, or because cinema, by its very apparatus, resembles the tourist imaginary. And noir cinema, like noir literature, reinforces the primitivist fantasies of antitourism, the lingering panic that erases neighborhoods in yet another way. Occasionally, comedies about "the good life" in the wasteland seem to describe the urban vernacular, but generally these are about West Side opulence, as in *Shampoo*, or *Down and Out in Beverly Hills*, or *L.A. Stories*. They are very much an extension of the world-view that the film community itself applies to the city, not about neighborhoods. And then there are classic ethnographic fictional films, like Charles Burnett's *Killer of Sheep* (1978),[5] about a man's survival while working for a slaughtering house – but a scant few.

Compare this erased vision of neighborhoods to films set in New York. Little Italy may be folding into New York's Chinatown, and good-guys going off to the suburbs, but those "mean streets" still register with audiences as quaint, ethnic beehives. The films may not be accurate. I do not believe that gentler films about New York neighborhoods, like *Moonstruck* or *Smoke*, were intended to be "accurate." Simply put, do not shop movie scripts about L.A. neighborhoods. That "stuff" is identified by movie insiders as a New York story, about doing the right thing, about tenements, slum lords, candy stores.

I am not implying, however, that L.A.'s neighborhoods have no public record at all; quite the contrary. The photo archives of vernacular Los Angeles are indeed gigantic, running into millions of images, mostly collections left by real-estate firms or by newspapers;[6] but also the highly respected work of Max Yavno,[7] William Reagh,[8] Will Connell;[9] along with hundreds of thousands of common photographs, particularly of Bunker Hill;[10] and photo projects like Power of Place by Delores Hayden,[11] or the Encyclopedia Persona by Kim Abeles.[12]

However, these cannot compete with hundreds of movie melodramas where downtown is a backdrop,[13] particularly noir classics of the early fifties that use railroad tracks for an ambush or a hideout, or Broadway near the Third Street tunnel for a murder, or Main Street as a suitably grim place to lay down and die; and dozens more, not always so grim. Echo Park Lake since the seventies has become an imaginary Central Park, in *L.A. Stories*, and so on. The El Rancho Market in Echo Park dresses well as a Hispanic burger joint. Some locations are simply easier to transfigure than others, for heavy equipment to be positioned, or cheaper to rent; and they therefore figure more powerfully in the public record, while others never appear. Indeed, Los Angeles remains the most photographed and least remembered city in the world, and will most likely stay that way.

Of course, cinema erases urban locales throughout the world, in historical dramas set in Jane Austen's England, or E.M. Forster's colonial India, or Satiyajit Ray's version of a Tagore novel. Historian Geoff Eley calls "the political project of ... forgetting" a genre in itself in Britain; "another country [is] subtly displaced from the present."[14] The working class in particular are "dehistoricize[d], depoliticize[d]," and "editorialize[d]" across the media, in films, television, autobiography, fiction, and "all manner of public imagery (including, most obviously, the tourism-directed national heritage industry)."

In 1950, Jules Dassin's *Night and the City* received bad reviews in the London press because it was such a travesty in its locations.[15] The harried crook (Richard Widmark) hops a bus at St Martin's Lane, one of the few streets in central London that has no public transport. He runs from the center of London to Hammersmith Bridge in such a short time that even a marathon runner couldn't have managed it. Film historian Richard Whitehall gave me this anecdote, and explained, thinking of the response to Hollywood's *Pride and Prejudice* (1938), and others like it: "We looked at visions of Victorian England, or even of Mrs Miniver's wartime Kent in the same way as American westerns. And perhaps even in American westerns, there was more truth than in these films about upper-class England." Much the same can be said of British documentaries during the Great Depression (Eley's principal example in the essay quoted above). *Housing Problems*, by Edgar Anstey and Arthur Elton, may be the only documentary of the thirties that clearly defied the upper-class tourist mode. Instead, it concentrated on the East End of London: on gritty interviews with local residents; on the daily grind. (Of course, both Anstey and Elton came from the upper classes. Sir Arthur actually inherited his title.)

In 1945, when Rossellini's *Rome Open City* appeared, it was greeted by critics throughout the world as "realist," with its use of non-actors, its grittiness, its hand-held camera wandering at street level. Today, of course, the viewer may be struck by how many scenes were still influenced by Hollywood melodrama – for example, those involving the Gestapo. Even the structure of character in film, like all areas of film grammar, bears witness to Hollywood films infecting the history of World War II.

Speaking even more broadly, film is a chronicle form. Every technical element helps make allegories about social imaginaries. That is its genius, its Rembrandt effect. Without the absence in shadow, there would be no contour. "Forgetting," then, is inherent to the script, the shots, the effects. To explain what I mean, let me pause for a few examples from film theory about forgetting, then conclude with more on Los Angeles.

Haunted Imaginary: Erasure Off Screen

A movie can present only a small proportion of the scenes in a novel, for example. However, what is left out "exists" off screen, and is sensed by the viewer. This phenomenon – phantom diegetic memory – has generated another field of memory theory, about erasures in film, particularly in avant-garde and documentary cinema, as well as later Hitchcock films and film noir. While much of the theory involves Lacan, another canonical source has been Sartre's *The Psychology of the Imagination*,[16] on the phenomenology of erasure. Film historian John Orr uses Sartre very clearly in the following:

> The imaginary [as conceived by Sartre] is not the real, yet in filmic terms can be just as immediate as the real. Modern film plays endlessly and in different ways on this ambiguity. It knows the immediate image is questionable. It also knows the real is haunted by the imaginary.[17]

The central question is simple enough: who or what resides just beyond the frame, as the spectator might see it? Is it camera and crew, ten people out of costume working in a warehouse of film equipment? Or is it the rough cut of the film that has been erased, compared to the edited version that remains? Surely the "offscreen" must have "ambience," generated by good cinematography. But most of all, the offscreen suggests the audience itself, watching the apparatus of film at work. As Christian Metz explains: "Everything out of frame brings us closer to the spectator."[18] For Metz, this chain of identifications constitutes the *cinematic imaginary*. This imaginary is highly unstable; it changes continuously in the viewer's mind – what Bill Nichols calls "the anthropology behind the scenes."[19]

Migration of Memory: Erasure On Screen

In some films, the narrator "forgets" *on* screen. More specifically, a *migration of memory* is basic to the plot. Through flashback and voice-over, the narrator's account reverses and decays, jumping from one place in time to another. The classic example of migration of memory is probably Resnais' *Hiroshima Mon Amour* (1959): the narrator and both of the central characters analyze how history erases the experience of memory; and in turn, why that erasure can be useful, to help the individual remove the trauma of remembering. As Michael Roth explains: "That which is unforgettable is that which cannot be remembered, cannot be recounted."[20]

Direct Address in Colonial Los Angeles

Recently, I was part of a graduate student's film about "forgetting" in Los Angeles. In Temple-Beaudry, I showed him grassland where houses used to be, next to oil wells surrounded by chain-link fences. Across the street, a man with a Mayan face was selling pizzas door to door. As soon as he noticed the camera, he asked to be filmed. The student was quite pleased. What came out, however, was somewhat surprising. The man stared down the camera for what seemed minutes. With a gentle dignity, shoulders back, chest out, he could have been posing for a daguerreotype, or a piece of sculpture.

He was exaggerating an effect common to ethnographic films: direct eye contact, reminiscent of Vertov's Soviet documentaries of the twenties, or those of the Egyptian filmmaker Attetyat El Abnoudy, about street people in Gaza (*Mud People*, 1971), or local families (*Permissible Dreams*). The camera becomes an unsettling Westernizer, pretending to capture rituals that are pre-cinematic. What it captured in this case, however, was not ritual but erasure, two imaginaries in mutual incomprehension. The man's memory of Central America could be sensed off screen, while the camera remained out of reach for him, more than just across the street. I wonder how deeply this, or any film, can go into the shocks currently affecting (or afflicting) Los Angeles?

What these examples suggest is the utter instability of cinema as a formal record, and the fact that audiences enjoy this paramnesiac sensation, as memory dissolves. The mood of erasure is fundamental to the spectator's pleasure. Perhaps, in Lacanian terms, this pleasure restores the audience to the point where the mirror stage and the Symbolic Order are held in tension.[21]

Furthermore, the layering of erasures is essential to moving the narrative along, to its simultaneity, its unreal solidity, its anarchic orderliness. However, beneath the charming effect lie the actual sites where a film is shot. These cannot surface, even when they are in plain view; and they are very rarely sensed offscreen either. Once a city or an event is enshrouded by this pleasure, there is almost no way to make it visible again. Film, therefore, is a form of tourism even more totalizing than anything the boosters in Los Angeles devised. That may be why the remembered L.A. is continually mis-identified as "Hollywood," no matter what television news may say. Even Rodney King's face being crushed by police batons became a form of Hollywood, as I will explain.

One of the last Hollywood films to bear witness to the erasure of downtown Los Angeles was *Farewell My Lovely*, shot completely on location for forty days in 1975. The period ballroom, Myron's, downtown served as the nightclub for the opening sequence. Mrs Florian's home was sited close to where Chandler imagined it, on Vermont Avenue. The Queen Mary was overhauled, and taken out of dry dock for the film, since the old gambling ship, the Rex, was long gone. Even traffic lights, street signs, were altered to accord with old photographs.

The crew shot in actual hotel rooms on skid row downtown. A long search for Florian's Bar led to Jack's Bar on Sixth Street – again, not all that far from the original Florian's in Chandler's novel. Also, "the fact that when you went downstairs or stepped into the street you might well get knifed for two bucks in your pocket – produced the kind of performances we needed."[22]

But in the midst of these filming problems, Hollywood was formally notified that forties Los Angeles had essentially disappeared. As publicity material for *Farewell My Lovely* indicated (1975): "Unless there is a radical change in public policy, a few years hence it will be utterly impossible to film a 1940s story in the streets of Los Angeles... Architectural remnants of the era are fast disappearing along with open spaces and clean air."[23]

All We Are About to Forget on Video

The old man had disappeared years ago. His daughter, Janice, finally located him on Fifth and San Pedro, "in the skid row section of Los Angeles." With the video camera running, she asked him if he recognized her. He said that she did resemble his daughter faintly. The cumulative effect of the past fifty years had shattered his memory. He had been interned at Manzanar during World War II, resisted, suffered nervous breakdowns, undergone shock therapy. "Silence was the keeper of memories," Janice explains in voice-over (Janice Tanaka, *Who's Going to Pay for the Donuts Anyway?* 1992).

There is a considerable body of independent video about what Tanaka calls "the Department of Amnesia" – how political manipulation has invaded our collective memory.[24] Mostly this is represented through video montages, like imagos. In Rea Tajiri's *History and Memory* (1991), propaganda clips about the internment camps are set beside interviews with relatives who suffered there, but who fortunately do not quite remember all the details. In Woody Vasulka's *The Art of Memory*, clips of murders and wars are processed into 3D animation, then curled like wet film on an invisible surface, to float on a figure-ground ambiguity – as false history.

Tanaka talks about the "constant rewriting of memory in order to grow, to review the experience through different points of entry."[25] In my introduction I compare this "re-entry" to notes for a novel not written, a crossover of many discursive media at once. Even the five senses are unreliable sources; the video "sees" what can be sensed only in its absence. Tanaka worked on a television program about a local poet blinded by gunfire as an adult. Trying to find the sites he wrote about, she was surprised how often they were already gone, except of course in the poetic paramnesia of his mind's eye – not as untruths, simply as sufficient distortion to keep them vivid.

It is crucial that a video on "forgetting" should never memorialize erasure while condemning it. It should keep re-entering a street where forgetting takes place. Imagine a "forgetful" re-edit of Walther Ruttmann's *Berlin: Symphony of a City* (1929), but not nearly as fluid, closer to Jem Cohen's trackless video symphonies set in Middle Europe, or New York,[26] and now Los Angeles (a work in progress). Points of view should scatter into trails like subplots from incomplete novels, re-entries like the *Comédie Humaine* as hypertext. That would capture how collective distraction seems to operate, today in particular. When I say *today*, consider what a primitive moment we live in: a clownlike plantation economy, with a new euphemism for every new cruelty, from "downsizing" to the "war on drugs." You may not have job security, but you get a remote control for your television set. For a world as ruthlessly distractive as this, I am calling for less elegance and more confessional uncertainty, on behalf of all that we are about to forget.

B-ROLLS: TV SCREENS

For four years, I consulted regularly for television documentaries about Los Angeles. The sum of that experience was numbing. At one meeting in 1989, a producer decided that there was no point doing a show on the Watts Rebellion because, in his words, by the summer of 1990 there would be so many twenty-fifth anniversary retrospectives on Watts that the entire problem would be redundant by the Fall, when our show might run. The round table of consultants rose to disagree. They explained almost in unison that conditions in South Central were even more desperate than in 1965, that a new round of political explosions was inevitable. But the producer simply shook his head benignly. Once a story is covered by too many shows, it is used up. Retrospective is retro.

On another occasion, an executive producer told me that whatever problem I wanted to select for a documentary, I had to be sure that I could find a "B Roll" for it – that is, existing footage to run on top of the voice-over. When I explained that some crucial issues do not have very much existing footage, he simply warned me – green newcomer that I was – that if no clips could be found, the story did not exist. To which I asked: "Does this mean that events with a lot of existing footage are more real than events without?" What a ridiculous question! "It exists there if the B-Roll is there." He was trying to be hard-boiled, in an industry obsessed with the art of the bottom line. If you cannot fill the screen with photos or a clip, then any event, no matter how important to the world, is not "a story."

The few documentary scripts I saw during those four years reflected the same oversimplification, as did the shoots I watched in studio. Historical events must be redesigned to fit a fictive format, the pretense that fact is more exciting if it arrives like a movie melodrama:[27] that makes events "accessible" – for whom is not always made clear. The screenplay should read like a fictional movie, with a central "character" and a cinematic "conflict." If an issue is too hot to ignore but cannot fit into "story," and there is no B-Roll, then a talking head must be found, an expert.

I have been a talking head on a few occasions – another chastening experience. The interviews are taken very quickly, because time is money. Setups are expensive. Second thoughts afterward rarely make it into film. And your "talk" has to fit into the B-Roll to follow.[28]

In November 1993, for a news special during sweeps week, I was interviewed on Citywalk, the outdoor mall that "parodies"[29] and at the same time deodorizes the image of Los Angeles. In "bites" of no more than thirty seconds, and preferably as short as fifteen seconds, I tried to summarize for the camera what Citywalk represents. Three bites were chosen, and I managed to say close to what I had intended. However, the editing destroyed the meaning, so I wound up sponsoring precisely the opposite of what I had said.

In the version that aired, the newscaster opened with what presumably was a balanced view of the subject. Will Los Angeles lose its public life, she asked? Will people prefer to visit public spaces that resemble theme parks? Will we choose Citywalk or the streets of Los Angeles? Behind her voice-over (B-Roll), the camera flashed an MTV jumpcut montage of Citywalk, ripe with color and quirky angles. Then, as the B-Roll for

L.A., it cut to a crime scene in noir lighting. That left two choices for the couple planning a night out: either wander in safety through Citywalk, or stay in L.A. and watch a corpse being loaded into an ambulance.

How far does this B–Roll tourist reading of social problems go? It certainly is going straight to CD-Rom, and into the electronic super-highway. The ripest example I have seen began with lines out of a pulp novel: "The first body was found at 3 A.M., tortured and mutilated." That is the opening in bold type to an ad for the new CD-Rom entitled *Daryl F. Gates' Police Quest: Open Season*. "You can't get any closer to the crime without a badge."[30] "Authored by the most experienced cop in the world," this journey takes you into sinister streets in "all-new ultrarealistic digital photography shot on location throughout Los Angeles and Southern California." It is "a story ripped from today's headlines." "An unprece-dented dimension of realism," said the *New York Times*.[31]

This game is a digest of tourist promotion, consumer panic and the language of media news. First it weaves clichés from movie crime, where the player is positioned as an LAPD officer down these dark streets. There is "another body in another alley ... but this one is your ex-partner." The crime is ghastly, but everyone is highly clinical, not even mourning a fellow cop who was stripped and mutilated. "Play this one by the book and you might stop a serial killer before he or she strikes again."

Your narrator is Daryl F. Gates, the police chief in exile, less than a year after he was fired by the city of Los Angeles for racist policies, and for what – beyond the euphemisms – amounts to incompetence. But he was "the most experienced cop in America," suddenly another Philip Marlowe, not a radio personality running a talk show in Orange County, as he did for a while, where he became even better known for extremely conservative political positions.

Finally, to make the package complete, *Police Quest: Open Season* (also called *Reality*) was directed by Tammy Dargon, a former producer of the television "real-life" series *America's Most Wanted*. Computer industries are merging with political pressure groups, very much in the way that tourism merged with downtown businessmen in Los Angeles. And the result is advanced paramnesia, a state of simultaneous distraction similar to what happened downtown, and which is about to take place throughout the United States. *Open Season* was a worldwide hit. Even in China, this CD-Rom was among the most pirated. Its sequel, *Police Quest: Swat* was also a success.

Regarding the packaging of *Open Season*, at least one of the advertisements that I have seen is modeled on the opening sequences from *Blade Runner*.[32] And on the back of the plastic case itself – added to what is called "An Authentic Police Tactical Simulation" – is the following: "Train as a member of the most elite[33] law enforcement group ever created. Learn the tactics, equipment and communication techniques..." This, along with the abridged manual of the LAPD itself, repeats precisely the image that Gates had promoted for over a decade, of the "high-tech" supercop, proud to be aloof, even Olympian. In the next chapter, I examine how this image dissolved after 1991. Yet it apparently survives without a break in cyberspace, a phenomenon I discuss in the Conclusion.

As the game progresses, the corpse of a naked white police officer who was tortured while in "South Central" is scrutinized by the investigating team. This includes one female officer who responds continuously to any prodding by the cursor with threats of harassment suits, as if she were dragged into the department through affirmative action. On succeeding levels, one gets to the station house, and from there, intermittently, hears speeches by Daryl Gates on the proprieties of law enforcement. There is no mention whatsoever of looting, 1992. That is forgotten – pure wish fulfillment and denial, not even a social imaginary; for who in 1993, only months after the Uprising, could imagine that it did not even take place?

With conservative majorities in Congress, and in many state legislatures, we are about to witness erasures of public institutions on a scale not seen in American history since the Civil War. And much of it may well be recorded like interactive video games, like boosterist innocence, as "state of the art digital photography and stark realism." Realism, by the way, refers specifically to the "real" photographs that were scanned, then digitally altered; this then is "real" Los Angeles, a B-Roll of another kind.

Objects like *Police Quest* will become popular political history in time. At least they will not corrupt within five or ten years, like so many of the disks being used today. Nor will they vanish in "cy-blivion" through a chat line, or on the ever disposable Web. Laser technology is the latest in a two-thousand-year-old pursuit of complete recall without decay of memory.

I enjoy watching the B-Roll fall apart. During the collapse of the Soviet Union, I was shown tapes from Lithuanian television, just as the Russians burst into the studio. The coverage was extraordinarily fresh somehow. Then I was told why: we were seeing the backs of people's heads. The camera was out of position, according to the grammar of on-the-spot reporting. Since then I have always wondered if part of the shock of the Rodney King video was that it showed too many officers from the back, where the camera is not expected to be: it was video verité.

In the next chapter, I will enter the imaginaries wrought by the King video, and by the shock to the LAPD since 1991. Now even the hand-held camcorder has developed its own grammar. Along with scenes of looting, it has become the ultimate B-Roll on Los Angeles, across the media.

NOTES

1. David Thomson, "Palos Verdes," *Film Comment*, vol. 26, no.3, May–June, 1990, p. 17. *Criss-Cross* was directed by Robert Siodmak, the esteemed director of noir (*The Killers*). The only "credited" screenwriter was Daniel Fuchs, a gifted novelist as well (e.g. *The Gangster*, adapted to the screen in 1947). And the cinematographer Frank Planer had just finished *Letter from and Unknown Woman* by Max Ophuls.

There is a curious twist to the locations: Bunker Hill sloped toward foothills much more in 1948 than it does today, even into Temple-Beaudry. Therefore the neighborhood ambience being fictionalized (Lancaster's parents, their house, etc.) probably borrows a lot from the presence of those other areas, suggesting a much less barricaded look, more like a small town. This is important to remember: that there was a comfortable pedestrian access from downtown to the west. The boundaries between downtown and neighborhoods directly west, particularly those below Temple Boulevard, were not as fixed as they became after Bunker Hill not only lost its upper hundred feet but was also walled off from north to south. Thereafter, streets just west of this "wall," like Court Street, lost the easy slope that allowed them to continue up into downtown. Clearly downtown would have "sprawled" west if not for the Harbor Freeway and policies by the CRA.

2. David MacDougall, "The Subjective Voice in Ethnographic Film,' in Leslie Devereux and Roger Hillman, eds, *Fields of Vision* (Berkeley: University of California Press, 1995).

3. Paula Rabinowitz, *They Must Be Represented: The Politics of Documentary* (London: Verso, 1994), p. 17.

4. A student documentary of Bunker Hill was made at USC in 1955. That may be the only other film record of neighborhood life itself in the years right before it was torn down. See also the remarkable opening sequences in Joseph Losey's *M* (1950).

5. Also Burnett's feature *To Sleep With Anger* (1990), about a man of dubious past coming to stay with old friends, and disturbing the balance of community around them.

6. See Regional History Center at UCLA (*L.A. Herald*); the Huntington Library; the Security Pacific Collection and others at the downtown public library; and boosterist photo collections at the Museum of Natural History library. And, of course, Dawson's Bookstore on Larchmont, and the redoubtable expert on L.A. photography and rare books, Michael Dawson.

7. Yavno's work, particularly of the forties and fifties, influenced by the social re-alist styles of the thirties, is mostly at the Center for Creative Photography in America.

8. Reagh's work – over 40,000 negatives and photos of the general downtown area primarily, taken from 1939 to the late eighties – is housed mostly at the Cal-State Sacramento library.

9. Connell photos, particularly of artists and writers in Los Angeles, are at UCLA Special Collections. A vast photo collection for the film industry is maintained at the Academy of the Motion Picture Arts and Sciences Library; a photo record of sites and locations is held at the archives for the Paramount Studios, and at other studios.

10. For common photos of Bunker Hill, see the photo collection at the Huntington Library.

11. See Delores Hayden, *The Power of Place: Urban Landscapes as Public History* (Cambridge, MA: MIT Press, 1995).

12. Shown at the Santa Monica Museum of Contemporary Art.

13. The following is a partial list of films using Los Angeles, beyond those already mentioned in the text:

Features since 1940 where downtown appears on location, and not simply as an establishing shot of City Hall, or simply the building where characters enter: *Act of Violence* (1949, Bunker Hill and below: final scene; mostly set in the emerging suburbs, like *No Down Payment*, 1957); *M* (Losey version, 1950, Bunker Hill: opening); *DOA* (1950, along Wilshire to Broadway, then final shootout at Bradbury Building on Broadway); *Kiss Me Deadly* (Bunker Hill; also the beach); *Repo Man* (warehouse district).

Double Indemnity establishes downtown at Olive Street, but most of the film was shot on the lot, except for a brief excursion to Jerry's Market across from Paramount, on Melrose, and an establishing shot along Franklin and Vermont.

Studio locations dominate *Murder My Sweet* and *The Big Sleep*. Probably *This Gun For Hire* reveals more of L.A. (though presumably set in New York). So too, *Blue Dahlia*. I discuss some of the use of office towers, etc. in Chapter 4.

Dozens of films have used Union Station, including a feature *Union Station* (1950), and e.g. *The Postman Always Rings Twice* (both 1946 and 1979 versions), *Chinatown*, *The Last Tycoon*, *Blade Runner*.

By the seventies, except for period films, downtown loses its importance, as I explain. So in *The Long Goodbye*, Marlowe is essentially in West Hollywood and points west of there. So, too, with *Shampoo*, *California Split*, *The Fortune*, and even as early as *Point Blank* (1968).

Practically every police film passes through downtown in one scene or another, like *The New Centurions*, *To Live and Die in L.A.*, *Internal Affairs*.

Many films select fantasy architecture in a shot, like a scene in *Zabriskie Point* of the Farmer John mural of happy pigs near downtown.

Most films about Hollywood present very little of Los Angeles directly, and more of the studio lots, and the elegant, decadent hillside mansions toward the west of the basin. *Sunset Boulevard*, however, was shot on Wilshire Boulevard, and considerably farther east, in a mansion owned at the time by J. Paul Getty.

Except for *Colors*, most films set in South Central use locations there.

Among foreign films using Los Angeles are *Smog* (1962, Rossi); *The Loved One*; *The Model Shop* (1969, Demy); *Lion's Love* (1969, Varda).

For the silent era, the list is too immense. The comedies tended to use the streets even more than did the dramas: early Chaplin (Sennett and Mutual), Harold Lloyd,

Ben Turpin, Laurel and Hardy (though much was shot in Culver City). Roach even had a studio lot up in Bunker Hill.

14. Geoff Eley, "Distant Voices, Still Lives" (in Robert A. Rosenstone, ed., *Revisioning History: Film and the Construction of a New Past* [Princeton: Princeton University Press, 1995], p. 31), quoting Roger Bromley, *Lost Narratives: Popular Fictions, Politics and Recent History* (London: Routledge, 1988), and using David Lowenthal's *The Past in a Foreign Country*.

15. Interview, Richard Whitehall, 1991.

16. Jean-Paul Sartre, *The Psychology of Imagination* (London: Methuen, 1972). Most editions seem to rely on the translation from 1948 (New York: Philosophical Library).

17. John Orr, *Cinema and Modernity* (Cambridge: Polity Press, 1993), p. 87.

18. Christian Metz, *The Imaginary Signifier*, trans. Britton et al (Bloomington: Indiana University Press, 1982; orig. 1977), p. 55; also pp. 44–5.

19. Bill Nichols, *Blurred Boundaries: Questions of Meaning in Contemporary Culture* (Bloomington: University of Indiana Press, 1994), pp. 65–7.

20. Michael Roth, "Hiroshima Mon Amour: You Must Remember This," in Rosenstone, ed., *Revisioning History*, p. 98; also in *The Ironist's Cage* (1995).

21. A useful summary of debates on psychoanalytic theory in feminist film studies: Constance Penley, *The Future of an Illusion* (Minneapolis: University fo Minnesota Press, 1989).

22. Stephen Pendo, *Raymond Chandler on Screen: His Novels Into Film* (Metuchen: Scarecrow Press, 1976), p. 179.

23. Ibid., p. 181.

24. For a review of new independent video on "forgetting," see: Michael Renov and Erika Suderburg, eds, *Resolutions: Contemporary Video Practices* (Minneapolis: University of Minnesota, 1996), introduction, chs 1, 8.

25. Interview with Janice Tanaka, November 1996.

26. Among Jem Cohen's videos: *This is a History of New York* (1987); *Buried in Light* (1994)

27. The critical debate on melodrama, particularly in feminist theory, is a bit broader than the way I mean the term here. I take it literally at its "word:" melody-drama in England, and its application from the 1820s onward, a variation of opera and gothic story that rapidly is accommodated to the moralistic ideology of mid-nineteenth-century England. In *Seven Minutes*, I trace how this cautionary poetics mutates into Hollywood cinema by the thirties, and is translated into Disney animation by 1935–37, or as "anti-melodrama" in Warners' chase cartoons. I also feel that noir fiction of the mid-thirties, particularly by James M. Cain, was specifically anti-melodrama, and understood that way by mass readership. Therefore noir is an inversion of poetic justice; in noir the hero is "maudit" (cursed), and so is poetic justice; "the law is just, but it just ain't fair." As a further irony, this anti-melodrama resembles Aristotelian poetics and Greek theater in its fatalism.

28. Clearly, I was discovering first-hand what Adorno and Horkheimer identified as the "mummification" by mass culture, in essays from the thirties onward, particularly in *Dialectic of Enlightenment* (1944), completed during their stay in Los Angeles. For an overview, see Miriam Hansen, "Mass Culture as Hieroglyphic Writing: Adorno, Derrida, Krakauer," *New German Critique* 56, Spring/Summer 1992, an issue devoted to Adorno.

29. The expression used by John Jerde, its architect, for yet another documentary where I was a "talking head," for the BBC, on the History Of Shopping (1995).

30. From an advertisement that ran in many computer magazines.

31. *Daryl F. Gates' Police Quest Collection: The Four Most Wanted*, instruction and installation manual (Bellevue, Washington: Sierra Collectors Series, 1994), p. 112. Review excerpted from *Interact* magazine (article by Nancy Smithe Grimsley), on why Gates was selected by Sierra for CD-Rom: Ken Williams of Sierra felt that "the press had sort of painted the guy as a real dictator." He found Gates "a perfect gentleman, and a real personable family kind of guy," who had a popular radio show, and (like Williams) was a fan of Rush Limbaugh. Gates also liked surfing: "Any 60 plus old guy who took the time to go surfing every morning can't be all bad, so he made the mental decision to sign him." Williams felt that Gates "had been pinned as the fall guy for the whole Riot thing."

32. *Daryl F. Gates' Police Quest.*

33. The term "elite" is telling. It was crucial to the LAPD image for generations, where they were indeed among the models for law enforcement around the country. Of course, elite also implies elitist; and perhaps that there were not many, that it has always been a remarkably small police force compared to others.

CHAPTER ELEVEN

THE IMAGINARY L.A.P.D.

In the 1930s, "Two-Gun" Jim Davis, the chief of police, used to invite residents in Echo Park to watch him shoot a cigarette out of the mouth of a young officer.[1] That frontier image of the LAPD disappeared in scandal in 1938. The corruptions of the vice squad, and attempted assassinations of enemies of the mayor, brought down the Shaw administration, and swept in a reform mayor, Fletcher Bowron. During the Bowron years, 1938–53, scandals involving police were minimal, though some vice officers claimed that the house was still not clean. Local gangsters like Tony Cornero had simply franchised their interests to Las Vegas. Mickey Cohen still had clout downtown.[2] Overall, however, the "reformed" LAPD was popular, at least with whites. The new image seemed scientific, and, like myths about the FBI, above reproach – cops who cannot be bribed. The kindest way to summarize it would be a chilly professionalism under the tenure of those who followed Two-Gun Davis: James Parker, Ed Davis, and then Daryl Gates. Finally, with Gates leaving under a cloud, that social imaginary – for whites essentially – has dissolved in the nineties.

Even if problems at the LAPD were solved by 1997, their image might remain sour for the rest of the decade. Not that a solution is imminent: political infighting has brought police reform almost to a standstill.[3] That generates even more cine-myths about cops going crazy, acting guilty and depressed. In 1995 alone, sinister readings of the LAPD were crucial to the plot in four mainstream films: *Devil in a Blue Dress*; *Virtuosity*; *Strange Days*; *White Man's Burden*. Also in 1995, equally dark images of the LAPD were unmistakable in urban legends, law cases, local shootings, and in news coverage. In all of these, a few cues repeated with considerable regularity: (1) the schizo-homicidal cop; (2) videos that "undermine" the LAPD. These cues always refer back to 1991–92, and two memorable imagos: the video of the King beating, and television coverage during the days of looting.

Distrust of the LAPD utterly rescripted the O.J. Simpson trial, particularly once Mark Fuhrman took the stand. Fuhrman's impassive face became a savage icon on dozens of front pages throughout the USA, Europe, Asia and the Middle East. Even the federal government felt compelled to respond, with leaks that the Justice Department had begun inquiries into his career.[4] In L.A., the struggles between the police chief[5] and the mayor were recoded according to Fuhrman − temporarily Fuhrmanized. Do we need more cops immediately on the streets, or fewer Fuhrmans?

Simpson's defense portrayed Fuhrman as a "nigger"-baiting cop from Simi Valley who planted a bloody glove to implicate "O.J." As one radio pundit explained: "It's as if Fuhrman were on trial for the beating of Rodney King. The hatred of the police runs that deep, at least among blacks in L.A." Like a noir film, Fuhrman's psychological tics were revealed in flashback from court transcripts, while greasy paparazzi fought for position at "O.J. City" across from the courthouse steps. Even stranger still, Fuhrman had imagined his life as a movie. Years before the trial, he was taped at great length by screenwriter Laura Hart McKinney.[6] Clearly he exaggerated on these tapes − but where? He detailed scenes of intense police brutality.

Newspapers ran psychological portraits about Fuhrman at work. Fellow officers claimed that he did not behave in a racist manner in front of them, though indeed he was chilly, and almost seemed to model some of his mannerisms on Clint Eastwood's portrayal of Dirty Harry: "No expression. No nonsense ... there was no way for the public to know whether he liked them or not."[7] When asked to comment on the Fuhrman tapes, which described the LAPD as pathological bullies and racists in the late seventies, one Latino officer said: "I was shocked. I just didn't believe it."[8] Another said that "the bottom line ... is that if he is that way there must be more just like him... That is the most frightening thing about all of this."

Fuhrman's profile began to resemble that of a serial killer: He was always very polite when he showed up at work. Like Jim Thompson's psychopathic sheriff in *The Killer Inside Me*, he pretended to solve crimes that he himself committed, and then covered up later by behaving normally in the precinct. He was above the law, like the murderous L.A.

cop in the movie *Unlawful Entry* (1994). His victims had no recourse. The total Fuhrman package was so infuriating; it stood in for all the unfinished problems of 1992. To non-white jurors, his presence reminded them that institutional racism was not being addressed. Meanwhile, many white respondents on talk shows hoped that "we" could put Fuhrman and 1992 behind us.

AUGUST 1995

If I blended all these half-fictions about the LAPD in 1995, they would add up to a scenario something like the following. An LAPD officer has been struggling close to the point of nervous breakdown. He is so divided internally that he cannot help but become a criminal himself – as well as a victim. That means a cop is metamorphosed into Rodney King during a hellish carnival similar to the looting and vandalism in 1992. The disruption outside matches his dissolving identity inside. Meanwhile, embarrassing mistakes by police are recorded on hand-held video, or lit by helicopters overhead.

The helicopter repeats as a vital piece of staging here, throughout the media, like a malicious theatrical machine in a revenge melodrama. It is as divided in meaning as the LAPD: partly for surveillance; partly for liberation from surveillance. It is the truth-seeing eye; or the panoptical gaze of a murderer; even the flight to freedom for criminals, as in helicopter chases in *Die Hard III*, *Broken Arrow*, *Mission Impossible*. Helicopters catch or kill rogue cops.

George Holliday had needed helicopter light in order to record King being pummeled nearly to death. Helicopters became the medium used for overhead television coverage of the looting in 1992;[9] footage that incriminated and embarrassed the police. I also notice migrated memories about choppers during Vietnam (revisited by way of *Apocalypse Now*, *Platoon*, *Forrest Gump*), when helicopters were first popularized as fundamental tools for war and policing; as well as firebombing and napalm.

By contrast, during the eighties, helicopters were praised as one of the proud symbols of imperial distance between the LAPD and the street. Not so proud for residents below, of course. The sound of helicopters flying low at night, to scan for undesirables, became a standard – and very odious – experience in non-white neighborhoods in Los Angeles. (Ice T calls them ghetto birds.) Its pulsating effect suggested thoughtless power. Indeed, in movies about the LAPD, the psychological breakdown of characters often occurs near the vibrating of helicopters at night, like a giant insect, a species insensitive to civilians, unable to hear or care.

I am building a fiction here, merging dozens of sources into a single chronotope. It helps me clarify how the social imaginary of the LAPD "vanished," as backstory to movies in 1995. But, more importantly, it emphasizes a vital distinction within all these mythemes or half-fictions: they never say what replaced the LAPD social imaginary from the eighties. They simply re-enact the *vanishing itself*.

VIRTUOSITY

In late July, a week before the Fuhrman testimony began, the movie thriller *Virtuosity* opened to mixed reviews, and to more commentary about hellish Los Angeles. The setting was close to "O.J. City," around the Courts Building downtown, but set in 1999. The view was updated by computer. Mattes for extra high-rises were slipped into the background, like a fall of hair, to heighten the density and the morbidity. Areas just beyond downtown, as always, were treated as unholy blanks. The streets immediately east and west of the high-rises resembled Morocco, where the poor live like Bedouins.

But downtown is not the pulse point of the story. The flashiest scenes are set in a computerized VR simulator, designed for the film inside the *Spruce Goose*[10] hangar, based on production sketches where a police station is modeled to look like a prison bloc. The screenplay was inspired by real VR technology, the OZ military simulator program, which uses nanotechnology[11] to make cyber creatures called "Woggles" who "think on their own." Of course, whatever cuteness a name like Woggles suggests was filtered out, to make what the director called "the cold war meets Sega."[12] What cold war would that be? Certainly not Soviet moles or CIA hit men. This was an LAPD cold war. In place of Berlin Walls, he relied on nightmare imagos from 1991 and 1992 in Los Angeles.

The two lead characters are both psychological disasters "built" by the LAPD. The first, Parker Barnes, is a black cop found guilty of police brutality, then dumped into prison. The second is purely electronic: he lives on a screen, in a computer program named Sid.7, at the LAPD lab. The files of many serial killers were merged into his personality, to make him a super-psychopath. Predictably, "Sid" escapes from the screen into the real world, thanks to gullible geeks inside the LAPD. In fact, bad cops help him escape – a severe embarrassment if the truth came out.

Both Parker and Sid (particularly Sid) are descendants of the *Robocop* genre, familiar but updated for post-1991 Los Angeles, down to camera angles, key plot points, even the character inversions. They are conflicted to the point of rage, forced to carry multiple identities put inside them by the LAPD, which drives them to madness. Parker Barnes is a particularly contrary blend. He is both Stacy Koon – the white sergeant who led the King beating – and Rodney King. He enters prison Koonlike, a cop who got violent; but is brutalized until he becomes Rodneylike, a scowling black convict. Guards force Parker to fight to the death against a neo-Nazi skinhead, as gladiatorial diversion, hopefully to kill off another "nigger" nuisance. Instead, Parker beats the skinhead to death; and, as penance, must re-enact the stages of the cross we associate with Rodney King. Clubbed to the ground, he is forced to crawl on all fours to protect his face. Even my thirteen-year-old son felt this scene reminded him of the King beating. And so did many film critics, who cite it in reviews.

But this is only the most obvious re-enactment of events since 1991. Others much fainter are buried inside the cinematography, particularly in the use of an unsteady camcorder. The hand-held camcorder has become a metonym for the LAPD falling to pieces, in swerving light. Even the tremble of light is crucial to the effect, which brings me back to George Holliday's video, and the helicopter light.

The sociopathic Sid is the LAPD's worst nightmare, a blend of George Holliday with Charlie Manson. He uses a camcorder to taunt the police, having it record him torturing a man to death. Then, his snuff video is sent to television stations, who beat police to the crime scene. Finally, to "heighten" insecurity about law enforcement, while the LAPD tries to regroup, the camera pans overhead as if from a helicopter. Once again, the streets are not safely policed during a riot. Once again, media choppers record another of Sid's massacres. This blood bath resembles, perhaps not intentionally, the demonstrations that preceded the looting downtown in 1992. Sid interrupts a political rally at Parker Center, the actual site of the first demonstrations on 29 April, before slaughtering everyone in sight. Helicopters churn overhead, following essentially the same camera angles they used in 1992. The police, as before, "lose" the city in front of millions of viewers.

For the obligatory conclusion, Parker Barnes and Sid meet in a death struggle on a roof near City Hall. They fall through thousands of square feet of shattering glass, which Sid uses to regenerate his severed body parts. His flesh is made entirely of computer chips, again from the lab of the LAPD.

The internal conflict of Parker Barnes bears a strange resemblance to the public persona assigned to Fuhrman: a policeman double-coded as both criminal and victim. An old plot turn has been updated, about cops who fall apart. Parker suffers a low-grade nervous breakdown, swinging from depression to overreaction (explosive vengeance). He is utterly divided, even by the standards of a noir anti-hero. The muddled authorities have wrongfully scapegoated him for every conceivable crime: for being a rogue cop; for being a black convict. When we see him early on, he is brooding, and in dreadlocks. He looks precisely like the stereotype of the black male held in a racist prison system. Later, after his release, he struts like another Dirty Harry – white-identified, roguish – just gun-crazy enough to kill a lunatic like Sid. In ten scenes at least, he switches to both sides of the law-enforcement equation, as if cops and street kids get their rage from the same place.

Much of this seesaw is handled by flashback. One memory in particular repeats: it shows Parker much younger, happily married, and father of a lovely daughter. Then it switches to another ominous, unsteady video, made by a mass murderer who is taunting Parker much the way Sid does now. "This one's for you, Parker," the murderer says, while he slits another victim's throat. Finally, Parker's professional self-control snaps. He fails to arrive at a crime scene in time to save his own family. He is condemned to watch them get blown up. Blind with rage, with one arm sheared off by the explosion, he forgets that he is LAPD and behaves like a victim seeking revenge (not unlike the final scene in Usual Suspects, also from 1995, and also shot downtown). Parker's blind reflexes take over. He senses people behind him. Suddenly he spins, overreacts, and fires his automatic pistol wildly at a news team, killing an innocent woman.

That gets him thirty years in prison, and a descent into Mandingo racism. At the same time, the slaughter of his family, like a video with a mind of its own, has been transferred into Sid's memory. Sid, the Dionysian psychopath, exploits it, once he knows that Parker is after him – to drive Parker crazy yet again. But, as poetic justice requires, Sid fails, and is obliterated.

In the final scenes, Parker senses that the "real" cause of Sid's reign of terror will never be made public. None of the brass will let the scandal out. What is worse, the same bastards who covered up the mistake will probably reactivate the same vicious program all over again. So he throws the Sid chip off a building. We see it get pulverized into glass by an oncoming truck.

On the surface, the plot reads like a Geraldo talk show: cops who go crazy; the brass who cover up. But there is a danger in oversimplifying how collective memory turns up in a movie. Most of the resemblance was probably not intended directly by the scriptwriters or the director, particularly in a film that goes through twenty incarnations before it becomes a product. At best, it is the collective memory of an entire production team over a work schedule running up to four years.

Many scenes are derivative, straight out of "neo-noir" of the eighties, like *Robocop*, *Blade Runner* or *Alien*. But the representation of the police has been updated. In eighties noir, even cyberpunk, the stories about the evil packaging of cops are less ambiguous. They suggest that police, however demonic, are stable, integrated smoothly into the capitalist infrastructure, like cyborgs. That is not what I find in *Virtuosity*. It deals more with the dissolution of a package, the symbolic history of a public relations disaster. It is an allegory about the psychological instability immediately after the older promotional image of the LAPD – a social imaginary – dissolves.

REVERSE ANGLE: BLACK NOIR AND DEVIL IN A BLUE DRESS

Devil in a Blue Dress had already finished its run by the time *Virtuosity* opened; but it had very similar elements, now from a distinctly black POV, a black director (Carl Franklin), from a novel by a black author (Walter Mosley). It also highlights one scene that is crucial to all these films: the disposable black man beaten to the ground by white authority – but with differences.

Mosley pays homage to the black experience from 1945, particularly the novels of Wright, Himes and Ellison; and most of all to the African-American workers who migrated west during the war, then were ruthlessly ignored by the media until the Watts Rebellion. It is fundamentally a story about institutional racism. Easy Rawlins is cornered by the LAPD in *Devil in a Blue Dress*; then cornered even more desperately by red-baiting FBI in *A Red Death* (1991). His struggle to possess his anger reminds me of a spectacular passage by Chester Himes in *If He Hollers Let Him Go* (1945). By the late forties, Himes' scene of the black man against the wall was a familiar trope in mass fiction. But usually it was set in the rural south, not in Los Angeles. The lurid paperback cover (1949),[13] makes that plain enough: the black man Bob Jones (who bears an uncanny resemblance to Himes himself) is positioned as the wrongly accused, the uppity "negro." Bob has been backed into the lower corner of the picture, stares fearfully at a tousled blonde woman, described in the publisher's blurb as "a tough blonde from Texas." She points him out as a rapist to angry white workers streaming through a framed doorway. There is little in the picture to identify Los Angeles, or the industrial defense industry during the war, where the novel is set. It could be a small rural town. It clearly resembles the Erskine Caldwell South, an allegory broad enough to attract readers across the country.

In Himes' novel, Bob Jones dreams that he is lying in the middle of Main Street in downtown L.A., in front of the Federal Building.

> Two poor peckerwoods in overalls were standing over me beating me with lengths of rubber hose. I was sore and numb from the beating and felt like vomiting; I was sick in the stomach and the taste was in my mouth. I was trying to get up on my hands and knees but they were beating me across the back of my head at the base of my skull and every now and then one would hit me across the small of my back and I could feel it in my kidneys. Every time I got one knee up and tried to get the other one up I couldn't make it and would fall down again and I knew I couldn't last much longer.[14]

The "peckerwoods" stopped out of pity. But "somebody laughed and I looked around and saw two policemen standing by a squad car to one side nudging each other and laughing." And the "hard, cultured" voice of the president of the shipping company where Bob works tells the rednecks to "Continue! It's an order." "So they started beating me again and I was hoping I would become unconscious but I couldn't." Bob catches himself rolling in bed, trying to wake up from his dream, but somehow not soon enough. "They keep beating me not quite to death."

Needless to say, this scenario, already so familiar in 1945, plays ominously like the King video itself, but consider also the noir POV of the *non-white* narrator here: in staging Bob's way of seeing, Himes emphasizes the expression on the policeman's face, a very important touch, almost standard in black crime fiction – the *leer* of the officer watching from a car. It clarifies the edge of the city where blacks should not cross. Donald Goines wrote sixteen novels about black criminal life in L.A., many while in prison, where he was murdered in 1975. In his last novel, *Inner City*

Hoodlum (1975), small-time thief Johnny Washington drives his old Chevy up "the steep bank" of the Fourth Street exit, into the "deserted, cavernous canyons of downtown Los Angeles. The streets were empty and dark. Everyone had fled the urban center the moment their work day had ended. Very few would dare to stay in the downtown district after dark."[15]

Johnny's friend Buddy feels "the whole fucking place is ours for the asking." They prepare to break into boxcars. However, as a standard precaution, they notice "a squad car cruising slowly north on Main Street. Quickly, [Johnny] turns south and passes the two policemen casually. He sees their white suspicious faces peering at him from the interior of the black and white." The war of nerves between the LAPD and the black driver is as essential to these stories as Philip Marlowe toughing it out with a smart hood. The body language of the meeting identifies the intensely fragile distance that must be maintained between the races, or the iron fist will simply drop on you.

Of course, this black POV has been updated for the nineties. The black detective is more an insider facing institutional racism. The leering L.A. cop is more like his white boss, who tokenizes and victimizes him. In the post-riot detective novel *You Can Die Trying* (1993) by Gar Anthony Haywood, the plot centers around a conspiracy to manipulate physical evidence at the scene of the crime. Private eye Aaron Gunner learns that innocent blacks are to be blamed, because at the top Police Chief Bowden is "the biggest and baddest LAPD cop of them all." A very delicate ballet is needed for a black police officer not to get caught in this net himself.

> Being made to feel answerable to the whole of one's race was a burden few white men ever had to shoulder, yet it was a black man's birthright from day one. To wander too far from the beaten path of conformity, daring to expand upon what some people insisted were the unalterable parameters of blackness was to purchase the guilt of treason, and for some that guilt could be so incessant as to be crippling. Aaron Gunner [the black detective] was no such victim, but he had felt the sting of the phenomenon more than once.[16]

URBAN LEGENDS:
POLICE CALLS, POLICE OVERREACTION

On 29 July 1995, the weekend after *Virtuosity* was released, a fourteen-year-old boy was shot by a policeman with a record of overreacting under fire. Antonio Guttierez was apparently holding a T9 semi-automatic pistol when an officer opened fire, in the mostly Latino district of Lincoln Heights, northwest of downtown. A riot ensued for three days, as neighbors – and his mother, who was a witness – insisted that Guttierez was only carrying a flashlight, or that he had tossed away the weapon. What struck me most about the story was that six rounds were fired, four into his shoulder and back, presumably while he was spinning from the impact.

I was told by a young military specialist who had been on alert in San Diego during the "riots" of 1992 that soldiers in combat often get so "keyed up" under fire that they simply fire until the noise stops – empty a clip absent-mindedly, as if screaming for relief. A week after the shooting, I asked him what he had heard about Lincoln Park. His story fitted the police version, but he added another strange twist by saying: "The officer exercised reasonable control. A lot worse goes on." "A lot worse" implies that nineteen rounds in a clip might be fired before judgement is restored. My wife told me that a Salvadoran student of hers remembered his brother being shot "nineteen times in the head by a policeman." I can imagine how many rumors emerge out of agonized memories like that. The number of cases of wrongful death by police and by officers in the sheriff's department have cost the county and the city tens of millions of dollars in court. A sheriff's department raid at a Samoan wedding festival in 1989 led to a $15 million verdict in August, 1995.

Increasingly, the institutional intransigence of the LAPD appears in the news without the sense that someone has intervened on their behalf, to mute the nastiness. Therefore complaints about the top brass itself become an ongoing editorial, in various "think pieces" beside the headline story. The policeman who shot the young Guttierez had been recommended for release by the Christopher Commission four years earlier, along with forty-one other officers considered too violent, most of whom were still on active duty. That opened up old wounds. Why didn't the brass get rid of this man? Where was Internal Affairs? Why was the new mayor, Riordan, unable to work with the new police chief, Williams?

Then came the material released to the press about Mark Fuhrman, on his years at the Hollenbeck detail, in Lincoln Heights. In medical interviews from 1981, he said – again as if a split personality – "I was a good policeman. Something happened to me." When Fuhrman asked for a stress disability release in 1983, he told the pension commissioner that while working in Hollenbeck, he "tortured [suspects] … When I would choke out somebody, I would try to break their necks, period." In the taped interviews with Laura Hart McKinney, he was even more graphic:

he and partners pounded suspects' faces to "mush," pushed one down the stairs, left a blood-spattered apartment in ruins.[17] One report by a police psychiatrist in 1982 recommended that Fuhrman be re-educated, but the psychiatrist said later that "the problem is with the department. If they got this report and didn't do anything ... they must have liked him there and wanted him back."[18] This quickly became international news, with juicy exploitation of entire sections of Fuhrman's testimony in newspapers around the world. "Is the police department as jaundiced as the Fuhrman tapes suggest?" asked *Newsweek*. "Segments of the LAPD remain encrusted with a culture of racism and sexism."[19]

By 9 August, Mayor Riordan had appointed two new members to the police commission – to push reforms – while Chief Williams had begun intensive investigations, even of shootings involving Fuhrman as far back as 1978.[20] But that failed to stem the crisis, particularly after some of the Simpson jurors went on television afterward blaming the sloppiness of the LAPD, and the racism of Fuhrman for tainting the prosecution's case.

Promises of new training programs designed to reduce fatigue and alienation at the LAPD drew a sneer. New job fairs for the LAPD got mixed reviews. More awkward statistics continued to haunt the news: almost 40 per cent of the Department's field officers and 36 per cent of its sergeants had less than four years on the job. They were raw, because "specialized units were bleeding the institutional heart out of patrol."[21] Even more telling was the news that 83 per cent of the LAPD did not reside in Los Angeles, and most lived between twenty and fifty miles away, in distant white enclaves like Simi Valley or Santa Clarita – very suburban-identified, often deeply alienated from the inner-city residents they served.

From station house to the streets, very little routine was in place for "community" policing, for cops "walking" a beat. This detachment had been justified as high-tech professionalism. Attempts to improve relations with poor neighborhoods were notoriously uneven. The LAPD was still desperately understaffed: less than half the ratio of other large cities, in an area many times larger. And within the department itself, shortages aggravated the struggle over resources, over who got which plum assignment. For that and other reasons, there was a class structure and racial separation among the brass that bred a xenophobia about outsiders who interfere. We "protect" our own – the famous "code of silence." Perhaps similar problems exist in every city police department. The sum of these revealed a pattern, which repeats continuously, in the way calls were handled.

First, residents experienced sluggishness and withdrawal, almost utter in-activity; and then, just as suddenly, like warriors fighting to claim a beach-head, the police exhibited flashes of violent overreaction.

In Lincoln Heights, since 1994, there had been pressure by local groups and by the local councilman to force the police to be more helpful. Gang incidents had increased in number for almost a year. Many in the neighborhood asked for a storefront substation similar to those in every other area in the Hollenbeck police district. Lincoln Heights community leaders complained that there were not enough Latino officers, that community-based policing was not working yet, that rights violations were endemic, that "frustrations are running high." Once again the ex-pression "open season" appeared, to suggest careless racist disregard by the police. At the same time, the distrust of cops ran very deep. In the words of councilman Mike Hernandez, "The police have no credibility because there is no communication."[22]

The memory of a shooting in 1991 was still fresh in people's minds. The slaying of Arturo (Smoky) Jimenez by sheriff's deputies in the nearby Ramona Gardens had sparked a summer riot that presaged what happen-ed citywide in the spring of the next year. Later, the Jimenez family was awarded $450,000 in a wrongful death suit. A similar legal action was filed on behalf of the Guttierez family. As a civil-rights attorney in Lincoln Heights explained, "The situation on the Eastside is very similar to the situation in South Central with the black community."[23] The explanation given by police was very revealing. Captain Haggerty of the Hollenbeck district – a veteran of riot policing in 1992 – said:

> When people get in oppressed situations, because of the economy and lack of jobs, they tend to lash out. And when they lash out: at the police. We're the most visible presence... We are not the problem. We are stuck dealing with the results of the problem.[24]

The subtext here sounds familiar. Whenever the police identify them-selves as victims in much the same voice as the criminals they catch, I immediately sense a grave problem, and not simply because of shootings and sweeps – the dramatic overreactions – but in the daily routine: in the way calls are answered, in the assumptions about which potential suspects need to be watched, and who can be trusted. When cops exclaim that they feel martyred, it tends to mean that they have made very few allies; that, in their minds at least, no bridges exist; and, above all, that the brass are perceived as not managing the problem, that working conditions and

morale are bad. Another comment by Haggerty echoes the same problem: "We've never had anything like this" – suggesting brass who are out
of touch with daily needs, and who just want to keep a lid on it. Never
before? It reminds me of the cycle of callousness followed by withdrawal
and then overreaction that can spark riots. It also generates urban legends
about abuse, until at last it seems that neither the residents nor the police
can win for losing.

In 1981, a small riot broke out on Ridge Way in Angelino Heights. Five
youths in mohawks howled at the moon for an hour or so, then vented
their rage on the newly arrived Vietnamese – mostly curses and rocks.
Police came to clear the street, then stayed for about an hour. I sat on a
stoop watching, while a policeman pointed to my house as the probable
cause of all the problems. I told him that he was two years behind. The
"gang" who used to live there had moved to Glendale after their mother
sold me the property. For a moment I thought a useful conversation was
coming. I could let him know that the police helicopters occasionally
circling my building were wasting their time. But clearly I was supposed to
say nothing at all. There was a long pause. He turned to another neighbor
and said: "If you feel you need to get a gun, I'll understand."

A few months later, a rock was thrown through another neighbor's
house. The couple inside were too upset use the phone, so they asked us
to call the police. Once again, I waited outside at a corner of Ridge Way
for a squad car to arrive. When I saw it approaching, I flagged it down;
this initiated ten minutes of overreaction and absurdity. With startling
abruptness, I was nearly arrested for standing and waving at night. In a
monotone, they advised me to assume the position. Then they pulled my
wife into the street as well, for possible arrest, when she stood in her
nightgown at the front door. Finally, speaking in complete sentences,
trying to sound as Anglo as possible, I made them understand that while
I did look somewhat "Mexican," I was not in fact the boy who had
thrown the rock, but only the person who had called them. This seemed
a letdown. Very abruptly, they jumped into the car and drove off. No
report was made, not even a written description of who threw the rock.
I thought I was watching a Keystone Comedies routine. In my mind's
eye, I remember their rifles out of open windows, and the squealing of
tires. I realize that this must be an exaggeration, but the sense of absent-
minded persecution stays with me.

I was very angry when I called the police yet again, this time to
complain. Once more, I used my deepest WASP voice, to make certain

they knew I was a concerned citizen who wouldn't go away. Finally, an hour later, another squad car stopped at my neighbor's house. A husky blond sergeant emerged and went straight to work. He wrote down every detail, and then asked if we wanted a yellow copy. Finally, after hearing my "allegation," he admitted that some police were indeed losing their edge lately. He leaned toward me, almost intentionally ignoring the neighbors sitting three feet away. He didn't seem to care that they were young Mexican-Americans when he said: "Our problem is minority hiring. It's forcing us to lower our standards." Ignoring the sudden chill from us, perhaps assuming it meant we were actually taking him seriously, he asked me to call the police academy "on Monday," and voice my support for what sounded essentially like white supremacy. I looked at my neighbors, who didn't seem at all surprised.

Callousness, withdrawal, overreaction: these stories stick in my mind while I look through my notes on the "riots" in 1992, on the two extremes in the image of police that have made their way erratically into movies like *Virtuosity*, or even into the Simpson trial – spit-and-polish professionalism at the precinct, opposed by nervous breakdown on the streets. In the eighties, the middle class generally presumed that police were high-tech professionals. Obviously, what high-tech meant depended on where you sat – which class, which place, which race. If you lived in a poor neighborhood, police were abusive and gruff too often, like machines. In wealthier districts, high-tech might suggest that cops were simply well trained, and had fancy equipment, closer to the boosterist image reinforced during the Olympics in 1984. Indeed, that high-tech social imaginary has dissolved, leaving nothing coherent in its place, except an unfixed paranoia. No wonder the story in *Virtuosity* seems more about divided memories than about efficient all-seeing law enforcement; all-seeing was an "old" image, from the eighties, about ruthless "fascist" police, as in *Robocop*, and not as appropriate in the wake of 1992.

I can place the precise moment when the shift became obvious: during the Rebellion, there was a rumor that the fires had to be master-planned, that flyers were distributed by gangbangers beforehand, even with addresses – to outsmart the LAPD. I kept asking myself why that much preparation was necessary. Based on the image the police had in my neighborhood, it seemed that the media was overestimating how street-wise and high-tech the police were. I remember saying to friends that it was difficult to imagine why looting needed to be "planned." "Synchronize watches." "Let's go over those blueprints again." Reporters may have been seeing too many eighties' crime films.

The fires seemed to erupt in a sequence, as if designed by teams; but really, most of all, they looked like the cat and mouse game between youth and police that had been ongoing for years, where the police tended to lose control, often seem to withdraw, then just as often overreact. Only the scale was different. There were also rumors that gang members had car phones to track the police, and could maintain a fairly coordinated system of counter-surveillance. I wondered if that was needed, based on the evidence of the demoralized cops I had seen. Most of all, I knew that this was *not* an event radiating out of Florence and Normandy, as the media tended to say throughout the world. It started in many "pulse points" (a hot term for a few weeks). Based on pulse points in areas that I knew, like the revolt in Pico-Union/Westlake or the looting in East Hollywood heading west, it was clear that the looting – the sheer carnival and tragedy of it – involved parallel sets of events, and that once again the police were unable to keep track, except through overreaction, preceded by a strange, almost depressed, withdrawal.

To the media, L.A. is often imagined as a city without neighborhoods. That myth distracted many reporters from noticing the multiple history unfolding here – the extraordinary differences from one mile to the next, their separate ethnic demographics, unique job patterns and investment cycles – instead of simply the melodramatic issues, such as where gangs hung out, who shot whom, or what graffiti really said.

The "rioting" was not only largely unplanned; it was also extremely random in many ways, with pockets that were surprisingly peaceful. However, these quiet spots, particularly in poor neighborhoods, were not the kind of story to carry in the midst of a disaster. In fact, Angelino Heights and Echo Park were generally so quiet that I heard crickets all night (the curfew stopped freeway traffic). One shoe store on Sunset Boulevard was looted, but the empty boxes were found stacked like pizza cartons after a teen party in front of a house on Kensington Avenue, at an address that everyone seemed to know.

Back in the eighties, I used to groan when I read the flashy publicity on the LAPD. It seemed to cover up the extraordinary incoherence and combat weariness that I was noticing, or hearing about first-hand – the usual neighborhood rumors. But in 1992, the lid was off. One interview after another had stories about cops looking confused, out of position, withdrawn, careless, even ignoring firefighters. I wondered how the officers I had watched from the Ramparts Division behaved; if they were shocked and unprepared, like soldiers in a citywide combat zone without a contingency plan. Many cops used to chat about policing as if they were Indian scouts looking for hostiles, reading graffiti like hoof prints and smoke signals. Even the officers I met who had a genuine investment in doing a sensitive and fearless job often hinted to me in some way that they felt one step behind, and extraordinarily mismanaged.

That same ambivalence surfaced in interviews I read about police inside the Uprising. Officers consistently repeated how abandoned they felt. Even their phrasing reminds me of the despairing cop who told me in 1981: "I feel as unappreciated as the kids I arrest." Here is one sampling:

> *The public* wants protection, but doesn't realize the violence involved.
>
> *The community* doesn't want to accept blame, so [it was] passed on to the LAPD.
>
> *Politicians* and *media* would never blame [themselves], so blame police – scapegoat.
>
> Community is saying we did nothing – but that's what they [politicians] wanted.
>
> Media encouraged belief and police are [the] easiest focal point for frustrations.
>
> The *upper brass* did not let the patrol officers do their job. If we would have went in there in the beginning with force we would not have had the disturbance grow as large as it did.
>
> We were lacking leaders! The *command post* was a black hole that sucked officers in, but couldn't spit them back out.
>
> ... the command staff had brain farts.[25]

Someone I showed this to said it resembled badass rhetoric after the fall of Vietnam, a comparison worth taking seriously, since many police served in that war. But their distress was hidden from public view during the eighties. The media generally gave police high marks, particularly in the afterglow of the successful 1984 Olympics. They are described as spartans aided by futuristic technology (super helicopters, surveillance radar), a fierce army of last resort, prepared to keep L.A. from becoming another Vietnam.

1991–92: PROMOTION AND DAMAGE CONTROL

Much of this amounted to sheer boosterism of course – carefully staged news briefings and press conferences. But it seemed to work, along with a militant brinkmanship. Whenever cases of police brutality broke into the headlines, like the Eulia Love shooting in 1979,[26] or the furore over lethal choke holds in 1986, a well-orchestrated press conference was called. The brass were protected. Chief Gates would make an edgy (or double-edged) statement, then ask the city council for support, and get it. First, he would make some kind of public apology, agreeing that there are "occasional" excesses, though not institutional ones. Then, in the same breath, he would stand firm, warn everyone that L.A. cops must be left to do their job professionally, that they are implacable and honest. For example, during the gang sweeps of 1988, out of the 25,000 who were arrested by the LAPD, and 25,000 more by the Sheriff's Department,[27] many were innocent black and Latino bystanders; and some of these bystanders were shot. Internal Affairs recommended that twenty-five officers be suspended. Gates said to the press: "The officers were trying to do the right thing – to solve the gang problem, to solve the narcotics trafficking problem. Unfortunately, while doing the right thing, they were doing it in the wrong way."[28]

Gates continued more or less with the same strategy through the spring of 1991, after the King video was broadcast on 3 March, admitting that he, like President Bush, was shocked by the video, but that oversight agencies had better see this as a bizarre exception to the rule. At first, it seemed that Gates – and therefore the police – would weather the entire mess. Their problems were distracted by a larger story: the collapse in March of Mayor Bradley's black/liberal coalition that had dominated city politics for a generation.[29] In effect, the enemy-of-my-enemy became a kind of neutral friend. Those who hated Bradley's handling of the city were not as harsh toward Gates, whom everyone knew Bradley was trying to squeeze out of office. City Council split behind Bradley's demand in April that Gates resign.

Nor did polls indicate voter fright in the April elections.[30] Gates' support actually rose among whites in April, though it plummeted among blacks, Latinos, Jews and white women. The signals were plain enough, but not considered definitive, at least certainly not by the media, not even in July when the report by the Christopher Commission reinforced what the King video seemed to make self-evident: a casual brutality among the police, suggesting an ongoing policy, and enormous gaps in the chain of command.

During this false spring, promotional literature like the annual report from the LAPD continued as it had. Police were still hyped as incorrupt-ible masters of high-tech; there was no mention of the scandals by name.

The Training Division announced a new Judo Tactical Communications Course, code name Verbal Judo:

> By using such Verbal Judo Skills as representation, translation, paraphrasing and persuasion, police officers can clearly differentiate between situations that call for communication or when words demonstratively fail, situations that require the use of physical force.[31]

Along with Verbal Judo, a pilot program was unveiled called Arraignment By Video. That meant literally making arrests interactively – on a large monitor, teleconferencing from the Parker Center, which handled 37 per cent of all felony arrests, to the Municipal Court a mile away.[32]

Not until the fall did this boosterism fail completely. Months later, reporters at the *L.A. Times* listed the chain of events that finally obligated them to treat the LAPD much more harshly: first, in November the City Council angrily approved $7.1 million to settle dozens of claims of police brutality and excessive force, "boosting total payments for the year to a record of more than $13 million."[33] A week later, the Korean shopowner Soon Ja Du was given five years probation for the killing of Latasha Harlins. A little more than a week after that, four of the officers involved in the beating of Rodney King were ordered to trial. Three days after that, "LAPD officers fatally shot a twenty-eight year old black man, Henry Peco, who allegedly ambushed them while they investigated a power outage, prompting a standoff with more than 100 residents of the Imperial Courts housing project in Watts."[34]

Throughout May, retrospectives on the collapse of the LAPD's image became standard front-page news; even the *L.A. Times* ran a special ten-page insert.[35] The devastating Christopher Commission was quoted regularly, with its demands to revamp the citizens' complaint system; overhaul the police commission; limit the police chief's term of office; shift toward "community oriented" policing; require more psychological screening of officers, at hiring and regularly afterward; and, finally, set up cultural awareness courses for officers.[36]

Stanley Scheinbaum, president of the L.A. Police Commission explained to the *L.A. Times* that he had tried on various occasions during the "Riots" to get a police briefing:

> I didn't reach any of them because they were all deployed in various places... The situation was out of control... On the same block as the Wilshire Station on Venice Boulevard there were about three or four or five burnouts within 200

or 300 yards... But there wasn't much they could do at the station because almost everybody was out in the field, deployed.[37]

From there, the slide was utterly precipitous. It seemed that the video camera had been invented to mortify the LAPD. On 29 April, Daryl Gates was taped at a fundraiser against Proposition F, the police reform initiative that passed anyway in June, just in time for the tenure of new police chief Willie Williams. On CBS television, he rankled when asked why he was in Bel Air that night of all nights, rather than staying at his job. Gates swore that he had just popped in for five minutes. However, when the tape was released, it showed him lingering there in tuxedo for nearly half an hour, and possibly much longer, while L.A. burned. I remember someone saying to me that week: "I keep imagining Gates in bed having nightmares about camcorders. Giant rotating heads chase him. Tapes rewind the sound of Stanley Scheinbaum getting the last laugh."

In May, to diminish the impact of those damning videotapes, the "No On F" forces spent about $500,000 for a video of their own, a television spot featuring Reginald Denny. Over the footage of four blacks beating up the white truck driver, a voice-over blamed *non*-LAPD leadership for the unrest, showing the mayor, a black councilman, and the Police Commission president. Then, in front of television overheads of looting, a text flashed: "The police wanted to do their job. They weren't allowed."[38] However, according to one newspaper, "within a week, all the local TV stations were refusing to run the ad... A poll in the Los Angeles Times days before the election showed Prop. F leading with 61 percent in favor... In addition, Gates' disapproval rating [had grown to] a whopping 81 percent."[39]

That was rock bottom for damage control at the LAPD. In late June, a high-profile editorial in *Editor and Publisher* stated that editors of the *Los Angeles Times* were openly criticizing the way their newspaper had covered the "riots," stalling coverage of police brutality until the problem exploded after the King verdict on 30 April.[40] That same month, the *Washington Journalism Review* faulted the entire newspaper industry for missing the underlying realities behind the crisis in L.A.: racism, poverty and political insensitivity.[41] This came apparently after a panel of minority journalists filed a paper showing that racism among the press had obscured urban crises that should have been discussed long before the civil unrest.[42]

From May into the fall, reporters could sample data from dozens of "riot" conferences in practically every college and meeting hall in Southern California. By the spring of 1993, at least twelve separate volumes had been published on the Rebellion, going into considerable detail and arriving at what I understand as the root causes:[43] the loss of 70,000 manufacturing jobs in South Central from 1978 to 1983, coupled with huge cutbacks in public services during the Reagan years, further strained by the vast immigration from Mexico and Central America – a pressure that afflicted the aggrieved areas most of all – and, finally, as the immediate cause, *sweeps* by police.

But there lies the sore spot: using the term "sweeps" retrospectively. That is the space where *distraction* continued, despite the media blitz. The sweeps did not stop; they simply were not part of the promotion anymore. They were what was supposed to be hidden. The only conference that covered this missing piece was that organized by the ACLU in late June.

"Sweeps" and curfews had been a fundamental policy during the Gates era, with precedents as far back as 1942, during the Zoot Suit hysteria.[44] The idea is to round up as many young men as possible who might be involved. As some officers explained: "Pick 'em up for anything and everything." "Mess around with them."[45] Tag teams would check for even mild auto violations. Simply the wrong clothing might be enough. The problem could then be sorted out at the station. The important thing is to get names on the blotter; then the blanks can be filled in. The number of black youths in poor neighborhoods who have police records is astounding: one in four, if not higher.[46] As Mike Davis wrote in 1990: "As a result of the war on drugs every non-Anglo teenager in Southern California is now [according to police] a prisoner of gang paranoia and associated demonology."[47]

Possibly the largest sweep in L.A.'s history started on 30 April 1992 and ran for weeks, even though the police seemed utterly neutralized – "impotent, paralyzed," as Joseph McNamara of the conservative Hoover Institute said.[48] In fact, they were anything but paralyzed. The world's press and television forgot to notice that the police were continuing with a central policy that was "natural," given the structure and routines. The media gloried in the number of buildings lost, in the sheer financial cost,[49] even in the trend momentarily toward more sociologically driven and scholarly journalism. At the same time, reverting themselves to old boosterist tendencies, newspapers and television ran numerous pieces on the Rebuild L.A. Committee, a blue-ribbon charity – and promotional – operation; they then ran photos almost daily of the genial and stolid face of the new police chief, Williams. The sum of this suggested a genteel mopping-up operation, the end of nasty business as usual. That was clearly what so many sorely hoped for. And yet, business was very usual indeed.

When the rioting began, a curfew was established, first limited only to South Central, since it was assumed that 1992 would follow the patterns of 1965, and stay inside black neighborhoods. In fact the looting very quickly jumped past South Central, starting fiercely in five locales that I saw. It became apparent that this was a drive-by insurrection. Only a citywide curfew could stem it, and allow for the primary police weapon to take over – massive sweeps. As the rioting grew during the second day (Thursday), new policies gave police absolute authority. "Mere presence" *outside* during curfew was grounds for arrest, with high bail and harsh sentences.[50]

The overcrowding in the jails reached hazardous proportions by the third day. Virtually no one was being released. The usual bail for a misdemeanor like breaking a curfew was increased from $250 to more like $15,000, so that essentially no one picked up who was poor could leave. If the defendant had no previous record (almost two-thirds did not), the bail was set at $8,000. One Inglewood judge set bail as high as $50,000 for "looters:" "In his court, one person was charged with a felony and $50,000 bail for stealing sunflower seeds from a convenience store."[51] Finally, many of the homeless were caught in the curfew net simply because they had no home but outdoors. .

It became a numbers game: thousands shoved into jails and holding tanks;[52] at least 5,633 "formally" arrested. Most were Latino males (51 per cent). Only 36 per cent were African-American males, and 13 per cent "female" or Anglo.[53] That figure of 51 per cent Latino is crucial here; it repeats in practically every report I have read. Consider the problem: Proposition F was on the ballot, the police in purgatorial shame, the public hungry for results. It became apparent early on at the district attorney's office that less than half those detained could be sent for trial, which was not unusual for sweeps anyway. For there simply was not enough evidence. And since many of the innocent were being scooped up with the guilty, the resulting evidence was too contaminated to make strong cases in court for that many defendants at once.[54] Less than half had any police record at all. But clearly the public demanded a monumental number of convictions, because even in polls the police were held very much to blame for the unrest.

One reliable way to show results *fast* was to concentrate on illegals from Latin America: work with immigration authorities to deport defendants who were undocumented aliens, and avoid having to try them for looting. Very soon, over nine hundred cases were transferred to the INS. This ran counter to established practice. Usually, someone who is cited for a violation, or arrested, did not have to reveal immigration status. Otherwise, harassment for deportation could get utterly out of control, turn into a witch-hunt for anyone who looks illegal, has a Mexican face, or drives a "wetback" car. Clearly, a near witch-hunt already operates between the INS, the Sheriff's Department, and the highway patrol, to snare drivers transporting illegals from the border into other counties, or looking as if they might. The pursuits can get dangerous. "High-speed chase syndrome" has led to hundreds of accidents and cases of police abuse – and finally to another embarrassing video, this time taken from a media chopper in March 1996: fifteen seconds of sheriff's officers clobbering immigrants. The passage of a statewide anti-immigrant referendum in 1994, Proposition 187, was seen as license for such activity, and even led to legal Latinos getting harassed at the County Medical Hospital. But 1992 added to the legal mess as well, along with risks that accompany the use of the National Guard as city police.[55]

Indeed, the problem can shift locales and venues very easily. In 1992, the principle of the sweep shifted to immigrants to camouflage the deep shock felt by police that week, a post-traumatic meltdown[56] confusion about who gave the orders and how not to incite another riot. On television, this shock came across as extreme apathy. By the hour, reports on television showed LAPD frozen, making embarrassed "retreats." In one video, which was recycled a lot, a squad car pulls up in a dark street, and turns away ("turns tail," as one announcer put it), as if in retreat. That one appeared on Channel Five local news, and was broadcast as far as Reno and San Francisco.

Consider how soothing it was, after the traumas on the streets, simply to get names on the blotter – an indexical sport, like body counts during the Vietnam War, or bomb tonnage during the Gulf War; or camouflaging the demolition of a neighborhood by releasing sanitized models of high-rises that will replace it. Keep the rules simple: since the streets had to be cleared quickly, curfew-breakers were often picked up by category and proximity (blacks, Latinos, the homeless) and were detained for weeks. The more who pleaded guilty the better. No one wanted more cases of police brutality to inflame the newspapers, or cause more rioting. However, no one could afford to let thousands simply walk. Thus, to help the statistics, a large number of those detained were given a harsh choice: either wait in jail for thirty days before any chance of trial, or plead guilty; no contest. Afterward, by avoiding a trial, you could apply time served to the sentence, even get probation. As a result, hundreds simply pleaded to go home.

This returns me to a central thesis for this section of the book: that "breaking stories" on television are mostly a form of distraction. Loops of a disaster that morning are replayed from morning to night on television, but the immediate present is lost: long-term causes; the uneventful events, the camouflages, even people just out of the frame. In all forms of photo memory, the camera records explosions as they happen – presence – but not the present.

SEPTEMBER 1995: STRANGE DAYS

In September 1995, at the time of the Simpson verdict, the film *Strange Days* was released, to mixed reviews. Like *Virtuosity*, it is set in the year 1999 in downtown Los Angeles. Even more than *Virtuosity*, it inserts memories of events from 1991 and 1992. The principal character, Lenny, is a former LAPD officer who is now a self-destructive dealer in illicit virtual reality disks. Mostly about kinky sex, they transmit orgasms and simulated murder through a VR headset that resembles a portable hair-dryer, or a hat for an electric chair. Lenny's identity is disintegrating. He is disappearing into his videos, trying to reimagine the woman who got away. Like all addicts to these disks, he loves his flashbacks, his acid burn.

The cops are evil or inept, particularly two who strongly resemble Stacey Koon and Laurence Powell. They leer with a fleshy insolence, like suburban *fascisti* fresh from Santa Clarita or Simi Valley. They are loose cannons who kill Jeriko 1, a gangsta rapper with a mystique like Malcolm X; this is essentially a glamorized reference to the gang truce of 1992, and to the panic it spread. Many police worried that it would organize into a holy war against the LAPD. In *Strange Days*, that becomes a distinct possibility, and the motive for assassination. With Jeriko dead, however, comes the risk of yet another riot, which would start downtown around the Bonaventure Hotel, that icon of panoptical – and postmodern [57] Anglo elegance and hubris. If the Bonaventure were to be overrun, particularly just as the clock strikes the year 2000, a millenarian riot might begin – the big one that might sweep away Los Angeles as we know it.

Lenny discovers he is a moral agent after all, after stumbling upon the truth of Jeriko's death. The truth is housed in a pocket-sized VR disk that recorded the assassination. Typically, the truth is an unsteady medium shot, about the same distance from the bullet that killed Jeriko as George Holliday was from Rodney King's cheekbone. But once the truth is on Lenny's side, the action accelerates. While the party grows, he splices his way through one catastrophe after another. He learns that the woman who was his heart's desire is a weak bitch controlled by a murderous VR drug lord. Then he discovers that she has been two-timing her drug lord, and really loves Lenny's closest buddy, another LAPD cop who turns out to be a murderous shit.

Luckily, Lenny has someone remaining in the movie that he can love, who can save him: Mace (as in bludgeon), a black lady chauffeur who pines for Lenny, while using her martial arts to knock his enemies unconscious. She definitely knows good from evil, and persuades Lenny to give her the assassination disk, though it will probably spark a huge riot. She will deliver it to the chief of police, the only honest executive left in the LAPD. However, Mace is too black, and too much a chauffeur to get through to the chief. What is worse, as the price for her uppityness, she has to undergo the Rodney King ritual of stoning. The Koon/Powell psychopaths cheer viciously, while she is beaten by mobs of sadistic young Anglo cops. We witness her calvary through the legs of onlookers, as if in a fish-eye of George Holliday's video again. Meanwhile the pulse toward riot keeps rising. The lights are near absolute meltdown. But at last, as always in these films, instead of rioting, all goes well. After a lavish twenty minutes that feels like a jumpcut washing machine, as the clock strikes midnight we see a helicopter overhead, in a sea of confetti. The millennium has arrived safely. Between hyperventilated action scenes, Lenny has realized that Mace is the love of his life. Exeunt.

Critics unanimously called *Strange Days* an indictment of the LAPD; and the filmmakers at least feigned surprise. Jay Cocks, the co-screenwriter, said that "Mark Fuhrman just snuck up behind us." "This is not a story of the LAPD as a bunch of maniacs, but as an organization of power. Racist behavior and abuses exist in any organization of power."[58] The director, Kathryn Bigelow, added that both "the good and bad" of the LAPD are presented, "an entire spectrum of behavior." *Strange Days* merely raised "to the level of myth" the reality of Los Angeles as a "flashpoint society" (another code word used in media coverage of 1992).

The director of the new "no frills reality" television series *LAPD* sounded cautious as well, saying that the LAPD is "one of the best police departments in the world," and that he had the full cooperation of Chief

Willie Williams. Reality television is slanted anyway, he added. "The officers know they're being followed by a camera crew."

By 1995, a sub-industry for media and the LAPD had developed. To achieve accuracy, *Strange Days* director Bigelow hired a consulting firm known as Call the Cops, founded in 1988 by Randy Walker, who had spent ten years on an L.A. SWAT team. He followed essentially the same call for forgiveness of the LAPD: "People in all professions … make errors in judgment." "Thousands of hours of good police work can be overshadowed by negative rumors." This is similar to the comment of Edith Perez of the Police Commission, when told of the federal grand jury about the Fuhrman testimony:

> As a practical matter, [the investigation] is going to be distracting. But this department has been through a lot of distractions, and this is critical to restoring confidence in the department.[59]

After Simpson was acquitted, the Fuhrman case became a rallying cry for celebrity murder trials. Rumors spread that the Menendez Brothers, in their retrial for the murder of their parents, were planning a defense based on the ineptitude of the LAPD (it failed: the brothers were found guilty). In Philadelphia, police officers were brought up on charges of tampering with evidence. The furore accompanying demands for reform of the LAPD led to another study, the Bobb report, which found that there had been very few changes: fewer beatings; more pepper spray instead of batons; more diversity in hiring. Otherwise, the department remained in confusion, "a ship in mid-passage, but not certain to reach port." What a migrating image of despair – clearly a noir myth.[60] It offers no solutions but forgetfulness after the headline dies down. That is why Marlowe can "solve" a case but rarely prevent a crime. The crime is long-term and causal. It moves geologically, like continental plates, in cycles that far exceed the hot-button coverage of a disaster.

DECEMBER 1996

I attend an "audience survey" pre-screening of the movie *L.A. Confidential.* I will be polled along with other 18–54 year olds on its potential box office appeal, whether it has enough "drama," "action," and a good ending. The film is better than some, shimmering with the usual noir gore. The epic sprawl of James Ellroy's novel about fifties L.A. has been condensed into a cop opera about good-hearted but corrupt LAPD detectives – and the prostitutes they know – caught in a web of deceit, made even uglier by the macabre struggle over 25 pounds of heroin. Still, it is the best movie ever made about the lies in building the "high-tech" image of the LAPD – wildly exaggerated, but with a Scorsese-like opening montage about how images are falsified. As always, the murders center on the western end of downtown, particularly Bunker Hill. Every ten minutes or so, cops troop back to Echo Park to find another body, or to capture blacks raping Mexicans – into the zone of hopelessness. Afterward, the audience is asked to write down comments. Two men, as they leave, decide that the story is not "true to life" because "there's just no good guys."

NOTES

1. Based on interviews with old residents. Also see chs 4 and 5 in *To Protect and Serve: The LAPD's Century of War in the City of Dreams* by Joe Dominick (New York: Pocket Books, 1994); and particularly James Fife and Jerome Skolnick, *Above the Law* (New York: Free Press, 1993). And, for comparisons with other police departments, Paul Chevigny, *The Edge of the Knife* (New York: The New Press, 1995).

2. On corruption during the Bowron years, see Charles Stoker, *Thicker 'n Thieves* (Santa Monica: Sidereal Company, 1951).

3. Jim Newton, "LAPD Reforms Fall Far Short, Study Charges," *L.A. Times*, 31 May 1996, p. A1.

4. Jim Newton and Ronald Ostrow, "Federal Probe of L.A. Police Moving Forward," *L.A. Times*, 7 November 1995, p. B6.

5. Code word "rogue" cop, as in unusual. John Schwada, "Williams Promises 'Biopsy' of Fuhrman," *L.A. Times*, 6 September 1995, p. B1.

6. Headline stories in *L.A. Times*, 30 August 1995.

7. Greg Krikorian, "Co-Workers Paint Different Portrait of Mark Fuhrman," *L.A. Times*, 8 November 1995, p. 14.

8. Ibid. See also 30 August 1995, p. A1.

9. Seven local television stations had their helicopters in the air at once during the looting.

10. The same *Spruce Goose* that Howard Hughes flew into the New York World's Fair in 1939. It may still be the largest flying machine ever assembled, so the hangar is immense, like a steel-ribbed basilica.

11. Nanotechnology uses computers to build micro-systems one atom at a time. Presumably, in the future, these systems might be inserted into the body directly, or become self-perpetuating creatures.

12. "Shot by Shot," *Premiere*, September 1995.

13. The first paperback edition of *If He Hollers Let Him Go* was published by Signet Books, New American Library, 1949. The illustrator was James Avati, the leading "cover

artist" of the day, whose reputation grows (interview with Jeffrey Browning, a specialist in L.A. literary history, 1996).

14. Chester Himes, *If He Hollers Let Him Go* (New York: Thunder's Mouth Press, 1986; orig. 1986), opening to ch. 9, p. 69. The short introduction by Graham Hodges is useful. See also: Peter J. Rabinowitz, "Chandler Comes to Harlem: Racial Politics in the Thrillers of Chester Himes," in *The Sleuth and Scholar: Origins, Evolution, and Current Trends in Detective Fiction* (New York: Greenwood Press, 1988); John N. Swift, "Chester Himes, The Fiction of Exclusion, and Los Angeles' Other Geography of Desire," in pamphlet anthology *Writers of the Historic Wilshire Boulevard* (Los Angeles Cultural Affairs Department, *c.* 1991).

15. Donald Goines, *Inner City Hoodlum* (Los Angeles: Holloway Publishing Company, 1975), pp. 7–9.

16. Gar Anthony Haywood, *You Can Die Trying* (New York: Penguin Books, 1993), p. 19. See also Gary Phillips, *Violent Spring*.

17. Paul Feldman and Robert J. Lopez, "Fuhrman Case: How the City Kept Troubled Cop," *L.A. Times*, 2 October 1995, p. A16.

18. Ibid.

19. "Up Against the Wall: The Explosive Fuhrman Tapes Put the LAPD Under New Scrutiny," *Newsweek*, 4 September 1995, p. 24.

20. Jean Merl, "Mayor Appoints Two Civic Leaders to Seats on Police Commission," *L.A. Times*, 9 August 1995, p. B1.

21. Dominick, *To Protect and Serve*, p. 339. In the revised paperback edition (1995), two chapters have been added on the Simpson trial, as additional hooks. On the cover is a blurb that says the LAPD helped O.J. get acquitted.

22. Patrick J. McDonnell and Robert J. Lopez, "Tense Times in Lincoln Heights," *L.A. Times*, 7 August 1995, p. 12.

23. Ibid.

24. Ibid. Some community meetings followed, also coordination at the funeral – perhaps early signs of changes in policy. For fictional account of policing at Hollenbeck decades ago, see Joseph Wambaugh, *New Centurions*.

25. Terri Harvey-Lintz, "Psychological Effects of the 1992 Los Angeles Riots: Post Traumatic Stress Symptomatology Among Law Enforcement Officers," dissertation, UCLA, pp. 106–9.

26. During an argument with police over an unpaid bill, Eulia Love was shot and killed. This case became a rallying cry among Afro-Americans in Los Angeles.

27. Dominick, *To Protect and Serve*, p. 324. Operation Hammer as it was called began in response to the driveby murder of a young woman Karen Toshima, in the white Westwood district.

28. Martin Schiesl, "Behind the Badge," in Norman M. Klein and Martin J. Schiesl, eds, *Twentieth Century Los Angeles: Power Promotion and Social Conflict* (Claremont: Regina Press, 1990), p. 189. Also in Dominick, *To Protect and Serve*, p. 336: of thirty-five officers ruled to have shot people unnecessarily, only two were fired; there was "no consistent pattern of punishment."

29. Raphael J. Sonenshein, *Politics in Black and White: Race and Power in Los Angeles* (Princeton: Princeton University Press, 1993), pp. 212–14.

30. Ibid.

31. *1991 Los Angeles Police Department Annual Report*, p. 10. The expression "verbal judo" might also have a slightly derogatory meaning, as in the quote from Chief Tom

Reddin, in reference to events about 1982, gathered by Joe Dominick (*To Protect and Serve*, p. 298): "Hand-to-hand combat is a lot simpler than having to deal with verbal judo."

32. Ibid., p. 8.

33. Ibid.

34. "Understanding the Riots," Part 1, *L.A. Times*, 11 May 1992, p. T11.

35. Ibid.

36. Ibid.

37. "Understanding the Riots," Part 3, *L.A. Times*, 13 May 1992, p. T2.

38. Laureen Lazarovici, "Prop. F Wins Big," in *Inside the L.A. Riots: What Really Happened. Why It Will Happen Again* (Los Angeles: Institute for Alternative Journalism, 1992); adapted from an article in *The L.A. Weekly* (co-sponsor of the anthology).

39. Ibid.

40. *Editor and Publisher*, 27 June 1992, p. 7.

41. Reese Cleghorn, "The Riots: Searching for Truths and Reality," *Washington Journalism Review*, vol. XIV, no. 5, June 1992.

42. George Garneau, "Bearing the Burden of Blame: Neglected Coverage of Race Relations Made Los Angeles Riots a Surprise," *Editor and Publisher*, 9 May 1992, p. 11.

43. By 1996, over fifty volumes had appeared, and up to a thousand articles and government documents. Among the most useful sources are: the ACLU report, *Civil Liberties in Crisis* (based on conference, 23 June 1992); *Understanding the Riots* (a record of many articles from the *L.A. Times*, useful for hour-by-hour summaries); *Beyond the Ashes* (the Los Angeles Business Journal, some demographics, and eighties history); Manuel Pastor, *Latinos and the Los Angeles Uprising: The Economic Context* (the Tomas Rivera Center, a scrupulous job); *Inside the L.A. Riots* (Institute for Alternative Journalism, essentially the *L.A. Weekly* coverage, see footnote 26); *New Initiatives for Los Angeles* (Senate Task Report, provides a sense of what information made its way to Washington); *To Rebuild Is Not Enough* (California State Assembly Report, 28 September 1992, in the spirit of policy alternatives, while that spirit lasted); Joel Kotkin and David Friedman, "The Los Angeles Riots: Causes, Myths and Solutions" (*Commentary*, February 1993); James H. Johnson et al., "The Los Angeles Rebellion: A Retrospective View," *Economic Development Quarterly*, November 1992; Allen J. Scott and E. Richard Brown, "South-Central Los Angeles: Anatomy of a Crisis (Working Paper, Lewis Center for Regional Policy, June 1993); Kathi George and Jennifer Joseph, *The Verdict is In* (San Francisco, Manic D Press, a Bay Area point of view, including poetry and personal essays). Many of these sources and others are cited in the anthology edited by Mark Baldassare, *The Los Angeles Riots: Lessons for the Urban Future* (Boulder, Colo.: Westview Press, 1994). See also Sue Hamilton, *The Los Angeles Riots*, 1992; Erna Smith *Transmitting Race: The L.A. Riot in Television News*, 1994; Mychal Wynn, *Enough is Enough: The Explosion in Los Angeles*, 1993.

I also would recommend the articles written by Mike Davis during this period (1991–94), in pamphlets, various anthologies, the *Nation*, *L.A. Times*, *L.A. Weekly*, and *New Left Review*. See also Lynnell George's collection of essays, *No Crystal Stair* (London: Verso, 1992), and Anna Devere Smith's interviews, as the text of her one-person show *Twilight: Los Angeles, 1992; On the Road: A Search for American Character* (New York: Bantam/Doubleday, 1994; based on performances from 1993). Raphael Sonenshein, Martin Schiesl and Joe Dominick are cited elsewhere in this chapter. Finally, see the anthology *City in Turmoil* edited by Norman M. Klein and Martin J. Schiesl (forthcoming, 1997); and James H. Johnson and Walter Farrell, "The Fire this Time: The Genesis of the Los Angeles Rebellion of 1992," *North Carolina Review* 71, June 1993.

44. Beatrice Griffith, *American Me* (New York: Houghton-Mifflin, 1947) p. 17.

45. Dominick, *To Protect and Serve*, p. 325.

46. In 1995, the figure quoted regularly was one in three black youths in prison or on probation. So I am being quite conservative.

47. Mike Davis, *City of Quartz: Excavating the Future in Los Angeles* (London and New York: Verso, 1990), p. 284.

48. *International Herald Tribune*, 6 May 1992, p. 4. The coverage in Europe was more about effects on US politics, on the upcoming presidential elections, or on the international business community. McNamara was formerly the police chief of San José.

49. Mike Freeman, "Riots Boost May Ratings in L.A." (up to 36 per cent in a sweeps month), *Broadcasting*, 1 June 1992, p. 20.

50. *Civil Liberties in Crisis*, p. 15.

51. Ibid., p. 29.

52. Estimates vary: around 13,000 were detained. Gail Diane Cox, "A Staggering Load," *National Law Journal*, 18 May 1992, p. 1.

53. Ibid., p. 45. See also Pastor, *Latinos and the Los Angeles Uprising*, p. 9 (50.6 per cent).

54. See the ACLU report, *Civil Liberties in Crisis*, cited in footnote 43; also Moran, "Curfew Laws Jail the Innocent and the Guilty," *L.A. Times*, 7 May 1992, pp. B3, 6.

55. The use of army as police classically leads to human-rights abuses, because armies are trained to search out the enemy by category and location, very similar to sweeps. However, in the case of 1992 in L.A., clearly there were not many examples of the National Guard arresting or detaining; most of that was done by the police themselves. Also, the National Guard, late in arriving, were greeted in a friendly way almost wherever they went. But the implication, if normalized, remains worrisome. I was told that an Army unit trained in urban warfare was on alert in San Diego – among various contingency plans involving the military if matters continued to get out of hand.

56. Harvey-Lintz, *Psychological Effects of the 1992 Riots*. The bibliography makes an important point about police under fire. Studies from the eighties found that nearly 30 per cent of police suffered from severe stress disorders (p. 31), at least 12 per cent from PTS (perhaps as war veterans). Apparently, psychological support systems for police remain limited; they simply do not fit the mystique of the tough crime fighter.

57. On the Bonaventure Hotel, see Chapter 2, n.34.

58. Richard Natale, "Hollywood and LAPD: A Romance on the Rocks," *L.A. Times*, 28 October 1995, pp. F1ff., F8.

59. Newton and Ostrow, *L.A. Times*, 7 November 1995, p. B6.

60. Reese Cleghorne, "The Riots: Searching for Truths and Reality," *Washington Journalism Review*, June 1992.

PART V

CONCLUSION

CHAPTER TWELVE

SUBURBAN NOIR
AND CYBERSPACE

Beginning with crime writers like Ross Macdonald in the late forties, the suburb became a new zone of noir ruination. After all, the suburbs immediately after the Second World War were also decayed: "By daylight, the long, treeless street of identical houses looked cheap and rundown. It was part of the miles of suburban slums that the war had scattered all over southern California."[1] Finally, in the seventies, *The Rockford Files* became the first television series about L.A. suburban noir, about con men and sleazy boosters in the San Fernando Valley or Malibu. The show was also about the ruins of the left, so essential to the inspiration for noir. The producer of the *Rockford Files*, Roy Huggins, had been identified as a hostile witness during the McCarthy hearings, but always felt he had not been hostile *enough*, that he had still played it safe.[2] In the casting of this show, many former blacklisted actors and writers were hired, as if the erasure left by McCarthyism and the Cold War guilt still remaining were a hidden motif on the set, hidden irony in the production. The character Rockford, played by James Garner, had been jailed unfairly and was trying to rebuild his life. In many of the scripts, as in Ross Macdonald's stories, a crime forgotten for twenty years is resurrected; new murders reveal the path back to forgotten murders.

Suburban noir is more directly about consumerism and deviance than simply anti-tourism. And this translates into cyber-noir as well: Larry Niven's "Dream Park" novels show an Anaheim of the future where Disneyland has become ringed with brothels, drug dealers – a Gehenna literally quarantined from the rest of California, to sell pleasure in much the way that L.A.'s Chinatown was forced to accept legalized prostitution in the 1890s.

The sinister reading of Disneyland, as part of the suburban noir aesthetic, began as a sub-industry in the sixties, from anti-Mickey comic books to noir anti-Disney[3] crime novels like *Carny Kill* (1966) by L.A. writer Robert Edmond Alter:

> Tourist traps turn ... the coast of Florida into a glittering façade... They hide the naked sight of the hundreds of thousands of voracious cash registers behind the tinsel ... a big, bristling, brawling take-off on the Disneyland idea out in Southern Cal. You might almost call it a steal.[4]

However, "start scratching the surface and the dirt you find under your fingernails is the same grime you'll find in any clipjoint." Theme parks, the "Westworld" phenomenon, become a new critique of boosterist enthusiasm: the great Disney berm off the freeway in Anaheim. In the final scene of the novel *L.A. Confidential*, James Ellroy positions death in the fifties inside an amusement park ride, like an alternative ending to Hitchcock's merry-go-round crushing the psychopathic Bruno in *Strangers on a Train*:

> They were found last week together, on Dream-a-Dreamland's Grand Promenade. There were no notes, but County Coroner Frederic Newbarr quickly ruled out foul play. The means: all three had ingested fatal quantities of a rare antipsychotic drug.[5]

The source for much of this Disneyland-as-hell imagery was probably the carny fiction of the forties, like the macabre classic *Nightmare Alley* by William Lindsay Gresham (1946), adapted into the film starring Tyrone Power, which followed a string of B-carny films from *Freaks* (1932) onward. But in its suburban mode, this consumerist rage passes from the performer-as-criminal to the audience itself. The suburbanites whom Nixon would include in the "moral majority" for his 1968 campaign already appear in their antipodal darker form, as vengeful and deviant, in fifties noir. In the film *Act of Violence* (1950), a real-estate developer hides from his past as a Nazi collaborator, then falls apart, like Main Street downtown, when his sins catch up with him in the final scene, until at last he dies on the street (long shot of whirl of faded newspapers).

Philip K. Dick wrote a curious novel about consumer rage in the fifties' suburbs of Southern California. He delivers a much darker place than John Cheever's New England. Midway in the novel, a long-suffering suburbanite is mugged, robbed, loses some teeth, and is consumed by a vision of "crooks, swindles of every kind," a huge list of grievances a page long, about loan offices, banks, "Pachucs smashing store windows," defective equipment of all sorts, bad chiropractors, "Communism taking over, Red Cross blood with syphilis germs in it, Negro and white troops living together... He saw the whole world writhe with hair, a monstrous hairy ball that burst and drenched him with blood. 'Shit,' he said, walking along the sidewalk, his hands shoved down into his pockets. Gradually he got control of himself."[6]

Another noir variant emerges out of James M. Cain's Glendale in the novel *Mildred Pierce* (1941), where the suburb is a world of dysfunctional working-class families. In the sixties, Joan Didion writes about spousal murder in San Bernardino, in her remarkable blend of the fictive mode and the documentary essay, "Some Dreamers of the Golden Dream:"

> This is the California where it is possible to live and die without ever eating an artichoke, without ever meeting a Catholic or a Jew. This is the California where it is easy to Dial-a-Devotion, but hard to buy a book. This is the country in which a belief in the literal interpretation of Genesis has slipped imperceptibly into a belief in the literal interpretation of *Double Indemnity*, the country of the teased hair and the Capris and the girls for whom all life's promise comes down to a waltz-length white wedding dress and the birth of a Kimberly or a Sherry or a Debbi and a Tijuana divorce and a return to hairdressers' school... Here is where the hot [Santa Ana] wind blows and the old ways do not seem relevant, where the divorce rate is double the national average and where one person in thirty-eight lives in a trailer. Here is the last stop for all those who come from somewhere else, for all those who drifted away from the cold and the past and the old ways.[7]

Finally, suburban noir becomes a book of apocalypse in the final chapter of Mike Davis's *City of Quartz*. As Davis often mentions in lectures, many postwar working-class suburbs have become slums, but their realities are still ignored. Since 1993, a spate of articles have appeared about murder in San Bernardino, which is now rated as the fifth most dangerous city in the United States – hardly just the trailer-park white dystopia that Didion describes. Inside San Bernardino County, Davis chronicles the attempts at survival in the town of Fontana – what he calls "the junkyard of dreams." He begins his cautionary tale in the forties essentially,[8] when boosters declared that the 1940 census "Proves Fontana, Top Agricultural Community in the United States." There was then a turnabout when Fontana became a steel-mill town, until Kaiser left in the eighties. Afterward, the city fell into viciously corrupt redevelopment schemes that practically bankrupted it. Today it is a "junkyard" of industrial and consumer projects that went sour, and serves as little more than a fuel stop for trucks off the San Bernardino Freeway.

In all these examples, and any number of others, from novels by T. Jefferson Parker's (*Laguna Heat*) or Carolyn See's Pacific Palisades, or Sue Grafton's exurbia, even Fay Kellerman's West Side, there are themes very similar to the stacks of noir xeroxes and noir paperbacks on downtown L.A. that dominate the back of my garage. They are tales about erasure, about fast money, corrosive land deals, deviant tourism, and revenge in the mall. Caravans of newcomers pour into poly-nucleated edge cities, the internationalization of the suburbs. Global capital reconfigures its mode of production, as industry sprouts up along the suburban freeway routes. By the nineties, downtown often seems no further than your modem; it could be located in small town Nebraska, or in Ventura County.

And then there is the ultimate complaint, that suburbs and far suburbs (exurbs) have erased boundaries, "the loss of visibility or legibility," similar to the complaint about downtown and industri-opolis. Out of this erasure comes a noir fury. The prototype for suburban noir in cinema is probably *Rebel Without a Cause*, since so many of these stories involve teenagers in a state of rage, like the cult classic *Over the Edge*: suburban ennui at a suburban high school brings on a zero-for-conduct mass revolt and massacre.

And now, at last, in the chain of exurban extension, cyberspace is the next suburb. The best guideed tour of suburban cyberspace is probably by architect and critic William J. Mitchell, who has provided a clever guidebook to the cyburbs, in his ironic handbook *City of Bits*. He begins by saying that "the incorporeal world of the Net has its own mechanisms for coding and class construction."[9] Within that construction are "bit cities" and "soft cities" that are placeless and borderless."[10] "This will be a city unrooted to any definite spot on the surface of the earth." Mitchell goes on about how "asynchronous" it will be, and "disembodied," with "fragmented subjects who exist as collections of aliases and agents." He could have been describing the imaginary L.A. freeway *circa* 1970, and the themed environments that go with it. He then takes us through museums, trading floors and the like, into the digitalized agora, and finally into the cognate on the Net for shopping malls and Disneylands, except that here the places are "semi-public."[11] Much of the core debate centers on this erasure of privacy, on whether the obsession with the Net will ultimately be about finding a secured identity that cannot be rolled into the semi-public realms of the disembodied. Instead, the surveillance – the program on alert – will guard, not reveal. In semi-public digital neighborhoods – chat lines with scripts people sign on to, where city exists as text – the players become fictions and facts simultaneously to each other.[12]

Power and identity are automatically hybridized. Text and space are intertextual, as are work and play, public and intimate, male or female (be any avatar – imaginary creature – you want). By 1994, there were already "virtual" rapes on chat lines, where a man took over the persona of a character that a woman invented. Now, with more vivid chat rooms, the paramnesiac love affairs will probably get even stranger, a blend of Oprah, soap opera and medieval carnival. And with towns on the Web, tourists are invited to escape into a cybernetic democracy that isn't really there. For now, it still looks crude, filled with anthropological absurdities.

Generally, despite the attempts at critique of the Internet and the World Wide Web, the process is so young that one feels as if Edwin S. Porter were visiting to tell you about the rules of the Edison patent in 1902. Fundamentally, at this stage at least, and very likely for years to come, the promotion of computers tends to camouflage in a mode that reminds me of the great California Sunkist campaign in Iowa (1907). Clearly, many of the same tourist evasions will generate many of the same erasures that I have found in the history of Los Angeles.

Cyber sales is fundamentally a form of boosterism, a sunshine strategy with tens of thousands of advertising home pages, and a sprinkle of the rest. Like boosterism, it builds a social imaginary that distracts attention from the widening class structure and the global restructuring of economic power. Like earlier booster campaigns, it has a master-planned millenarianism, about life after slums. It assumes that industrial decay will stop at the boundaries of the ghetto; that what happened to inner cities was historically unique, and could never infect the exburbs, much less the World Wide Web.

To camouflage this problem, digitalized boosterism, like its earlier forms, uses memory as political erasure. In the cyber-culture, whether for banking, sim-sex, gaming or shopping, the voluble gigabyte of memory is the medium of exchange. Like an improved snow blower or toaster, computerized marketing is a more convenient way to forget. Instead of sending out bulldozers, one merely presses Delete. It is the digitalization of forgetting, not the end of the assembly line.

NOTES

1. Ross Macdonald, *The Name is Archer* (New York: Warners Books; orig. 1946), p. 142.

2. Victor S. Navasky, *Naming Names* (New York: Penguin Books, 1981; orig. 1980), p. 282. Roy Huggins was a major television producer for decades afterward.

3. Norman M. Klein, *Seven Minutes: The Life and Death of the American Animated Cartoon* (London: Verso, 1993), pp. 249–50.

4. Robert Edmond Alter, *Carny Kill* (Berkeley: Black Lizard Books, 1986; orig. 1966), p. 1.

5. James Ellroy, *L.A. Confidential* (New York: Mysterious Press, 1990), p. 490.

6. Philip K. Dick *Puttering About in a Small Land* (Chicago: Academy Chicago Publishers, 1985), pp. 100–101. This novel was written in the fifties but unpublished; it was discovered among Dick's papers.

7. Joan Didion, *Slouching Toward Bethlehem* (New York: Dell Publishing, 1968), p. 4. The essay appeared earlier in the *Saturday Evening Post*.

8. Davis, *City of Quartz*, pp. 389–435.

9. William J. Mitchell, *City of Bits: Space, Place and the Infobahn* (Cambridge: MIT Press, 1995) p. 10.

10. Ibid., pp. 24, 151, 160.

11. Ibid., p. 129.

12. Ibid., pp. 118ff.

WHERE IS FORGETTING LOCATED?

While preparing the Introduction to this volume, I read up on memory theory, to find a genealogy for the "history of forgetting." In early drafts, my sources fit into an orderly and enclosed narrative, like intellectual history before the 1970s. However, the subject itself – theories of forgetting – is unquestionably a social imaginary as well. From Plato to Freud, many parallel imaginaries reappear, which were then put into practice as mnemonics (rhetoric), and finally as therapy (psychoanalysis). Forgetting takes place – or "a" place, but where precisely no one seems to be certain, except by the evacuated trail it leaves.

The term "distraction" in cognitive psychology describes that contradiction. I added the adjective "simultaneous," to emphasize the paradox of forgetting – *simultaneous distraction* – and assigned two formats: (1) In order to remember, something must be forgotten. (2) The place where memories are stored is coexistent with its own erasure, and therefore too unstable to have boundaries.

In other words, to use an image from computers, an individual remembers by making a backup file that is different than the original. The act of recall cannot take place without corrupting this original file in some way, because the backup writes over the earlier data. It is a binary with a life of its own, a blemish in a quadrant. This blemish erases the original as soon as memory is activated or even while a "file" is inert. That is what was meant by distraction. Only severe mnemonic discipline can slow this decay, the contrariety of two ruining each other as quietly as a computer corrupts a file. In the West, mnemonics was designed to prevent distraction. Schoolchildren were taught the methods for millennia, based on an architectural imaginary. Two hundred guests are announced. The master remembers each by where they stand in the hall. Even after the hall burns down, he can recite the names of charred bodies by where they fell.

A hermeneutics of memory and forgetting evolved, particularly after mnemonics was restructured during the Renaissance, and then much more drastically after the seventeenth century, and again after 1870. In all examples I found, the paradox of distraction is central, either as a symptom, a sensation, a sign of madness, or "proof" of where the unconscious is located. Here is a gloss on some of these, a genealogy of forgetting, but also a social imaginary.

The first Western writing on the paradox of distraction is usually credited to the Greeks, and afterward to Roman systems for building memory (mnemonics). Both Plato and Aristotle imagined memory as a waxen substance inside the soul, easily inscribed but just as easily effaced, particularly if the wax were thick or muddy. Some degree of effacement (forgetting) was, as many systems repeat thereafter, inescapable.[1] For example, *aporia*, the inability to know how or where to begin, was considered a symptom of effacement (oblivion), to be resisted through mnemonic discipline. "Artificial memory" protected against this sort of loss, but not easily. Remembering was arduous. It required imaginaries as solid as an aqueduct. From the Romans through the Renaissance, students were trained to fight *aporia* through "memory theaters," a spatial imaginary that kept knowledge from drifting into oblivion.

To a well-trained Roman rhetorician, the order of hundreds of names – or of thousands of lines from Virgil – could be stored in *loci*, inside warehouses imagined like walls of facts, standing firm while oblivion lay all around. Similarly, as described in Yates's classic study on the "art of memory," the Renaissance scholar Guilio Camillo actually wanted to build a memory theater out of wooden boxes (each holding files).[2] It was to be similar in design to the seven gangways of the Roman stage, but with inscriptions on each pillar, and sub-headings that connected the mind with the planets. Camillo was blending Roman theory with the Renaissance interest in occult redefinitions of Christianity, by way of the cabbala and Hermetic philosophy. In England, the scholar Robert Fludd designed what he hoped would be a memory room, like a gentleman's waiting area inside a larger space that may have been modeled on Shakespeare's Globe Theatre. To exercise the memory and keep it available, five doors were supposed to be imagined – the memory places where the powers of the Zodiac released truth.

By the seventeenth century, mnemonics was given a much more empirical topology, not at all resembling a room or a building, but just as solid; more like a clerk's ledgers, with sheets neatly scripted and stacked. Memory storage resembled books rather than architecture. In the era of much longer print runs, memory *libraries* seemed more indelible protection against fading. Yet, no matter how the evidence was stored, the models mostly returned to the same paradox.

Descartes identified the seat of intellectual memory in the pineal gland; the folds of the brain confused the information held there, distorting it with fictions and phantasms. This potential misfortune was balanced by the flow of animal spirits in the blood, like a tidal rhythm.[3] Descartes was presenting what amounts to a theory of perfectibility, a very fragile gift that nature has provided humans in their struggle against forgetfulness. This Cartesian cynicism was deeply ingrained in the ethic of the Enlightenment – that humans are essentially absent-minded, and reason must constantly be engaged or else oblivion wins. John Locke's view was particularly extreme; he warned that no matter how tenacious, even miraculous, some memories are, "there seems to be a constant decay of all our Ideas, even of those which are struck deepest, and in the minds the most retentive." If ideas are not "renewed by repeated Exercises of the Senses, or Reflection on those kind of Objects ... the Print wears out, and at last there remains nothing to be seen."[4]

It is indeed a curious subtext to "the age of reason" (of La Mettrie, d'Holbach, and so on), that even Locke, the most widely read exponent of orderly nature, should find such disorder in memory. Locke's image of the mind as blank slate is frequently cited as the paragon that induces learning, that brings forth the natural and convivial entrance into the social contract. But this slate was also in a continual state of erasure, even while the world continued to write so efficiently upon it. There is no innate knowledge, and human knowledge is fragile. The soul, in effect, guards reason against oblivion.

Memory can be clouded by what Hobbes called "the decay of sense" – "compounded imagination ... when from the sight of a man at one time, and of a horse in another, we conceive of a Centaur."[5] In Hobbes's dissection of the brain the act of remembering was continuously filtered through false impressions, which leads to violence and willful disregard.

Voltaire is particularly savage in his satire "Memory's Adventure" (1775), which shows how humans will not be innately peaceful (and certainly not Lockeans) once their memory dissolves. The fable is set in ancient Greece (as seen by the gods) – obviously the Paris of Louis XV. Mortals prove disappointing to the gods, as always. They display so much contempt for memory that, finally, the Muses punish them with utter forgetfulness. This brings on vast social calamities: thievery by servants, the loss of speech, rampant sexual outrages. Finally, Mnemosyne, goddess of memory, takes pity and restores what was lost, but with a warning: "Imbeciles, I forgive you; but *this time* remember that without the senses there is no memory, and without memory there is no mind." [6] However, due to court intrigue and a foolish rector at the University of Paris, very few take her seriously enough. Pandemonium returns.

In the eighteenth century, the most famous debunking of reasonable memory appears in Sterne's *Tristram Shandy* (Book II, chapter 2), where Tristram rails against critics who read Locke the wrong way, who do not "look down into the bottom of this matter", how memory works "in man's own mind". For there exist three causes of "obscurity and confusion": "dull organs;" "slight and transient impressions made by the object when the said organs are not dull;" and (the now classic phrase) "a memory like unto a sieve, not able to retain what it has received."[7]

If we jump to the nineteenth century, the theme of memory loss moves from a satirical jibe to center stage. It clearly takes on an exotic reading in Romanticist allegories about fading feudal memory; in Gothic Romances; in robinsonades about shipwrecked souls with schizoid memories; in hundreds of sources where characters forget under the psychological impact of isolation. Poor Prince Friedrich of Homburg drifts at the edge of madness, unable to be certain if he is sleeping or awake.[8] Shelley's Ozymandius, the dissolving king made of sandstone in the desert, stands as an inversion of Mnemosyne. In Shelley's version, the king's mind, sculpted in oblivion (like a memory trace), mistakenly imagines that mind will be remembered. Clearly, Romanticism gloried in the ruin of memory, as part of an epistemic shift that eventually found its parallels in modern literature and mass culture alike – an increasingly psychological reading of the fugues brought on by memory decay.

The full impact of this shift to an "exotic forgetfulness" is more evident in the period 1850 to 1885. During those years in Europe certainly, there is a bounty of literature on the alienation of memory, which is identified generally by critics since the 1960s under the Baudelairian heading "modernity."[9] As part of the transition from Romanticist to modernist literature, these stories tend to lurch like fractured autobiographical journeys – not Romantic adventure stories about warfare in exotic North Africa, but adventures about solipsistic inaction, into disoriented confessions by solitary figures unable to leave their house. Many of these afflicted are still, of course, highly exoticized characters, generated by what Baudelaire called "natural opium." There remains something of an internalized orientalism to forgetting. Schizoid memory has afflicted the characters like sudden fevers, of the sort acquired in North Africa or in Polynesia. They contemplate how vivid the fevers of forgetting can become, when the "orgy" of memory induces temporary or permanent insanity. The range of characters in novels includes Goncharev's Oblomov,[10] and Huysmans' des Esseintes.[11] These novels center around the image of memory as brittle, as cracking or tearing the seam of story until at last, there is inaction. They became the foundation that the young Proust read, in that sense helped give permission to Proust's opus a generation later.

The exotic of memory lapse is evident in popular horror tales as well, like Maupassant's *The Horla* or Stevenson's *Dr Jekyll and Mr Hyde*. These, along with late Romantic tales, like those of Nerval in the 1850s, clearly return to the theme of simultaneous distraction: the narrator is possessed by a phantom double inside, who interrupts at will, serves as a companion, a replacement and a censor. For example, in the short novel *Aurelia* by Nerval, the patient records, as if through a diary, the false sense of omnipotence he felt during a nervous breakdown. "Everything," he explains, "took on a dual aspect, no more reasoning bereft of any logic, no more memory erasing the fainter details that reach me. Only my actions, seemingly disengaged, stood ready to submit to this so-called illusion."[12]

By the 1880s, even when the psychology of learning emerged as a field of clinical research, more humane as well as more positivist (but sometimes just as repressive as earlier), the enemy identified once again was memory loss – amnesia; and secondarily false recollection, or paramnesia. Ebbinghaus's Forgetfulness Curve (1885) indicated how quickly memory decays – what is now called working or short-term memory.[13] The curve quantified the learning of nonsense syllables, which in turn are forgotten mostly within the first hour, leaving a trace that can be relearned faster, but through different paths, because the original is virtually lost.

But here, too, no cure was found, only the annoyance of distraction. In the century since Ebbinghaus, the vast majority of studies on learning essentially agree that memory is afflicted *simultaneously* by forgetting. It does not disappear merely through disuse, but through *interference*, either retroactive or proactive; through distraction.[14] Treatments for forgetting still rely on encoding within different cognitive contexts, back to memory theaters, but using nonsense words. Except under surgery, the instant of loss remains indistinct. No memory is released, or stored, without some degree of erasure. This is particularly true of episodic memory of past events. The record is always filled with omissions, encoded after a period of "secondary indifference."[15] Two of the dominant models that explain why we forget our early childhood are "blockade" and "selective reconstruction."[16] Therefore a memory "trace" may satisfy the urge to remember, but not the urge to remember the "facts." In a text from 1978, psychologists write:

> It is an oversimplification to envision images [in the mind] as enduring fixedly, as if preserved in amber. In fact, imagery may undergo myriad evolutionary transformations before it is utilized, and people's style of coding may shift drastically as task requirements alter, even if the same external stimuli are presented.[17]

Most of all, as in centuries past, despite all the scientific models about forgetting that doctors in turn apply as a social imaginary, no one has yet located precisely where in the brain the complete chain of a single memory is lost – or even what a memory looks like physiologically. The term most frequently used is "engram," but that soon acquired an occult meaning – very much a social imaginary – once it entered mass culture. In Scientology, the engram is a mystic godhead, located through the E meter like secrets from the pyramids. The myth of engram takes on the powers of a tonic sold by mail order, or in the case of Scientology a corporate marketing of positive thinking – science as the fiction of the iron-clad ego.

The German biologist Richard Semon coined the term "engram" in 1904, to identify a structure in the cerebral cortex where memory must be stored.[18] To Semon, this was primarily a "location," a surface excited by stimuli, and stamped. The neural tissue was "engrammed," or "engraphed," inscribed as if by an engraving tool. However, the engramming left only a trace, not a complete record. There was no way to retrieve it whole. Semon insisted that memory components, whatever they were, easily split apart, and could be delivered only as fragments.

And today, nearly a century later, despite a raft of competing theories, the mystery remains. Each memory is stored either at a precise location, or sympathetically along a web of functions. It may be guided by hormones — emotional effect; or by the hippocampus (initial temporary storage); or simply be built like muscle tissue inside synapses. The precise "cerebral topography" cannot be identified; there is only what the evidence shows — a set of axes crossing on a graph.[19] And when they cross, the graph dissolves a bit. It decays immediately after an experience is stored, and then a second time when the memory is retrieved. To spark the engram some neural tissue is changed physically. Part of its structure is scorched, or reconfigured, a trigger set off by a cue. Therefore to release its cargo the neural code inside the engram must be altered. The more traumatic the memory, the more radical the changes. In psychologist Erwin Strauss's words: "What has happened is undone."[20] Afterward, a coping mechanism takes over, or else the memory is lost altogether. The original can never be put back precisely as it was, only reprogrammed in some way — repositioned like baggage switching planes after a stopover, where the bags have been opened by customs.

I can feel the fictional image intruding into the scientific realm at this point. However, there is reason to argue (at least in Foucauldian terms) that the social imaginary of forgetting, even its clinical version, came out of literary fiction as much as the sciences. But that is not the heart of my argument. I am using this background more as a reminder that research is an unstable fiction (and often uses fiction itself). Like novels, it merges fact into an imaginary construct, even when the subject is the site of memory in the brain. Semon's work arrives at the end of a century of popular novels and philosophy specifically on the subject of mnemonics, as a kind of gothic imaginary of the body and the self. Sources from German Romanticism (Herder, Schiller, and so on) were still cited often in mass culture, much the way cinema is cited today. As I explained earlier, the Romanticists glorified the act of forgetting: the exoticism of memory decay, as dream and fairy tale, the fetish of paramnesia — false recollection as a virtue. Distorted memory was praised as the tool of the artist, even as the soul in the afterlife, the dream inside the dream. In 1810, Schelling wrote:

> [In the afterlife] there will be a kind of forgetfulness, a Lethe, but with a different effect: when all the good arrive there, they will have forgetfulness of everything evil, and thus of all suffering and pain; the wicked, on the contrary,

will have forgetfulness of everything good. And further, it will surely not be the power of memory as we possess here; for here we must first interiorize everything, whereas there everything is already interior. The phrase "power of memory" is too weak to capture the sense.[21]

The disoriented memory took on the power of redemption. In mass culture, there even were how-to books, parlour tricks about free "association" in the safety of the home. Freud was given one of these potboilers at the "provocative age" of fourteen, and devoured it. He kept it in his library for fifty years, the only volume he saved from his boyhood. The author, Ludwig Borne, was "the first ... into whose writings he had penetrated deeply." One short essay, "The Art of Becoming an Original Writer in Three Days," is cited most of all, not as a major source but more as banal coincidence. However, Borne's technique does, by sheer accident, vaguely resemble free association. It recommends writing for three days on end, "without fabrication or hypocrisy, everything that comes into your head. Write down what you think of yourself, of your wife, of the Turkish War, of Goethe, of Fonk's trial, of the Last Judgment, of your superiors." Afterward, you will be "out of your senses with astonishment at the new and unheard-of thoughts you have had."[22]

During Freud's childhood and early career, the vogue for such books was at its strongest: theories on what made one thought spark another in a surprising way – a practicum on "creative juxtaposition;" how to develop creative memory. One key source undoubtedly came from research on "association," stemming from the writing of David Hartley in the eighteenth century, and a network of British and German psychologists after 1850.[23] By the 1880s, "association" groups in England would convene to argue whether fresh ideas came by contiguity or by similarity. At Oxford in 1877, Walter Pater fretted that many students, misreading his work, had taken associationism too far and grown anxious searching for a "hard gem-like flame" through the "devouring" whirlpool of sensations.[24] Pater, like Henri Bergson, must be classified as a spokesman against "forgetting."

In Paris a generation later, Bergson lectured to students at the Collège de France on exercises for recovering the phantom of memory, in its "pure duration." To cite cases of "pure memory," he referred to popular mnemonics, systems of "mental photography," and associationism (which he found too fragmenting: "To picture is not to remember").[25] Popular mnemonics (from variety acts to books) were thrown into the same context with clinical research. Clearly by the 1890s there was a massive body of published work across the literary markets on how to stave off the alienation of memory (modernity). And just as clearly, there were modernists on both sides of the debate.

The contentious object was the impression itself, that twinkling in the present when a memory invades (simultaneous distraction). This imperceptible duration can strike the mind as solidly as a stroke of paint (Cézanne's cones and cubes), but will also be very startling and precipitous; and is often described as a metonym for modernity. Bergson compared it to a phosphene: after the eyes close, a glowing after-image decays against a darkened background. The inside of the eyelids convert into a screen for a Melies trick film, or an Émile Cohl white-line cartoon. Proust compares the impression to "a searchlight beam cutting out or illuminating the side of a building."[26] The past is contained in a material object, most famously in the scent of tea on a madeleine that releases a chain of association (impressions), but in a conflicted coexistent way. This conflict – the present fading into the object that brings the memory – is essential to Proust's technique, despite his fundamental belief in pure memory. Consider the homeliest parallel, simply to emphasize that this technique problematizes in a way similar to distraction: does Proust's expression "temps perdu" translate as "time erased," or "time recovered"? Was "impression" a sign for memory decaying, or memory as eidetic, so vivid it was stable, almost metaphysically present?

That term "impression" has a curious link to theories on how one forgets. From translations of Aristotle, to the work of David Hume in the 1750s, it suggests how memory disorients ideas. By the nineteenth century, it falls under the broad canopy of what was called association – "impression" as milisecond, that precise instant when distraction is perceived. In 1857, a Swedenborgian mystic named Garth Wilkinson came up with an associative method called "impression": "the first mental movement, the first word that comes."[27] Impression increasingly implied randomness; it is "involuntary" (Proust's phrase); or it endangers representation of the real, as in the phrase "the inconstancy of the impressionist image" that Monet still remembered as late as 1915 as a stinging attack on his paintings.[28] Therefore his work of the 1870s may have been attacked not simply as artistic blasphemy, but also in the context of a medical crisis discussed in newspapers as well as medical journals: the emotional hazards of random memory.

Even the term "unconscious" is linked directly, even etymologically, to debates on how lost memories leave impressions. In the 1870s, three authors independently developed the term "organic unconscious memory" (Eduard Hering, Thomas Laycock, Samuel Butler).[29] At the same time, dozens of clinical papers appeared on forgetfulness and the insane, in Germany and the United States in particular. They represent a shift among physicians in the way forgetting was diagnosed, away from Romanticist elegies toward a new science on forgetting – not as release, more as a battery of symptoms caused by anxiety and inhibition. The treatises on forgetting tended to support one central ideological assumption: that the healthy person was equipped with nearly complete recall, ready to take on rational work and family.[30] Memories were stored somewhere in a narrative chain, even though they came in fragments. As Theodule Ribot explained: "In showing how memory is disorganized, it shows us how memory is organized."[31]

By contrast, amnesiacs were sociopaths. In clinical descriptions, they resemble the sinister Victorian photographs of the mad, their eyes sunk in martyrdom, the physiognomy of self-erasure; lost memory is a scar left from childhood, or by injury, even by the barbarism of modern life, by worry and loneliness. Functional amnesia – referring to psychologically *motivated* amnesia, loss *not* caused by brain injury – became the paradigm for treating many other diseases of the mind (depression, neurasthenia). Like all memory impaired, only more so, functional amnesiacs could not face up to trauma. They buried it instead. However, where and in what form it was buried became a crucial question for treatment, leading to problems described in Freud's early work.

Freud's theories on Screen Memory (1889) were his first broad set of papers on memory "displacement." Next, and more fundamentally, the seventh chapter of *The Interpretation of Dreams* (1900) remains an essential document for memory studies on repression, along with his analysis of childhood amnesia in *Three Essays on the Theory of Sexuality* (1905), and finally the work on memory lapses in conversation and other daily exchanges in *The Psychopathology of Everyday Life*, based on work dating back to 1888. These became the cornerstones of Freud's theories on how one forgets through repression or displacement (1889–1905). To these, he added essays on how memory is retrieved (memory traces), how psychic energy "cathects" memory into visual metaphors in the preconscious, with erratic results, like an electric current that regularly shorts out or surges.

Essentially, in Freud's symptomatology, guilt is the culprit. Guilt inhibits and camouflages. It inflects the way the story is remembered, condensing its narrative, erasing its details, masking its significance, displacing it onto another story altogether. This crisis also implies a threat to the empirical method itself, which by definition must be able to retrieve original memory (as in group history or personal history), even after the memory has been erased. The paradox of first memory returns in various forms throughout Freud's writing, from dream theory (latent content) to parapraxis, to theories on taboos.[32] If an adult (or a social group) suffers from childhood amnesia (about the childhood of the self or the society), does that original memory stay preserved somewhere anyway, like oil in a jar? Or does it decay, even disappear; or can it be condensed or displaced inside another interiorized story, as an inexplicable detail? There must be a permanent lexicon somewhere in the mind.

In 1925, Freud suggested a "mystic pad" in the unconscious, where memories that are endangered can be written down securely. However, the mystic pad might be clay, and could be smoothed away, erased yet again (which takes us back to the problem of engram, and to Plato). Also, Freud was continually aware of the need to forget as a form of emotional release. If the mystic pad worked too well, and recall were magically preserved, that might induce more problems.

There lies the crux of the problem for the historian of mass culture: the act of writing cannot be privileged. The writer cannot locate the received image in the "mind of the group" any more than the scientist can find the site of memory itself. As Derrida explains, in homage as well as criticism to Freud, the mystic pad was an attempt to separate memory from "psychical responsibility," but "writing is unthinkable without repression."[33] Freud's struggle to defend recorded memory against repression only expanded the problem. It implied that all forms of writing were also fictional, that no memory aid could preserve without leaving gaps. And in fact, for Derrida, the gaps – the faintly erased – were precious; they were the spaces where relief from repression was possible. Derrida defends opacity against transparency, using aspects of Freud's struggle to protect knowledge against repression – not in the way Freud intended, of course, more in reverse. At any rate, whichever side one takes (Freud or Derrida), the oil in the jar remains impure. The act of forgetting is complicit at all times with recollection, in dreams, in public, in conversation, in writing, probably in the synaptic byways themselves.

The reference to Derrida takes me to the other side of the ledger. Unlike Freud, many late-nineteenth-century modernists *defended* the act of intentionally forgetting. This continues as a century-long debate on whether inscription (recording) is *supposed* to erase memory, what Derrida later summarized as *différance*: to inscribe erasure within the act of writing. If memory (that is, impressions) is random, then writing must find beauty by escaping to the random: for example, Mallarme's famous experiments on chance as poetic diction; the term "la mystere" in Symbolist fiction; Nietzsche's "active forgetting" (*On the Genealogy of Morals*, 1887). Nietzsche describes forgetting as the peaceful state that blanks the mind to allow incorporation. Forgetfulness allows the will to discharge, and energizes memory itself:

> ...active forgetfulness is like a doorkeeper, a preserver of psychic order, or repose, and etiquette: so that it will be immediately obvious how there could be no happiness, no cheerfulness, no hope, no pride, no present, without forgetfulness. The man in whom this apparatus of repression is damaged may be compared ... with a dyspeptic – he cannot have done with anything ... forgetting represents a force, a form of robust health.[34]

As I explain in the introduction, in the twentieth century, particularly as an article of faith in poststructuralism, in modern and postmodern literature, the sheer body of writing against mnemonics is much larger than the empirical studies. Among Futurists and Surrealists, distraction is defended as simultaneity,[35] as the marvelous. Louis Aragon writes:

> As soon as one thinks about something else, it's all over. Impossible to get back to my starting point, and between the thread and the needle I find myself in a desert at some undetermined stage of the universe.[36]

Very often, Surrealist writing is designed as a testimony in self-erasure. But in the hands of Latin American writers, Surrealist anti-mnemonics is taken one step further, toward epic, to identify the *sensation* when an entire world dissolves, or is forgotten. The writer begins with an object that contains memory – a computer, a library, a book in parchment. The character is inscribing within it, while the system corrupts, and begins to fade. The conclusion of Gabriel García Márquez's *One Hundred Years of Solitude* is a classic sample of this device in action: "Before reaching the final line ... he already understood that he would never leave that room, for it was foreseen that the city of mirrors [or mirages] would be wiped out by the wind and exiled from the memory of men at the precise moment when Aureliano Babilonia would finish deciphering the parchments..."[37]

NOTES

1. David Farrell Krell, *Of Memory, Reminiscence and Writing: On the Verge* (Bloomington: Indiana University Press, 1990), pp. 13–83. This source proved by far the most thorough and the most insightful on the relationship between memory theory and Western philosophy, comprehensively researched by a scholar of ancient philosophy. It reviews the sources from the seventeenth and eighteenth century, and concludes with Heidegger, Nietzsche and Derrida. It is in many ways a journey through the incarnations of a single model of memory – the engramming on wax.

2. Frances A. Yates, *The Art of Memory* (Chicago: University of Chicago Press, 1966), p. 140. This must be the most cited secondary source on memory theory: familiar to medieval scholars, to European historians, and to contemporary critics. The Camillo memory theater is particularly fascinating; it includes a fold-out diagram. See also J. Spence, *The Memory Palace of Matteo Ricci* (1984).

3. Krell, *Of Memory, Reminiscence and Writing*, pp. 61–3.

4. Ibid., p. 77. From Locke's *Essay Concerning Human Understanding*, Book II, Part X. Mary Warnock's *Memory* (London: Faber & Faber, 1977) has a useful section on Locke, pp. 70–71. Her study provides more background on nineteenth-century philosophical sources, some of whom Krell does not emphasize. The final chapters (6 and 7) in Warnock have additional material on autobiography and diary as modern responses to the crisis of memory; a reminder that many of the problems we assign to postmodern theory have deep echoes in nineteenth-century literature that was not strictly the novel, the sources for Roussel and later Bataille, for example – the layered travel fiction, the complex personal journals that were so much a part of the writer's market, and may become so again, one can hope.

5. Thomas Hobbes, *Leviathan* (London: Collier Books, 1962), p. 24. This appears early in chapter 2 ("Of Imagination") in Part I.

6. Voltaire, *Candide, Zadig and Selected Stories*, trans. D. Frame (New York: New American Library, 1961), p. 328. This passage is one paragraph below the end of the story.

7. Further down the same page (Book II, chapter 2) of Sterne's *Tristram Shandy* (after comparing Dolly's wax imprint from a thimble to Uncle Toby's memory, as always going awry – clearly a signal of Sterne's having read memory theory since the Greeks): "What it did arise from, I have hinted above, and a fertile source of obscurity it is – and ever will be, – and that is the unsteady use of words, which have perplexed the clearest and most exalted understandings."

8. Kleist's *Prince Frederick* is a curious play to watch as well, because the director has extraordinary power over the diegetic fact of the story, without changing the lines at all. Do the events really happen or not? It is a building of the imaginary as distraction, one fiction positioned before the other.

9. Modernity has become an all-purpose alternative to "modernism" in contemporary criticism. I do not see it at all as a synonym. My sense of the term is taken from Baudelaire's essays on the Painter as the Hero of Modern Life, in essays in 1846 and 1859: at the instant when the eternal and transitory meet, one distracts the other; in literary terms, it is the suture when trauma, brought about by urbanization/Haussmanization/industrialization (etc.) alters perception (also, the trauma of distantiation, alienation). Clearly, Marshall Berman, T.J. Clark, and many others have written at great length on

these issues. The broader implications in Nietzsche, in the transitions from the Second Empire definitions of modernity to those during the Symbolist era, are a massive subject in themselves, much broader than the range of this book, particularly in the uses of the term "modernity" since 1968 in cultural theory and art criticism. For my narrower purposes here, one question remains, even in 1997: to what degree has scholarship as a form of literature – and scholarship about mass culture – applied the permissions of nineteenth-century modernity – how to describe the context of distraction?

10. The popular response in Russia of the 1860s to Goncharev's novel is striking – the sleeper who cannot awaken, and therefore cannot act upon the world. His is the purely interiorized reading of bureaucracy and class as hopelessly entropic, an erosion of memory.

11. Huysmans' *À Rebours* was an event in French (decadence) and English literature (aestheticism). The man of overrefined taste cannot act upon the world except through simulation, through a gesture that distracts the original. I am aware that much of this book is about des Esseintes' persona – another classic in the history of white male panic: the fear of lost potency; the need to ritualize power because it seems continually threatened. Huysmans is describing the fading rituals of the aristocratic class, modeled partly on the fashionable Baron Montesquieu, whom Proust also describes fictionally. One question that strikes me, in relation to my project here is: what is the transition that this rather uneven novel points toward? The novel of sociability (for example, Jane Austen; even Balzac or Stendhal) is replaced by the novel where the social is distracted – remembered/forgotten – by private ritual.

12. This is located at the top of section III in the first part of Nerval's *Aurelia, ou la Rêve et la Vie* (1841, 1853). I referred to my little Tchou edition, *Poèmes et Prose*, 1969, p. 100. The recent translation by Kendall Lappin seems very solid (Santa Maria, Calif.: Asylum Arts Publishing, 1991).

13. While Ebbinghaus's Forgetfulness Curve is mentioned as a crucial moment in every psychology text on memory that I found, the three books that best clarified the broader issues for me were: Endel Tulving (one of the central figures in contemporary cognitive psychology), *Elements of Episodic Memory* (New York: Oxford University Press, 1983); Michael M Gruneberg and Peter Morris, eds, *Aspects of Memory* (London: Methuen, 1978); John Kihlstrom and Frederick J. Evans, eds, *Functional Disorders of Memory* (Hillside, N.J.: Lawrence Erlbaum Associates, 1979).

14. Roger M. Tarpy and Richard Mayer, *Foundations of Learning and Memory* (Glenview, Ill.: Scott, Foresman and Co., 1978), pp. 258–60.

15. Endel Tulving, *Elements of Episodic Memory* (Oxford: Oxford University Press, 1983). Much of this book centers around the contrast between semantic memory and episodic memory. Clearly, the subject of my project is episodic memory, which is more unstable. The arguments are first very carefully laid out, in pages 1–78; then the history of empirical evidence on these issues is presented; and, finally, we return to the conceptual framework on p. 123; for example: "Why have our psychological theories of memory had so little to say about the mental experience of remembering, the subjective feelings of veridicality and awareness of pastness of remembered events, and the relation of the experiences, feelings, and awareness to overt memory performance?" (pp. 125–6).

16. Sheldon H. White and David B. Pillemer, "Childhood Amnesia and Development of a Socially Accessible Memory System," in John F. Kihlstrom and Frederick J. Evans, eds, *Functional Disorders of Memory* (Hillside, N.J.: Lawrence Erlbaum Associates, 1979), p. 34. Note also the sense that children do not remember "narratively" until six

or eight years of age, which presumes that we know what "narrative" means as a fixed system.

17. Ted Rosenthal and Barry Zimmerman, *Social Learning and Cognition* (New York: Academic Press, 1978), p. 255.

18. Daniel Schacter, *Stranger Behind the Engram: Theories of Memory and the Psychology of Science* (Hillsdale, N.J.: Lawrence Erlbaum Associates, 1982), chs 6 and 7. From Tulving, *Elements of Episodic Memory*, p. 159: "In the General Abstract Processing System, engrams possess functional properties rather than structural ones. Structural properties of memory traces imply their conceptualization as entities can at least be imagined to exist independently of their function; functional properties, on the other hand, can be identified and described without postulating any such independent existence."

19. One of the more thorough recent summations on the state of new work on memory simply indicates that there are many "locations" at once, and that measurements continue to improve, while clinical practice lags behind. Nelson Butters, Dean Delis and John Lucas, "Clinical Assessment of Memory Disorders in Amnesia and Dementia," *Annual Review of Psychology*, vol. 46, 1995, pp. 493ff. Also: the links between "distraction" and chaos theory, or uses of the term "heteroglossia" – theoretical and scientific models about locations as collapsed signs.

Various terms have come and gone: less interest in Interference Theory," more in Schema Theory (how abstraction leads to inaccurate memory); the fragility of memory in "context," distortions, reconstructions, flashbulb memories (overwriting a memory – see Chapter 10 above). A number of recent works should be cited here. They deal with the construction and the imaginary of memory; memory distortion; "confabulation;" implicit memory (a far more neutral model for sublimated or repressed memory than the term "unconscious," and also more suitable for computer-like imaginaries about memory); and, finally, the history of memory theory: Daniel L. Schacter, ed. *Distorting Memory* (Cambridge, Mass.: Harvard University Press, 1995) (excellent survey, with a fine introduction); also Schacter's *Searching For Memory: The Brain, the Mind, and the Past* (New York: HarperCollins, 1996), with a very clear analysis of "implicit" memory; the three-volume series on *The Psychology of Memory*, edited by Peter E. Morris and Martin A. Conway, particularly Volumes I and III, which include essential articles by many key figures, from Bartlett to Schacter. Also, since 1980, the books by Michael Kammen on memory and history; Michele Simondon, *La Mémoire et L'Oubli* (1982), on the Greco-Roman sources in philosophy and myth; Matt Matsuda, *Memory of the Moderns* (1996); Ulrich Neisser and Eugene Winograd, eds, *Remembering Reconsidered: Ecological and Traditional Approaches to the Study of Memory* (Cambridge: Cambridge University Press, 1988), particularly on how events are misremembered.

20. Krell, *Of Memory, Reminiscence and Writing*, p. 90; from Erwin Strauss, *Phenomenological Psychology* (New York: Basic Books, 1966), p. 96.

21. Krell, *Of Memory, Reminiscence and Writing*, p. 50; in Schelling's *Stuttgarter Privatvorlesung* (VII, p. 47).

22. Sigmund Freud, "A Note on the Prehistory of the Technique of Analysis" (1920), in *Therapy and Technique*, edited by P. Rieff (New York: Crowell-Collier Books, 1963), p. 193. See in the same volume, Freud's essay on "fausse reconnaissance." It is difficult to find any volume of Freud's writing that does not return to his applications of the theory of displacement, which in turn refer back to his work on memory.

23. Schacter, *Stranger Behind the Engram*, pp. 167–9.

24. Judith Ryan, *The Vanishing Subject: Early Psychology and Literary Modernism* (Chicago:

University of Chicago Press, 1991), p. 28.

25. Henri Bergson, *Matter and Memory*, trans. N. Paul and W. Palmer (New York: Humanities Press, 1978; reprint of 1911 edition [London: Unwin]), p. 173.

26. Marcel Proust, *Swann's Way*, trans. S. Moncrieff and T. Kilmartin (New York: Vintage Books, 1981), p. 46.

27. Freud, "A Note on the Prehistory of the Technique of Analysis," p. 192.

28. Claude Monet in his famous letter to Gustave Geffroy, "To Paint... Paint" (*c.* 1915), in Robert Goldwater and Marco Treves, eds, *Artists on Art from the XIV to the XX Century* (New York: Pantheon Books, 1945 [reprinted 1972]), p. 315.

29. Lancelot Law Whyte, *The Unconscious Before Freud* (London: Julian Friedmann Publishers, 1978), p. 170.

30. I should emphasize "*nearly*" complete recall. Hypermnesia, the disease of too much memory, was also studied in considerable detail, in late-nineteenth-century France for example, as described in Michael Roth's splendid essay "Remembering Forgetting: *Maladies de la Mémoire* in Nineteenth Century France," *Representations*, Spring 1989: "With hypermnesia, however, memory becomes an agent of disorder, overwhelming the present" (p. 60). This issue of *Representations*, edited by Natalie Zemon Davis and Randolph Starn, concentrates on "Memory and Counter-memory." All the articles are valuable for the historian interested in memory theory.

31. Ibid., p. 56. Ribot was an influential professor of psychology at the Collège de France.

32. For example, much of Freud's argument in *Totem and Taboo* is designed to overcome the theories about decay of memory that nominalist anthropologists (his term), like Andrew Lang describe. In "nominalism," speech itself, more than psychological repression, decays original memory. Culture, therefore, is identified as entropic by its very nature. As an example, Freud quotes Lang on how the proper names of taboos are forgotten – in Lang's view as the inevitable erosion brought on by social memory. This argument from Lang sounds to me like a simplification (and exoticization – Lang, after all, edited fairy tales lovingly) of culture as catabolic (diminishment as a result of development), rather than metabolic (building up through development). In the spirit of the Gothic and Celtic Revivals in England at the end of the nineteenth century, collective memory is understood as continually eroding, because it came through oral tradition, where memory cannot be fixed on written records. The crisis built into this theory is evident. If folklore is a treasure because it decays through everyday speech, like a stream pulling away banks of soil, is that decay desirable? Or is it something that the Victorians of Lang's generation should resist using written "Grammar," lest industrial England go the way of feudalism, fall into ignorance of recorded history? (Sigmund Freud, *Totem and Taboo*, Part IV, section on "Infantile Recurrence").

33. Jacques Derrida, *Writing and Difference*, p. 226. In the same paragraph: "It is no accident that the metaphor of censorship should come from the area of politics concerned with deletions, blanks, and disguises of writing, even if at the beginning of the *Traumdeutung*, Freud seems to make only a conventional didactic reference to it. The apparent exteriority of political censorship refers to an essential censorship which binds the writer to his own writing." On p. 222 he writes: "A slate, whose virginity may always be reconstituted by erasing the imprints on it, does not conserve its traces." More narrowly, in terms of my project in this book, Krell devotes chapters to Derrida's theories of writing as erasure.

34. Friedrich Nietzsche, *The Genealogy of Morals*, Second Essay, section 1.

35. As the reader undoubtedly knows, simultaneity is a term used often by the Futurists, even in the titles of their paintings; it is applied to the Cubists and to others — the representation of more than one time/space at once.

36. Since the Surrealist material on forgetting, as well as Expressionist material, is too vast for the subject of this book, I selected a sample that seemed too apt to pass up. Jacqueline Chenieux-Gendron, *Surrealism*, trans. V. Folkenflik (New York: Columbia University Press, 1984), p. 129. In researching for this project, the classic documents on the Surrealist use of distraction that fit the most easily were Aragon's *Paysan de Paris*, and Breton's *Nadja*, both written in 1927, at the moment when interest in Freud among Surrealists was at its height: the intercutting of document and diary as free association (automatism). As literature, these are practically structuralist, almost clinical, docu-novels applying a cinematic method. They catalogue in print, like a high-speed photograph or even Vertov's Kino Eye, a point vivid enough to show the multiples of distraction still present, before the process of erasure disoriented them. Examples include the arcade described by Aragon; the photos as disjointed references to "chance encounters" *not* with Nadja but with places she left, or failed to pass by. They point out the instant when affinity generates automatism — the rushed montage through a train window, convulsive beauty, a mental connection that lasts only a moment. Not surprisingly, the novels by Woolf and Joyce attack parallel problems during the same years, at least in terms of literary technique, if not intention.

37. Gabriel García Márquez, *One Hundred Years of Solitude*, trans. G. Rabasso (New York: HarperCollins, 1970; orig. 1967), p. 422.

BORGES' FATHER

I prefer to end a book on forgetting with a fragment from an interview with Jorge Luís Borges, during a visit to Harvard in 1968. He began to think back to his childhood, and to his father, a lawyer with a passion for the psychology of memory. Many years before, his father remarked that he thought he could recall his childhood when "we first came to Buenos Aires, but now I know I can't."[1] "Why?" Jorge asked.

His father answered with a theory of forgetting that lingered with his son for decades afterward. "I think if I recall something," his father said, "for example, if today I look back on this morning, then I get an image of what I saw this morning. But if tonight, I'm thinking back on this morning, then what I'm really recalling is not the first image, but the first image in memory. So that every time I recall something, I'm not recalling it really, I'm recalling the last time I recalled it, I'm recalling my last memory of it. So that really, I have no memories whatever, I have no images whatever, about my childhood, about my youth."

He illustrated what he meant by building a stack of coins. After piling one on top of the other, he said: "Well, now this first coin, the bottom coin, this would be the first image, for example, of the house in my childhood. Now this second would be a memory I had of that house when I went to Buenos Aires. Then the third one another memory and so on. And as in every memory there's a slight distortion, I don't suppose that my memory of today ties in with the first images I had." Then, finally, his father grew more pensive, and added, "I try not to think of things in the past because if I do I'll be thinking back on those memories and not on the actual images themselves." It saddened Borges' father to think that there were no true memories of his youth.

The interviewer cut in at this point, to learn more of what Borges meant. Do you mean "that the past was invented, fictitious?" he asked. To which Borges agreed. He was an old man himself, thinking back on his father at the same age. "That it can be distorted by successive repetition," Borges explained. "Because if in every repetition you get a slight distortion, then in the end you will be a long way off from the issue. It's a saddening thought. I wonder if it's true, I wonder what other psychologists would say about that."

NOTE

1. Richard Burgin, *Conversations with Jorge Luis Borges* (New York: Avon Books, 1970; orig. 1968), p. 26.

INDEX